T0331246

## Economics of Electricity

This comprehensive and up-to-date book explains the economic rationale behind the production, delivery and exchange of electricity. Cretì and Fontini explain why electricity markets exist, outlining the economic principles behind the exchange and supply of power to consumers and firms. They identify the specificities of electricity, as compared to other goods, and furthermore suggest how markets should be optimally designed to produce and deliver electricity effectively and efficiently. The authors also address key issues, including how electricity can be decarbonized. Written in a technical yet accessible style, this book will appeal to readers studying power-system economics and the economics of electricity, as well as those more generally interested in energy economics, including engineering and management students looking to gain an understanding of electricity-market analysis.

**Anna Cretì** is Professor of Economics at the Paris Dauphine University, senior research associate at the École Polytechnique and external affiliate of the Siebel Institute at the University of California, Berkeley. She is the Scientific Director of the Climate Economics Chair and the Natural Gas Chair at Paris Dauphine University. She is the author of numerous articles in international peer-reviewed journals.

**Fulvio Fontini** is Professor of Economics at the Department of Economics and Management, University of Padova (Italy). He has been co-chair of the ESS task force of the Council of European Energy Regulators (CEER), and member of several task forces of CEER and the Agency for Cooperation of Energy Regulators (ACER), where he was seconded as national expert. He is the author of numerous articles in international peer-reviewed journals.

# Economics of Electricity

## Markets, Competition and Rules

ANNA CRETÌ
Université Paris Dauphine, PSL Research University, France

FULVIO FONTINI
University of Padova, Italy

# CAMBRIDGE
## UNIVERSITY PRESS

University Printing House, Cambridge CB2 8BS, United Kingdom

One Liberty Plaza, 20th Floor, New York, NY 10006, USA

477 Williamstown Road, Port Melbourne, VIC 3207, Australia

314-321, 3rd Floor, Plot 3, Splendor Forum, Jasola District Centre, New Delhi - 110025, India

79 Anson Road, #06-04/06, Singapore 079906

Cambridge University Press is part of the University of Cambridge.

It furthers the University's mission by disseminating knowledge in the pursuit of education, learning and research at the highest international levels of excellence.

www.cambridge.org
Information on this title: www.cambridge.org/9781107185654
DOI: 10.1017/9781316884614

First published 2019

*A catalogue record for this publication is available from the British Library*

*Library of Congress Cataloging in Publication data*
Names: Cretì, Anna, author. | Fontini, Fulvio, 1970– author.
Title: Economics of electricity : markets, competition and rules / Anna Cretì, Universite de Paris IX (Paris-Dauphine), Fulvio Fontini, Universita degli Studi di Padova, Italy.
Description: Cambridge, United Kingdom ; New York, NY: Cambridge University Press, 2019. | Includes bibliographical references and index.
Identifiers: LCCN 2019005623 | ISBN 9781107185654 (hardback : alk. paper)
Subjects: LCSH: Electric utilities. | Electric power production. | Electric power consumption.
Classification: LCC HD9685.A2 C74 2019 | DDC 333.793/2–dc23
LC record available at https://lccn.loc.gov/2019005623

ISBN 978-1-107-18565-4 Hardback
ISBN 978-1-316-63662-6 Paperback

# Contents

# Figures

# Tables

# Acknowledgments

Several people have contributed directly or indirectly to this project. Clearly, none of them is responsible for what is written here. We would like to thank Carlos Battle Lopez, Côme Billard, Silvia Blasi, Severin Borenstein, Silvia Concettini, Nicolas Gruyer, Cristian Lanfranconi, Salvatore Lanza, Katrin Millock, Paolo Mastropietro, Michele Moretto, and Dimtrios Zompas.

Fulvio Fontini wishes to thank the University of Paris Dauphine PSL (LEDA CGEMP) for financial support and kind hospitality during his visiting period.

Let us finally thank those without whom this work would not make sense: our students at Barcelona Graduate School, Bocconi University, Climate Economics Chair, École des Mines, École Polytechnique, European Electricity Markets Chair, Natural Gas Chair, Padova University, Paris Dauphine University, Toulouse School of Economics. Their enthusiasms, questions, doubts and remarks have helped to inspire this textbook.

# Introduction

What is the *Economics of Electricity* about? This is an interesting question that has no easy answer. We could take the safe path and claim that it is the study of the electricity markets. But, as economists already know, there is already a specific economic field devoted to the study of industries, called Industrial Organization. So, are there any specific features of the economics of electricity that justify a reference textbook? We believe so. It is true that the economics of electricity is, after all, just another applied study of economics; but the way the models and tools that are (or should be) in the hands of any well-trained economist are applied in this field makes all the difference. There are specific features of power systems, accruing from the laws of physics and the way power systems have been created and developed throughout history, which require a careful understanding before applying economic analysis. Moreover, they imply that the standard approaches of economics, such as welfare maximization and competition studies, when applied to the electricity sector, also drive new and interesting results. For instance, economists are trained that competition induces a selection of technologies and therefore only the most efficient players survive in the market. In the electricity sector, however, it is natural for technologies with different efficiencies to coexist; actually, this is even a desirable feature. Every student knows that an equilibrium with a negative price makes no sense. In electricity markets, this may occur. And we could continue, but we do not want to reveal all now. Just read the book through, and you will find those interesting results yourself.

One final word about a second question that might require a preliminary explanation. To what extent is this textbook new? There are other textbooks on electricity markets, or power systems, or electricity sector regulation, such as Biggar and Hesamzadeh (2014), Hunt (2002), Kirschen and Strbac (2004), Perez-Arriaga (2013), Stoft (2002). They are excellent references, and we have also made use of them. However, we think that a comprehensive yet accessible textbook on the economics of electricity is missing. This is the purpose of this book, aimed at all those who have a basic training in economics, perhaps in Industrial Organization, but who lack the specific knowledge required in applying economic models to the electricity sector. We aim to bridge this gap, and, we assure you that studying it will be worthwhile. It is a rewarding experience; at least, it has been for us.

## Content of the Book

The book contains an exhaustive and up-to-date discussion of electricity economics. It seeks to address questions such as: What are the properties of electricity as an economic commodity? What are electricity markets, why do they exist, and how do they work? What are the economic principles behind trade, supply, transportation and distribution of power to consumers and firms? Are there any specific aspects of the economic analysis applied to electricity systems? How are the different markets organized and why? How should they be optimally designed and what elements should be taken into account to deliver electricity effectively and efficiently? How can electricity production be decarbonized?

The style of the book is technical, yet accessible to all those who have a basic training in economics. The main and most widely accepted tools of economic analysis are used. An introduction to the basic elements of power system elements and engineering is also provided, to help most economics students to become acquainted with the basics of electricity that have to be taken into account when delivering meaningful and useful analysis of the sector. Moreover, students in the field of engineering, political sciences, and physics, who have already had introductory courses in economics will be able to follow the rationale of the analyses developed and gain insights into the economics of electricity systems.

The structure of the book is modular. It spans twenty-seven chapters, grouped in eight parts. The sequence we have chosen reflects a logical path that helps teaching courses on electricity economics. It can be undertaken sequentially from the first to the last chapter, or sub-sequences could be constructed depending on instructors' needs.

Several chapters discuss and provide concrete references to real-world cases that refer to the concepts developed and explained in the text. Moreover, quick exercises developed as simple examples help to understand the various theoretical concepts that are introduced. At the end of each chapter, the learning outcomes focus on key-point messages.

Part I – Chapters 1 and 2 – presents an introduction to energy and electricity. Chapter 1 covers definitions and unit measures. It deals with the definitions of energy, electricity, and power; energy sources and carriers; unit measures and energy conversion principles. Chapter 2 presents a brief history of electricity and electricity markets. Examples on energy unit measures and conversion help students unfamiliar with those concepts to become acquainted with them. The fundamental notions of electricity production costs are then detailed.

Part II – Chapters 3, 4 and 5 – covers the basic features of the power systems and the design of electricity markets. Chapter 3 describes the Electricity Supply Chain (ESC), divided into production, transmission, dispatching, distribution, metering and retailing; it describes their features and specificities. Chapter 4 distinguishes between the physical and economic delivery of electricity. Chapter 5 describes four different market arrangements under which the ESC can be organized. The time structure of the economic delivery of electricity, from production to real-time, is also explained. Chapter 6 is an overview of the main principles of regulation in the power sector, a brief yet useful reference to understand the specific problems of regulation in electricity.

Parts III to V are linked by a progressive removal of simplifying assumptions, toward a more accurate and realistic description of the electricity sector.

Part III – Chapters 7 to 11 – considers simplified isolated markets without network congestion. Chapter 7 looks at main characteristics of the load (or demand) and power generation. Chapter 8 explains demand-supply matching. It presents the basic tool for analyzing the principle of optimal dispatching, namely, the concept of Economic Dispatching, in centralized markets. While Chapter 8 takes the point of view of a fully integrated monopoly, Chapter 9 describes the welfare maximization solution of a central planner, when load is time-varying. Chapter 10 shows under which conditions a full market solution replicates the optimal planned one. Chapter 11 is devoted to specific markets delivering services whose aim is to ensure stability and reliability. In particular, we study how balancing services can be exchanged effectively and efficiently. At the end of Part III, we provide a link to a web-based platform that introduces a market game. This simulation replicates the features of a stylized power exchange. The exercise allows interested readers to become acquainted with the technical side of power plants (technologies, costs, efficiency, maintenance, $CO_2$ emissions, varying load) and practice the profit-maximization strategies and the market consequences studied in this part.

Part IV – Chapters 12 and 13 – explains why electricity markets are vulnerable to market power. The arguments are developed both from a theoretical and an empirical point of view. First, the main models of market power are analyzed (Chapter 12). Then the issue of market power measurement is discussed (Chapter 13).

Part V – Chapters 14 to 18 – introduces the economic analysis of transmission networks, both internally and for import and export of energy. Chapter 14 introduces the basic problem of finding the optimal dispatching in a two-nodes network, by means of nodal pricing. The notion of congestion is also introduced. The consequences of Kirchhoff's laws in meshed networks are considered in Chapter 15, using the simple three-nodes case as a reference. Chapter 16 describes the concepts, characteristics and properties of nodal and zonal pricing in practice. Chapter 17 tackles the issue of network expansion and the incentives to invest in transmission capacity. Chapter 18 shows the complexity of setting transmission rights, either physical or financial, and the possibility of risk hedging with transmission rights and contracts for differences.

Part VI reviews the characteristics and specificities of electricity retailing markets. Chapter 19 is an overview of theoretical models of competitive electricity retailing activities, whereas Chapter 20 is devoted to practical examples and implementation issues in different countries.

Part VII tackles the issue of investments in generation capacity. Following the same approach as in Part III, in Chapter 21 the optimal investment problem in a planned setting is introduced first, followed by the competitive market analysis. In real-world situations, however, incentives to invest can be sustained by specific mechanisms to remunerate capacity. The theoretical comparison of generation capacity investments with and without remuneration schemes is carried through in Chapter 22. Then, various existing capacity remuneration mechanisms are presented and discussed in Chapter 23.

Part VIII explains the role and importance of the environmental dimension in the electricity markets and the evolution of the electricity system, with reference to demand-side advances and innovation at the production, transmission and distribution levels. Long-term decarbonization scenarios are presented in Chapter 24. The role and features of renewable electricity production are considered in Chapter 25. The issues arising from the integration of non-programmable energy sources in electricity systems are studied in Chapter 26. Finally, Chapter 27 focuses on the Electricity Supply Chain evolution, with regard to smart grids and new retail services.

## Possible Teaching Sequences and Sub-Sequences

The content of the teaching depends on the length of the course, its level, audience and students' backgrounds, as well as on the instructor's interests. Teaching all of the chapters would require a full-length semester course of sixty hours or more. While this might sometimes be required, several sub-sequences can be taken out of the structure of the content of the book.

A typical masters-level course for economics students can be served by teaching Parts I to V, possibly also including Part VII. If the teaching material has to be shared with other topics in energy economics, typically gas markets, Parts II and V can be left out, and Parts I, III, IV taught. When the class focuses on competition and regulation in electricity markets, we recommend including Part V, and perhaps skipping Part II. There are also classes on "Energy and Environment." In this case, the teaching material would be Parts I, II, IV and VIII. Second-year masters students in energy economics could go for Parts I to VI. If students are familiar with the basics of power systems, they can skip Part I and, depending on their background, also Part II. Undergraduate students can refer to Parts I to IV of the book.

# Part I

# Introduction to Energy and Electricity

Energy economics is the branch of economics that analyzes energy markets. Electricity, being a form of energy, is contained in the field of energy economics. Thus, electricity economics is that part of energy economics that refers to electricity markets, namely, the modalities and features through which electricity is produced, sold and purchased. We will study it following both a positive and a normative approach. The former refers to the several ways in which electricity markets are effectively designed around the world, as well as the possible different steps through which the electricity sector has progressively been opened to competition. The latter answers the question about how electricity markets should be designed, taking into account an idealized world (first-best analysis) as well as the several constraints posed by different real features across the world and across various electric systems (second-best analysis). However, before undertaking such a task, we should explain what electricity is. Indeed, we believe that the nature and physics of electricity have specific characteristics that have to be clearly understood in order to have a clear picture of the constraints that they pose to the way electricity can and should be traded. In Chapter 1, we explain what energy and electricity are and the nature of their relationship. Then in Chapter 2 we specify the characteristics of electricity as a type of energy and briefly consider the evolution of the set of appliances, tools and technical apparels that enable it to be exploited.

# 1 Basic Principles, Definitions and Unit Measures

## 1.1 Introduction

In this chapter, we explain the meaning of energy and electricity. We introduce tools and concepts that will be needed in the following chapters. Indeed, the physical laws that govern electricity constrains the economic activity of players. In order to understand why, we need briefly to describe the basics of energy and electricity.[1]

## 1.2 Basic Principles of Energy

Electricity is a shortcut word for electric energy. It is a form of energy. But, what is energy? There are several possible definitions. In brief, energy is whatever enables a body to do work. Work, in the physical sense, is a displacement against a resistance; we thus have a possible definition of energy, as stated in Newton's second law of motion:

DEFINITION. **Energy:** *the capability to do work, i.e., a displacement against a resistance*:

$$E = F \cdot x; \tag{1.1}$$

where $F$ is a force, measured in Newtons, and $x$ is a displacement, measured in any unit measure of distance, such as meter. Therefore, energy, $E$, is measured in Newton-meters. It is also measured in joules, where one joule corresponds to one Newton-meter:

DEFINITION. **Joule:** *the work done, or energy transferred, by an object when a force of one Newton displaces it for one meter.*

The above definition refers to work done, or energy *transferred*. Where is that energy transferred? In order to understand, it is useful to distinguish between usable work and residual heat, where the former could also be usable heat, while the latter is the residual heat that is always generated when some energy does work but cannot be captured in any useful way. Let us explain this concept better. We have said that the energy that exerts

---

[1] This chapter presents just an introduction to the topic. For a more thorough discussion, see Shepherd and Shepherd (2014).

a force does *work*. Heat is energy that does not carry out work. A force is the product of mass ($m$) and acceleration ($a$):

$$F = m \cdot a. \tag{1.2}$$

For the case of linear motion, acceleration is the rate of change of velocity ($v$):

$$v = \frac{dx}{dt}; \tag{1.3}$$

$$a = \frac{dv}{dt}; \tag{1.4}$$

where the unit measure of velocity is meters per second (or any other ratio of distance over time), and acceleration is meters per second squared (it is simply the derivative of distance per time over the same unit measure of time). Therefore, we have:

$$E = m \cdot a \cdot x;$$
$$E = m \cdot \frac{dv}{dt} \cdot x;$$
$$E = m \cdot \frac{dv}{dx}\frac{dx}{dt} \cdot x; \tag{1.5}$$
$$E = m \cdot v \cdot \frac{dv}{dx} \cdot x.$$

Equation (1.5) shows that energy is the product of the linear momentum, i.e., the (linear) velocity that holds the mass, and the term $\frac{dv}{dx} \cdot x$, which represents the applied force that gives rise to the relative change in the velocity, for a given distance.

A mass possesses two kinds of energy: potential energy and kinetic energy. The first depends on the position of the mass, the latter on its motion. The potential energy is given by the gravitational force, applied to a mass at a given height ($h$) above a given plane:

$$E_{P_e} = g \cdot m \cdot h; \tag{1.6}$$

where $g$ is the gravitational constant, whose value is $g \cong 9.81 \ m/s^2$ (note that it is an acceleration). We say that a mass of one kilogram, placed at a height of one meter, that receives a constant acceleration of one meter per second squared, has a potential energy of one joule. The kinetic energy associated with a linear motion depends on the mass and the velocity by means of the following equation:

$$E_{K_e} = \frac{1}{2} \cdot m \cdot v^2. \tag{1.7}$$

Equation (1.7) shows that linear momentum is nothing other than the rate of change of kinetic energy with respect to velocity: $\frac{dE_{K_e}}{dv} = mv$. From Equations (1.5) and (1.7), we can easily see the relationship between kinetic energy and work done:

$$W = \frac{dE_{K_e}}{dv}\frac{dv}{dx} \cdot x;$$

$$W = \frac{dE_{K_e}}{dx} \cdot x.$$

(1.8)

The work done, i.e. the energy transferred, is just the change in the kinetic energy between any two locations (i.e. for a given displacement).

Both kinetic energy and potential energy satisfy the principle of conservation of energy stated in the first law of thermodynamics, namely, that the internal energy of a system equals the work done by the system, and therefore total energy remains constant. Heat goes from hot to cold bodies, thus establishing the irreversibility of energy transfer in natural processes, as stated in the second law of thermodynamics. An example can usefully explain how these two laws are related to the energy concepts that we are introducing in this chapter and why they are important. Consider the short experiment described in the Example 1.1:

---

**Example 1.1 A Simple Experiment** Let us perform a simple experiment. Please, stand up (if you are reading this book seated in a public library or if you believe you might disturb someone around you, please don't do it, just imagine it!) and let the book fall to the ground. Then, take the book again, and continue to read it.

Done? Well, what has happened? We suppose you heard some noise. Why? Where does the sound come from? Figure 1.1 works out the experiment from the energy point of view.

---

Figure 1.1 represents the energy of the book that falls at different points in time: 1) when you were holding it in your hands standing up; 2) right after you left

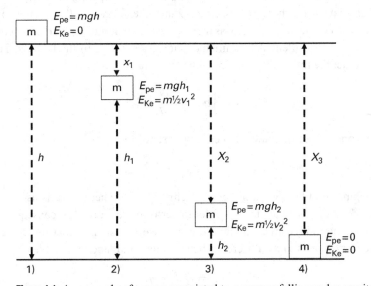

**Figure 1.1** An example of energy associated to a mass $m$ falling under gravity

it falling to the ground; 3) a few instants before it hit the ground; 4) after it hit the ground.

We can see that at point 1 all the energy of the book is potential energy. It is the product of the mass of the book, the height at which you are holding it in your hands and the gravitational constant. As soon as you release it, it starts falling, running some distance $x_1$, and therefore reducing the remaining height to $h_1$. Some of the potential energy, namely, the difference between the whole potential energy $m\,g\,h$ and the actual $m\,g\,h_1$, is converted into kinetic energy, measured by $\frac{1}{2}\,m\,v^2$. Obviously, the speed increases with the distance $x$, reaching its maximum just before the book hits the ground. At point 4, the book, after hitting the ground, has no more energy: there is obviously no kinetic energy (there is no velocity when the book lies on the ground), and no potential energy either, given that the ground is the datum plane (the height is zero). But the book has done work, i.e., there has been some energy that has displaced its mass through the distance $x$. Where has it gone? All the energy, i.e., the work done, which was accumulated in the change in the potential energy from zero (when the book was in your hand) to its maximum (right before it hit the ground) has been transferred to the system that contains the book (the room where you are doing your experiment) in several forms corresponding to different lengths of electromagnetic waves, namely, sound, heat, light, etc. This is why it is important to distinguish between work and residual heat. The energy transferred to the system cannot be recovered; it is somehow lost.

Let us have a further look at the consequences of the laws of thermodynamics. The second law of thermodynamics, stated differently, affirms that total entropy of an isolated system always increases over time. As a consequence, the energy transfer in a system is irreversible. Entropy, roughly speaking, can be defined as the amount of energy that cannot be converted into work. It is a measure of the spontaneous molecular disorder. It can be understood starting from the definition of change in entropy: $dS = dQ/T$, where $S$ is entropy, $Q$ is heat and $T$ is the temperature (in degrees kelvin). Note that heat is not the same as temperature: the former is the amount of energy capacity (to do work either directly as thermal warming or indirectly through conversion in some other form of energy), while the latter is a measure of the hotness. Therefore, entropy is just the ratio of the heat over the temperature:

$$S = \int dS = \int \frac{dQ}{T} = \frac{Q}{T}. \tag{1.9}$$

The second law of thermodynamics simply states that:

$$dS \geq 0. \tag{1.10}$$

A machine, or a heat-work system, is defined by the energy that is used in it when doing work or that is added to it in order to perform the work. The consequence of the first law of thermodynamics applied to a heat-work system is that the energy of the machine corresponds to the difference between its initial and the final heat:

$$E = Q_I - Q_H; \tag{1.11}$$

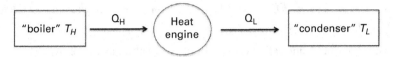

**Figure 1.2** The ideal Carnot machine

Where $Q_H$ is the initial heat and $Q_L$ is the final one. According to the second law of thermodynamics, heat goes from hot to cold bodies, and not vice versa. We can describe the heat transfer in an ideal machine by means of the so-called Carnot machine, represented in Figure 1.2.

Assume there is an original source of energy stored at temperature $T_H$. Call it the boiler (to ease the metaphoric interpretation of the heat-work machine as a heat pump, for instance, a sink where water is boiling). The original energy is $Q_H$. The machine carries out work in the engine; for instance, the steam that derives from the boiling water is used to rotate a turbine. The amount of energy is $E = Q_L - Q_H$ (notice that this figure is negative because it represents the energy that is extracted from the machine, not added to it). Then the temperature cools down, for instance the steam temperature is reduced to $T_L$ (steam is condensed in the condenser, which could as well be the atmosphere where it is released into). Notice that entropy is reduced when the liquid flows from the boiler into the engine, since heat is subtracted from $T_H$, while it is increased when the hotter liquid (or steam) flows into the condenser, since heat is added to $T_L$:

$$S = \int dS = -S_H + S_L = \frac{Q_L}{T_L} - \frac{Q_H}{T_H}; \tag{1.12}$$

Where $S_H$ is the entropy of the energy transfer from the boiler to the engine, while $S_L$ is the entropy added to the system when energy is added to the condenser. Given that $dS \geq 0$ we have:

$$\frac{Q_L}{Q_H} - \frac{T_L}{T_H} \geq 0;$$

$$\frac{Q_L}{Q_H} \geq \frac{T_L}{T_H};$$

$$1 - \frac{Q_L}{Q_H} \leq 1 - \frac{T_L}{T_H};$$

and recalling that $E = Q_H - Q_L$ we have:

$$\frac{E}{Q_H} \leq 1 - \frac{T_L}{T_H}. \tag{1.13}$$

The left-hand side of the equation above represents the ratio of the energy output of the machine over the energy input. We can call this term the efficiency of the system, usually denoted by $\eta$:

DEFINITION. *Energy Efficiency (η): the ratio of the energy output of a system over the energy input.*

The right-hand side ratio is the ratio of the final temperature over the original one, measured in kelvin. The absolute zero kelvin is not reachable in a physical system, therefore the right-hand side will always be less than one. Equation (1.13) then shows that the efficiency of an energy system, albeit theoretical, will always be less than one, i.e., it is not possible to fully convert all energy input $Q_H$ into usable work. Some of it will always be lost, i.e., transferred to the environment where the system is placed.

Notice that the efficiency stated in Equation (1.13) is a theoretical one, also called Carnot efficiency, since it corresponds to the application of the second law of thermodynamics to a theoretical machine. In reality, the efficiency of a machine will be far less than the Carnot one, since further losses are employed in all energy transfer processes. But in any case, Equation (1.13) shows that all energy transfer processes inevitably imply some inefficiency, which can be reduced by improving the process, but never eliminated.

## 1.3    Primary Energy Sources and Energy Carriers

There exist several forms of energy that can be classified on the basis of their properties (energy forms), or on the basis of the substances that contain the energy (energy sources):

- Energy forms: mechanical, chemical, thermal, radiant, nuclear, electrical.
- Energy sources: coal, oil, gas, uranium, hydro, biomass, wind, solar, geothermal, ocean energy.

Like all taxonomies, this is artificial, and the frontiers of the definitions are rather weak. For instance, thermal energy is also referred to as heat, while radiant energy can be referred to as light and electromagnetic radiation, even though electromagnetic radiations of different length are indeed heat, light, sound, electricity, etc. Moreover, a given energy source can be classified in one or more energy forms. For instance, uranium is the only source of nuclear energy that we are able to convert through fission of its nucleus into electric energy, while solar energy is indeed radiant energy but also thermal and electrical energy.

Electrical energy is energy due to the movement of electrons induced by electromagnetic force, as we will explain in Chapter 2. In this chapter, it is useful to introduce a further classification of energy that helps to analyze the specificities of the electricity sector. We can consider different levels of energy usage, either directly or through some transformation. In particular, it is useful to distinguish between primary energy sources and secondary energy sources, also called energy carriers:

DEFINITION. *Primary energy source: an energy source that can be directly used in some system.*

DEFINITION. *Energy carrier: an energy source that derives from the transformation of some primary energy source.*

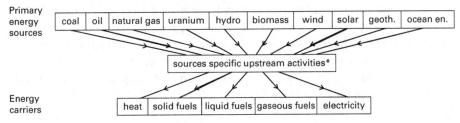

* = depend on sector specific investments. For hydrocarbons: prospecting; exploration; extraction; refining; distribution.

**Figure 1.3** Primary energy sources and energy carriers
*Source*: our adaptation from Sims et al. (2007), Figure 4.1.

The above definitions require some further comments. All energy sources, when used, are converted; after all, this is what we have seen in the description of the Carnot machine. Therefore, all sources require some system to be used. These energy sources can be directly used, in the sense that they exist in some form and can be used in the system. The energy carriers, on the contrary, do not exist as energy sources, but are the product of the conversion of some primary energy source into some other form of energy. From the point of view of economics, energy carriers are intermediate products of some primary transformation process. They are produced in order to be further used. Electricity is an example of an energy carrier.

Figure 1.3 helps to understand the difference between primary energy sources and energy carriers. The figure shows that primary energy sources of different forms can be transformed to give rise to different energy carriers. For instance, from hydrocarbons we can obtain heat by burning coal, oil or gas, but also from biomass or geothermal energy. Liquid fuels, such as gasoline or diesel, are derived from the refining of hydrocarbons, but also from coal (called Synfuel), natural gas or biomass. Gaseous fuels come from the cultivation of gas fields, but also from the refining of other hydrocarbons or even from biomass. The economic activities that allow the usage of primary energy sources are called upstream activities. For hydrocarbons, these are the activities of prospecting, exploration, extraction refining and distribution. For other primary energy sources, not all of these activities are relevant, while some other parts of the upstream activities require significant investment to obtain the carrier, such as research and development for ocean energy, for instance or cultivation for biomass

Electricity, as an energy carrier, is obtained from the conversion of several primary energy sources. These primary energy sources are transformed into fuels that are then further converted into electricity through power generation. For instance, oil or coal can be burned to generate heat that is converted into electricity in thermal power plants, or the potential energy of water contained in a dam is converted into electricity exploiting the kinetic energy of water through hydropower production. Note, however, that any energy conversion implies some loss of energy. Therefore, for the case of electricity, we must consider losses due to the efficiency rate of power production, as well as the losses due to the efficiency of the whole process of making electricity available to end consumers, called Electricity Supply Chain (ESC) (see further below). The efficiency of the ESC is sometimes referred to as system efficiency. The reason why it is useful to convert primary energy sources into electricity even if this implies losses, or sometimes even converting some other energy carriers into electricity for instance by burning gas or gasoline in engines, will be apparent when explaining the properties and characteristics of electricity as an energy carrier.

## 1.4     Energy Units and Energy Measures

Recall the following definitions of multiple of units as stated in the International System of Units[2] (SI):

**Table 1.1** Multiples in SI units

| Factor | Name | Symbol |
|--------|------|--------|
| $10^3$ | kilo | K |
| $10^6$ | mega | M |
| $10^9$ | giga | G |
| $10^{12}$ | tera | T |
| $10^{15}$ | peta | P |

We have already encountered the joule as the unit measure of energy. However, there are other possible unit measures for energy. Some of them derive from the way the energy concepts were discovered and defined throughout history. A first important equivalence is between joule and watt-second (Ws):

$$1 \text{ Joule} = 1 \text{ watt-second.} \tag{1.14}$$

What is a watt-second? In order to understand this we have to explain the relationship between energy and power.

DEFINITION. **Power**: *the time rate of the work done by the energy.* $P = \dfrac{dE}{dt}$.

Power is an instantaneous (timeless) measure of the rate of conversion of energy, i.e., of doing work. Therefore, power and energy are linearly related to the time:

$$E = P \cdot t. \tag{1.15}$$

The unit measure of power in SI is the joule per second [J/s], called the watt [W]. Using the second as the unit measure of time in SI, we have the equivalence stated in Equation (1.14).

There are other measures of power, such as the horsepower [HP], an old British power unit: $1 \text{ HP} \equiv 745.7 \text{ W} \equiv 0.7457 \text{ kW}$.

---

[2] See Taylor and Thompson (2008).

Some unit measures of energy are calories and British Thermal Units [BTU]. A calorie is defined as the amount of energy needed to raise the temperature of one gram of water by 1 degree Celsius. It corresponds to 4.1868 joules. The BTU is defined as the amount of energy needed to raise the temperature of one pound of water by 1 degree Fahrenheit. It corresponds to 1055.06 joules.

Using Equation (1.15) we can express power using all measures of energy. If time is expressed in seconds, its multiples are hours, days, etc. It is common to relate power to calories considering kilocalories per hour [kc/h], and 12,000 BTU per hours, called tonnes of refrigeration [12,000 BTU/h].

Similarly, it is possible to convert multiples of watt-second using the equivalences of times. For instance, we know that there are 60 seconds in a minute, 3,600 seconds in an hour. Therefore, 3,600 watt-seconds correspond to 1 watt-hour.

Time units are additive. Any combination of power and times that give rise to 3,600 watt-seconds correspond to one watt-hour. For instance, the power of 3,600 watts that generates energy for one second corresponds to 1 watt-hour. But we can also have one watt-hour if we have a power of 1,800 watts that does work for two seconds, since $1,800 \cdot 2 = 3,600$, or any other possible combination of power and time that give the same result.

There exist other unit measures for energy that take into account the average energy embedded in several energy sources. The purpose of these measures is to express the energy content of different primary energy sources using a common unit measure. Indeed, there exist several types of substances that we call coal, oil, gas, etc. depending on the different specific weight, sulfur content, caloric power, and so on. These sources have been standardized with respect to the energy content, and then all primary sources but oil converted in fractions of energy with respect to the energy content of oil. This latter is called Tonne of Oil Equivalent.

DEFINITION. *Tonne of Oil Equivalent (TOE): the amount of energy embedded in a standard tonne of oil.*

It is also common to express the equivalence in terms of barrels of oil equivalent [BOE] rather than tonne. Taking into account that there are 158.987 liters in a barrel, using a standardized specific gravity of 0.88 (i.e. 1 l = 0.88 kg) we have a conversion of 1 BOE = 0.14 TOE. Obviously, for the oil itself the unit measure is rightly termed as just Tonne of Oil or Barrel of Oil.

## Learning Outcomes

- Energy is the capability to do work. In physics, it is the force that makes a displacement against a resistance. It is measured in joules. The force depends on the mass; a mass possesses potential energy and kinetic energy.

- Energy follows the laws of thermodynamics. In the conversion process of potential energy into kinetic energy, some energy is transferred to the system in which the work is done in a form that cannot be recovered, called heat.
- The Carnot machine can be used to show that energy efficiency, namely, the ratio of energy output of a machine over the energy input, must be less than one because of the first and second laws of thermodynamics.
- There are several forms and sources of energy. Depending on the usage of energy, we can distinguish primary energy sources, directly used in energy systems, and energy carriers, derived from transformation of primary energy sources.
- There exist several unit measures of energy. One joule is equivalent to one watt-second, namely, the power of one watt for one second. Power is the instantaneous rate of conversion of energy. The International System has standardized the equivalences between the several unit measures of energy and of power.
- A Tonne of Oil Equivalent is a unit measure of primary energy based on the average energy content of oil, as a reference for primary energy source.

# 2 Introduction to Electricity: Brief History of the Power Industry

## 2.1 Introduction

Electricity is a man-made product. Of course, this is a false statement: electricity is a form of energy that exists in nature. But the way this energy has been developed and adapted in order to provide useful services is indeed an invention of mankind. The structure of the technical relationships that enabled the generation and provision of electricity to consumers, that we call the electricity system, was established at the end of the nineteenth century and has undergone a continuous process of evolution and adaptation ever since. There are several components of the complex system that allow the provision of electricity in a useful way to consumers. We describe the Electricity Supply Chain (henceforth, ESC) in Chapter 3. However, before doing so, we detail here the specific characteristics of electricity as a type of energy, and how the ESC has been developed from its early days. Moreover, we briefly review the main features of the technologies that allow the generation of electricity in the ESC.

## 2.2 Basic Principles of Electricity

Electricity is a form of energy.[1] It is the energy that allows work to be carried out through the ordered flow of electrons. The word ordered here plays a crucial role. Recall Equation (1.15) and the definition of power. For the case of electricity, power is the product of voltage and current:[2]

$$P = V \cdot I; \tag{2.1}$$

where $P$ represents power, measured in watts, while $V$ stands for voltage, measured in volts and $I$ for current, measured in amperes. What are current and voltage? Consider the following definitions:

DEFINITION. *Current: the instantaneous ordered movement of electrons through a medium.*

DEFINITION. *Voltage: the differential in electric potential between two elements.*

---

[1] As before, for more on the basic principles of electricity see Sheperd and Sheperd (2014).

[2] This is true for Direct Current, and only partially true for Alternating Current. See further below.

A useful comparison can help understand the relationship between voltage and current. Electric energy is the energy that derives from the movement of the electrons through a medium, also called a conductor. This movement can be induced by several factors, such as a magnetic field for instance or the electric imbalances of atoms that are not in a state of electric stability. We can imagine the flow of electrons through the conductor, for instance through a cable, as the flow of water in a pipe. Even though this metaphor could be misleading, since the flow of current can be reversed, as we shall see later, it helps visualize the voltage and the current. The former is like the pressure of the water on the pipe, the latter the flow of water through it. Voltage is sometimes called "potential difference," "electric potential difference," "electric tension" or "electric pressure." The first two terms in particular refer to the definition of voltage as the difference in potential electric energy between any two points per unit of electric charge (either positive or negative). There is electricity if there is the potentiality of having electrons moving through a mean, and this potentiality is indeed what voltage is. Two aspects are worth emphasizing. The first is that, obviously, a potentiality is just a necessary condition to have energy flowing, but not a sufficient one. If there is no current, there is no energy delivered and therefore no electricity. The second aspect is that a voltage is a timeless measure, since it refers to the potentiality of energy flow, not the flow itself.

We have mentioned the term "ordered" movement in the definition of electricity. What does this mean? In order to understand it, let us imagine electricity as a flow of electrons, generated by an impulse (whatever it is) that proceeds through a conductor, for example a cable. When electrons "flow," they induce the electrons of the atoms of the cable to move from atom to atom, as if they were "pushed" by the movement. But some electrons of the conductor would move randomly, colliding among themselves, and thus instead of pushing the electrons of the cable (e.g. copper) to jump from one atom to the other, they would simply collide among them. This random movement would increase the heat of the cable, but would not turn out into a useful work. The latter would be the activity that can be performed thanks to the ordered movement of the electrons at the end of the circuit. For instance, this movement of electrons generates an electromagnetic field, and this can be transformed into mechanical work. This is called an **electric engine**. Or by capturing and storing this movement of electrons in a properly designed device, made of specific metals; this is called a **battery**.

Thus, like any form of energy, some of the electric energy is not converted in useful work, but simply lost as heat in the system. The amount of such a loss, or vice versa, of the relative share of useful work that can be done, depends on the characteristics of the medium through which the electrons flow, and in particular on its resistance:

DEFINITION. **Resistance**: *the measure of the difficulty that the electric current has in passing through a conductor. It is measured in ohms.*

Resistance[3] is linked to voltage and current through the following equation, called **Ohm's law**:

$$R = \frac{V}{I}. \tag{2.2}$$

This is not always true for all materials, but it is mostly true. Therefore, Ohm's law can be regarded more as an empirical regularity rather than a proper physical law. The opposite of resistance is called **conductance**, and is a measure of the ease with which current passes through the conductor. It is important to understand that resistance depends on several aspects of the conductor, and in particular on its intrinsic ease or difficulty in passing the electric current through it. This intrinsic property of the materials is called **resistivity** and its inverse is **conductivity**. Resistivity (or conductivity) is an intrinsic property of the material while resistance (or conductance) depends on the resistivity (conductivity) as well as on the length and the surface (cross-sectional dimension) of the material. The relationship between resistivity and resistance is given by the following equation:

$$\rho = R\frac{A}{l}; \tag{2.3}$$

where R is the resistance, $\rho$ is the resistivity of a given material, $A$ is the cross-sectional area of the material, $l$ its length. A resistance of one ohm for a surface of one meter squared and a length of one meter gives a resistivity of one ohm-meter.

Some materials have a low resistivity and thus, for a given sample (surface and length) a rather low resistance. They are said to be "good" conductors, such as copper and aluminum. Some others, characterized by a complex molecular structure, have a high resistivity, a low conductivity and therefore for a given sample they show a high resistance: they are insulators, such as rubber and wood. By solving Equation (2.2) for resistance it is apparent that the same level of resistance could be obtained with two different conductors, adjusting their respective surface and length. For instance, say there are two conductors of different resistivity, $C_1$, with a lower $\rho$ and $C_2$ characterized by a higher $\rho$. Assume that their length and shape is given, for instance, they are cylindrical cable of one meter each. In order to have the same resistance, $C_1$ can be of a smaller surface, while $C_2$ must increase the diameter of the cable by the square of the radius in order to overtake the higher resistivity.

We have already mentioned in Equation (2.2) the relationship between voltage and current, and what voltage is, using the hydraulic metaphor developed earlier in the text. However, a further element should be taken into account when thinking about the relationship between voltage and current, which depends on the resistance. It is not the voltage itself that determines the flow of energy, but the voltage drop, namely, the difference between the voltage at the beginning and at the end of a circuit. As in a pipe, it is not the pressure itself of the liquid that determines its flow, but the difference between

---

[3] The counterpart of resistance for AC circuits is called "Impedance." It has both a magnitude and a phase. See further below for definition of AC and phase.

the pressure at the beginning of the pipe and the pressure at the end. Even if at the beginning there was a high pressure, if there was also a concomitant high pressure at the end of the pipe that contrasts the inflow pressure, there would be a limited flow. This limited flow has to overtake the resistance of the medium through which it is flowing in order to pass. For instance, if the pipe is full of sand, there is a much higher resistance than if the pipe is empty. This is the role played by the resistance.

We have seen that the useful work performed by the electric energy is the work due to the ordered flow of electrons through the medium (i.e. it is the current that matters): whenever there is a need for electricity there is the need for current. The path of the electron flow is called **electricity circuit**. The intermediate point of a circuit in which electrons face a resistance (i.e. the point in which they are "used"), is called electrical load, or simply load:

DEFINITION. *Load: the portion of an electricity circuit that consumes electric energy.*

Sometimes, the load takes the form of a resistance. A high resistance induces a high amount of heat and a limited current flow. A matter with high resistivity implies that a lot of energy is converted into heat by that material itself. But this is exactly what might be needed, for instance, if the load is a resistor that is designed to convert the electrical energy into heat or light (which are just electromagnetic waves of different length), as in an incandescent light bulb or a heater. By combining Equations (2.1) and (2.2) we can calculate the amount of power dissipated by the load, depending on the resistance and the current, by the following equation:

$$P = R \cdot I^2. \tag{2.4}$$

The difference in the electric pressure (i.e. the voltage), determines the current flow through Ohm's law. This is true (for those materials for which Ohm's law is respected) for Direct Current (DC), while it is more complex for Alternate Current (AC). But, what are DC and AC currents? Recall that the current is a signed quantity. The negative sign denotes the power source, since electrons conventionally have a negative charge. The positive sign denotes the point of the circuit in which electrons return back (i.e. leave the circuit). The load is in between the negative and the positive poles. In DC circuits, current always flows from the negative to the positive node. In AC circuits, current reverses its direction and it flows first from the negative to the positive pole and vice versa. The time of such a reversion is called a period, and the number of complete cycles is called **frequency**. The unit measure of frequency is hertz (symbol Hz). The normal frequency of electric systems is 50 Hz in Europe, 60 in the United States.

For AC systems, Equation (2.1) needs to be adjusted. It is not correct to refer to just a single power for AC. Other concepts have been developed, that are linked among themselves: the apparent power, the active power and the reactive power. Let us see what they are. Assume that voltage and current have a sinusoidal shape. If the load in an AC circuit was just resistive, the voltage and the current invert their polarity at the same time. Therefore, their product would always give a value that is either positive or null. Equation (2.1) would then provide an exact measure of a system power. This power is what we call **active power**. In this case, we say that the system provides only active power. However, when the current and voltage are not at the same phase, there are values of current and voltage whose product is negative. This is called **reactive power**. A reactive power does not denote useful work that can be done for the load, but rather subtracts the possibility of providing energy to the load from a given power generator. The extreme case would be voltage and current out of phase with a 90° angle, since for two half cycles the product of voltage and current would provide positive figures and for the other two halves negative figures that exactly counterbalance the positive one. Thus, on average, we would have a zero value for active power. But energy has been produced and transmitted. Where has it gone? It has inverted its flux completely, going from the power generator to the load and back, thus providing zero useful work, just wasting all the energy heating the conductor. In this case, all the power would just be reactive power. The degree of difference between current and voltage expresses the phase. Its symbol is conventionally the Greek letter $\varphi$. For AC, Equation (2.1) needs to be replaced by:

$$P = V \cdot I \cdot \cos \varphi. \tag{2.5}$$

Equation (2.5) measures active power. When current and voltage are in phase, $\varphi = 0$, and $\cos \varphi = 1$. Equation (2.5) coincides with (2.1), which holds true for DC. There would be no difference between active power in an AC circuit and power in a DC one: all power is just active power. However, if current and voltage are not in phase, $\cos < 1$, and the power supplied (which is active power) is lower than the maximum possible one, the difference is the reactive power. This maximum possible power level is expressed by the concept of **apparent power**, which is the magnitude of the vector sum of active and reactive power. In Equation (2.5), active power is given by the product of current and voltage, (when these are calculated as root mean square (r.m.s.)[4]). The ratio of active power over apparent power is called the power factor $PF$, and it coincides with $\cos \varphi$:

$$PF = \frac{active\ power}{apparent\ power} = \cos \varphi. \tag{2.6}$$

Power factor is a useful summary statistic. It measures, in a circuit, for a given voltage, the fraction of the current supplied that is doing useful work, the complement to one being just reactive power. In a large circuit, or system, it is apparent power that matters when designing it. Indeed, unless the load is purely resistive, every increase or reduction of the power by adding or subtracting a power generator or a load changes the apparent power, not just the active one, depending on how this load or generation is phased with the rest of the system.

The typical current of a modern electric system is a three-phase AC current; namely, there are three main conductors and a central neutral one (the positive pole), and in each conductor there is the same voltage, but of one-third out of synchronism with each other at each point in time. This might seem complex (since it requires synchronizing each

---

[4] The root mean square is the square root of the mean of the values squared.

phase to every possible increase or decrease of the load), but it is extremely flexible for domestic or industrial usages.

The three-phase current is obtained (in its simplest format) by rotating a magnet or electromagnet, called the **rotor**, surrounded by three coils of wires, called the **stator**. This apparel is called a three-phase **alternator**. On the contrary a DC current, which is the current that flows from two materials of different electric potentiality through a mean (as it happens in a battery) can be generated, in its simplest form, in a **dynamo**. The dynamo is a power generator in which a coil of wire rotates between a magnet (or electromagnet). Why has AC current been invented, and why is it widely used in every electric system? In order to answer these questions, we should briefly review the history of the development of the electricity industry. All in all, an economic issue has determined the "supremacy" of AC over DC current in modern electricity systems.

## 2.3      Brief History of the Commercial Development of Electricity

The commercial usage of electricity began in the nineteenth century. It is still widely used today and will probably continue into the future. The electricity era, as it has been named, has been anticipated, supported and fostered by a vast number of scientific discoveries and technological developments. We will not provide a full account of the history of electricity here.[5] We focus only on the economic causes and consequences of the electrification of economic systems.

There have been three main "killer applications" that have pushed the usage of electricity around the world: 1) electric lighting; 2) the development and usage of electric engines; 3) the "portability" of electricity through the development and usages of batteries and the usage of electricity for transportation services.

1) *Electric lighting*: The need for lighting, when there is no sunlight (as occurs at nighttime or in closed rooms) has always been a human need, generally tackled by means of burning some natural or mineral oil. However, this had its drawbacks in terms of large externalities (smoke, danger) and above all high cost, due to the limited efficiency of lighting by means of burning. In the nineteenth century, public lighting started to be developed by means of coal and gas lighting, followed by carbon arc lamps,[6] which would use electricity to provide lighting. Again, this was rather expensive, and its management and operation was extremely labor intensive. The crucial development proved to be the introduction, by Thomas Edison,[7] of the

---

[5] There are several interesting books on this. We suggest, for instance, the vivid account written in the chapter on electricity by Everett et al. (2011).

[6] A carbon arc lamp is a lamp that produces light by an electric arc between carbon electrodes in the air. It was invented by Humphry Davy (see https://en.wikipedia.org/wiki/Humphry_Davy) at the beginning of the 1800s, and commercialized around 1870. It is the basis of modern fluorescent lamps.

[7] Thomas Alva Edison was an American business and inventor. He invented and/or developed, among other things, the phonograph, the motion picture camera and the light bulb. He is regarded as one of the greatest American inventors, as well as a successful businessman. He also founded the General Electric Company, which is still one of the largest companies in the world (see https://en.wikipedia.org/wiki/Thomas_Edison).

incandescent light bulb, which was far more reliable, lasted longer and was much more flexible than carbon arc lamps. They started as a status symbol for rich people, but technological developments enabled huge cost reductions: after its introduction into the market, in just three years the cost of lamps dropped by more than 90 percent. The spread of electric lighting had a dramatic consequence: it allowed many people among the working classes and even poor people to get rid of the day-night constraint and it reduced risks and health dangers. In economic terms, it pushed labor productivity and increased welfare. It had another consequence, which is extremely relevant for the evolution of electricity systems. Adding new customers created large economies of scale, since it was far cheaper to serve new additions of lamps by extending existing electricity circuits served by some power plants. The basics of the electricity system supply chain were established. To begin with, it seemed natural to serve lighting through Direct Current. After all, lamp light is the simplest example of a resistance in a DC circuit. Edison was in favor of DC, but it was soon replaced by AC systems, invented by Nikolas Tesla[8] and developed by the Westinghouse Electric Corporation together with the spread of the electric engine, which is the second "killer application" we review here.

2) *Electric engine*. The electric engine inverts the scheme used in power generators to produce electricity: the latter converts rotating energy into electricity; the former turns electricity into rotating force. It is possible to power an engine with DC and AC. Tesla showed how to use an AC current in the electric engine, and laid down the foundation to use the three-phase AC in electric motors, which is the standard that continues to be used today. The crucial element was the high efficiency of the energy conversion, that in AC three-phase engines can reach up to 90 percent. This led to their widespread usage in factories. A cheap and flexible source of energy was available for use in the textile industry, mechanics, manufacturing, and similar industries. Moreover, the AC current could be used by picking up any of the three phases in small electric engines, which, albeit being less efficient than the three-phase ones, would still provide cheap available energy to engineer and mechanize some tasks which hitherto had been provided by human labor: it was the beginning of what eventually became the widespread diffusion of domestic usages of electric engines for cooling (refrigerators), washing, and similar applications. The development of the electric engine came hand in hand with the spread of AC systems. Both DC and AC systems had several advantages: the former was flexible enough to be used with lamp lights and could be backed up by batteries. The latter was sufficiently powerful to provide energy for engines, and could still be used for lamplights. Albeit more complex, however, AC had a crucial advantage over DC which eventually determined its widespread adoption. The voltage of an AC current can be very

---

[8] Nikola Tesla (see https://en.wikipedia.org/wiki/Nikola_Tesla) was a Serbian inventor, mechanical and electrical engineer who emigrated to the United States, where he would eventually become a naturalized citizen. He carried out several fundamental studies on electricity and electromagnetism, and developed patents. In particular, he pioneered the research and development of the AC motors and polyphase AC systems that he eventually licensed to the Westinghouse Electric Corporation.

efficiently increased and decreased in a **transformer**.[9] The loss of energy in modern transformers can amount to a very few percentage points. As we have seen in paragraph 2.2, in order to be transmitted electricity has to overcome resistance of the line though which it is transported, and this, for a given resistivity of the conductor and a given length of the cable, depends on the voltage. Recall Equation (2.1): a given amount of power implies a small amount of current, at a high voltage, while at a low voltage it entails a much higher amount of current. When the voltage is low, for a given resistivity of the conductor and a given length, it is necessary to increase the size of the cable to the square of its radius to overtake the resistivity and transmit the current (or, to put it differently, too small a cable would simply get burned without being able to transmit the electricity). On the contrary, by increasing the voltage a cable with a much smaller diameter can be used to transmit power. This advantage has determined the "supremacy" of AC over DC. Current is what is needed by end users. By using transformers, AC current can easily and efficiently be increased in voltage, which allows power stations to be sited at a distance from the end users. This flexibility, in turn, pushed the use and deployment of hydropower to produce electricity, which was typically located far away from end users. Moreover, it allowed disentangling the locational choices of industries from the places where the primary sources were available. The length of transmission cables increased, as well as the size of power stations. Then, by reducing the voltage at stations close to the end users, the current needed by devices could be forwarded to customers with a (relatively) low loss of energy. The structure of modern electricity systems was thus laid down.

3) *Transportation services* and services made available through stored electricity. Another fundamental impetus to the usage of electricity came from the development of batteries and electricity used for transportation services, which would benefit from the development of batteries (as well as from the spread of electricity systems). Indeed, batteries could provide electric energy that could be transported and used where needed. This proved to be extremely useful for the communication industry (i.e. the telegraph), which had been established following the exploitation of discoveries and innovations relating to electromagnetism and its usages. Moreover, it became apparent that batteries could be used not just to deliver electric energy (DC), but also to store electricity when produced, by transforming electric energy back into chemical energy. This fostered the development of vehicles that could use electricity as a source of energy for transportation. At the end of the nineteenth century, most vehicles that did not harness the power of animals were powered by batteries. Even though automobiles were later replaced in large part by vehicles powered by internal combustion engines (not to be confused with external combustion engines, such as steam boilers), this did not happen for some large transportation vehicles, such as trolley cars and trains, that also began to be employed around the end of the nineteenth century for public transportation. The reason was that for small vehicles, such

---

[9] A transformer is an electrical device that transfers electrical energy between two or more circuits. Transformers are used to increase or decrease the voltages in AC circuits.

as private cars, the tanks of fuels used in internal combustion engines allowed storing a much larger amount of energy per unit of weight (using gasoline or diesel) as compared to the joules stored in a battery. Together with the growth of a network of refueling stations, this made internal combustion engines more convenient than electric engines for private transportation needs. However, for those vehicles for which the storage space was not an issue or for which it was economically convenient to lay down a fixed electric circuit (i.e. for those vehicles designed to run along a fixed track), it was convenient to use the electric engine, even backed by a pile of batteries. Thus, public transportation means were being developed, such as city trolley cars and trains, which had fewer externalities (less smoke, less dirt), were more flexible (less time to be heated up and used), implied lower maintenance costs and were safer than those run by animals or by external combustion engines. They could also be used in long underground tunnels, thus fostering the use and development of the first underground systems. They continued to be conveniently used even when internal combustion engines started to replace electrical vehicles, even in the form of hybrid vehicles. Indeed, hybrid vehicles, which we tend to think are an outstanding example of modern transportation systems, were quite widely used from the early days of public transportation and still are. For instance, diesel trains use internal combustion engines to charge batteries that provide energy to an electric engine. They were also used for those applications that depended crucially on the absence or the possibility of controlling emissions, as for submarines, for instance.

## 2.4    Introduction to Power Generation Technologies and Costs

In Chapter 1, we explained the differences between primary and secondary energy sources. Electricity is a secondary energy source, since it is derived from the transformation of some other primary energy source. Notice, however, that in several statistics, such as in the primary energy source statistics of IEA (IEA, 2017a), the electricity produced from hydropower or nuclear power is accounted for as a primary energy source. The idea expressed by such a classification is that the energy potential of water or of nuclear power is not captured in any other way than by transforming it into electricity, and thus it is accounted for as primary energy. Even though such a classification is in our opinion somewhat confusing, it makes clear that electrical energy is obtained by means of some technical device that allows one of the various types of energy, such as chemical, mechanical, thermal, kinetic, and so on, to be transformed into electricity. These technologies have been developing throughout the history of electricity systems, as we have briefly described in the previous section, and they are continuously evolving. In this section, we do not aim to provide a full description of the technical aspects of these technologies, but just to identify some of their features that have relevant consequences for the electricity industry.

Electricity is produced in power stations, also called power plants, or simply plants. These can be industrial farms where some fuel is converted into electricity by first converting the chemical energy incorporated into the fuel into thermal energy ("burning the fuel") and then converting the thermal energy into electrical energy. The latter is obtained by means of a turbine, that converts the thermal energy into a rotating force applied to a generator (a dynamo or an alternator). For this reason, power plants are sometimes also referred to as power generators, or simply generators, although this is not precise since a generator is just a component of the whole power plant. This is the simplest scheme of a thermal power plant. There are obviously large and small power plants, ranging from several hundred Megawatts (or even some Gigawatts) to very small portable generators of a few watts. The basic working principles are the same. Plants are often fueled by hydrocarbons, such as coal, natural gas or oil, but they can also work by burning some other energy source such as biomass, peat, lignite, and so on. One possible way of classifying plants might thus refer to the nature of the primary energy sources that fuels them. It is possible that the fuel used is not renewable, or it can be a Renewable Energy Source (RES), depending on its relative rate of (re)production:

DEFINITION. ***Renewable Energy Source (RES):*** *An energy source whose rate of reproduction is either instantaneous or takes place at a time scale comparable with its rate of depletion.*

The energy embedded in the solar radiation that reaches the Earth can obviously be considered renewable, since it is continuously produced by the sun, at least for a span of years that is long enough not to be of concern to the human species. The energy released by burning some biomass can also be regarded as renewable, depending on the rate of reproduction of the biomass compared to its rate of depletion. For example, burning wood logged from so-called short-rotation forests (i.e. trees cultivated to be logged every few years), can be considered a renewable form of energy production, while logging spontaneous, secular forests clearly is not. Like any classification, the definition of reproducibility can also be criticized and has some overlapping grey areas, which are mirrored in the several possible legal classifications of what can be regarded as a renewable primary source. A typical example is the case of urban waste. If we consider that human life on earth (in particular in urban areas) somehow naturally implies the production of some waste, this can be regarded as a renewable production. If we do not agree with this point of view, we might not include urban waste in RES. Power plants that do not use RES are classified as conventional thermal power plants. A specific category of thermal power plants uses uranium as a primary energy source in purpose-built reactors, converting the thermal energy released by the fission of the atoms of uranium isotopes into electrical energy. The reactor and the control devices are much more complex than conventional thermal power plants, but the working principle is very similar. These plants are called nuclear power plants.

There are also other ways of capturing and converting energy into electrical energy, such as the kinetic energy of wind or water or the radiant energy of the sun. These RES fuel wind power plants, photovoltaic or solar thermal power plants and hydropower plants.

Plant characteristics can be described from an economic point of view by calculating the different components of their costs and grouping them into costs that vary according to the different amount of energy produced and those that do not, dependent on the energy produced. The former are variable costs, while the latter are fixed costs. It is possible to summarize plant characteristics by means of a cost function $C_i(Q_i)$ that represents the power plant's $i$ costs in a given period, for instance in a year, as a function of the quantity of energy $Q_i$ that it produces in that period, measured in some unit measure of energy (e.g. MWh). The cost function can assume several possible specifications, depending on the technology of the power plant, the type of fuel used, size, age, and whether it produces several energy outputs, such as electricity and heat, for instance, or a single one, electricity. A simple functional form for the cost function is the *linear one*:

$$C_i(Q_i) = FC_i + Fl_f \cdot a_{f,i} \cdot Q_i; \tag{2.7}$$

$$\text{with: } \underline{Q_i} \leq Q_i \leq \overline{Q_i}$$

where:

- $FC_i$ are the fixed costs of the plants, i.e. the overall cost of planning, financing, building and maintaining the plant, regardless of its energy production. These costs are calculated over the entire useful predicted life span of the plant and attributed to each period (i.e. each year, by a proper amortization). The costs encompass economic risk, as well as a proper remuneration of all activities involved in the business of setting up and managing the plant. In real-life applications, this is typically included in the financial cost components. The annual amortized quota of the fixed costs is also referred to as the Capital Rental Cost (CRC), to highlight the fact that in a perfectly competitive financial market an investor who would like to enter into that business by, say, renting a plant would face that amount of financial cost every year to do so.
- $Fl_f$ is the price of the fuel $f$ which is used by the $i$th plant. It is measured in terms of money per unit of energy of the fuel, for instance, \$/GJ. In such a simple specification, it is assumed that there exists just one type of fuel that can be used to generate electricity. In this case, the plant is called mono-fuel. In several thermal power plants, however, it is possible to use different types of fuel to generate the thermal energy that is converted into electricity. These are called multi-fuel plants. In these cases, the cost function has to be extended to describe this technical characteristic. For instance, in the case of a dual-fuel plant, Equation (2.7) should be replaced by the following specification: $C_i(Q_i) = FC_i + Fl_f \cdot a_{f,i} \cdot Q_{f,i} + Fl_k \cdot a_{k,i} \cdot Q_{k,i}$, where clearly $f$ and $k$ are two different fuels and $Q_{f,i}$ and $Q_{k,i}$ denote the amount of electricity produced by plant $i$ using fuel $f$ and $k$, respectively.
- The coefficient $a_{f,i}$ is the parameter that represent the effective energy efficiency of the plant. It is the effective ratio of energy input over the energy output of the plant. It depends on the plant maximum or theoretical efficiency, as described in Chapter 1. However, note that the latter is purely a technical parameter, while the former depends on the way the plant is built, managed and operated, and is lower than the maximum technical efficiency. Its unit measure depends on the way the energy content of the fuel and the electric energy

output are measured. For instance, if the energy of the fuel is measured in GJ and electricity is in KWh (or a multiple), its unit measure would be GJ/KWh.

- $Q_i$ and $\overline{Q}_i$ are the lower and upper limit of production possibilities, given by the technical constraint of the plant. In this simple specification, it is assumed that there exists a maximum possible level of production, typically given by the generator capacity, and a minimum one. In some technologies, this minimum could be zero (or close to), such as for the case of photovoltaic production, for instance; in other technologies, this minimum is close or almost equal to the maximum one, as happens for units of coal or nuclear power plants, that, once they start their production, occurs at a given positive (and often large) level. See that the cost description of Equation (2.7) implies that it is not technically feasible for the plant to produce at a level lower than $Q_i$ or higher than $\overline{Q}_i$. This is expressed by assuming that the cost is infinite beyond those levels: $C_i(Q_i) = \infty$ for $Q_i < Q_i$ or $Q_i > \overline{Q}_i$.

The marginal cost of the plant described in the Equation (2.1) is:

$$\frac{\partial C_i(Q_i)}{\partial Q_i} = Fl_f \cdot a_{f,i}, \text{ for } Q_i \leq Q_i \leq \overline{Q}_i \tag{2.8}$$

This makes apparent that the plant described in Equation (2.7) has the characteristics that the cost of providing an additional watt-hour is constant throughout its operational range and depends just on the cost of the fuel and the plant efficiency rate. This is an assumption that is often made, for instance when describing plants' bids in liberalized electricity markets. However, it is in general too simple a description of the characteristics of the plants. Indeed, the whole functional form described in Equation (2.7), can hardly capture all the features of the various possible technologies of power plants. For instance, it is quite possible that a plant has more than just a lower limit or an upper production limit, but rather several possible production ranges, within which there are different efficiencies, captured by distinct parameters $a_{f,i}$. This is the case of a piecewise cost function, which can be described, in its simplest case of a two-step piecewise function, as:

$$C_i(Q_i) = \begin{cases} FC_i + Fl_f \cdot \widehat{a}_{f,i} \cdot Q_i \\ FC_i + Fl_f \cdot \widetilde{a}_{f,i} \cdot Q_i \end{cases} for \begin{array}{l} Q_i \leq Q_i \leq \widehat{Q}_i \\ \widehat{Q}_i \leq Q_i \leq \overline{Q}_i \end{array} \tag{2.9}$$

with $\widehat{a}_{f,i} < \widetilde{a}_{f,i}$ and $Q_i < \widehat{Q}_i < \overline{Q}_i$.

The two-step piecewise cost function describes the existence of two possible ranges of operation, and that producing above the threshold $\widehat{Q}_i$ implies that there is an increase in the variable costs (e.g. because of a rise in the maintenance cost or in the risk of damage that implies some extra safeguarding measures, or an increase in the need for cooling of transformers, and so on).

The example described in Equation (2.9) is that of a two-step linear cost curve. There could be several more steps in the piecewise cost function. Indeed, a more general functional form that represents a continuous and smooth version of a multiple-step piecewise linear cost function is the quadratic one:

$$C_i(Q_i) = FC_i + Fl_f \cdot a_{f,i} \cdot Q_i^2, \text{with } \underline{Q_i} \le Q_i \le \overline{Q_i}. \tag{2.10}$$

The marginal cost function of the plant described in Equation (2.10) is:

$$\frac{\partial C_i(Q_i)}{\partial Q_i} = 2Fl_f \cdot a_{f,i} \cdot Q_i \ , \ \text{for } \underline{Q_i} \le Q_i \le \overline{Q_i}. \tag{2.11}$$

This marginal cost function shows that the marginal cost is not constant, as was for the case of the linear cost function, but rises within the plant's operational range.

A common aspect of the plant's cost description represented by the plant's cost function, whether linear or quadratic, is that it is (implicitly) assumed that those costs are to be conceived as constant throughout the period to which the total cost function refers. For instance, if the cost function refers to a year, the total cost function specification implies that its parameters are constant for all possible fractions in which the year can be divided, such as months, days, hours, minutes, and so on. In other words, the description of a power plant through its own total cost function is a static description. This is a clear limitation. There are some costs that the plant incurs, depending on its status, that do not depend on whether the plant is producing electricity or not. These are called **quasi-fixed costs**. Examples of quasi-fixed costs are those costs that a plant has to face to be able to produce electricity, even if it is not doing so. For instance, a plant could be burning fuel just to remain warm, and by doing so staying connected to the system, even if it is not producing electricity (i.e. it is not adding electricity to the system). Or it might be that a plant is burning some fuel to generate a current in a dynamo that is used to excite the electromagnet in the alternator. Even if the turbine connected to the alternator is not working and thus is not producing electricity, such a plant would be burning fuel just to be ready to produce electricity when needed. These are called **no-load costs**.

The cost function of Equation (2.4) can be augmented to describe the no-load costs. However, in order to do so, we need to pay attention to what $Q_i$ means. We have described it as the quantity of electricity that a plant produces. There is, however, a difference between the amount that is produced in a given period and the amount that can be produced in that period when considering it before producing. The former is a calculation done *ex-post*, the latter is an evaluation *ex-ante*. If a plant could be started on and off with no time lag or specific cost, there would not be any difference between what was produced in a given year in the past and what could have been produced in that year (note that we do not mean the maximum that could have been produced in that year). However, if we were to distinguish the cases in which a plant was not able to produce from situations in which it was able to produce but has not, we would need a more structured representation that described cases in which the plant is off from cases in which it is on but not injecting electricity into the grid. That is to say, there is a difference between a situation of zero production and a situation in which it is on, but not injecting electricity into the grid, for some technical reason. We therefore couple the term $Q_i$, that denotes as before the quantity that is produced by a given power plant, with the variable $Q_i^\circ$, that denotes the amount of electricity that can be produced. $Q_i^\circ = 0$ means that the quantity that can be produced is zero because the plant is off; $Q_i^\circ > 0$ denotes that the quantity that can be produced is greater than zero because the plant is on, but not necessarily injecting power into the grid. The cost function of Equation (2.10) becomes:

$$C_i(Q_i) = \begin{cases} FC_i & Q_i^\circ = 0 & Q_i = 0 \\ FC_i + Fl_f \cdot b_{f,i} & \text{with} \quad Q_i^\circ > 0 & \text{and} \quad 0 \leq Q_i < \underline{Q_i} \\ FC_i + Fl_f \cdot (a_{f,i} \cdot Q_i^2 + b_{f,i}) & Q_i^\circ > 0 & \underline{Q_i} \leq Q_i \leq \overline{Q_i} \end{cases} \quad (2.12)$$

The description in Equation (2.12) makes it apparent that the term $Fl_f \cdot b_{f,i}$ denotes the no-load cost. See that, consistently with the notation on $\underline{Q_i}$ being the lowest feasible level of production, in Equation (2.12) it is assumed that the plant cannot generate power below it.

Another case of quasi-fixed costs are **start-up costs**. Several thermal power plants have the characteristics that they need some time to be heated up before they can produce, and this time can range from a few minutes (in the case of small hydropower plants) to several hours (as for large thermal power plants or nuclear power plants). In order to describe them in a cost function, we need a dynamic representation of the costs. Suppose, for instance, that time is divided into equal periods, say hours, and that the plant is heated at hour $t_l$, but it requires $z$ more hours before it becomes operative (i.e. before it can inject electricity into the grid). In these hours, it burns fuel just to warm up. The cost function representation would be:

$$C_i(Q_i) = \begin{cases} FC_i & t < t_l \\ FC_i + Fl_f \cdot e_{f,i} & \text{with} \quad t_l \leq t < t_{l+z} \\ FC_i + Fl_f \cdot a_{f,i} \cdot Q_i^2 & t > t_{l+z} \end{cases} \quad (2.13)$$

Where we have not specified the production limits for simplicity of notation and it is obviously assumed that the plant can produce only once its heating-up period of $l+z$ hours has passed.

## Learning Outcomes

- Electricity is the energy that makes a work through the ordered flow of electrons. It is the product of Current, Voltage and time. The amount of useful work that is done, and conversely of energy that is lost as heat, depends on the resistance of the medium through which electrons flow. Ohm's law relates resistance to Voltage and Current.
- The Electricity Circuit is the representation of the flow of electrons through a medium. The intermediate point of the circuit where electrons meet a resistance is called load. Current flows from a negative to a positive pole of the circuit. It is called Direct Current (DC). It can also revert the flow from the two poles. It is the Alternate Current

(AC). Frequency measures the number of times current reverts its flow in a circuit. It is measured in Hertz. AC circuits have active and reactive power.

- The commercial usage of electricity was developed over the course of the nineteenth and twentieth centuries. Three main services were (and are still) provided: electric lighting, workforce given by electric engines and transportation and telecommunication services. The AC system has been adopted worldwide as the standard for power transmission.
- Electricity is produced in power plants. They are industrial sites where primary energy sources are transformed into electricity, which is an energy carrier. The cost of this transformation is represented by means of cost functions.
- Costs can be fixed or variable. There are several possible cost functions, depending on the level of technical complexity of power production. Simple cost functions are linear and can have fixed capacity ranges. More complex cost functions can be quadratic, piecewise, and can have quasi-fixed costs such as no-load and start-up costs.

# Part II

# The Basic Design of Electricity Systems and Markets

In this part we describe the basic structure of delivering electricity to end consumers, from the standpoint of the physical properties of electricity and the economic relationships between the different bodies that are active in the delivery of electricity. First, in Chapter 3, the structure of the electricity system, namely the grid, is described. The way electricity is conveyed from the production phase to end consumers alongside the different elements of the electricity system, called the Electricity Supply Chain, is introduced and explained. Then, Chapter 4 focuses on the possible economic arrangements through which energy is exchanged in the electricity system. The physical delivery of electricity through the grid is coupled with economic delivery, in which there are players who acquire the right to be served by electricity in exchange for a payment, and producers who have the right to generate electricity in exchange for payment. This is what a market does. In Chapter 5 four possible market arrangements are described and analyzed, based on different degrees of vertical separation alongside the Electricity Supply Chain. Moreover, the time structure of electricity markets and the way the different transactions are matched to real-time power delivery are presented. Finally, Chapter 6 presents an introduction to regulation in the power sector. Indeed, even if several parts of the Electricity Supply Chain can and have been liberalized, this has not occurred everywhere in the world. Moreover, several parts of the Electricity Supply Chain still need to be regulated because of their monopolistic features.

# 3 Electricity Systems and the Electricity Supply Chain

## 3.1 Introduction to Electricity Systems

In order to describe the electricity system, we need to define its basic elements, starting from the most elementary feature, the node:

DEFINITION. *Node: a point of a circuit where two or more elements of the circuit meet.*

Nodes are also referred to as buses. They are points in which different elements of the electricity systems are connected among themselves. A node can be the junction point of a plant and a line, or the point where a load is connected to a line, or the point where one line is linked to another line, and so on. The positive current sign denotes the node toward which current flows, while the negative sign the node from which it flows. This characteristic allows us to distinguish the node in which electricity is created and introduced into the system from the node that uses the electricity, namely, in which there is a resistance that uses the current for some final use (lighting, electric engines and so on). The former are the generation nodes, the latter the loads. The generation nodes are where there is a plant connected to the system. Even though there is a difference between a generation node, that refers to the connection point between a power plant and the electricity system and the plant itself, which might be made of several generators, for simplicity we will not distinguish between a generation node and a power plant and treat the injection point as a single point in which electricity is produced. Similarly, we will consider the load as a withdrawal point[1] without paying attention to the final use of the electricity (i.e. the purpose for which electricity is required).

With the definition of the node just provided, we can now provide a definition for the electricity system:

DEFINITION. *Electricity system: the set of all the components that are interconnected in an electric circuit.*

---

[1] Note to the reader: it should be clear by now that the term "withdrawal" is to be understood in the economic sense, namely, acquiring it for some end-use, not in physical terms, since electricity continuously flows into the systems and is continuously re-injected to maintain its balance. If this point is not clear, you should re-read Chapter 2.

The electric circuit of an electricity system is typically large, in the sense that it serves several loads, possibly located in different geographical places, and in which there are typically different plants, also possibly located in distinct geographical places. In this case, it is also commonly referred to as the electricity **grid**, or just grid, to highlight the network nature of the electricity system.

The electricity system is composed of the following elements: power plants; load; and transmission and distribution networks. We describe them here.

### 3.1.1    Power Plants

As mentioned, power plants are also called generators or power generators. We have already reviewed the different plants' characteristics in Chapter 2. There are several possible technologies, sizes and capabilities of power plants. Some of them require and withdraw electricity from the electricity system as well as injecting it, while others do not. The former are classified as power plants, as long as they are net providers of electricity to the system. In some cases, power plants are built and operated to produce electricity for internal usage, for instance, because they are connected to a factory that requires it, and only residually release the extra energy that is not needed for the electricity system. In this case, they are classified as **self-producers**. There is no clear-cut distinction between producers and self-producers, because there is no single specification of what a residual production is. In different electricity systems, there are different definitions of what self-producers are and how they are to be distinguished from other power plants. Self-producers are not to be confused with those plants that generate two energy carriers at the same time, such as heat and electricity. These are called **Combined Heat and Power** (CHP) plants. From an economic perspective, a CHP plant is a plant that produces multiple outputs. The treatment of multiple-output production functions is quite complex and typically requires the application of some operational research algorithm to find the optimum between the multiple inputs and outputs. A shortcut is to evaluate which one is the primary output (e.g. electricity is the plant's main production and heat is a by-product), and optimize the production decision with respect to the primary output, treating the other one as a parameter. This is the case, for example, for those plants that release heat for the heating needs of some consumers, as it is for **district heating**. In this text, we will treat power plants as single output plants.

An important feature to keep in mind is that every power plant that is connected to an electricity system is made of two main components, no matter how big or small it is: the generator, that converts the energy potential of some primary energy source into electricity, and the transformer (or inverter[2] in the case of DC plants such as photovoltaic panels or batteries). The latter is the physical interface with the grid. A crucial characteristic of the interconnection between a power plant and an electricity system is that the electricity generated by the generator has to be in phase with the electricity of the system. As discussed in Chapter 2, the transmission system operates (almost always and almost everywhere) in AC. Consider what happens when the power plant starts up.

---

[2] An inverter is an electronic device that converts DC into AC.

Suppose, for instance, it is a hydropower plant or a gas-fired plant. It starts rotating the turbine using its fuel, whether this be water or natural gas (or whatever). This activates the alternator. It is possible that the alternator is already using the current that it receives from the grids to excite the electromagnets, or perhaps the plant might be using some fuel to do so with a dynamo. Once it is running, it starts generating electricity. The voltage of electricity is increased in the transformers. However, before connecting the plant to the grid, there is the phase of synchronization, in which both the voltage and the frequency are to be aligned to the grid. Once it is in phase, it can start releasing electric energy into the grid. At this point it is effectively producing. When it is producing, it is continuously facing changes of voltage and frequencies coming both from the grid and from itself because of its own operation (e.g. because of changes of some physical parameters such as the temperature, the heat, the type and availability of fuels and so on). Therefore, it has to be continuously managed, in order to maintain its alignment with the grid. The alignment was once made manually, and it is now mostly performed by electronic devices. However, even if the speed of the synchronization is changed, the basic principles of operation remain the same as those of the early days.

From an economic perspective, a power plant connected to the grid generates two elements: a product and some externalities to the grid. The former is the power that is needed for the load, namely, the active power. The latter can be positive externalities, whenever new current added allows some new load to be served, or negative ones, whenever a change in the generation implies changes in the voltage or in the frequency. Moreover, new generation can also provide reactive power, and this can be a positive or negative externality depending on whether such a reactive power is needed to avoid a voltage drop, or conversely needs to be offset by a load able to balance it.

## 3.1.2    Load

As previously noted, the load is the point of the electricity system in which the current is used to perform a function. However, it is also common to refer to the load as the amount of electricity that is needed for that work.

It is possible to classify the load according to several possible parameters. A first classification refers to the nature of the final use of the electricity that it uses, namely, if it has to be used as an input in production activities or as a final product to be consumed. In the first case, we refer to it as an industrial load, while the rest is a residential load. Another classification groups load according to classes of average consumption over a certain period, such as a year. In this case, there are several possible classes that one can refer to. For instance, in Europe, the following classification is used to define annual consumption bands of households:

(i) very small: annual consumption below 1,000 kWh;
(ii) small: annual consumption between 1,000 and 2,500 kWh;
(iii) medium: annual consumption between 2,500 and 5,000 kWh;
(iv) large: annual consumption between 5,000 and 15,000 kWh;
(v) very large: annual consumption above 15,000 kWh.

While for industry there are five bands ranging from annual consumption below 20 MWh to annual consumption above 150,000 MWh.

Another classification refers to the level of voltage at which it is connected to the electric system. Generally, large consumers, and industrial consumers, are connected directly to the high voltage or extra high voltage lines, while several small and residential consumers are connected to the grid at relatively low voltages (i.e. a few kV). There are several possible classifications for voltage levels. IEEE[3] defines low voltage as less than 1kV; medium voltage from 1kV to 72.5 kV; high voltage up to 230 kV, and extra-high voltage above this figure. In the United States, ANSI[4] refers to voltages up to 600 V as low voltage; from 600 V to 69 kV as medium voltage; from 69 kV to 230 kV as high voltage and above this figure as extra-high voltage.

Another feature of the load has more to do with its physical characteristics than to the voltage of interconnection or the consumption levels. In AC systems, the load might be resistive or inductive. A *resistive load* is a load that has just a resistance, such as a lamp light, for instance. It opposes the flow of electrons and has no effect on the phase of electricity. An *inductive load*, on the contrary, is a load that generates a magnetic field (and stores electricity in it) and by doing so changes the current and voltage out of phase. Electric engines are inductive because of their construction. Indeed, in reality almost all loads have some resistive and inductive properties, which implies that the load can generate reactive power and influence the power factor of an electricity system, as much as a plant (which is rather obvious, being part of the same physical system). Thus, we reiterate that in the economic analysis the load has to be treated in much the same way as a power plant, since both can impact the electricity system, generating consequences (i.e. externalities), for the whole system For instance, an increase in load generates a negative externality, since it induces a change in voltage and frequency that needs to be counterbalanced.

The load shares another common feature with plants: their contribution to the grid, whether negative (i.e. the absorption of electricity from the grid), or positive (i.e. provision of electricity to the grid), needs to be measured. This is done by using **electricity meters**. Electricity meters, or just meters, are devices built in order to measure the amount of electric energy consumed by a load. Recall that electric energy is measured in watt-hours (or multiples): energy is a dynamic concept. The meter can measure and report the amount of energy consumed in a given period of time. Traditionally, this period was conceived to be long enough to allow it to be read by users or providers of the energy. These are the traditional meters that just provide a progressive numerical measure of the watt-hours consumed. Every time the meter is read it shows how much energy has been consumed since the last time it was read. But, clearly, this leaves open the question as to when that amount of energy was consumed, given that the same amount of watt-hours can imply a large amount of power for a short period or a small amount of power for a prolonged period. More modern meters can calculate the energy consumed in short time periods and take stock of them. They are

---

[3] Institute of Electrical and Electronics Engineers. IEEE (1996).
[4] American National Standards Institute. NEMA (1995).

called **smart meters**. For instance, they can calculate the energy consumed in each hour and group this information according to several possible classifications of the hours, such as day-night hours, day of the week-weekend hours, and so on. Indeed, very modern meters can even calculate the amount of energy consumed almost instantaneously; namely, for very short time intervals (seconds or even less) and immediately provide this information for the user. These are called **real-time meters**. In any event, regardless of how smart meters are, they are an essential feature of every electricity system.

Even though load and generation share some common features, it is in principle easy to distinguish between them, looking at whether they are net absorbers of energy or net providers of energy to the grid. The former refers to a load that is connected to the grid but that has also some power production facilities installed. For instance, this might be a residential home with photovoltaic panels installed, which on average consumes energy, but where during some hours the production of energy is higher than the consumption and thus it turns into a net provider of energy to the electricity system. It is important to know whether the meter allows calculation of the amount of energy consumed separately from the amount of energy produced, or if it just measures the net withdrawal from (or contribution to) the grid. In this latter case, we talk of **net-metering**. This is an aspect that can be relevant, for instance, if the production of energy is remunerated at a different price from the consumption of energy, which happens when there are subsidies to production or consumption.

### 3.1.3  Transmission and Distribution Networks

Electricity is conveyed from the plants to the load trough a medium, which eases (by opposing a limited resistance) the ordered movement of electrons from generation to resistance (and back). This is called a **transmission line**. Several transmission lines form a **transmission network**. It is common to distinguish the network on the basis of the voltage level at which it operates. Strictly speaking, the transmission network, is high-voltage, while the network of cables that conveys electricity from the high voltage one to domestic usages is called the distribution network. The transmission network can transmit AC or DC. In modern electricity systems, the current generated and consumed is AC. The transmission network takes the form of overhead transmission cables or lines. They consist of cables made of material with a low resistivity, such as copper or aluminum, not covered by insulation. In modern transmission networks, they are almost always made of aluminum. Underground transmission lines are also sometimes used, whenever it is not feasible or too costly to rely on overhead lines. Due to the costs of insulation and excavation, underground transmission lines are costlier than overhead lines. Another difference between underground AC and DC lines is that long AC underground cables have high capacitance, which reduces their ability to transmit power. Therefore, for long underground transmission needs, High-Voltage DC (HVDC) transmission lines are preferred, since they have no capacitance. In general, decisions on whether to use AC or DC for new transmission lines depend on their respective costs: if the DC line is planned to connect two AC systems, it requires specific terminals at both ends of the line which are more expensive that AC ones. Thus, HVDC lines have higher economies of scale with respect to length, compared to AC lines, and this determines the break-even distance between one technology and another.

The transmission network is composed of transmission lines, power plants and substations,[5] where voltages are increased or decreased. It also encompasses several devices that allow the transmission of electricity and the control of power. The main ones are

- **capacitors and inductors**: (small or big) devices that store electricity in an electric and magnetic field, respectively, and allow shifting the phase of current and controlling the power factor;
- **circuit breakers**: automatically operated electrical switches designed to protect an electrical circuit from damage caused by excess current;
- **SCADA systems**: Supervisory Control and Data Acquisition (SCADA); these are systems used to control plants, allowing them to switch on and off system elements in or out of the system.

A system made of several AC lines, namely, a transmission network, must be kept synchronized. An area made of several AC lines where there is the same voltage and where electricity is synchronized is called a **synchronous grid or area**. In North America, it is termed **Interconnection**. There are several synchronous grids in the world. In the United States and Canada, the main synchronous grids are the Eastern Interconnection, serving the eastern United States and Canada; the Western Interconnection, covering the western United States, Canada, and northwestern Mexico; the Texas Interconnection; and the Quebec Interconnection. In Europe, there are five synchronous areas: Continental Europe, Nordic, Baltic, Great Britain, and Ireland-Northern Ireland. Other large synchronous grids are the IPS/UPS, that covers Eurasia, grouping the network of twelve former Soviet Union Countries including Russia plus Mongolia; the Australian National Energy Market (NEM), that groups the networks of eastern and southern Australia's States (Victoria, Queensland, New South Wales, South Australia, Tasmania); and the Indian National Grid. Thus, there are countries that are grouped in large super-national synchronous grids, while other countries are split into more than one synchronous grid. In China, there are three main synchronous areas; in Japan there are two synchronous areas, with different frequencies, for historical reasons.

Synchronous grids are managed, regulated and overviewed. The managing activity is performed by the **System Operator** (SO). The role of the SO will be discussed in the Paragraph 3.2.2. The overview and regulatory activity can be performed by several entities that may or may not coincide with SOs. For instance, in the United States there are eight regional Reliability Councils (RCs), overseen by the North American Electric Reliability Corporation (NERC) that have oversight of SOs; in Europe SOs are grouped

---

[5] The term "substation" derives from the need to distinguish it from power plants, which are sometimes referred to as power stations. Throughout this book we prefer to refer to the latter as power plants, and refer to substations as transformers, even though strictly speaking, substations denote the places where transformers are.

in the European Network of Transmission System Operators for Electricity (ENTSO-E) that operates in each synchronous area through the Regional Groups (RGs). Figure 3.1 below shows the synchronous areas and the RGs in Europe and the interconnections and the RCs in North America.

A caveat must be placed here on the use of the term "interconnection." In the United States, it is common to refer to synchronous grids as interconnections. However, in Europe, it is more common to distinguish transmission lines that are inside a transmission network from those transmission lines that link one transmission network to another and use the term **cross-border interconnections,** or simply, interconnections, to refer just to the latter. Thus, in Europe interconnections are simply taken as synonymous with cross-border interconnections. However, there is a slight indeterminacy at to what "border" means in this terminology. Clearly, there is a border wherever two synchronous grids are linked by an interconnection. However, the border might as well be an administrative border, such as a State border, or the term interconnection might also

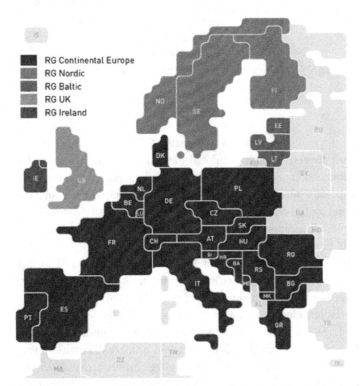

**Figure 3.1** European and North American synchronous grid

*Source*: ENTSO-E, year 2010 (Europe); NERC (North America). Note: this information from the North American Electric Reliability Corporation's website is the property of the North American Electric Reliability Corporation and is available at www.nerc.com/AboutNERC/keyplayers/Publ ishingImages/Interconnections%2024JUL18.jpg. This content may not be reproduced in whole or any part without the prior express written permission of the North American Electric Reliability Corporation.

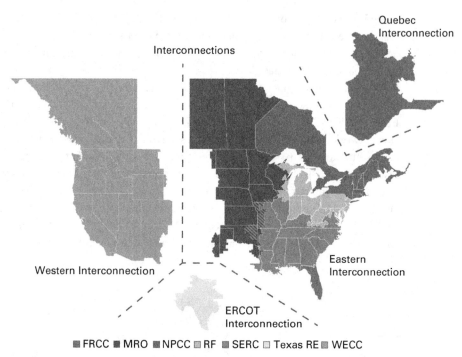

**Figure 3.1** (cont.)

indicate the physical link between two parts of the same synchronous grid, i.e. two networks, that are connected by a limited transmission capacity. In this book, we shall treat interconnection capacity or transmission capacity as being synonymous. The existence of limited interconnection capacity even within a single synchronous grid is relevant for the definition of market zones, a concept that we will describe further in Chapter 16. The economic analysis of interconnections and their expansion and planning will be discussed in Chapter 17.

The **distribution network** is the network of transformers and lines that delivers electricity to final consumers. It is linked to the transmission network at substations, where voltage is reduced from high-voltage to medium voltage; it is then further reduced at local substations close to end users' premises and delivered to them at low voltage. The low voltage lines connecting end users can be overhead lines or underground. The medium-voltage distribution level is called primary distribution; the low-voltage level is secondary distribution. Secondary voltage differs across distribution networks worldwide. In Europe, it ranges from 220 to 240V while in the United States it ranges from 100V to 127V, as in Japan.

Although similar to the transmission network, the distribution network has two distinctive features that influence its economic analysis. The first is that the topology of distribution networks depends on the geographic dispersion of the users that are (or need to be) connected. Users should be grouped as much as possible in substations in order to exploit economies of scale, because substations are quite costly. However, at the distribution level, substations, particularly at the secondary level, must be close to the end users in order not to avoid losing too much energy in transmitting it at low voltage. Thus, it is natural to observe the emergence of several distribution networks that are geographically unconnected. The second distinctive feature is that end consumers, particularly residential consumers, typically need just a single-phase AC connection. This allows greater flexibility for distribution connections, but also produces more instability, since the power flowing on each of three lines is different and this might create imbalances. Interruptions and accidents that occur at the distribution level can therefore be more frequent than those at transmission level, but are less disruptive, in the sense that they occur at a lower scale and affect a smaller number of users.

The architecture of the distribution system that we have described here is the traditional one, whose design derives from the early days of electricity systems. However, the emergence of new features enabled by technological progress, and in particular the possibility for the load to be simultaneously a load and a generation, creates additional problems for distribution lines. Indeed, these were designed to deliver electricity from the transmission network to the end users, while the new challenges imply that they are frequently asked to invert their role and act as a generation point vis-à-vis the transmission system. We shall discuss this in Chapter 27.

A common characteristic of all electricity systems is that all energy transmission implies some loss of energy. We have already seen that this is due to the resistivity of the transmission line. The loss depends on the "disordered movement" of the electrons. Transmission and distribution lines are designed to minimize the transmission and distribution losses.

The flow of energy in a system, which includes the losses, respects the physical principles of current and voltages summarized in **Kirchhoff's laws**:

DEFINITION. *Kirchhoff's first law: At any node in a circuit, the sum of currents flowing into that node is equal to the sum of currents flowing out of that node.*

DEFINITION. *Kirchhoff's second law: The sum of all the voltages in the network is zero.*

Kirchhoff's laws imply that at any time the system has to be **balanced**. This means that the effective power at the injection points, plus the losses, must always be equal to the resistance of the loads. Therefore, whenever there is a change in the load somewhere along the system, this has to be compensated by a change of the opposite sign somewhere else on the circuit. In particular, if more power is required by some load, this must be instantaneously injected by some generation connected to the same system (taking into account the losses), and the same for reduction of loads or generation. Any failure in respect of this principle generates an imbalance, that would alter the frequency of the system, damaging the appliances of the systems.

This is a major difference between electricity and any other good or service, which has crucial consequences for the design of electricity systems and electricity markets.

## 3.2      The Electricity Supply Chain

The components of the electricity system are grouped together in the *Electricity Supply Chain (ESC)*, which describes the functions that all agents undertake in the electricity system. The description of the ESC thus focuses on the who-does-what of the system, rather than on its technical characteristics. The ESC can be disentangled in the following five functions: production, transmission, distribution, metering and retailing and dispatching.

### 3.2.1     Production

Production is the generation phase. As we have seen, typically, plants of different technologies contribute to it. Some have large fixed costs, and rather low variable costs. This is the case with large thermal power plants, such as coal-fired power plants or nuclear plants. Other plants, such as oil-fired plants, have quite low fixed costs. However, due to fuel costs and their efficiency rate, their variable costs are rather high. For RES plants, variable costs are typically small or null, whether these are the opportunity cost of using water in hydropower plants in a given hour or the just the variable cost of maintenance for wind power plants or photovoltaic plants. For the latter, in particular, maintenance costs are fixed, thus there are no variable costs. However, not all RES plants have low or null variable costs. Plants that use biomass as fuel can have high variable costs. As for the fixed costs, large hydropower plants (i.e. hydropower plants that rely on large dammed reservoirs), have huge fixed costs, while other RES power plants have smaller fixed costs, depending on the technology and the site where they are located. It is interesting to point out that hydropower provides a storage of energy, albeit just potential energy. This is the role of the reservoir created by the dam. This capacity can be augmented by *pumped storage*: when the electricity value is low, pumped storage plants can invert the production cycle and instead of having the water running from the reservoir to the turbine, it can pump the water up into the reservoir. Even though from an energetic point of view pumping water has a negative energetic balance (remember the Carnot machine in Chapter 1: every energy conversion implies some energy waste), it is an operation that is implemented to obtain an economic positive balance: electricity is acquired to pump water when it has a low value and is produced when it has a higher value. Apart from storing electricity in batteries, pumped storage is the only large means of storage of electricity (or better, electric energy potential) that can be used in electricity systems.

### 3.2.2     Transmission

Electricity transmission or electricity bulk transmission is the activity of moving electricity from generating sites to substations. It is the activity of managing the electricity transmission system, or grid, in order to let the power be transmitted. It is performed by entities called System Operators (SO). There can be different possible configurations for

SO, which in particular refer to the ownership of the grid and planning and executing the grid extensions and updates (which might also include removal or changing of some existing line or device). It is possible that the ownership of the transmission grid is separated from its usage and control. In this case, the SO is called the **Independent System Operator** (ISO). Under the ISO scheme, generally grid expansion and planning are undertaken by the grid owner, typically under the supervision of some entity, which might also be the ISO itself. It is also possible that the grid is owned and managed by the SO, which is then called **Transmission Service Operator** (TSO). In this case, the grid expansion is typically planned and/or supervised by a third entity, such as a Regulatory Authority. A further distinction is whether or not the TSO is owned by the plants' owners. If it is not, the TSO is under **Ownership Unbundling**. This is however a rough taxonomy, and there may be other mixed models with responsibilities and roles for planning, executing and operating the grid differently attributed from the scheme described here.

The SO operates the grid in order to allow the power to flow in a secure way. This means issuing **orders**, which are real-time commands to the transmission system devices, loads and power plants to maintain the grid in the prescribed range of frequency and voltage and transmitting the required amount of power. If the load is not instantaneously met by the power generated, an **imbalance** occurs. Imbalances must be compensated, since power injected and withdrawn from the grid must coincide. Whenever it is not possible to match injections with withdrawals, the latter must be cut. This is called **load shedding**, which occurs whenever it is not possible to keep the grid balanced by using all possible existing instruments and asking plants to adjust their production. It is thus a programmed, or at least managed, event undertaken by the SO. Load shedding is also termed controlled load curtailment or rolling blackout. The latter term should not be confused with whole-system **blackout**. A blackout, also called **power outage** or power blackout occurs whenever there is a loss of power in some area due to an unforeseen or unmanageable event that makes the electricity system so unstable that it breaks up. In the electric system, even if the load is shed somewhere, there is always current flowing in it; the load is not served exactly because of the need to maintain the system operational. On the contrary, in a blackout the current is no longer flowing through some part of the system. Thus, a blackout is a pathological status of the electricity system, which in principle should hardly occur, while we shall see that load shedding, albeit rare, is a physiological and to some extent even desirable event. Blackouts can be very long, disruptive and affect a large network area. Moreover, it can take a lot of time for the electricity system to recover from it, once it has occurred. For this reason, the management of the grid is done in such a way to minimize the risk of blackouts occurring.

### 3.2.3   Distribution

Electricity distribution is the activity of moving electricity from substations to end consumers. It is performed at medium and low voltage, by entities called **Distribution System Operators** (DSOs). DSOs are similar to SOs, with the crucial difference that they typically do not control (or share control with) power plants, except for those connected at low and medium voltage, if any, which are however typically smaller than power plants connected to transmission grids and thus have less chance of being controlled remotely from DSOs. A crucial responsibility of DSOs, performed on the distribution network, as well as for the SO on its own gird, is controlling **quality of supply**. In the electricity sector, quality of supply, or power quality, refers to controlling the voltage, frequency and shape of the waves (voltage and current), in order to maintain them in the predefined ranges. Even though the terminology refers to quality of supply of electricity, it is effectively the quality of the voltage that is controlled. This makes clear the difference between controlling quality of supply and controlling power (i.e. making sure that the power in the grid is always balanced). When there is a large and sudden drop in voltage, a **brownout** occurs. Brownouts (the term deriving from the dimming of light bulbs when voltage drops) can also be very damaging for end users' apparels.

## 3.2.4    Metering and Retailing

Retailing is the activity of selling electricity to final users. In order to do so, a prerequisite is that the electricity used is somehow measured. In the early days of the electricity system, Edison would not measure the electricity consumed as such but would proxy it by counting the numbers of apparels that used it. He would charge consumers on the basis of the light bulbs that they would buy (and replace given their short life duration), but this soon proved to be extremely inefficient, since it limited the usage of electricity, and resulted in an inefficient way of measuring electricity consumption (light bulbs could break for several reasons). Thus, it soon became clear, and remains the case, that what matters for calculating the electricity sold is the amount used, not the purpose for which it is used, and that this could be done by metering it. Traditionally the activity of metering referred not just to installing traditional meters, but reading them from time to time, which implied employing personnel to do so. As explained above, this is less common nowadays, at least for those systems where smart meters are installed.

Retailing is an activity that can be performed by several possible entities, separated or not from those that perform the other tasks of the ESC. It can be (and often is) undertaken by the DSO, since often the meters that are installed are owned by the DSO itself. In those systems where retailing is separated from distribution, it is a DSO responsibility to release the data on electricity consumption to the retailers.

Retailing activity involves more than just metering. One further service is invoicing, which is, of course, the counterpart of metering. However, if retailing occurs in a competitive way, there is typically more than just metering and invoicing, since loads become **customers**, and are treated as such, using all possible marketing tools, such as the price (making tailored offers), customer relations, products (meaning selling more products than just the ordered movement of electrons (i.e. electricity), but also energy efficiency services, advice, other energy carriers, other products) and so on.

When there are several possible retailers, competing for the same customers, namely, when there are **retail electricity markets**, it is common to refer to retailers as **suppliers**.

In this case, the term "retailers" can be used in a strict sense to denote those suppliers that need to buy electricity from some sellers in order to resell it to the end consumers. This distinguishes retailers from other suppliers that own some generation or that can anyhow provide electricity directly to end customers. Note, however, that this distinction is not strict, and sometimes the terms "retailers" or "suppliers" are used interchangeably. In this case, they can also be denoted as **retail suppliers**. A general term denoting the activity of all those who sell electricity to final customers is **Load Serving Entities** (LSEs).

It is important to note that the term "suppliers" in electricity market economics is used in a different sense from the standard economic usage: in the latter suppliers are those who participate in the supply side of the market (i.e. those who *produce* a good). In electricity economics, suppliers are LSEs (i.e. those who *buy* the good "electricity" to provide it to customers). This point will be explained in Chapter 4. The analysis of the markets where such an exchange takes place is at the core of the analysis of Part VI of this book.

### 3.2.5   Dispatching

Dispatching is the optimal selection of power plants and loads, under transmission and operational constraints. It is important not to confuse transmission with dispatching. Transmission refers to allowing the power to flow under predefined parameters, while dispatching means taking decisions according to some optimality criterion that will allow the energy to flow. Optimality means selecting *ex-ante* an ordering criterion (i.e. cost minimization or profit maximization). This will be discussed in Part III. System operations work through orders, while dispatching works through **schedules** which are rankings of power plants and loads following a predetermined criterion. Thus, schedules select which power plants have to produce and which load has to be served.

The activity of dispatching is performed by the dispatcher. In order to perform the dispatching activity, the dispatcher must take into account several parameters, such as power plant characteristics and availability, grid topology and status (namely, how many lines are there, their status, how many losses there can be and so on) and the forecasted loads (both quantity and location on the grid). The dispatcher can coincide with the SO or not. If they are distinct entities, the dispatcher issues schedules and the SO executes them. If they coincide, they are obviously performed by the same entity.

### 3.3   Representing the ESC

Figure 3.2 describes the ESC. The transmission line at high voltage is drawn as a thick bold vertical line. Nodes are represented by dots. Distribution lines at medium or low voltage are drawn as thin lines. In the figure, as an example, we have drawn two distribution networks, serving typically residential and small industrial customers at low voltage; each distribution network foresees a specific metering and retailing activity. There is also a load that is directly connected at high voltage (i.e. it has its own transformer), which is the typical case for large industrial consumers. There are two power plants connected, at two distinct nodes, to the transmission grid, while there is just

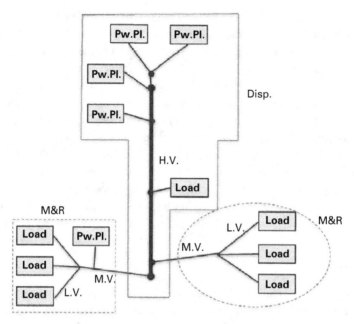

**Figure 3.2** A schematic representation of the ESC

one node connecting two power plants. Given that there is just one node, these two are effectively two units of the same power plant. There is one power plant that is connected at medium voltage to the distribution network on the left of the picture. The fact that there is no node drawn denotes that this plant is not dispatched by the SO, but is rather controlled by the DSO on the left. Finally, note the continuous line denoting the area of dispatching. The dispatcher does not control the final residential customers (or the power plant connected at low voltage), but just the plants connected to the transmission network and the distribution network (at the relevant substations).

Note that this scheme is a general overview of the possible ESC that exist worldwide. Even though, for didactical purposes, it is useful to distinguish the four aforementioned functions, this does not mean that in real-life examples they are always separated and performed by different entities. It is quite possible that a single body undertakes all four ESC functions, or that transmission and dispatching are performed together, or that only generation is separated, and so on. The next chapter describes four possible taxonomies of electricity systems based exactly on possible ways in which the four functions are separated or grouped together.

One final consideration about the ESC refers to the scheme described in Figure 3.2. As noted, the scheme of the ESC has remained substantially the same from the start of the electricity era until now. However, technological progress has allowed the emergence of new entities and agents performing different roles at the same time, such as producers and load or SO and plants, and so on. This is questioning the very structure of the classification proposed here for the ESC. We still believe that it has its merit, if for no other reason than that technological changes do not take place worldwide at the same rate and this scheme will remain useful to describe the ESC of several countries for a long time. However, it is also possible that it will become outdated at some time in the future, perhaps quite quickly. Possible future configurations are discussed in Chapter 27.

## Learning Outcomes

- The electricity system, or grid, comprises all the components that are interconnected in the electricity circuit, such as power plants, load and transmission and distribution networks.
- Electricity flowing into the grid has to respect the physical principles of current and voltages summarized in the Kirchhoff's laws. This implies that the electricity system must always be balanced, namely, that the effective power at the injection points, and losses, must always be equal to the resistance of the loads.
- The Electricity Supply Chain (ESC) specifies the role of each agent in the electricity system. The ESC consists of the following five functions: production, transmission, distribution, metering and retailing, dispatching.
  - Production: the phase of electricity generation.
  - Transmission: the activity of moving electricity from plants to the distribution network.
  - Distribution: the activity of moving electricity from transmission lines to end consumers.
  - Metering and retailing: metering is the activity of measuring the consumption of electricity; retailing refers to selling it to final users.
  - Dispatching: the activity of selecting power plant and loads, under transmission and operational constraints.

# 4 The Four Market Designs of the Electricity System

## 4.1 Introduction

This chapter describes the possible market structures of the electricity system, that is to say, the different ways in which participants in the electricity system can interact. The different entities that act in the ESC have specific roles. In different market settings, their activities may be attributed to different entities, or belong to a single body who would perform some or all of the functions along the ESC. Following a taxonomy originally proposed by Hunt and Shuttleworth (1996), it is possible to group the different market structures that represent the way electricity is exchanged in the ESC, on the basis of the degree of vertical integration of the entities that operates along the ESC, in four models, described below. Each of them is described by a figure, in which in addition to the stylized electricity system, described in Chapter 3, the market arrangements are reported. They are represented by dashed circles, that represent the agents that operate in the market, and dashed arrows, that describe market monetary fluxes, namely, payments across market agents.

## 4.2 The Vertical Integrated Industry

Figure 4.1 represents the electricity system as a vertically integrated industry. The electricity system is encompassed in a single circle representing the vertical integrated industry. Consumers (i.e. loads), can obtain electricity from just one agent. This entity would perform all the activities of the ESC: it would have power plants generating electricity, would manage the grid acting as an SO and as a DSO would dispatch its own plants. Note that the electricity system described in the picture is an isolated one, meaning that there are no interconnection lines with other electricity systems. If these existed, they would be managed by the vertically integrated company, possibly together with the SO of the other system, since there is no one but the vertical integrated industry that is allowed to import or export electricity.

The vertical integrated industry need not be characterized by the existence of a single company. There can be several companies, for instance owning different plants, a separated SO, and so on. However, it is crucial for a vertical integrated industry to hold some agreements among these bodies to act as a single entity. Clearly these agreements could be legal or contractual, for instance there could be a single holding company owning all the companies that are active on the ESC, or there could be other

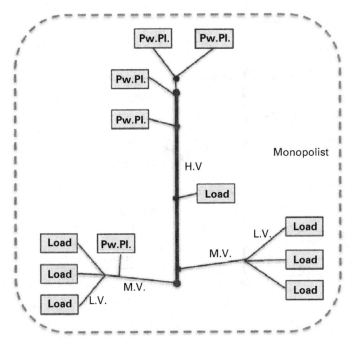

**Figure 4.1** The vertical integrated industry

forms of agreements. These companies therefore behave as a single monopolist in the electricity market. As with any monopoly, the monopolist faces a demand curve for electricity. The demand curve for the case of the load has specific features that we will discuss in Chapter 7. It is enough to note that is quite rigid, thus exposing customers to a high degree of exploitation from the monopolist. To avoid this shortcoming and to guarantee efficiency, it is common to regulate the price that the load pays for the provision of power by means of **tariffs**. Electricity tariffs will be discussed in Chapter 6. Note that the payment from the load to the monopolist is not described in the picture because it is not a market transaction, but rather a payment for the provision of a regulated service.

The vertical integrated industry represents the current status of all those electricity industries worldwide that have not undergone liberalization or been opened up to the market. Clearly, the reality is more complex than how it is stylized in the model represented here, but the basic elements coincide: a single body, possibly regulated, does everything from generation to the delivery of electricity.

## 4.3    The Single Buyer Model

Figure 4.2 represents the single buyer model. In this model, some or all plants can be independently owned and managed by several entities, which are called **Independent Power Producers** (IPPs). There is a single company that performs

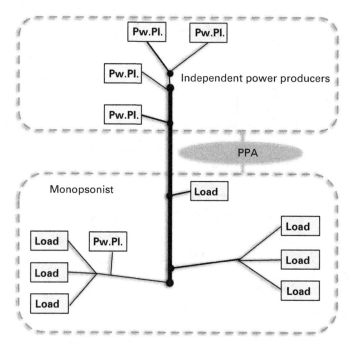

**Figure 4.2** The single buyer model

all other activities of the ESC. It would be the SO, the DSO, and the dispatcher of the system (plus producing if it owns some power plants). This company is thus called a **single buyer**, to emphasize that it is acting as a monopsonist vis-à-vis the IPPs. It is theoretically possible that, instead of having several IPPs, there exists just one owner of all the power plants, distinct from the single buyer. In this case, the situation depicted would be a bilateral monopoly, rather than a monopsony. However, this is a rare situation. Indeed, the single buyer model is often adopted as a first step toward the market opening for vertical integrated industries. If the vertically integrated industry is split to form a single buyer who still owns some power plants, while some other plants are divested to the market, this entity is termed as the **former incumbent**. There are three main ways in which generation capacity can be divested to the market: i) ownership unbundling; ii) tolling agreements; iii) Virtual Power Plants.

i)   **Ownership unbundling**. In this case, some plants are physically divested from the incumbent plant and sold to new entrants in the market. There are several possible ways in which this divestiture can take place, ranging from private agreement among the parties to open competitive auctions. The crucial element, however, is that after the divestiture these power plants must compete among themselves and with the single buyer.

ii)  **Tolling agreements**: a type of rental contract, in which the owner of some primary fuels, called the toller, writes a contract with the power plant owner so that the latter agrees to convert the fuel into electricity for a predetermined fee. These contracts are mutually beneficial whenever the toller can acquire the primary fuel at a better rate than the power plant owner, but does not have or want a power plant to convert it into electricity.

iii) **Virtual power plants**. These are contracts in which the owner of the power plant maintains its ownership, but sells to the buyer the right to use them to produce electricity. VPP contracts must specify two main components: the price at which this right is sold, called VPP premium, and the price at which the energy that the plant will produce will be remunerated. The premium is expressed in terms of money per kW (or multiple), since what is effectively sold is the capacity to produce energy, which is measured in terms of power. The energy price is expressed in terms of euros per kWh, or multiples. Moreover, VPP contracts must specify the respective parties' obligations, and the applicable penalties in the event of non-compliance, namely, missed energy payments or unavailability of the plant, since in the VPP scheme, the management and operation of plants remain the plant owner's responsibility.

When a single buyer model is adopted, a market is created for power exchange between the single buyer and the power plants. Therefore, there are monetary exchanges that go in the opposite direction from the power flow: power goes from producers to load; load pays a tariff to the single buyer that remunerates all its activities, namely, purchasing power from IPPs and transmitting/distributing it. The single buyer has to remunerate the IPPs for their commitment to generate electricity whenever requested by the dispatcher (the single buyer itself). This monetary exchange is represented in Figure 4.2 by the dashed arrow going from the single buyer to the IPPs. The contractual arrangements established between them are called Power Purchase Agreements (PPAs). These PPAs can take the form of any contractual arrangement between the parties, specifying the terms at which the single buyer will call the IPPs to produce electricity and the payment for this.

## 4.4    The Wholesale Market

Figure 4.3 represents a common market arrangement for several electricity markets, in which the single buyer is split into distinct bodies: an entity that operates the grid and dispatches electricity (i.e. the SO); distinct entities, one or more, called Distribution companies (DisCos), which bundle the activities of electricity distribution and monitoring and retailing together. There can be several DisCos, one per each distribution network, or just one.

Figure 4.3 describes the payments that each agent makes in this scheme. These payments refer to just the power that is produced by IPPs and used by the loads. In the previous chapters, we have seen that in order for the power to flow, several other activities must take place, undertaken by the SO and the DSOs. These activities, namely, the dispatching service, transmission and system services, and the distribution services (which include metering and retailing, in the wholesale market model) are remunerated by the load, but are kept distinct from the payment of the power itself. The power flowing from plants to load is remunerated in the place where the needs, expressed by the loads,

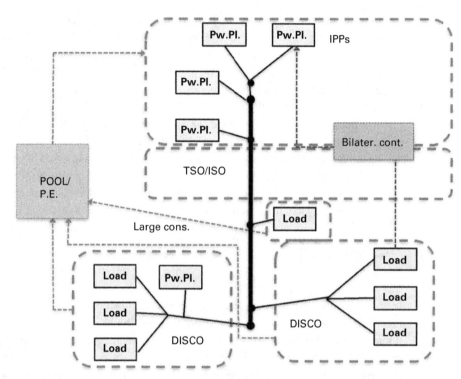

**Figure 4.3** The wholesale market model

meet the production possibilities, brought by the plants. This place is called the
**Wholesale Power Market**, or simply wholesale market. This market is termed wholesale to distinguish it from the retail market, which will be introduced in the next section.

There are two main models that can be adopted to organize exchanges in the wholesale market: the **pool** and the **power exchange**, defined as follows:

DEFINITION. ***Pool****: a wholesale power market where all those who exchange power are
asked to participate. Thus, the pool involves the compulsory participation of IPPs and
the load.*

DEFINITION. ***Power Exchange****: a wholesale power market where plants and the load can
exchange power before its effective delivery. Thus, a power exchange is voluntary in nature.*

Both pools and power exchanges are centralized marketplaces, in the sense that there
is a body that organizes it, setting the rules of power exchanges, the characteristics that
agents have to respect to be able to participate, and how the economic settlement takes
place. This body is called the **Energy Market Operator** (EMO). The EMO may also be
the SO, but in most cases, it is a distinct operator. For the wholesale market model, when
a power exchange is set up, plants can also enter into Over-The-Counter transactions
with the buyers, autonomously choosing the terms of trade. These are called **Bilateral
Contracts**. These bilateral contracts, together with the schedules that arise from
exchanges in the power exchange, or if there is just a pool, the schedules that occur in

it, have to be communicated to the dispatcher. This means that the dispatcher, namely the agent who decides who to call to produce energy, has to be informed and takes into account the proposed dispatch that arise from the economic arrangements among the agents. Given that when power flows it does so at a speed close to the speed of light, following Kirchhoff's laws, it would not be possible to decide the economic arrangements of the exchanges simultaneously with the physical exchanges that take place. For this reason, the economic exchanges typically take place before the real-time delivery. For the same reason, there must also be rules that specify the roles and responsibilities of the parties involved whenever the planned economic exchange cannot be respected by the physical flow of power. This is done in the *ex-post* balancing and in the settlement phase. The different timing of electricity markets will be analyzed in the next chapter.

Another important distinction between pools and power markets, that relates to their different compulsory nature, relates to the economic counterpart of each agents' participation. In a power exchange, agents, being the IPPs or loads, participate voluntarily. This means that they express their market participation by communicating their willingness to pay, or be paid, to use or generate electricity, for load or IPPs, respectively. This willingness to pay or receive is grouped in the loads' or plants' **market bids**: offers to pay in exchange for power, or power in exchange for a payment, for loads and plants, respectively. In a pool, where participation is compulsory, it is harder to set the proper terms of exchange between power and the monetary payment, for both the plants and the load. In a theoretical setting, IPPs should receive remuneration for their ability to produce power. Thus, remuneration for plants depends on their cost function. The same principle should also apply to load. In this case, the load cost refers to the opportunity cost of not being served by the power. This is called Value of Lost Load (VOLL). This concept will be analyzed in Chapter 9.

However, there is a crucial problem in a pool as to the EMO's knowledge of the costs of the IPPs or load, due to the asymmetry of information between plants, load and the SO. For this reason, when a pool is adopted, the role of EMO is often attributed to the SO of the system, since it is supposed to have lower asymmetry of information on generation costs than any other agents. For instance, pools are often created whenever there is a change from model 1 to model 3 (perhaps with some plants that are still owned or managed by the SO). In this case, there must be a regulation that specifies how to communicate and control *ex post* the costs of the IPPs. For the same reason, in a pool the load is often not allowed to participate: it is calculated as a fixed quantity by the SO, grouping all the loads together. Another approach that can be applied in order to ease problems of asymmetries of information, is coupling the compulsory participation with the possibility of expressing market bids, rather than just costs. This somehow erases the distinction between the pool and the power exchange model. In Part III we will review the optimality criterion of dispatching, based on costs, as in a pool, in Chapter 8, allowing load to change overtime in Chapter 9, and based on bids in Chapter 10. This latter is the reference model of electricity market that we consider in this book.

Note that in Figure 4.3, DisCos participate in the wholesale market. This is a distinct feature of the wholesale market model: no consumer can participate directly in the power market; only distribution companies can buy electricity on behalf of their customers (and distribute the power to them). However, such a strict model is often relaxed in reality by allowing some load to participate. In this case, we can still refer to it as a wholesale market only model, provided that the load that is allowed to participate directly is not served by a distributor. We have considered this case in the picture drawing the dashed arrow that connects the high voltage load (directly linked to the transmission line) to the wholesale market. However, this distinction also becomes less stringent in real-life applications of the wholesale market model: often, some type of load, even if connected at medium or low voltage, is allowed to buy power without having to rely on its own distributor to do so. This is typically done by looking at consumption thresholds. In this case, the model moves toward a fully liberalized wholesale and retail market model, as described in the following paragraph.

## 4.5   The Wholesale and Retail Markets Model

Figure 4.4 describes the wholesale and retail markets model, also called the fully liberalized model. A distinctive feature of this model is that all the tasks performed by agents in the ESC are unbundled and attributed to distinct bodies, not just those referring to generation and transmission, but also electricity distribution and retailing. Thus, at the distribution level, there are no DisCos; they are split into separated entities: one that

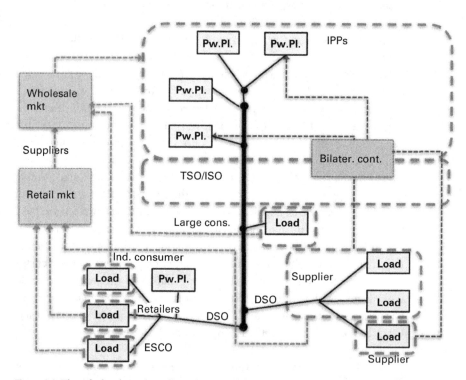

**Figure 4.4** The wholesale and retail markets model

plays the role of the DSO, and one or possibly several suppliers that compete among themselves to retail electricity to final customers. Note that there could be a single supplier created in each distribution network, by splitting each DisCo in a distributor and a supplier. However, there can be a retail market only if there is competition in it; for this to be the case, when just one supplier is created per each distribution network, this supplier must be allowed to compete with the other suppliers on the other distribution networks to serve energy to the final customers. Obviously, when there are several retailers and/or suppliers competing among themselves in each distribution network, there is an increased possibility of effective retail competition. Retail market competition will be analyzed in Chapter 19.

Figure 4.4 describes several possible market arrangements that can occur at the distribution level. The right-hand side describes the roles of suppliers, who can group load, and can acquire energy in all the ways that are allowed in market settings to serve their customers. However, it is also possible that consumers operate directly on their own behalf to acquire energy, regardless of their voltage or consumption level. This is described in the left-hand side of the graph. Moreover, consumers can either operate directly at the wholesale level, or ask some intermediary to do it on their behalf. These are called **retailers**, exactly because they acquire energy at the wholesale level and resell it at the retail level. **Energy Saving Companies** (ESCOs) are one specific type of retailer. These are retailers who sell energy saving services to their customers, sharing with them the benefits of the energy saved through contractual agreements. In a fully liberalized market an ESCO can operate by selling power to its customers, having acquired it at the wholesale level (either in a centralized market or through bilateral contracts).

Fully liberalized wholesale and retail markets are different to a fully vertical integrated industry. It is the market design, for instance, of the European countries, which however differ with respect to the effective degree of competition that suppliers have in the retail markets.

## Learning Outcomes

- There are different market structures of electricity markets depending on the degree of vertical integration of the entities that operates along the ESC. Four models can be identified: the Vertical Integrated industry; the Single Buyer model; the Wholesale market model; the Wholesale and Retail markets model.
- In the Vertical Integrated industry there is a single entity or a set of entities that are tied by contractual or legal arrangements and perform all the activities along the ESC. There is no completion in any part of the ESC.
- In the Single Buyer model some or all plants can be independently owned and managed by several entities, the Independent Power Producers (IPPs). There is a single company that performs all the other activities of the ESC. Thus, there is competition only among IPPs, who face the monopsony of the single buyer.
- In the Wholesale Market model the Single Buyer is split into several bodies; an entity that operates the grid and dispatches electricity and one or more Distribution

companies (DisCos). Transmission is fully unbundled from generation. Electricity is purchased by distribution companies on behalf of their end users, and sold by plants at the wholesale level in power exchanges that can be arranged as pools or power markets. The price that end consumers pay for the electricity that is purchased by suppliers is not established in a market but is regulated.

- In the Wholesale and Retail market model all the tasks performed along the ESC are unbundled and attributed to distinct bodies, including electricity distribution and retailing. DisCos are split into distributors and suppliers. There are also independent retailers. All of them have to acquire energy at the wholesale level and resell it in the retail market.

# 5 Energy Products and the Time Dimension of Electricity Markets

## 5.1 Introduction

In the previous chapter, we described the four possible market arrangements based on the separation of roles that each agent plays in the ESC. We have also seen, when discussing the wholesale market, that economic exchanges cannot take place at the same time as the delivery of power to customers. This is a feature that does not refer just to the wholesale electricity market. It is possible to set up markets that provide not just power, but all the services required to deliver this power. These markets take place at a different point in time, before the real-time delivery of electricity. Therefore, we can categorize electricity markets according to the services they provide to the electricity system, namely, electricity itself or services to allow the delivery of the electricity, or on the basis of the distance in time from the moment of contractual exchange to the moment of electricity delivery. The former taxonomy distinguishes between energy, ancillary services and generation capacity. The latter specifies the time structure of electricity markets.

## 5.2 Energy, Ancillary Services and Generation Capacity

We have already explained that power is linked with voltage and frequency, and that in AC current power is made of real and apparent power. In the electricity system, any perturbation to the system by an external factor or by a change in load or generation implies a change in these parameters. It is the role of the SO to keep the system operational, respecting the system and transmission constraints, namely, the acceptable range of frequency, voltage and power factor. Whenever there is a need for intervention, the SO must use one or more tools provided by all the systems and devices that constitute the electricity system, including loads and plants. The services provided by these systems, that are needed to deliver power in a safe and secure manner, are called ancillary services.

DEFINITION. *Ancillary services: services needed to deliver power in a safe and secure manner in an electricity system.*

Traditionally, there are three main categories of ancillary services: balancing services; reserves; voltage control services and system restoration services:

1) *Balancing services.* Balancing means all actions and processes through which the SO ensures the maintenance of system frequency within a predefined stability range. A balancing service is the service provided by those devices that allow the SO to keep the system balanced. Balancing services are thus supplied by production units, like small plants, that are able to cope with small, frequent imbalances. There are two types of balancing services: regulation services and load-following services. The former are able to handle rapid fluctuations in loads and small changes in generation. The latter handle slower fluctuations in loads.

2) *Reserves.* Generation capacity that can be used to produce active power in a given period of time and that has not been committed to generate energy in that period. Reserves are capable of handling large fluctuations in the availability of power that can threaten the stability of the system. They are provided by plants and are separated into spinning reserves and supplementary reserves. The spinning reserve refers to the capability of a plant to respond immediately to a change in frequency and provide the full amount of reserve very quickly. Supplementary reserves are categorized with respect to the time needed to respond and so they can be brought on line quickly. Another classification of reserves refers to their capabilities in terms of controlling the system, whether they are automatic or not, and whether this capability is located at local power stations or is centralized at the SO level. In particular, there are three categories of system controls: i) primary control: local automated control able to respond to any frequency change; ii) secondary control: centralized automatic control; iii) tertiary control: manual change in the dispatching in order to restore the secondary control. It is common to refer to the spinning reserve as the primary control, and to refer to the secondary and tertiary controls as the secondary and tertiary reserves.[1] Spinning reserves, are typically generated by keeping a power plant that is able to modulate its operational range operating at part load, being ready to increase it if needed. According to the possible classifications, the load can also provide a supplementary reserve, if it is able to be disconnected quickly. This is called **load interruptibility**.

3) *Voltage control services and system restoration services.* The former refers to those services that allow a transmission network to be kept operational by controlling reactive power. Both system devices, such as capacitors and inductors, and some types of plants and loads unit can provide these services. System restoration services refer to the need for most power plants, and in particular their alternator, to require power from the grid to be able to produce it. Therefore, in the event of blackouts, they are cut off the grid and cannot be restarted without it. Plants that are able to self-start without requiring power from the grid are those providing system restoration services.

Ancillary services are needed to provide useful electricity (i.e. electricity that can be used by end consumers). However, there is a prerequisite to providing electricity, that is,

---

[1] Not all scholars agree on this. In particular, Rebours and Kirschen (2005) propose treating spinning reserves as secondary control, rather than primary control. See also Rebours et al. (2007) for a worldwide classification of reserves.

there must be the possibility of generating electricity. In the electricity system, power is generated by power plants. However, power plants are also produced; namely, they are the results of some investment activity. Whenever some plants are called in order to provide ancillary services, that plant has to be there (i.e. it has to exist and be connected to the grid). This possibility is a result of the capacity of the plant. If there were not enough capacity to cope with the load, some load would have to be shed. Similarly, when some plants go off, some existing generation capacity has to replace it in order to keep the system balanced, or some load has to be shed. The generation capacity itself, therefore, can be interpreted as a form of service provided to the electricity system, namely, the possibility to produce power to keep the system balanced. Note that in order to keep it balanced, it is not strictly necessary to have generation capacity: the load can also help keep the system balanced if it has the capability and willingness to be shed. Therefore, the capacity services can be provided by generation capacity or load. There is also a third category of capacity that can provide capacity services, namely, the interconnection capacity. If a system needs power, this can also be supplied by another system through an interconnection. In Part III, we consider an isolated system, while we introduce the analysis of interconnections in Part V. The following is the definition of capacity services for non-interconnected systems:

DEFINITION. *Capacity services: the service provided by generation capacity of being able to generate power, or by the load of being able to be shed, in order to keep the system balanced.*

Both ancillary services and capacity services can be provided by market arrangements. Electricity markets do not refer just to power, but also to ancillary services and capacity. These markets can be classified according to their temporal distance to real time, the latter being the time at which electricity is generated and consumed. We have already noted that economic exchanges cannot take place simultaneously with power exchanges. The same is true for ancillary services and capacity exchanges. However, there can be several possible time arrangements for these exchanges, which can involve different agents. We discuss them in the next section.

## 5.3     The Time Structure of Electricity Markets

Figure 5.1 represents the different timing of the markets for energy, ancillary services and capacity.

The figure requires an explanation. On the horizontal axis, it displays the time. t0 denotes the time at which there is the exchange of power. This time is indeed a time interval: power flows continuously, but it is common to define a unit of delivery as a time interval during which power or the other services can be delivered. These time intervals can range from a few minutes to single hours and define the time nature of the products exchanged (i.e. if they are hourly products, quarter-hourly products, five-minute products and so on). The control of the electricity system during this time interval is the sole responsibility of the SO. There is a trade-off in the choice of the proper time

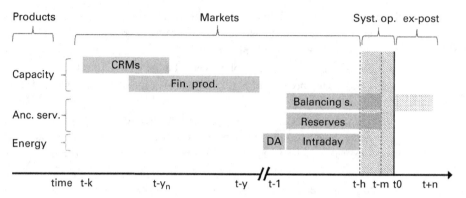

**Figure 5.1** The time dimension of electricity markets

interval: short time intervals (e.g. quarter hours or less) ease the work of the SO that has to balance the grid, but implies that a lot of time products are to be exchanged in the markets, while the opposite is true if hourly products are selected. Note that it is possible that these time products do not have the same time interval for all products: if power is exchanged in hourly products (i.e. energy in a given hour), ancillary services can have a quarter-hour structure, but other combinations are also possible. The time axis then reads, from t0 to the left, time units before the delivery. These time units can be minutes before t0 (denoted as t-m), hours before t0 (denoted as t-h), days (denoted as t-d) or even years before (t-y, t-$y_n$), up to several years before (generically denoted as t-k). To the right of t0, there are time units after the physical delivery, generically denoted as t+n. The period after t0 is denoted as *ex-post*, to highlight that what happens there occurs after the physical delivery. In the figure, there are the three products that can be exchanged, namely, energy, ancillary services and capacity; for each of them the figure represents when there can be market exchanges (described as "markets"), how long these market transactions can be (described by the length of the rectangles describing market transactions per each product) and when it is the SO responsibility to manage the grid in order to deliver energy (the dashed area denoted as "system operation"). The vertical solid line at t0 denotes the time of physical delivery, while the vertical dashed lines denotes the point in time before t0 beyond which no more transactions are possible and only the SO can operate to keep the grid balanced and deliver the energy in a secure and safe manner. This point in time is called **gate closure**. Obviously, the gate closure occurs before t0. There can be one gate closure for all products or one per each possible product, but obviously, there can be just one gate closure per each product at most. Gate closures can be close to real-time delivery, namely, minutes before, or distant to real-time delivery, namely, hours before. The two vertical dashed lines represent two possible gate closures. After the gate closure, no more market transactions are possible by definition. This does not mean that after the gate closure it is not possible for the SO to call for some service, but just that these services, such as balancing and reserves, would be directly commanded by the SO. This is called system operation. After the physical delivery, there is also the settlement period, in which market transactions are compared to the physical ones and cleared. We can see in Figure 5.1 that there are different durations for the markets of each of three products, energy, ancillary services and capacity. Let us consider them more closely.

## 5.3.1 Energy Markets

Energy is exchanged before the physical delivery. In Figure 5.1, the small light grey box with the DA tag represents an exchange taking place one day before the delivery. This is a common characteristic of several power markets. Indeed, it is so common that the market where power is exchanged is often called **Day-Ahead market (DA)**. For instance, in Europe, hourly energy products are exchanged in the day-ahead markets: they open in the morning, and close at some time the day before the delivery, generally at 12.00; energy to be delivered in each hour for the day after is exchanged between plants and suppliers (or load, DisCos, etc.). Two elements of these power markets should be emphasized:

i) Regardless of whether the energy markets take place one day before or several days before or just hours before, these markets are always forward markets: in these markets, forwards of energy specifically defined (i.e. power to be delivered at a given point in time in the future for a given duration) are exchanged; this implies that the day-ahead market is essentially a financial market, albeit with a physical delivery.

ii) The day-ahead markets are wholesale markets, in the sense that energy is exchanged at the wholesale level: plants and suppliers (or DisCos, retailers, load, etc.) participate in them, depending on the specific market structures adopted, as explained in Chapter 4. Retail markets have completely different time structures: in retail markets, typically energy is exchanged on a long-term basis (i.e. there are annual, multi-year or even perpetual contracts (terminable by one or both parties)).

The day-ahead market is often coupled with **intraday markets**. These are markets for the exchange of power that open after the closure of the DA market and close at the gate closure time (i.e. much closer to real-time delivery). The picture describes one distinctive feature of intraday markets compared to the DA market. In those markets where intraday power exchange possibilities exist, these last longer than those in the DA market. For instance, in several European markets, where the DA markets close at 12.00 the day before the delivery, intraday markets open straight after the closure of the DA and last up to a few hours before the delivery of each product, or each group of products. That is to say, electricity hourly products are grouped in sub categories (e.g. power for the first four hours of the day, power for the subsequent four hours and so on) and each intraday ends close to the delivery of that specific group of products; for instance, the gate closure time for the group of products power-for-the-last-four-hours closes at 21.00 of the delivery day, and so on. There are two other distinctive features of intraday markets:

i) in many cases only agents who have participated in the day-ahead market can participate to the intraday;

ii) the market rules, in particular relating to price formation, can be different with respect to those for the DA market.

The first point can be explained in the context of the rationale for creating intraday markets: they are created to allow market operators who have participated in the DA to adjust their positions. For instance, a plant that has participated in the DA and which has been scheduled (i.e. that its offer has been accepted in the market), may find after the closure of the DA market that it will not be able to generate some or all of its power for some technical reason. This implies that it will create an imbalance that will have to be tackled by the SO by activating some reserve (possibly purchased in the balancing or reserves market – see below). However, power for imbalances can be more costly than power for generation (again, this point will be explained more fully below). Therefore, an inefficiency can arise, which could be avoided if say it was possible to replace this expected unavailability with some other load before it becomes an imbalance. This is the kind of situation that intraday markets are there to address.

Constraints on participation are not, however, a feature of all intraday markets. When participation is free, regardless of whether or not the plants and load have participated in the DA market, the distinction between intraday and day-ahead becomes weaker. The specific feature of the intraday markets, on top of the price formation rule that will be discussed further below, is that traders can choose to trade at different periods of time, more or less close to delivery. Therefore, there is a sort of self-selection of trades among traders: the intraday trades that take place at the beginning of the intraday period will essentially have the same characteristics as DA trades and thus can be analyzed in the same way. The closer the time to the gate closure, the more the operators can make proper forecasts and will more confidently be able to predict whether they will be imbalanced or can provide balancing energy. Thus, trades close to the delivery at the intraday market essentially become balancing trades and the intraday markets essentially become markets for balancing services. However, intraday trades occur among market participants (i.e. between plants and load). Thus, in this case, intraday markets can be interpreted as markets for balancing services among market participants (i.e. plants and load), and not as markets for balancing services in which the market counterpart is the SO, as in balancing markets properly defined.

We have already noted that markets for energy before delivery are essentially forward markets. This is also the case for intraday markets. The similarity with financial markets helps to understand the second characteristic of intraday markets, as noted above. As with "pure" financial markets, they can be structured as markets with continuous trading or auction markets with an opening and a closing period. The former are markets in which agents place a market order. In the case of intraday, this is the willingness to generate or to buy load and the price at which this happens. The order is closed (i.e. there is a transaction), as soon as an order to purchase is matched with an order to sell at the same price (and vice versa). This means that several orders can be closed (i.e. matched at different prices). In auctions, orders are brought to the market in a given period; they are ranked by the auctioneer (the market operator in the case of intraday) from the highest to the lowest willingness to buy, for purchasing orders, and from the lowest to the highest price for the generating orders; then they are matched and cleared at the matching price (this point will be explained when economic dispatching is discussed in Chapter 10). Therefore, in auction markets there is a single price that is formed. The two types of markets have different pros and cons: continuous trading is an efficient way to organize markets whenever they have high liquidity, because it is easier for agents to close orders and agents do not have to wait for the closure of the auction for the execution of their orders. In contrast, when there is limited liquidity, they are riskier, in the sense that it can be less likely that transactions will be closed or they can be closed at different prices. For auction markets, the opposite is true: they are useful in providing a reference price for the transactions, but can be inefficient if the opening time is long and it forces agents to wait for the closing of the auction.

## 5.3.2     Ancillary Services Markets

Ancillary services are balancing services and reserves, as well as voltage control services and system restoration services. There is a first fundamental difference between the former two and the latter two. Balancing services and reserves are mostly offered by plants and can be provided by many types of plants. The latter two are provided either by devices that are under the control of the SO or by few types of plants. Therefore, it is not advisable to set centralized organized markets for voltage control services and restoration services. Generally, there are long-term bilateral contractual agreements between the SO and the possible suppliers of these services, under which the SO acquires the right to use them if needed. For balancing services and reserves, it is possible to organize markets for their exchange, or to impose their provision by some technical rules. The latter is less efficient, since there is no need to oblige all plants to supply them. Moreover, it is better to let those who are willing to offer these ancillary services to do so, as they will typically have a better knowledge of their costs than any possible regulator. As in any market, however, a crucial feature is to make sure that there is a competitive environment. A characteristic of balancing services and reserves markets, is that they are markets in which there is just one buyer, the SO. In fact, it is the SO who needs these services to allow power to flow within pre-defined admissible technical ranges. Therefore, these markets can be described as monopsonies. However, the monopsonistic power is mitigated by the possible limited competition at the supply side, since not all power plants can provide balancing services and reserves. The possible reduced competitive environment of ancillary services markets compared to DA markets makes the economic analysis of these markets analogous to the study of bilateral monopolies or oligopolistic markets rather than competitive ones. A common feature of the models developed to study these markets is that they emphasize strategic interaction settings and the impact of agents' market power on market outcomes. To reduce the possible exploitation of market power by plants in the ancillary services markets, they often rely on different market rules compared to those for DA markets, in particular in relation to price settlement and bidding rules. For instance, ancillary services markets often rely on discriminatory auction rules rather than uniform auction rules (see Chapter 12).

Ancillary services are used by the SO to acquire the services that it needs in order to deliver the power that has resulted from the DA market. Therefore, they are *ex-ante* markets. If this is rather obvious for the reserves, since there would be no meaning for an *ex-post* reserve (recall what a reserve is, capacity kept available to be used in case it is needed), there can be different market arrangements for balancing. Let us make this point clear by specifying the timing of the balancing process. When the DA market closes, a dispatching schedule is established: the set of power plants scheduled to provide power at t0 and the loads that will acquire power is selected. If intraday markets exist, this process starts at the end of the intraday. Thus, the market, either DA or intraday, determines who produces, who consumes power and at which price, for a given time interval (e.g. an hour). The result of the dispatching schedule, however, occurs before real time, and is fixed for a given time interval. The physical reality of the system, however, changes continuously. There is thus the problem of matching the result of the day-ahead schedule with the possibility of delivering energy in real time. This problem can be tackled in two ways.

One way is taking the results of the dispatching schedule as a constraint of the real-time delivery, and solving repeatedly, for very short time intervals before delivery (e.g. five minutes before real time delivery), a problem of cost minimization that also encompasses all the constraints posed by Kirchhoff's laws. This is the **real-time market** approach. Markets in the United States, such as the Pennsylvania Jersey Maryland (PJM)[2] for instance, work according to this paradigm.

Another approach is to rely on balancing markets. Under this scheme, the result of the dispatching schedule is communicated to the SO. The SO checks if this schedule is compatible with the forecast status of the grid for that period (e.g. an hour) verifying if power can respect all the constraints posed by Kirchhoff's laws. If not, it needs to alter the scheduled dispatching in the balancing market. The market arrangements of balancing services can be centralized, or bilateral. If there are centralized **balancing markets**, the SO uses them matching its need for balancing services, or possibly also reserves, with the willingness to supply balancing services and reserves by plants and load. If there are no centralized markets – the SO in order to keep the system balanced – calls those balancing services that it has either acquired on the basis of a previous long-term contractual agreement, established well before the real-time delivery, or that it can use thanks to a regulatory framework that imposes on the plants the obligation to provide them to the SO. The economic terms of the compensation, i.e. the price at which plants (or load) are remunerated for their services, which have not been established in the balancing markets, occur at the level that was predetermined in the long-term contractual agreements or at the regulated price.

The activity of using balancing services to adjust the day-ahead schedule is called **ex-post balancing**. It is represented by the dotted light grey area for the balancing services. *Ex-post* balancing should not be confused with **redispatching**, which is the activity of altering the generation and/or load pattern, undertaken by the SO, in order to

---

[2] PJM groups all or part of Delaware, Illinois, Indiana, Kentucky, Maryland, Michigan, New Jersey, North Carolina, Ohio, Pennsylvania, Tennessee, Virginia, West Virginia and the District of Columbia.

change physical flows in the transmission system and relieve physical congestion.[3] Thus, redispatching occurs before real time, when the SO receives the schedule of dispatching and sees that its implementation would infringe some physical constraint of the grid or imply an inadmissible zonal configuration (this point will become clear when we will analyze market zones in Chapter 16). On the contrary, *ex-post* balancing denotes the activity of using balancing services in order to operate the grid.

After the real-time delivery, the usage of balancing (and reserves) must be settled. This is described in Section 5.3. Balancing markets are analyzed in Chapter 11.

### 5.3.3 Capacity Markets

Capacity markets are the places where capacity is traded. A distinctive element of capacity markets, as compared to the energy and ancillary services markets, is that capacity is traded for its capability of being used to generate electricity, not for the electricity that it will generate. In other words, what is traded is the capacity of a power plant to generate electric current, or the possibility that the load must reduce its consumption, regardless of whether such a capacity will effectively inject power into the grid or reduce the withdrawals in real time. Therefore, a common feature of capacity markets is that the remuneration for capacity, independent of the possible market organizations, is expressed in terms of money per watt (or multiples), namely, money per power, not money per energy. In fact, it is the power that measures the possibility of producing energy. As discussed above for ancillary services, in interconnected markets the possibility to deliver energy is effectively provided not just by power plants and load (to be shed) installed in a given system, but also by the interconnections of that system with other ones. Again, we will start by considering isolated markets. Thus, capacity markets refer here to generation capacity and load only. There is much debate in the literature about whether capacity markets are needed to provide sufficient investment in the power sector, or if energy and ancillary services markets are enough to provide remuneration both for amortizing existing investments and planning new ones. We will discuss this point in Part VII. For present purposes, it is important to say that if capacity markets exist, they are opened a long time before real-time delivery, in order to give enough time for new investments to be undertaken.

There are two types of capacity market, long-term financial markets and physical markets. In physical markets there is an explicit remuneration for the commitment by the seller to physically install new generation capacity (or reduce the load). There are several ways in which such remuneration can take place. A general term referring to them is **Capacity Remuneration Mechanism** (CRM). CRMs are mechanisms that allow remuneration for physical capacity; capacity markets are the places where capacity is exchanged and remunerated through CRMs. CRMs are discussed in Chapter 22. CRMs are not the only way to support investments. The very nature of investment embeds a risk for the investor due to the temporal discrepancy between the time of the investments and

---

[3] This is the definition as stated, for instance, in article 2(26) of European Commission Regulation 543/2013 of 14 June 2013.

the realization of the profits that these investments allow. In the electricity markets, this risk is due to the time lag between the physical planning and realization of a power plant (or some energy efficiency device, for instance, that reduces the load) and the time of the delivery of power. For capacity investments, as for any investments, it is possible to develop all those financial instruments that allow risk hedging, setting derivatives that covariate with the underlying asset. In the case of capacity investments, the underlying asset is the energy that a given capacity can generate. Therefore, there are several possible derivatives on energy that can be traded in financial markets, such as futures and options. These derivatives are traded in **long-term financial markets**. It is important not to confuse financial capacity markets with day-ahead markets. In the former, derivatives are traded that have a long maturity date, up to a period of years, which are needed to hedge investment risks. In the latter, the products traded, even if they have the structure of forward contracts, have a much shorter maturity, at most one day. This book will not analyze financial derivatives on electricity, as they are similar to other financial products.[4]

Note that in Figure 5.1, we have represented CRMs and financial capacity markets by means of two slightly overlapping rectangles. This is not strictly necessary. The figure simply aims to highlight two common features of markets for capacity. The first is that they usually remain open for a significantly longer period than energy or ancillary services markets; the second feature is that CRMs can have a longer time perspective compared to financial markets, since financial derivatives can hardly be traded for a maturity longer than a few years, while CRMs may have a very long time to delivery.

## 5.4    The Settlement Process

Settlement means clearing the payment of an exchange. In general, in commercial goods markets, the settlement activity takes place at the same time as the physical delivery of the good. For instance, if a quantity $q$ of a good, say apples, is exchanged from A to B, B pays to A the contracted payment for this. If A delivers fewer apples, say only $q - x$, B will reduce the payment by the corresponding contracted price times $x$, which measures the value of the goods not sold by A to B. Even if the payment is postponed, it is nevertheless possible to link every settlement with the exchange of the goods and service to which it relates: B knows how many apples have been sold from A and regulates the payment accordingly. In power markets, this is not possible. The physical nature of electricity implies that electrons flow where they find the lowest resistance (this is the meaning of Kirchhoff's laws), regardless of the contractual agreement between the plant that has produced them and the load that has consumed them. Therefore, there must be a phase after the physical delivery in which all physical injection to and withdrawals from the grid are recorded and compared with the contractual agreements regarding energy exchange that were established *ex ante*. Then the differences are settled on the basis of the prices that have emerged in the markets. This

---

[4] A useful reference for studying them is Aid, 2015.

phase is called *settlement*. The settlement relates to the balancing, but it must not be confused with it: balancing is the use of energy to keep the grid balanced (i.e. to make sure that load and generation coincide). The settlement is done by first comparing the scheduled exchanges to those that have effectively occurred, and then clearing the economic value of this difference. The net difference between the scheduled and delivered energy in the settlement process coincides with the amount of energy that has been used by the SO to keep the system balanced. Example 5.1 helps to explain the settlement process.

---

**Example 5.1** Suppose there is a simple electricity system comprising three plants, Alpha, Bravo and Charlie, and two loads, Delta and Echo. Consider the exchange of energy for a given time period (e.g. an hour). Assume that there is a market in which ancillary services are exchanged. For simplicity, we refer just to balancing services, but the same can be said for reserves. There is a power exchange and also let agents be able to exchange power through bilateral contracts. Thus, we refer to model 4 in Chapter 4. The prices in these markets are 10 dollars per MWh in the power exchange; 12 dollars per MWh is the bilateral contact price and the price of balancing services is 15 dollars per MWh. Charlie and Echo have entered into a bilateral agreement and have communicated to the SO that Charlie will produce 150 MW, bought by Echo. Delta buys energy in the Power exchange, where Alpha and Bravo sell it. Load Delta is 250 MW, and the supply schedule foresees Alpha producing 50 MW and Bravo 200 MWh. Table 5.1 summarizes this data.

Note that in Table 5.1 the load is accounted for as a negative number to denote that it is a withdrawal of energy from the system, while injections by plants are expressed using positive figures.

Suppose now that the SO needs to balance this energy, for whatever reason; for example, because Echo consumes 50 MWh more, while Delta consumes 40 MWh less, so that there is a need of an extra generation of 10 MWh, and at the same time there is a reduction of power by Bravo of 20 MWh. As a result, in the balancing market, the SO needs to acquire 30 MWh more, and it happens that Charlie sells it, while Alpha is not able to change its production from the expected schedule. Table 5.2 reports the effective energy delivered, and compares it to the scheduled figures to measure the individual and system imbalances:

Note the imbalances line. Charlie provides 30 MWh more to the SO; thus it sells a balancing service to the SO. Also Delta sells balancing services to the SO, since it reduces its withdrawals of energy by 40 MWh. Conversely, Echo buys balancing

---

**Table 5.1** The energy schedule of Example 5.1

| Energy (MWh) | Generation | | | | Load | | |
|---|---|---|---|---|---|---|---|
| | Alpha | Bravo | Charlie | Tot | Delta | Echo | Tot |
| Scheduled energy | 50 | 200 | 150 | 400 | −250 | −150 | −400 |

**Table 5.2** Scheduled effective energy and imbalances of Example 5.1

|  | Generation | | | | Load | | |
| --- | --- | --- | --- | --- | --- | --- | --- |
| Energy (MWh) | Alpha | Bravo | Charlie | Tot | Delta | Echo | tot |
| Scheduled energy | 50 | 200 | 150 | 400 | -250 | -150 | -400 |
| Effective energy | 50 | 180 | 180 | 410 | -210 | -200 | -410 |
| Imbalances | 0 | -20 | 30 | 10 | 40 | -50 | -10 |

**Table 5.3** The settlement of Example 5.1

|  | Generation | | | | Load | | |
| --- | --- | --- | --- | --- | --- | --- | --- |
| Payments ($) | Alpha | Bravo | Charlie | Tot | Delta | Echo | tot |
| Sch. Energy | 500 | 2,000 | 1,800 | 4,300 | -2,500 | -1,800 | -4,300 |
| Imbalances | 0 | -300 | 450 | 150 | 600 | -750 | -150 |
| Tot | 500 | 1,700 | 2,250 | 4,450 | -1,900 | -2,550 | -4,450 |

services, increasing the load by 50 MWh, as well as Bravo, who, by producing less, is treated as if it buys balancing energy from the SO, since there will have to be someone else in the system that has to supply the energy that Bravo has committed to generate but is no longer generating.

Table 5.2 also helps to show what would happen if there were not enough ancillary services. For instance, if Charlie was not able to increase production up to 30 MWh, but could do it only for 20 MWh, the only possibility to keep the system balanced would be shedding 10 MWh of load.

The physical exchanges of energy and of balancing services must be settled. Remember that the prices for energy purchased and sold at the power exchange level, at the bilateral contracts level and for balancing services are different. This implies that some operators will gain more than they expected before balancing, while some will gain less or pay more; but the economic settlement must bring about a zero net surplus. Table 5.3 reports the economic account of the energy and the imbalances that form the settlement account for these transactions.

We can see that the payments foreseen as the results of the market arrangements have been cleared according to those market arrangements in full; in other words, regardless of whether or not they have then been fully executed. However, the imbalances generated by the differences between scheduled and realized programs are also cleared, so that all those who have benefited from these services will have paid them *ex post* to those who have produced them. In Example 5.1, the load Echo and the plant Bravo have benefitted from balancing services that have allowed them to consume more or generate less, while the power plant Charlie and the load Delta have produced those balancing services which have allowed the system to remain stable, and have received the payments for them. We can also see that, as expected, the settlement phase implies that the balance sheet must be in equilibrium of payments across all agents involved

The settlement process provides a full-market clearing, in the sense that it guarantees that those who produce receive the market value of what they produce, and those who benefit pay it. However, it is left to the market to let the value of those services emerge.

## Learning Outcomes

- Electricity markets can be categorized according to the nature of the services they provide to the electricity system, or the time-dimension, namely, the distance between the contractual arrangement and the real-time delivery. The former taxonomy refers to energy, ancillary services and capacity services. The latter specifies the time structure of different electricity markets, from close to real time to before delivery.
- Ancillary services refer to Balancing services, reserves and voltage control and system restoration services. Balancing services are services that the System Operator uses to maintain the system frequency within a predefined stability range. Reserves are generation capacity that can be used to produce active power in a given period and that has not been committed to generate energy in that period. Voltage control and system restoration services provide services that allow reactive power (voltage control) to be controlled and the possibility of providing power to power plants in order to let them start and generate power (system restoration).
- Capacity services refer to the possibility provided by the investment in generation capacity (or load) to generate power (or reduce load) in order to keep the system balanced.
- The time dimension of electricity markets distinguishes between markets for balancing services and reserves, intraday markets, day-ahead markets and long-term markets, both financial and physical. The closing time of a transaction is called gate closure time, beyond which no transaction can take place. After the gate closure, there is real-time delivery of electricity. After physical delivery, there is the settlement period.
- Day-ahead markets and intraday markets are forward markets that are relatively close to real-time delivery. Capacity markets are long-term markets where capacity instead of power is exchanged among market participants, namely, investors on the one hand and capacity users, either the suppliers or the SO, on the other hand.
- *Ex-ante* balancing is the activity of purchasing or selling balancing services by the SO. *Ex-post* balancing is the accountability *ex post* (i.e. after the delivery) of the balancing services used by the SO to keep the system balanced. Redispatching is the activity of altering the generation and/or load pattern after the gate closure undertaken by the SO in order to change physical flows in the transmission system and relieve physical congestion.
- The contractual arrangements between two parties, a plant and a load, might not be respected by real-time delivery. The settlement process guarantees that those who have produced receive the market value of what they have produced and those who have benefitted from power production pay for it.

# 6 Some Principles of Electricity Sector Regulation

## 6.1 Introduction

Until the beginning of deregulation in the twenty-first century in some countries, the economic activities of the electricity sector were treated as natural monopolies. In this chapter, we explain what this means. There are still many countries where this institutional framework has not changed. Several countries have electricity service providers that are regulated monopolies, both in the developing and developed world. Moreover, countries that have introduced competition at the wholesale and retail levels, still have some form of regulation of transmission and distribution networks, even though many recent innovations in electricity services are being introduced at the network level (see Chapter 27 on Smart Grids).

The main objective of regulation is to maximize welfare, aiming for allocative, productive and dynamic efficiency. Regulation requires generating incentives for regulated firms to produce efficiently, from both the cost and the quality point of view. Practically, the underlying objectives are usually set as the efficient pricing of services, the achievement of the firm's objectives at the least cost – and subject to budget constraint – allowing the regulated firm to recover its own costs, and the prevention of any market power abuse – passed on to consumers (through excessive prices). Regulatory instruments also encompass controls of quality, quantity and entry. In this chapter, we focus on pricing and some general issues of regulation applied to the electricity industry. We describe the reasons for regulating in Section 6.2, followed by the main rules governing tariffs in practice in Section 6.3, and providing some examples in Section 6.4. Interested readers can refer to Viscusi et al. (2005) for a broader analysis of regulation in network industries.

## 6.2 Why Regulate the Electricity Sector?

Over the history of the electricity sector, several waves of competition and regulation have been experienced worldwide. As we have seen, before the introduction of the AC standard at the end of the nineteenth century, many companies were selling electricity, locating production very close to loads. The development of the new transmission technology allowed the rationalization of production and transportation of electricity over longer distances. The rapid industrialization in the twentieth century made electrical transmission lines and grids a critical part of the economic infrastructure in most industrialized nations. By using common generating plants for every type of load, important economies of scale were achieved. Lower overall capital investment was required, the load factor on each plant was increased thereby creating increased efficiency, allowing for lower energy costs for consumers and increased overall use of electric power. In this context, it became clear that electricity was to be organized as a natural monopoly. This concept dates back to John Stewart Mill, who in 1848 had already published an analysis of natural monopolies, noting that, "(a) Gas and water service in London could be supplied at lower cost if the duplication of facilities by competitive firms were avoided; and that (b) in such circumstances, competition was unstable and inevitably was replaced by monopoly."[1]

DEFINITION. *Natural Monopoly: there is a natural monopoly when a single firm can produce a product or a group of products more cheaply than two or more firms.*

Technically, a natural monopoly exists in an industry where the costs are *subadditive* (Baumol and Bradford, 1970). That is, where two firms produce $Q_1$ and $Q_2$ respectively and the costs are as follows:

$$C(Q) = C(Q_1 + Q_2) < C(Q_1) + C(Q_2). \tag{6.1}$$

Subadditivity is not the same as economies of scale. Costs can be subadditive, even if diseconomies exist (near the total output $Q_1 + Q_2$). In the single product case, scale economies are a sufficient condition for subadditivity. In the multiproduct case, product-specific scale economies are not a sufficient condition. Economies of scope are a necessary but not sufficient condition for subadditivity. Even economies of scale and scope do not guarantee cost subadditivity.

A sufficient condition to have a single product monopoly is that the average cost curve falls at any observed quantity for all firms and that there are economies of scale. Consider the following example:

---

**Example 6.1  Natural Monopoly in Electricity Generation and Transmission** Suppose there is an integrated company that can generate and transmit electricity incurring the following costs:

- Fixed cost $F = \$60$ for building plant and connecting houses;
- Marginal cost $MC = m = \$10$
- Average costs $AC = m + F/Q = 10 + 60/Q$

We can see that the average cost declines as output rises. The total cost of producing $Q = 12$ by one firm is equal to $\$180$ (i.e. $AC \cdot Q$). If the single plant was replaced by two plants, given the demand, they would produce 6 each. The individual $AC$ for each of them would be 20, and the total (system) cost

---

[1] John Stewart Mill, cited in Garfield and Lovejoy, *Public Utility Economics*, 1964, p. 15.

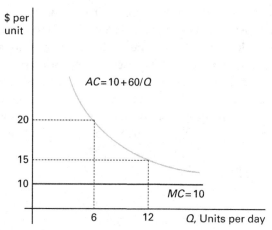

**Figure 6.1** Costs for a natural monopoly

would be $240, higher than before. Figure 6.1 (adapted from Carlton and Perloff, 2015) illustrates the example.

In order to assess whether companies in the electricity sector are in natural monopoly, we need to look at the different parts of the Electricity Supply Chain.

For power generation, the condition of being in a natural monopoly depends on the demand that plants face. According to Christensen and Green (1976), the average curve for US electric-power-producing firms in 1970 was U-shaped and reached its minimum at 33 billion kWh per year. Most electric companies operated in regions of substantial economies of scale, that is, for a quantity below 33 billion kWh. Figure 6.2 (adapted from Carlton and Perloff, 2015) illustrates this case. The demand function crosses the average cost curve below its minimum.

For example, Newport Electric produced 0.5 billion kWh/year and Iowa Southern Utilities: 1.3 billion kWh/year. These firms were natural monopolies. Others did not match this condition. For example, the largest electric utility in 1970, Southern, produced 54 kWh/year. It has been estimated that two firms could produce that quantity at 3¢ less per thousand kWh than could a single firm (Carlton and Perloff, 2015).

For electricity transmission (regardless of whether it occurs at high or medium/low voltage, i.e. for power transmission or distribution), there is little doubt that they are natural monopolies (Landon, 1983). They exhibit economies of scale – the average cost goes down as more demand is served through a single wire. Power lines exhibit very high fixed costs, but practically zero marginal cost. Once a power line is built, the marginal cost of serving an additional household with that same line is basically zero (ignoring power losses). Thus, the greater the number of households that can be served with a single wire, the lower the costs will be because the capital cost is spread out over more customers.

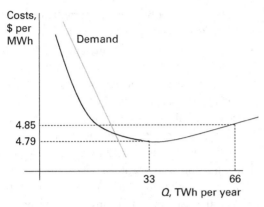

**Figure 6.2** Demand and natural monopoly
*Source*: adapted from Carlton and Perloff (2015).

As it turns out, it is also cheaper (per unit of electricity sold) to build higher-capacity power lines that serve a lot of demand rather than a large number of lower-capacity power lines. Table 6.1 provides some relevant data on transmission line costs.

**Table 6.1** Typical transmission costs

| Voltage cost (kV) | Capital cost (Thousand $/Miles) | Capacity (MWh) | Cost (million $/GW-mile) |
|---|---|---|---|
| 230 | 480 | 350 | 1.37 |
| 345 | 900 | 900 | 1.00 |
| 500 | 1,200 | 2,000 | 0.60 |
| 765 | 1,800 | 4,000 | 0.45 |

*Source*: Hirst and Kirby (2001), cited by Blumseck (2010).

Given that there can be relevant parts of the Electricity Supply Chain that are natural monopolies, a natural question that arises is how to price them.[2] Section 6.3 briefly tackles this issue.

## 6.3    Pricing Natural Monopolies

How can government regulate a natural monopoly so that it produces the efficient quantity? There are several options.

- *Marginal cost pricing rule* is a regulation that sets the price equal to the monopoly's marginal cost. The quantity demanded at a price equal to marginal cost is the efficient quantity. The regulator then sets a transfer in order to cover the losses, if it is allowed to do so.

---

[2] We shall discuss specific regulatory interventions in the retailing sector regarding last resort suppliers and other service obligations in Chapter 20.

- Where possible, a regulated natural monopoly might be permitted to *price discriminate* (i.e. to charge different prices to each consumer or group of consumers) to cover the loss from marginal cost pricing. The government might pay a subsidy equal to the monopoly's loss.
- The natural monopoly might charge a one-time fee to cover its fixed costs and then charge a price equal to marginal cost. The fixed charge may discourage some people from taking the service at all. The fixed charge may therefore cross-subsidize low users. To avoid this problem, *Ramsey Pricing* can be applied. Ramsey pricing derives from the problem of consumers' surplus maximization under the zero-profit constraint for a monopolist that sells a multiproduct. It stipulates that the markup on marginal cost of each product, that guarantees zero profits and no losses for the monopolist, is inversely proportional to the elasticity of demand, but smaller than it, depending on a constant smaller than one. Box 6.1 explains this point.

---

**Box 6.1** Ramsey pricing.

For simplicity, suppose that there are n independent demand functions for the n goods $(q_1, q_2, \ldots, q_n)$ produced by a monopolist: $q_i = D_i(p_i)$, for $i = 1, 2, \ldots, n$. The total revenue is $R(q_1, \ldots, q_n) = p_1(q_1)q_1 + \ldots + p_n(q_n)q_n$. The cost of producing these goods is $C(q_1, \ldots, q_n)$. The regulator maximizes consumer surplus over the different product markets:

$$\sum_{i=1}^{n} \int_0^{q_i} p_i(t)dt - C(q_1, \ldots, q_n). \tag{b.1}$$

subject to the constraint that revenue exactly equals cost (or that profit is a given constant). The first-order conditions are:

$$p_i - C_i = \lambda(R_i - C_i), \tag{b.2}$$

for $i = 1, \ldots, n$, where $C_i$ and $R_i$ are the partial derivatives of $C$ and $R$ with respect to $q_i$ and $\lambda$ is the Lagrangian multiplier on the constraint that revenues are equal to costs. This condition may be rewritten as:

$$\frac{p_i - C_i}{p_i} = -\frac{k}{\varepsilon_i}, \tag{b.3}$$

where $k = \lambda/(1 + \lambda)$ and $\varepsilon_i$ is the elasticity of demand for $q_i$. The price markup over marginal cost, $(p_i - C_i)/p_i$, results inversely proportional to the price elasticity of demand for that good. If $k = 1$, this condition is the standard monopoly price condition. If $k = 0$, this condition is the same as in competition.

These options ensure that the first-best outcome is achieved. Another alternative is to permit the firm to produce the quantity at which price equals (long run) average cost and to set the price equal to average cost – *the average cost pricing rule*. In Figure 6.3, the average cost pricing equilibrium corresponds to a price equal to $15, above the marginal cost pricing rule at $10.

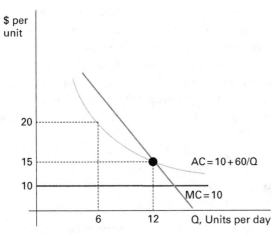

**Figure 6.3** Average cost pricing

However, regulation should preserve some efforts to minimize costs, by the monopolist. In practice, this depends on the strength of the incentives, the time horizon and the costs. If we assume that the transfer to the monopolist in the regulated scheme is equal to:

$$\text{Transfer } t = a + b \cdot Costs; \qquad (6.2)$$

we can summarize the different regulatory choices in Table 6.2, according to different values of the coefficient $b$.

**Table 6.2** Different forms of natural monopoly regulation

| Costs | Incentives | Time horizon | Impact of the incentives |
| --- | --- | --- | --- |
| 1. $b = 0$ | Regulation of the profit rate (*rate of return regulation*) | Ex post | Weak |
| 2. $0 < b < 1$ | Incentive contract | Periodically | Average |
| 3. $b = 1$ | Price fixing (*price cap*) | Ex ante | Strong |

If $b = 0$ in Equation (6.2), the transfer is fixed and decided after production, therefore the incentives for the monopolist to be efficient are rather weak. This contract is known as rate of return regulation:

DEFINITION. *Rate of return regulation (RoR): under this kind of regulatory contract, a firm must justify its price by showing that its return on capital does not exceed a specified target rate.*

For the RoR, the transfer of Equation (6.2) is equal to a predetermined rate of return of the firm's capital, which can be written as follows:

$$a = E + s \cdot RB, \tag{6.3}$$

where $E$ is the detailed cost breakdown of regulated company business; $RB$ is the rate base, usually set at the cost of capital; $s$ is established in rate hearing (in general $s = 10.5\%$). Under rate of return regulation, the financial integrity of the firm is always guaranteed, profits are monitored and there is no incentive to reduce service quality. However, there is no incentive to reduce cost and a high risk of accounting manipulation. In particular, this type of regulation can end up serving the self-interest of the firm rather than the social interest because the firm's managers have an incentive to inflate costs and use more capital than the efficient amount. The (potential) incentive to overinvest is the so-called Averch-Johnson (1962) effect.

If $b$ is below 1, there is the possibility to set an incentive contract that, if revised periodically, gives average incentives for efficiency.

Finally, if $b$ is equal to 1, the regulation is set *ex ante* and gives strong incentives for efficiency: typically, this is the price cap regulation.

DEFINITION. **Price cap**: *a price ceiling applied to the price that firms can set.*

The price cap rule specifies the highest price that the firm is permitted to charge. This type of regulation gives the firm an incentive to operate efficiently and keep costs under control. The firm has an incentive to minimize cost and produce up to the quantity that corresponds to the level of the demand curve that equals the price cap. The price cap regulation lowers the price and increases the quantity.

Under price cap regulation, the regulator defines an initial price $P_0$ (or a vector of prices if multiple products are produced by a regulated firm). This price (or a weighted average of the prices allowed for firms supplying multiple products or different types of customers) is then adjusted from year to year taking into account the expected inflation rate (i.e. the retail price index (RPI)), as well as a target productivity change factor $X$ that the regulator wants to pass to consumers.

Therefore, the price $P_1$ in period 1 is:

$$P_1 = P_0(1 + RPI - X). \tag{6.4}$$

A fixed price cap provides an incentive for regulated firms to decrease their costs of production. Furthermore, as Laffont and Tirole (1993) show, if a price cap is applied to a fixed weighted average of the revenues the firm earns from each product it supplies, the firm has an incentive to set the second-best prices for each service given the level of the price. But, in the context of asymmetric information – regarding cost production opportunities – a permanent price cap framework is not efficient with regard to the tradeoff between efficiency incentives and rent extraction (Schmalensee, 1989). Moreover, it is worth mentioning that if costs and service quality are positively correlated, a price cap approach creates an incentive to reduce service quality which is not suitable for consumers' welfare. Price cap regulation also suffers from the drawback that cost fluctuations are under the charge of the firm and that if X is set too high, the regulated firm can fail.

With respect to the regulation of distribution and transmission electricity networks, regulators apply cost of service in order to define the starting price $P_0$. Then, the price cap mechanism is operational for a period defined by the regulator (usually five years). As a pre-scheduled process, when the end of the contract period is reached, an assessment of the regulated firm's production cost is carried out and a new price $P_0$ and $X$ factor (target productivity change) are fixed. In the electricity sector, it is hard for distribution and transmission network regulated firms to estimate prices for consumers and services provided at distinctive network locations under an overall revenue cap. Price caps are more common as a cost incentive mechanism than as a tool to induce optimal second-best pricing of various network services. The reason is that implementing a price cap regulation for a service production is more difficult than, for instance, regulations in which just production costs are considered to reach efficiency. Moreover, price caps impose a significant burden on the regulator in terms of gathering information, and this is costly and time-consuming.

In practice, different regulatory approaches exist. In Europe, for example, only Belgium applies RoR, whereas Poland, Romania, Slovakia, Sweden and Turkey have opted for price caps. Hybrid models exists, as in Finland, Greece, Italy, Spain, Switzerland and the United Kingdom. Finally, broad incentive contracts characterize the approach of the Czech Republic, France, Germany and the Netherlands.[3]

Joskow (2014) argues that price caps are efficient at creating incentives for managerial efficiency and cost minimization, but weak at sharing the benefits of lower costs among actors. The cost of service approach is efficient for matching price and production costs, but it does not generate incentives for managers to decrease production costs, leading to excessive prices for consumers. According to the author, the optimal framework of regulation lies in between these two extremes. This optimal mechanism may include a profit-sharing approach, or a mechanism implying that the price fixed *ex ante* and charged by the regulated firm depends on realized costs savings (Lyon, 1996) so that failures of mechanisms presented are corrected. On this topic, Laffont and Tirole (1993) argue that the regulator can do better by offering the regulated firm a menu of cost-contingent regulatory contracts with different cost sharing provisions; the regulator can do even better than if it offers only a single profit sharing contract.

## 6.4 Electricity Tariffs and Bills

The final price paid by both residential and industrial consumers is regulated, if the firm is a natural monopoly, as it is for DisCos, for instance, or if some forms of consumer protection exist, or if there are transmission and distribution charges that are chosen by

---

[3] Survey by Ernest and Young, 2013, www.ey.com/Publication/vwLUAssets/Mapping_Power_and_Utilities_Report_2013/$FILE/EY%20European%20Power%20regulatory%20report%20FINAL%200513.pdf.

the regulator, even if generation and retail are competitive. We will further explain these concepts in Part VI.

Electricity tariffs can be different depending on the type of consumers, their load profile and their equipment. In general, tariffs for industrial customers are much more complex than those for smaller customers. There can be generation and demand charges, that reflects production and retail costs, transmission and distribution charges, environmental charges and sometimes charges for those services ensuring grid stability and reliability.

For example, the breakdown of a typical electricity bill for a domestic consumer in the United Kingdom, where there is competition in generation and supply and regulation in transmission and distribution, is as follows:[4]

- wholesale or energy costs 36.30 percent;
- network costs 27.59 percent;
- environmental and social obligation costs 14.79 percent;
- other direct costs 1.19 percent and operating costs 16.46 percent;
- supplier pre-tax margin -1.09 percent and VAT 4.76 percent.

In Australia, for instance, network costs are as high as 48 percent, whereas generation costs represent 25 percent of the bill.[5] In some cases a fuel adjustment component is also used. Clearly, we can find other situations, as for instance in North Carolina, where vertically integrated utilities are operational. The extent and the principles of regulation can be different; yet, the costs of regulated activities are generally passed on to end-consumers.

## Learning Outcomes

- A natural monopoly is characterized by a subadditive cost function. A sufficient condition to have a single product monopoly is that the average cost curve falls at any observed quantity for all firms and that there are economies of scale.
- The power generation can be a natural monopoly if the demand crosses the aggregate long run average cost below its minimum.
- Power lines exhibit economies of scale; they can be classified as natural monopolies.
- Monopoly pricing in practice can take different forms. Rate-of-return regulation (RoR) and price caps are the most common. Under ROR, the firms' return on capital cannot exceed a specified target rate. Under price caps, there is a ceiling on the service price.
- Regardless of the different forms of regulation, or their extent, costs are passed on to consumers under the regulated component of the electricity bill.

---

[4] Ofgem, www.ofgem.gov.uk/data-portal/breakdown-electricity-bill.
[5] Queensland Government, www.dews.qld.gov.au/electricity/prices/bill.

# Part III

# Simplified Isolated Markets without Network Congestion

Part III describes the way electricity markets are organized, focusing on the wholesale model. In order to highlight the basic features of the markets and the relationships between the physical characteristics of electricity and its impact on market design, we do not focus on the role and impacts that the electricity grid has on the markets. For the same reason, we do not consider here the different time dimensions of markets. Therefore, we begin our analysis with a stylized model that focuses only on demand and supply of electricity, without paying attention to the specific features of electricity transmission and distribution and assuming that load and power generation take place at the same node. This assumption will be removed in Part V. Moreover, we do not consider here aspects related to the availability of power plants, which is different from the possibility of dispatching them. In other words, we shall consider the set of power supply as given and assume that this set is enough to cover the load. We refer to a short-term analysis. We will focus on investments in power supply in Part VII.

The analysis performed in this part describes the buying–selling process that takes place in markets. In order to do so, we will start in Chapter 7 by considering the specific features of the load, on the one hand, and power generation on the other hand, since it has a crucial impact on the way power markets are set up and work. Then, we consider in Chapter 8 the simplest possible model of power dispatching, namely, one in which there is a fully integrated monopoly (model 1 in Chapter 4) and show the importance of power supply characteristics for the optimal decision for the monopolist. Chapter 9 presents the welfare maximization solution of a central planner when load changes over time, the economic dispatching rationale and what happens when there is not enough capacity to serve the whole load. In Chapter 10, the assumption of a centralized solution is removed and it is shown under which condition a full market solution can replicate the optimal planned solution. Finally, in Chapter 11, we will look at the characteristics of the markets of those services that are exchanged in real time, focusing in particular on balancing services, and how they coexist with wholesale markets.

One final word about notation. Throughout this book, $Q$ denotes energy, and $M$ generation capacity. Whenever it is not needed, we shall not distinguish between load and supply, since in real time they coincide. However, they are not the same things and it will often be necessary to distinguish the two. We shall do so using subscript letters, typically letter $i$, to denote supply by plants, of either load or capacity, and superscripts $m$ to denote the load demanded by a consumer $m$. Moreover, if needed, a superscript $d$ on the load, i.e. $Q^d$, shall identify the load (demanded). Finally, whenever needed, a further superscript $j$ identifies a given time period (i.e. a given hour).

# 7 Load and Power Generation

## 7.1 Introduction

Before looking at the economic organization of the electricity system, we have to look at some fundamental characteristics of demand and supply. The pattern of electricity demand, or load, has relevant specific features that need to be taken into account since they are fundamental in order to understand how electricity markets are set up and work. As we have said in Chapter 2, electricity is not storable and its consumption is affected by several factors, such as the temperature and economic conditions. This makes the load sensitive to the time at which it is consumed. Whenever someone turns on a switch, some extra load is increased and some extra power is introduced into the grid, corresponding to the electricity required by the device plugged to that switch. Moreover, an electricity grid always has some electricity flowing through it, which corresponds to the basic consumption of the grid itself, namely, of all the appliances and devices connected to the grid, including the power plants themselves. However, this electricity need, or consumption, is not constant over time. In this chapter, we study demand characteristics such as its time structure,[1] specifying the notion of capacity factor and load duration curve. We then turn to generation and detail the notion of fixed and variable costs, taking into account the time variability and availability of plants. Finally, we define the notions of average energy costs and average capacity costs.

## 7.2 The Time Structure of Load

To understand the time structure of the load, think about what most households do: when daylight fades they turn on the electric lighting; when the weather becomes cold or hot they turn on electric heating or cooling; at night, they would typically go to sleep turning off several devices, and so on. Most industrial consumers replicate these consumption patterns; for instance, when there are bank holidays several firms reduce or shut down their production; when orders rise, production increases and consequently more electricity is needed. These simple considerations should immediately show certain basic

---

[1] Since load changes over time it can be treated as a random variable. The same is true for electricity prices. There is a stream of literature that focuses on the stochastic properties of load and electricity prices. We do not discuss this argument here. For references, see Benth et al. (2008) and Weron (2007).

features of the electricity load, namely, that it has a minimum basic level below which it hardly goes and follows a periodic pattern. This is true for several possible time periods.

Consider Figure 7.1 which plots the hourly load from the first hour of the year up to the last hour, throughout the entire year, in a given (wholesale) market. The vertical axis reports the hourly load in MWh, the horizontal one the hour of the year. It refers to the Italian wholesale market in year 2012.[2]

There is a clear periodic pattern, albeit a complex one, and several time trends.

First of all, there is a weekly period, since at the weekend the load is smaller than the load during working days. This can be seen observing that there are fifty-two cycles in which load rises and falls, each corresponding to a week of the year. Note, however, that the amount of load of these cycles is not at the same level across the year. It rises in the first weeks of the year, in the winter. Then it declines during spring, and rises again in the summer with the notable exception of the decrease around the thirty-third week of the year, which corresponds to mid-August, a typical holiday period. Load drops again in autumn, but perhaps at a lower level than that of the previous spring, and rises when winter approaches, with the exception of the last week of the year, which is again another holiday period.

Clearly, these patterns signal that seasonal factors influence the load, due to external features such as weather conditions and calendar dates. Load is not constant even over years: if we were to extend this graph to more than one year we would observe other periodic patterns, relating to multiannual weather conditions (in particular as regards the level of yearly rainfall and summer hot spells), as well as to other factors such as the economic cycle. Also at a smaller scale we can observe a periodic pattern. Consider Figure 7.2, that plots the data of Figure 7.1 but for a given day of the year (the first Wednesday of March). The load reaches a minimum at night, rises during the day, reduces a little in the mid-afternoon, and then rises again in the early hours of the evening, before falling at night time. This pattern is consistent with the dynamics of that specific electricity system, characterized by an industrial load that follows a (mostly) daytime schedule and a domestic load that is needed mostly by households for lighting, cooking, etc.

When considering the load, we must pay attention to the unit measure of energy and power. Recall that energy is just power multiplied by time. Given that power is measured in terms of capacity, fixing the unit measure of energy is equivalent to predefining the unit measure of time. For instance, if we measure energy in terms of MWh, we choose to express time in terms of hours. If we choose joules, we select seconds as unit measures of time, and so on. Then, we consider a given period of time, or time spell. For instance, in Figure 7.1, we have considered one year. Clearly, we could have chosen any other period of time. However, once the unit measure of time and the time spell have been fixed, it becomes equivalent to express the load in that period of time in terms of energy or capacity. In other words, we can measure the load, say, in MWh, or in MW per each hour of the year. If we change the unit measure of time we would obtain different figures, but

---

[2] Strictly speaking, the picture does not show the amount of load effectively used in the market, but only that which is exchanged at the day-ahead level; however, for the sake of simplicity, we can ignore this aspect here and take it as an indication of the real power pattern in a given system.

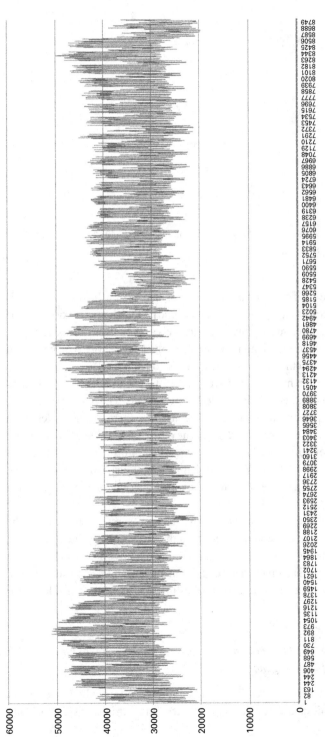

**Figure 7.1** A typical yearly load pattern

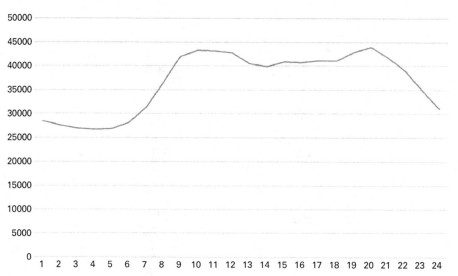

**Figure 7.2** A typical daily load pattern

the level of power of the load would not change. For instance, a load of 1 KWh is equivalent to 3,600 KJ (recall that 1 joule is 1 watt-second), but the power would still be 1 KW. For this reason, it is often more convenient to express the load in terms of power, not energy, even though in itself the load requires and consumes energy. The pattern of load during a given period, whether a day or a year (or any other period) in general shows two crucial features of power markets that we need to take into account in order to understand the structure and characteristics of electricity markets. The first is that there is always a minimum level of electricity in the grid (for instance, there was never less than 19.6 GW in the grid in our example of Figure 7.1). The other is that the load can increase several times above that level, but this happens very rarely. For instance, for the case of Figure 7.1, the load spiked up to 51.2 GW, but this happened for just one hour. These two features can be summarized in a single curve that shows the distribution of the load in the given period.

This curve could be constructed using the same unit measures as the axis of the original figure. However, it is more convenient to plot the inverse of the cumulative distribution of the load in a given period, against the cumulative distribution of the percentage of hours during that given period, instead of the hours themselves. The percentage of hours allows the unit measure of the time that is being considered for the analysis to be normalized.

Consider the following definition:

DEFINITION. *Capacity Factor: the fraction of time over a total amount of time in which there is a given amount of load or generation.*

Sometimes, the capacity factor, when it is referred to the load, is called load factor. However, we can ignore this distinction here, given that in an electricity system load and generation coincide in real time.

An example may serve to illustrate the capacity factor concept. Say that during one day (obviously of twenty-four hours) there was an amount of load of 10 MW for half of the hours of the day. The capacity factor of the 10 MW load would be 12/24 = 0.5. In practice, to calculate the capacity factor, it is enough to calculate the maximum of the time spell over which the analysis is conducted, for instance, 8,760 hours if it is an hourly load over the year (or 8,784 for a leap year as the one in Figure 7.1), and then divide all the subsets of the time spell for the considered time interval by that maximum amount, i.e. 1/8760, 2/8760, 3/8760, and so on, up to 8760/8760 which is obviously equal to one. Note that the capacity factor, being a normalized measure, is an a-dimensional measure (i.e. its dimension is 1, being hours over hours).

The capacity factor allows us to calculate and show the evolution of the cumulated distribution of the load. More precisely, taking the load as a random variable with a density function in a normalized [0,1] time interval, we can calculate the inverse of the cumulative density function of the load. We obtain a curve that shows all the pairs of capacity factors (on the horizontal axis) and the least amount of energy that was consumed for each given capacity factor (on the vertical axis). This curve is called the Load Duration Curve.

DEFINITION. *Load Duration Curve (LDC): the inverse of the cumulative density function of the load with respect to the capacity factor in a specific time interval.*

Figure 7.3 plots the LDC of the example in Figure 7.1. We can see that for the whole year at least an amount of 19.6 GW was consumed in each hour. But obviously, for some shorter periods of time, more electricity was consumed. For instance, for 50 percent of the hours, i.e. for a capacity factor of 0.5, 33.3 GW were consumed. At the highest level, an amount of 51.2 GW was consumed, but just in a single hour, i.e. for a capacity factor of roughly 0.0001 (1/8760).

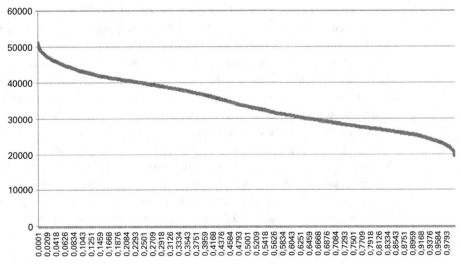

**Figure 7.3** The Load duration curve of Figure 7.1

The LDC, being a cumulative distribution of a random variable (the load), has an interesting probability interpretation. It measures the probability that the load exceeds a given level, for every possible level from its minimum to its maximum one. For instance, the fact that the load of 33.3 GW has a capacity factor of 0.5, means that there is a 50 percent probability that, over the year, in a given hour, the load exceeds 33 GW.

Note that, by fixing the time interval (e.g. a year (or whatever)), and the time units, it is possible to represent the LDC in terms of energy or capacity. From this point onward, whenever we need to represent theoretical LDC, we will use capacity unit measures on the y-axis.

The LDC curve is a fundamental tool for all electricity market analysis. It shows, for every electricity system, the minimum level of electricity that is always consumed and the maximum level of electricity that is consumed. The former is called base load, while the latter is the peak load:

DEFINITION. ***Baseload:*** *the minimum level of electricity load that is always present in an electricity system in a given time spell.*

DEFINITION. ***Peak load:*** *the highest possible level of electricity load reached in an electricity system in a given time spell.*

The definition of baseload and peak load refers to normal operational conditions. We have already discussed in Chapter 3 the difference between Load Shedding and Blackouts. Recall that blackouts are pathological situations of the electricity systems, in which the system ceases to work (at least for a while). Obviously, during a blackout, the load would be less than the baseload, being null or almost null. However, as noted, blackouts cannot be considered as normal operational conditions. Moreover, both definitions depend on the time units considered. For instance, the peak load from a theoretical point of view is the highest possible consumption in the time spell, but this level depends on the time interval at which consumption is measured (whether seconds, minutes, hours or some other time period). Moreover, the above definitions do not distinguish between the highest (or minimum) level of electricity consumed or produced, since it should be clear by now (if it is not, see Chapter 3) that in a given electricity system the level of consumption and generation coincide. However, it might sometimes be useful to distinguish between the highest possible theoretical level of electricity that would be reached if enough generation was available and the peak load that was indeed served in a given system. In that case, we would distinguish between the theoretical peak load and the effective one.

The LDC shows more than just the baseload and the peak load. It summarizes the profile of the load for a given time spell. For instance, if for every hour, the load was always at the same level, then there would be no difference between the baseload and the peak load, and the LDC would be a horizontal line. In contrast, if the daily load could be at two possible levels and during the day the load can be at either of those levels, and all days of the year were equal, the LDC would appear as a two-step curve, showing for how many hours of the year load was at the peak level and for how many hours at the baseload level, and so on. In summary, the LDC provides useful information on the load, showing that the full amount of load is not always present. Some load is almost always present, namely, the baseload plus the amount of load that has a very high capacity factor, say 0.9 or 0.8. This load can also be referred to as the baseload, and not just that very load that we have properly defined as baseload and that has a capacity factor equal to 1. Similarly, some load is required for very few hours. Also in this case, it is possible to term as peak load not just the very highest peak but all that load that has a very low capacity factor, say of 0.1 The LDC thus shows the frequency of the base load, the peak load and the load that is intermediate between these.

These considerations however are just preliminary. Where should the proper threshold of the capacity factor that identifies the baseload or the peak load be placed? What is the meaning of intermediate levels? The answer to these questions will be provided in Chapter 9, where we shall see that there is a specific criterion that we can follow in order to provide an answer to this question. This criterion is the efficiency with which generation can serve the load. In order to understand this, however, we must first consider the features of the supply side of electricity market, namely, the specific characteristics of the electricity production. This is the topic of the next section.

## 7.3     The Characteristics of Power Generation Costs

We have already discussed in Chapter 2 the features of power plants and their characteristics, and have seen that they can be summarized by means of their cost function. This is an aspect that is particularly relevant to identify the efficiency to which load is served in an electric system. Let us start by considering a simplified cost function, as the one reported in Equation (2.7):

$$C_i(Q_i) = FC_i + VC_i; \tag{7.1}$$

where $FC_i$ are the fixed costs of plant $i$, and $VC_i$ are the variable costs of plant $i$. Most of the time, we will assume that these variable costs are linear, that is, $VC_i = Fl_j \cdot a_{j,i} \cdot Q_i$. In this simple case, variable costs coincide with the cost of fuel $j$, $FL_j$, times the efficiency rate of the plant $i$ that uses fuel $j$, $a_{j,i}$ times the amount of energy produced. In general, and for the sake of simplicity, whenever it is not needed to specify the type of fuel and/or the efficiency rate of the plant we shall summarize $Fl_j \cdot a_{j,i}$ by means of a single variable cost parameter $c_i = Fl_j \cdot a_{j,i}$.

Even in this simple example we need to pay attention to the unit measures of the Equation (7.1). Costs occur over time. Therefore, as for the case of the load, it is necessary to predefine the unit measure of time and the time spell under consideration. For instance, we can choose the hour as the unit measure of time and the year as the time interval (this is indeed our default choice in this book, unless it is necessary to specify different time units or time spells). Variable costs obviously depend on the energy produced. In particular, in this simple case, $Fl_f$ has the unit measure of money per energy, e.g. [\$/GJ], the efficiency rate converts energy input in output, and thus its unit measure is energy [GJ/MWh] and the energy produced is obviously expressed in a comparable unit measure of energy, e.g. MWh in a given period, e.g. MWh per year, so that the unit measure of the variable costs is just money for the considered period (e.g. the year):

$$VC_i = Fl_f \cdot a_{f,i} \cdot Q_i.$$

$$\left[\frac{\$}{y}\right] = \left[\frac{\$}{GJ}\right] \cdot \left[\frac{GJ}{MWh}\right] \cdot \left[\frac{MWh}{y}\right] \tag{7.2}$$

Fixed costs, however, typically depend on the size, the technology and the age of the plants. They are the amount of money needed to build the plant or buy it/ rent it from a company. They are disaggregated in the rental cost of the capacity and the amount of capacity of the plant (see the explanations further below). The unit of measure of the rental cost is money per unit of capacity for a given period, say a year, e.g. dollars per Megawatt-year, since the capacity, namely, the power plants, lasts and can be used to generate electricity for several years. Therefore, the capacity has to be attributed to a given time period. Denote the yearly rental cost of plant $i$ as $YRC_i$. The capacity of a plant $i$ is denoted by $M_i$ (for simplicity of notation, we do not distinguish here between the effective level of capacity $M_i$ and the maximum possible level of capacity $M_i^{max}$; when we need to make this distinction, we will replace the former with the latter). The capacity is obviously measured in terms of power:

$$FC_i = YRC_i \cdot M_i.$$

$$\left[\frac{\$}{y}\right] = \left[\frac{\$}{MWy}\right] \cdot [MW] \tag{7.3}$$

The reader should note that the unit measure of fixed costs and variable costs are equivalent, namely, money in a given period (e.g. dollars per year). The variable costs by their nature are a flow, and therefore it is necessary to predefine for which period we are considering and measuring those variable costs. In Equation (7.2), the energy produced is expressed in terms of MWh for the given period, a year. Also for the fixed costs it is necessary to make an explicit reference to the time period of the analysis, in our case a year, since the fixed costs last for more than one year, and thus it is necessary to split the rental cost of the plant over its amortization period. In this way, the fixed costs have the same time dimension as the variable costs and can be summed up in the total cost function.

Having defined such a yearly total cost function, it is possible to calculate the average cost function. However, average with respect to what? We have seen that the fixed cost is independent of the production, and depends on the capacity of the plant, while variable cost clearly depends on the energy produced. Therefore, it is possible to calculate two concepts of average costs, average with respect to energy and average with respect to capacity. The former is the Average Energy Cost function that, once plotted in a graph, gives rise to the Average Energy Cost Curve. The latter is the Average Capacity Cost function and curve.

DEFINITION. *Average Energy Cost (AEC): the cost per unit of energy produced or producible.*

DEFINITION. *Average Capacity Cost (ACC): the cost per unit of capacity installed or to be installed.*

The AEC function shows the hourly (or for any other time reference) cost of plant per unit of energy delivered by that plant in the considered time spell. The ACC reports the hourly cost of the plant per unit of capacity that can deliver energy during that time period.

Let us see how to calculate the AEC and the ACC curve. As mentioned, it is necessary to choose the proper time horizon we want to use. We choose the hour (but any other time period can be used), thus we calculate the AEC and the ACC per each hour. Recall that from Equation (7.1) total costs are the sum of fixed and variable costs, and fixed costs from Equation (7.3) are given by yearly rental costs times the capacity. Taking into account that a year is made up of 8,760 hours, we can express the yearly rental costs as:

$$YRC_i = hRC_i \cdot 8760;$$

$$\left[ \frac{\$}{\text{MWy}} \right] = \left[ \frac{\$}{\text{MWh}} \right] \cdot \left[ \frac{\text{h}}{\text{y}} \right] \tag{7.4}$$

where $hRC_i$ denotes the hourly rental cost of plant $i$, i.e. the cost of renting in a perfectly competitive market one unit of capacity of a plant, such as plant $i$, in a given hour, which is equivalent to the hourly discounted amortized value of the capacity of plant $i$ over its expected (accounting) life horizon.

Using the definition of the hourly rental cost, we can write the total cost Equation (7.1) as the total cost in a given time spell, e.g. the yearly total cost:

$$yC_i(Q_i) = hRC_i \cdot 8760 \cdot M_i + Fl_f \cdot a_{f,i} \cdot Q_i \tag{7.5}$$

where we reiterate that the variable $Q_i$ denotes the yearly energy produced by plant $i$. Thus Equation (7.5) provides the yearly total cost of plant $i$. Its dimension is obviously money per year. Using the relationship between power and energy given by Equation (1.15) we can say that a plant $i$, whose capacity is $M_i$, over a year, produces an amount of energy such as $Q_i = M_i \cdot h_i$, with $0 \le h_i \le 8760$. Note that $h_i$ denotes the effective amount of time during which plant $i$ is producing in the given year, which can be expressed in terms of capacity factor as: $h_i = cf_i \cdot 8760$. Thus, we can rewrite Equation (7.5) as:

$$yC_i(Q_i) = hRC_i \cdot 8760 \cdot M_i + Fl_f \cdot a_{f,i} \cdot M_i \cdot cf_i \cdot 8760. \tag{7.6}$$

Equation (7.6) enables the calculation of the AEC function and the ACC function. The Average Energy Cost function in a given period, say a year, is given by the yearly Total Cost function divided by the yearly energy produced:

$$AEC_i = \frac{yC(Q_i)}{Q_i} = \frac{hRC_i \cdot 8760 \cdot M_i}{Q_i} + \frac{Fl_f \cdot af_{,i} \cdot M_i \cdot cf_i \cdot 8760}{Q_i};$$
$$= \frac{yC(Q_i)}{Q_i} = \frac{hRC_i \cdot 8760 \cdot M_i}{M_i \cdot h_i} + \frac{Fl_f \cdot af_{,i} \cdot M_i \cdot h_i}{M_i \cdot h_i};$$
$$= \frac{yC(Q_i)}{Q_i} = \frac{hRC_i \cdot 8760}{h_i} + Fl_f \cdot af_{,i}; \qquad (7.7)$$
$$= \frac{yC(Q_i)}{Q_i} = \frac{hRC_i}{cf_i} + Fl_f \cdot af_{,i}$$
$$\left[\frac{\$}{MWh}\right] = \left[\frac{\$}{MWh}\right] + \left[\frac{\$}{Gj}\right] \cdot \left[\frac{Gj}{MWh}\right].$$

The yearly Average Capacity Cost is obtained dividing the yearly total costs by the capacity:

$$yACC_i = \frac{yC(Q_i)}{M_i} = \frac{hRC_i \cdot 8760 \cdot M_i}{M_i} + \frac{Fl_f \cdot af_{,i} \cdot M_i \cdot cf_i \cdot 8760}{M_i};$$
$$= \frac{yC(Q_i)}{M_i} = hRC_i \cdot 8760 + Fl_f \cdot af_{,i} \cdot cf_i \cdot 8760; \qquad (7.8)$$

and by further dividing Equation (7.8) by the number of time units in the time interval (in our case, 8,760 hours in a year), we obtain the Average Capacity Cost for that period:

$$ACC_i = \frac{yACC_i}{y}$$
$$= \frac{hRC_i \cdot 8760}{8760} + \frac{Fl_f \cdot af_{,i} \cdot cf_i \cdot 8760}{8760};$$
$$= hRC_i + Fl_f \cdot af_{,i} \cdot cf_i; \qquad (7.9)$$
$$\left[\frac{\$}{MWh}\right] = \left[\frac{\$}{MWh}\right] + \left[\frac{\$}{Gj}\right] \cdot \left[\frac{Gj}{MWh}\right].$$

Note that both the AEC and the ACC functions are expressed in the same unit measures, namely, money per energy (in our case, dollars per Megawatt-hour) in the given time spell. The example below serves to illustrate the concepts of AEC and ACC.

---

**Example 7.1  The ACC and AEC of a Theoretical Power Plant** Suppose that there is a power plant whose fixed costs are 20 M\$, and that has an expected life of ten years. For the sake of simplicity, ignore the discounting factor and assume that the amortization implies a fixed cost per Megawatt per year, i.e. the yearly rental cost equals 20 K dollars per year. The hourly rental cost would be $\frac{20K}{8760} = 2.28$. Note that the unit measure of 2.28 is $\left[\frac{\$}{MWh}\right]$. Let us assume that the fuel cost and the efficiency rate provides the following figures: $Fl_f \cdot af_{,i} = 10$. Again, the unit measure of 10 is $\left[\frac{\$}{MWh}\right]$. The AEC would be:

$$AEC = \frac{2.28}{cf_i} + 10.$$ The ACC would be: $ACC = 2.28 + 10 \cdot cf_i.$

---

Both equations show the importance of the capacity factor: similar plants, with the same hourly rental costs, fuel costs and efficiency rates, will have different average capacity and energy costs, depending on their capacity factor. In particular, the higher the capacity factor, the lower the AEC and the higher the ACC. In the next chapter we will see the importance of ACC and AEC in finding the most efficient solution to serve a given load.

## Learning Outcomes

- Load has a complex time pattern: hourly, daily, weekly, seasonally and yearly. The amount of power serving the load in a time period (i.e. a year), can be described by the Load Duration Curve.
- The Load Duration Curve shows the probability that the load exceeds a given level for all possible levels of the load, from the minimum to the maximum level, during the given time spell.
- Baseload power is demanded for a large number of hours (i.e. with a large capacity factor), and a peak load power is needed for very few hours (i.e. with a low capacity factor).
- The cost of serving the load can be summarized by means of a cost function, that has fixed and variable components. The fixed components refer to the capacity installed, and variable components to the energy produced. To sum them up, it is necessary to express both components with money per unit of time.
- From the total cost curve, two average cost concepts can be derived and calculated: Average Energy costs and Average Capacity Costs. Both are expressed in terms of money per energy.

# 8    The Centralized Solution of Optimal Dispatching

## 8.1    Introduction

In this chapter, we analyze the problem of providing electricity serving the load from a variety of power plants in an optimal way. As usual in economics, the optimality criterion is the efficiency of energy provision. We consider Pareto efficiency, without taking into account externalities, public goods and distributional issues. Some of these aspects will be treated in Part VIII when we consider RES.

For the electricity sector, it is not easy to answer the above question. We have seen that there are several technologies and different power plants that can serve the load in a given period of time. Recall that the allocation of generation across plants derives from the need to dispatch electricity. Therefore, answering the question of how to select power plants in order to produce electricity is equivalent to providing a criterion for optimal dispatching. We shall start by making some simplifying assumptions, namely: the load is fixed for a given period of time and that the set of plants is fixed and given for that period of time.

Recall that throughout this section we are in a simplified setting that neglects network constraints. Thus, in this chapter we start by considering the simplest possible case, namely, the case of a dispatcher that owns or manages power plants and wants to serve a given load in an efficient way. This set up of the problem is equivalent to assuming that there is a monopolist that owns the power plant and that is also the dispatcher, who has the obligation to serve electricity in an efficient way. This obligation, for instance, is often implemented by specifying that electricity provision is a universal service, even though the latter also has several implications for network management and expansion and affordability of power provision that we do not consider here. We will consider the simplest possible setting (i.e. a monopolist that is either obliged or regulated and therefore cannot freely decide the price at which to provide power to customers). Therefore, the problem corresponds to identifying the efficient allocation of production in model 1 of Chapter 4. In the next chapter, we shall remove the assumption of a single monopolistic production, and consider what happens when there are several market agents. Finally, we shall also remove the hypothesis of a fixed load, and evaluate the market settings with demand and supply side participation. For this latter case, we will distinguish between market arrangements that occur *ex ante*, and effective electricity delivery.

Before starting the analysis, there is an important point that has to be understood about the unit measures of load and generation. We saw in Chapter 7 that in order to represent the load we need to fix the unit measure of time. We choose the hour as the unit measure of time. Define the load as $Q^m = M^m \cdot h$, where $m$ denotes the consumers (or group of consumers) that require(s) the load and $M^m$ is the capacity required by those consumers. Fixing $h = 1$ as the unit measure of time, we have $Q^m = M^m$. The same is true for the energy produced during time $h$. The energy generated by plant $i$ is $Q_i = M_i \cdot h$ where $M_i$ is the capacity of plant $i$. Therefore, having fixed the unit measure of time, providing energy or power is absolutely equivalent. In what follows, we shall use energy in the notation, since we believe it can be more intuitively understood, taking into account, however, that the analysis in terms of power would be exactly equivalent. Moreover, whenever not needed, we will omit subscripts and superscripts.

## 8.2          The Cost Minimization Problem with Two Power Plants

We start by assuming a fixed load. Clearly, this is a false assumption, as we have seen in Chapter 7. However, it holds for short time periods (i.e. for those periods in which the load has very limited changes). Assume there is a monopolist that has to serve a given load $\overline{Q}$, being able to manage $n$ plants. It is obliged to provide electricity. The analysis seen from the standpoint of the monopolist is equivalent to the analysis of a planner, who has to maximize the social welfare of consumers that use the load. Social welfare is $U(\overline{Q}) - C(Q)$, where $C(Q)$ denotes the total cost function to serve the load, and $U(\overline{Q})$ is the utility function of consumers that use the load $\overline{Q}$. We assume throughout this book that $U(\cdot)$ is a positive function with $U(0) = 0$ and $U'(\cdot) > 0$. Moreover, when load is fixed and constant, $U(\overline{Q})$ is also constant. The dual problem of the social welfare maximization is simply the cost minimization problem, i.e. $\min C(Q)$, where the constant $U(\overline{Q})$ can be ignored since the solution of the problem is independent of it.

The constraints of the cost minimization problem are extremely important and require careful analysis. Throughout this section, we assume that there is a fixed set of power plants, each one having a maximum capacity $M_i^{max}$ that is given. The overall installed capacity is able to cover the load (i.e. the capacity can produce an amount of energy for the considered time period that is enough (or more than enough) to serve the load). The time spell of the analysis is also given. It can be a year, a month, or an hour. If it was a year, the load $Q$ would be a yearly load, while it would be an hourly one if the time horizon of the model was the hour. Note that the installed capacity determines the maximum possible energy that can be produced in the time period. For instance, a plant with a 100 MW capacity that runs throughout the year with a full capacity factor will produce $100 \times 8{,}760 = 876$ GWh of energy in a year.

We do not consider the trivial problem in which there was a single power plant, since there would be no choice to be made. What would be the solution of the problem of cost minimization when there is more than one power plant that could be used? To answer this question, it is important to consider the differences between power plants. We start by assuming that there are different power plants, characterized by different costs. From this point onward, we shall make the assumption that costs have the simple structure represented in Equation (7.1), and that plants can be ranked according to their costs, so that the plants that have higher fixed costs have also lower variable ones and vice versa: $C_i(Q_i) = FC_i + VC_i$, with $FC_i > FC_j; VC_i < VC_j, i \neq j$.

We consider two cases below depending on whether each power plant is large enough to produce energy to serve the load or if more than one plant is needed. These characteristics of the power plants are expressed in the optimization problem by the slackness condition of the constrained optimization problems we discuss below. For simplicity of notation, we limit the analysis to a fixed number of plants, two or more, depending on the different cases treated.

## 8.2.1    Case I

There are two power plants, indexed by $i$, $i = 1,2$, each of which has a capacity higher than the load $\overline{Q}$. In other words; the load could be served by any of the existing power plants: $Q_i \leq Q_i^{max}$, with $Q_i^{max} \geq \overline{Q}$. The assumption $Q_i^{max} \geq \overline{Q}$ implies that there is enough capacity installed to serve the load. With a slight abuse of notation, we define $M_i \cdot h_i = Q_i$, with $h_i$ denoting the number of hours that plant $i$ produces in the predefined time period. Assume that $VC_1 < VC_2$. From Equation (2.8), it follows that $C_1'(\cdot) < C_2'(\cdot)$. The cost minimization problem can be written as:

$$
\begin{aligned}
&\min C_1\,(Q_1) + C_2\,(Q_2), \text{ s.t.}\\
&a)\ Q_1 + Q_2 = \overline{Q};\\
&b)\ Q_1 \geq 0;\\
&c)\ Q_2 \geq 0;\\
&d)\ Q_1 \leq Q_1^{max};\\
&e)\ Q_2 \leq Q_2^{max};\\
&f)\ Q_1^{max} > \overline{Q};\\
&g)\ Q_2^{max} > \overline{Q}.
\end{aligned}
\tag{8.1}
$$

Let us consider the meaning of the constraints: constraint ($a$) is the balanced load constraint; it simply says in this case that the production must serve the load, ruling out the possibility that some load is shed. Constraints ($b$) and ($c$) specify which plant has to be operational. The problem of turning on or off a power plant in the electricity system is referred to as the unit commitment problem (since in reality it is the power units of each plant that are being turned on or off). Therefore, constraints ($b$) and ($c$) are the unit commitment constraints. Constraints ($d$) and ($e$) refer to the technical limits of the plants; ($f$) and ($g$) correspond to the specific case we are considering here, namely, that in which each plant can serve the whole load. Note that this set of constraints is a minimal one; other constraints could be added, about the possibility or not of fractioning the production, the existence of ramps and the need to explicitly take into account the timing of production, the existence of no load costs. We ignore these features here, since even the simplest model is sufficient to make the essential point.

The Lagrange Equation of problem (8.1) is as follows:

$$\mathcal{L} = -C_1(Q_1) - C_2(Q_2) + \lambda(\overline{Q} - Q_1 - Q_2) + \mu_1 Q_1 + \mu_2 Q_2 + \delta_1(Q_1^{max} - Q_1)$$
$$+\delta_2(Q_2^{max} - Q_2). \tag{8.2}$$

The Kuhn-Tucker conditions at the equilibrium quantity $\overline{Q}$ are:

$$\frac{\partial \mathcal{L}}{\partial Q_1} = 0 \rightarrow C_1'(\cdot) + \lambda - \mu_1 + \delta_1 = 0;$$

$$\frac{\partial \mathcal{L}}{\partial Q_2} = 0 \rightarrow C_2'(\cdot) + \lambda - \mu_2 + \delta_2 = 0; \tag{8.3}$$

and the slackness conditions:

$$\mu_1 Q_1 = 0, \; Q_1 \geq 0, \; \mu_1 \geq 0;$$
$$\mu_2 Q_2 = 0, \; Q_2 \geq 0, \; \mu_2 \geq 0;$$
$$\delta_1(Q_1^{max} - Q_1) = 0, \; (Q_1^{max} - Q_1) \geq 0, \; \delta_1 \geq 0; \tag{8.4}$$
$$\delta_2(Q_2^{max} - Q_2) = 0, \; (Q_2^{max} - Q_2) \geq 0, \; \delta_2 \geq 0.$$

Note that it cannot be that $Q_1 = 0$ and $Q_2 = 0$, otherwise constraint (a) of problem 8.1 would be violated. Similarly, it cannot be that $\delta_1 > 0$, otherwise from the slackness condition we would have $Q_1 = Q_1^{max}$ which violates either constraint (f) or (a); the same is true for $\delta_2$ and constraints (g) and (a). Therefore, $\delta_1 = \delta_2 = 0$. The Kuhn-Tucker conditions simplify to:

$$C_1'(\cdot) = -\lambda + \mu_1;$$
$$C_2'(\cdot) = -\lambda + \mu_2. \tag{8.5}$$

Recalling that $C_1'(\cdot) < C_2'(\cdot)$, we see that a sufficient condition for Equations (8.5) to be true is that $\mu_1 = 0; \mu_2 > 0$, which implies that $Q_1 > 0$ and $Q_2 = 0$. In other words, the optimal solution corresponds to the case in which power plant 2 is off and power plant 1 is running, even though at a quantity lower than its maximum. Figure 8.1 represents this case.

We report the marginal cost of plant 1 and 2, in a Cartesian space where on the x-axis there is the energy that the plant can produce (measured in a given unit measure of energy, for instance, MWh) and on the y-axis the costs (measured in monetary terms per unit of energy, e.g. dollars per MWh).[1] We have already ranked marginal costs, and plotted energy (and power) production so that load is first served by the lowest marginal cost plant, then by the higher ones. Marginal cost is infinite at the plant's maximum capacity level since plants cannot generate energy beyond that level. The curve that is created summing horizontally the individual plants' cost curves is called industry supply curve (or just supply curve), since it is equivalent to the supply curve that a buyer would face in a market. Note that in our setting the

---

[1] Having fixed the time unit (i.e. $h = 1$), the graph represented on the money-capacity space would be absolutely equivalent.

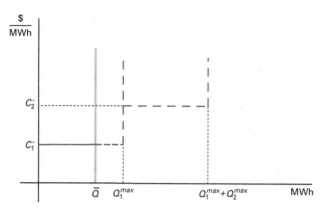

**Figure 8.1** Cost minimization with two power plants, such that $Q_i^{max} \geq \overline{Q}, i = 1, 2$

marginal cost is equivalent to the variable costs, these latter being linear. Ordering costs on the basis of the variable costs from the lowest to the highest is called merit ordering, and dispatching plants according to the merit ordering is called merit ordering dispatching:

DEFINITION. **Merit Order Dispatching**: *the dispatching of power ordered from the least variable cost power plant to those with higher variable costs.*

The solution to the cost minimization problem is provided by the merit ordering dispatching. Graphically, the dashed line represents the amount of energy that the plant can produce, while a solid line denotes the energy that the plant is indeed producing. The solid vertical line denotes the load. Note that at the equilibrium quantity the plant is producing less than its maximum: $Q_1 < Q_1^{max}$. This can be checked analytically, noting that the solution of problem 8.1 is such as $\delta_1 = 0$, which implies that $(Q_1^{max} - Q_1) > 0$.

There is an important implication here: recall that the electricity that plant 1 produces in the time period is $Q_i = M_i \cdot h_i$. The electricity that the plant could have been producing at its maximum was: $Q_1^{max} = M_i^{max} \cdot h_i$. However, note that energy is the product of two variables, thus we can write $M_i^{max} \cdot h_i = M_i \cdot h_i^{max}$. Therefore, at the equilibrium quantity $\overline{Q}$ plant 1 is producing $\overline{Q} = M_i \cdot \overline{h}_i < Q_1^{max} = M_i \cdot h_i^{max}$, which means that $\dfrac{\overline{h}_i}{h_i^{max}} = cf_1 < 1$. The capacity factor of the plant that is producing at the equilibrium is less than one. Note however, that this result does not imply that the plant is off for some time during the considered time spell. Given that the load is constant, for the required time spell the power plant 1 has to generate electricity. However, it is generating less power that it could at each point in time, and this is equivalent to saying that it has a capacity factor lower than 1.

The following example can help to explain the cost minimization problem and the capacity factor of the active plant.

**Example 8.1 An Example of the Equilibrium Allocation of Case I** Suppose that the load is equivalent to 876,000 MWh in a year. This is equivalent to saying that there is a constant load of 100 MWh each hour of the year. There are two power plants, each of which has a capacity $M_i = 150$ MW. The yearly total cost function of these plants has the following parameters, i.e. yearly rental cost and variable (fuel times efficiency) costs: $YRC_1 = 20,000 \left[\dfrac{\$}{MWy}\right]$, $YRC_2 = 10,000 \left[\dfrac{\$}{MWy}\right]$, $Fl \cdot a_1 = 40 \left[\dfrac{\$}{MWh}\right]$, $Fl * a_2 = 60 \left[\dfrac{\$}{MWh}\right]$. Thus, for the installed capacity, the total cost of electricity provision would be:

Producing by plant 1:    $\underset{(FC_1)}{\$3,000,000} + \underset{(VC_1)}{\$40 \times 8,760} + \underset{(FC_2)}{\$1,500,000} = \$4,850,400.$

Producing by plant 2:    $\underset{(FC_1)}{\$3,000,000} + \underset{(FC_2)}{\$1,500,000} + \underset{(VC_2)}{\$60 \times 8,760} = \$5,025,600.$

Using plant 1 the total cost is lower than using plant 2 or any linear combination of energy from plant 1 and 2. This latter point can be seen by simply observing that any MWh not produced by 1 and instead generated by 2 costs \$20 more. Note, however, that there is an inefficiency in the system due to the fact that there are two plants that each have their own fixed costs. Therefore, even if there is one power plant that is off, its total cost over the year is still present. Under this assumption, this system setting would be inefficient since the same electricity provision could have been reached at a lower total cost by simply avoiding installing the capacity of the plant that is off. Finally, note that the capacity factor of plant 1 is: $876,000/1,314,000 = 2/3$. The plant is using two-thirds of its capacity, which would be equivalent in terms of electricity produced to the case in which the plant was using its full capacity for two-thirds of the time (but clearly it is not since it has to serve the load for the whole year).

This result obviously extends naturally to the case of three or more plants, each being able to cover the load. The conclusion is simple: the load must be served by the plant that has the minimum marginal cost.

We consider now a situation in which no power plants have enough capacity to serve the load, therefore, both power plants will have to generate electricity. The question in this case is what is the optimal combination of generation that has to be produced from plant 1 and 2 that minimizes the cost.

## 8.2.2    Case II

There are two power plants, indexed by $i$, $i = 1,2$. Neither has a capacity higher than the load $\overline{Q}$: $Q_i \leq Q_i^{max}$, with $Q_i^{max} < \overline{Q}$. In other words; the load must be served by more than one power plant. As before, $VC_1 < VC_2$. The cost minimization problem can be written as:

$$\min C_1(Q_1) + C_2(Q_2), s.t.$$
$$a) \ Q_1 + Q_2 = \overline{Q};$$
$$b) \ Q_1 \geq 0;$$
$$c) \ Q_2 \geq 0;$$
$$d) \ Q_1 \leq Q_1^{max};$$
$$e) \ Q_2 \leq Q_2^{max};$$
$$f) \ Q_1^{max} < \overline{Q};$$
$$g) \ Q_2^{max} < \overline{Q};$$
$$h) \ Q_1^{max} + Q_2^{max} > \overline{Q}.$$

(8.6)

Comparing this with problem (8.1), note that now the signs of the inequalities in constraints (*f*) and (*g*) are reversed and a new constraint (*h*) has been added, which guarantees that there is enough capacity to serve the load.

The Lagrange Equation, the Kuhn-Tucker conditions and the slackness conditions are the same as those in Equations (8.2), (8.3) and (8.4). As before, it cannot happen that $Q_1 = 0$ and $Q_2 = 0$, otherwise constraint *a* of problem 8.6 would be violated. However, now, no plant alone can serve the load. Therefore, it cannot happen that $Q_1 = 0$ and $Q_2 > 0$, for otherwise either constraint (*a*) or (*g*) would be violated. The same is true for the case of $Q_1 > 0$ and $Q_2 = 0$, given constraints (*a*) and (*f*). Therefore, both $Q_1 > 0$ and $Q_2 > 0$, which implies that $\mu_1 = \mu_2 = 0$. The Kuhn-Tucker conditions simplify to:

$$C_1'(\cdot) = -\lambda - \delta_1;$$
$$C_2'(\cdot) = -\lambda - \delta_2.$$

(8.7)

A sufficient condition for Equations (8.7) to be true is that $\delta_1 > 0; \delta_2 = 0$. This implies that $Q_1 = Q_1^{max}; Q_2 < Q_2^{max}$. Now, plant 1, being the plant with the lower marginal costs, is producing at its full capacity, i.e. with $cf_1 = 1$. Plant 2, being more expensive, is producing with a reduced capacity factor: $cf_1 < 1$. Case II is described in Figure 8.2. We can see that now plant 1 is fully producing, while plant 2 is producing with a limited capacity factor.

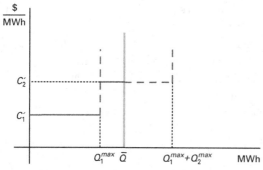

**Figure 8.2** Cost minimization with two power plants, such as $Q_i^{max} < \overline{Q}, i = 1, 2$

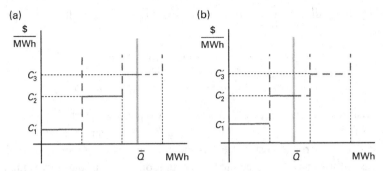

**Figure 8.3** Cost minimization with three plants. (a): all three plants are necessary; (b): two plants are sufficient

## 8.3 The Cost Minimization Problem with *n* Plants

Let us start from an example of three power plants, with costs ranked as $VC_1 < VC_2 < VC_3$. Two cases are of interest, one in which any pair of plants have enough capacity to serve the load, and that in which all three plants are needed (the other cases can be easily referred to those already studied here). Figure 8.3, panel (a), describes the situation in which all three plants are necessary. Figure 8.3 panel (b), describes the case in which two plants are enough. We can see that in panel (a), $cf_1 = cf_2 = 1$ while $cf_3 < 1$. In the case of panel (b), we have that $cf_1 = 1 > cf_2 > cf_3 = 0$.

The solution arises from the following rationale. Plants are ranked according to their marginal costs. Those with lower marginal costs are dispatched first and have higher or equal capacity factors to those with higher marginal costs. These capacity factors, depending on the load, can be 1 or less. The capacity factors of the plants with the highest marginal costs, depending on the load, can also be zero. This result can be shown analytically and extended to the *n* plants case. Assume there are *n* plants; each plant has a capacity range such that $0 \leq Q_i \leq Q_i^{max}$ and such that they can serve the load; however, some plants might not be needed to reach the level $\overline{Q}$. The Lagrange Equation of the cost-minimization problem would be:

$$\mathcal{L} = -\sum_{i=1}^{n} C_i(Q_i) + \lambda\left(\overline{Q} - \sum_{i=1}^{n} Q_i\right) + \sum_{i=1}^{n} \mu_i Q_i + \sum_{i=1}^{n} \delta_i(Q_i^{max} - Q_i); \quad (8.8)$$

with the Kuhn-Tucker conditions:

$$\frac{\partial \mathcal{L}}{\partial Q_i} = 0 \rightarrow C_i'(\cdot) + \lambda - \mu_i + \delta_i = 0, \forall i = 1, \ldots, n; \quad (8.9)$$

and the slackness conditions:

$$\mu_i Q_i = 0, \ Q_i \geq 0, \ \mu_i \geq 0, \ \forall i = 1, \ldots, n;$$
$$\delta_i(Q_i^{max} - Q_i) = 0, \ (Q_i^{max} - Q_i) \geq 0, \ \delta_i \geq 0, \ \forall i = 1, \ldots, n. \quad (8.10)$$

Then, depending on the load, we will have three solutions, that define three sets of plants:

$$(i) \; C'_i(\cdot) = -\lambda - \delta_i \text{ for those } i \text{ for which } \mu_i = 0, \; \delta_i > 0;$$
$$(ii) \; C'_i(\cdot) = -\lambda \text{ for those } i \text{ for which } \mu_i = 0, \; \delta_i > 0; \qquad (8.11)$$
$$(iii) \; C'_i(\cdot) = -\lambda + \mu_i \text{ for those } i \text{ for which } \mu_i > 0, \; \delta_i = 0.$$

The case of $\mu_i > 0, \delta_i > 0$ is ruled out since it violates the constraints. In Equations (8.11), there is a common parameter $\lambda$, which derives from the balanced load constraint. This is called system marginal cost, since it is the cost that the monopolist (or social planner) must pay at the margin to generate the last unit of watt-hour that serves the load.

DEFINITION. *System Marginal Cost (SMC): the cost for the electricity system of serving one unit more of the load.*

The SMC is the shadow value of the load constraint. It corresponds to the value of serving one infinitesimal unit more of the load. What Condition 8.11 shows is that at the equilibrium the SMC must be equivalent to the marginal cost of producing one unit more of power to serve the load. Note that this is a cost, which explains its negative value.

Solution (8.11) is the cost minimizing solution for the dispatching problem. It provides the optimal least cost dispatch. It shows that three solutions are possible: in solution (*i*), plants are active and producing at their maximum $Q_i = Q_i^{max}$. These are the plants whose marginal cost is less than the SMC, as shown by solution (*i*), since $\delta_i > 0$. The plants whose marginal cost equals the SMC, are producing at a *cf* lower than 1, as can be seen in the solution (*ii*), noting that $\delta_i = 0 \rightarrow Q_i < Q_i^{max}$. The equilibrium capacity factor is $\dfrac{Q_i}{Q_i^{max}}$.

Finally, plants whose marginal cost is higher than the SMC are not running, as can be seen in solution (*iii*), since $\mu_i > 0 \rightarrow Q_i = 0$. Therefore, the optimal least cost dispatch follows the merit order, it is a merit ordering dispatching, as defined before.

We can summarize what has been discussed in the following results:

---

### Result

The solution of the cost minimization problem requires the merit order dispatching of plants.

---

and

---

### Result

On the basis of the merit order dispatching, with a given load, the solution of the cost minimization problem implies that plants are:

- producing at their maximum if their marginal cost is less than the SMC;
- producing with a capacity factor less than one if their cost is equal to the SMC;
- not producing if their marginal cost is higher than the SMC.

---

If the cost functions of the plants were more complex than those considered here, like those described in Chapter 2, the solution would be more complex. In this case, a linear programming solution would identify the optimal set of plants and the level of production of each of them that minimizes Equation (8.8), taking into account the constraints of ramping, minimum and efficient quantity levels, no load costs and so on. However, taking into account all constraints, the optimal solution would still follow the same principle: for given constraints, the plant with lower variable costs produces more, and vice versa, so that the capacity factor of the plants follows the inverse ranking of the variable costs of plants.

## 8.4     The Welfare Maximization Problem with Several Consumers

So far, we have assumed that the load has a fixed level $\overline{Q}$. For simplicity of notation, we have treated the problem of cost minimization ignoring the constant $U(\overline{Q})$ since it does not change the results. We can show this here, considering also the case in which there were several consumers, each one requiring a different load. In other words, we consider here the problem of a load that can be changing across consumers, yet still constant at a given point in time. The problem becomes a welfare maximization problem now since the central planner (or the regulated monopolist) that has to serve different levels of load, has to take into account the utility of the load for consumers and the cost for power plants to produce it. We are still under the assumption that there is enough capacity to serve the maximum possible load. Let us write for simplicity of notation the load of consumer (or group of consumers) $m = A, \ldots,$ M as $Q^m$. Let the load of each of them be constrained between zero and a maximum: $0 \leq Q^m \leq \overline{Q^m}$. Moreover, the overall load is such that $\sum_{m=A}^{M} Q^m = \sum_{i=1}^{n} Q_i$. This is the balanced load constraint, that guarantees that the problem has a solution (different from zero). The welfare maximization problem would be:

$$\max_{Q^m, Q_i} \sum_{m=A}^{M} U^m(Q^m) - \sum_{i=1}^{n} C_i(Q_i), \text{ s.t. :}$$

$$(a) \ \sum_{m=1}^{M} Q^m = \sum_{i=1}^{n} Q_i;$$

$$(b) \ Q_i \geq 0;$$

$$(c) \ (Q_i^{max} - Q_i) \geq 0;$$

$$(d) \ Q^m \geq 0;$$

$$(e) \ (\overline{Q^m} - Q^m) \geq 0;$$

(8.12)

with $i = 1, \ldots, n;$ $m = A, \ldots,$ M, and $U^m(Q^m)$ denoting the utility function of consumers $m$. The solution to the problem, given the Kuhn-Tucker conditions, is as follows:

for the load

$$U^{m'}(\cdot) = \lambda + \theta^m \text{ for those } m \text{ for which } \rho^m = 0,\ \theta^m > 0;$$
$$U^{m'}(\cdot) = \lambda \text{ for those } m \text{ for which } \rho^m = 0,\ \theta^m = 0;$$
$$U^{m'}(\cdot) = \lambda - \rho^m \text{ for those } m \text{ for which } \rho^m > 0,\ \theta^m = 0;$$

(8.13)

for the generation:

same as in Equation (8.11);

where $\rho^m$ and $\theta^m$ are the slackness conditions associated to constraints (d) and (e), respectively. The multipliers $\theta^m$ and $\rho^m$ play the same role, for the load, of the multipliers $\mu_i$, $\delta_i$, respectively, for the generation, but with the opposite sign. Thus, the same principle of the generation applies to the load: the load with highest willingness to pay, i.e., highest marginal utility, is set at its maximum, and thus has a load factor equal to 1 (in this case, it is better to distinguish between load factor and capacity factor for clarity of message); it is dispatched first. The load whose marginal utility, i.e., the willingness to pay, is equal to the SMC, is the marginal load. It is dispatched with a load factor less than one. The load with a marginal utility lower than the SMC is not dispatched (i.e. it is set equal to zero). For generation, the solution is as before. The following result summarizes the finding:

---

### Result

When there are different loads with distinct utilities, with a given capacity, the solution of the welfare maximization problem implies that loads are:

- fully dispatched if their marginal utility is higher than the system marginal cost;
- dispatched with a load factor less than one if their marginal utility is equal to the system marginal cost;
- not dispatched if their marginal utility is below the system marginal cost.

---

For both load and generation, the reference parameter against which to compare the marginal cost and the marginal utility is the SMC. This is an important message. From the standpoint of the solution of the problem of cost minimization, or welfare maximization, load and power generation is to be treated in the same way, and ranked according to the marginal cost and marginal utility.[2] We shall see in the next chapter that this principle continues to hold, even if we allow the load to change over time.

---

[2] There is a caveat here. We have shown here the conditions for a technically efficient allocation. If the monopolist was not regulated, or if it was not forced to serve the load, the monopolist would produce maximizing its own profits, shedding load for all those levels of the load for which the customers' willingness to pay was lower than the marginal revenue of the monopolist. This is the well-known result of the allocative inefficiency of the monopoly. We shall consider load shedding and profit maximizing behavior in a competitive setting in Chapter 9, and discuss market power in Part IV.

## Learning Outcomes

- With constant load, welfare maximization and cost minimization coincide. In a given time spell the problem can be analyzed in terms of provision of energy or power.
- When there are different costs of energy provision, the efficient solution of the minimum cost problem requires ranking plants according to their marginal costs, from the lowest to the highest. This is called merit order dispatching.
- The rationale of the solution for the case of two plants extends to the case of several plants. The plants are to be dispatched according to their merit order, up to the point in which they serve the last unit of load that needs to be served. The cost of serving such a last unit of energy for the load is the System Marginal Cost.
- The system marginal cost is the shadow value of the load constraint in the cost-minimization problem. It provides the reference parameter for the merit order dispatching. All plants with marginal cost below the system marginal cost will generate at full capacity. Plants whose marginal cost coincides with the system marginal cost will produce with the capacity factor below one. Plants with marginal costs higher than the system marginal cost will not be called on to generate power.
- If load differs on the basis of the willingness to pay across customers, the same principle applies. Load with marginal utility higher than the system marginal cost is fully dispatched (i.e. it has a load factor that equals one). Load whose marginal utility coincides with the system marginal cost, is the marginal load and is dispatched with a load factor lower than one. Load whose marginal utility is below the system marginal cost, is not dispatched, and has a zero load factor.

# 9  Welfare Maximization with Time-Varying Load

## 9.1  Introduction

In the previous chapter, we tackled the problem of cost minimization assuming that the load in the given time spell was constant. However, in Chapter 7 we saw that load changes over time. Thus, the analysis of Chapter 8 can be considered as limited to the short run, namely, for those periods in which the load is constant, or at least has very limited changes so that it can be considered constant. In this chapter, we extend the analysis considering the case of load changing in a given time spell. Recall that we have shown that the problem of cost minimization is the dual problem of the welfare maximization one. Here, since the load changes over time, we explicitly take into account the utility of the load and the cost of serving it. Therefore, for clarity, the analysis here will be developed in terms of welfare maximization, even though from a formal standpoint welfare maximization or cost minimization are equivalent problems when agents are price takers.

In this chapter we use the following notation: $Q^{m,j}$ denotes the energy required by consumer(s) $m$ in the hour $j$. Whenever there is no need to specify the consumer, we will omit the superscript $m$.

We fix the hour as the unit measure of time, consider the year as the time-spell and let the load change over time in the time spell $T$: $Q^j \neq Q^k, j = 1, \ldots, T; k = 1, \ldots, T; j \neq k$. Note that fixing $h = 1$, $Q^j = M^j$, where the latter denotes the capacity required at time $j$. Since the load changes over time, it follows that $M^j \neq M^k$. Thus, the change in load can be expressed in terms of power.

We assume that the utility function is additive in the time, $U\left(\sum_{j=1}^{T} M^j\right) = \sum_{j=1}^{M} U(M^j)$,

and also the cost functions of all plants are additive in the time: $C_i(M_i^1 + \ldots + M_i^j + \ldots + M_i^T) = C_i(M_i^1) + \ldots + C_i(M_i^j) + \ldots + C_i(M_i^T)$. Notice that we have already assumed that costs are constant over time (since there is no time $j$ superscript to cost functions). In what follows, we consider the welfare maximization problem with respect to the capacity required by the load at time $j$.

There are $n$ power plants, with capacity $M_i^j$ each, such as $0 \leq M_i^j \leq M_i^{j\,max}$, with $M_i^{j\,max}$ denoting the maximum producible power by plant $i$ at time $j$. As before, we assume that marginal and average variable costs coincide. Variable costs are ranked from the lowest, that of plant 1, to the highest, plant $n$. We first assume that there is enough capacity to serve the load at every point in time: $M^j = \sum_{i=1}^{n} M_i^{j\,max}, \forall j = 1, \ldots, T$. This assumption will be removed in the last Paragraph of this chapter. We start from the two-hour case (i.e. $T = 2$), and then extend the analysis to the case of $T$ hours ($T = 8,760$ if the time period is the year). Note that in a given hour, the load is constant; thus, as noted earlier, the problem of welfare maximization coincides with that of cost minimization.

## 9.2    The Two-Hour Case

The welfare maximization problem is:

$$\max_{M_i^1, M_i^2} U(M^1) + U(M^2) - \sum_{i=1}^{n} C_i(M_i^1) - \sum_{i=1}^{n} C_i(M_i^2), s.t.$$

$$a) \sum_{i=1}^{n} M_i^j = M^j;$$

$$b) \ M_i^j \geq 0;$$

$$c) \ (M_i^{j\,max} - M_i^j) \geq 0;$$

(9.1)

with $i = 1, \ldots, n; j = 1, 2$.
The Lagrange Equation is:

$$\mathcal{L} = U(M^1) + U(M^2) - \sum_{i=1}^{n} C_i(M_i^1) - \sum_{i=1}^{n} C_i(M_i^2) + \lambda^1 \left( M^1 - \sum_{i=1}^{n} M_i^1 \right)$$

$$+ \lambda^2 \left( M^2 - \sum_{i=1}^{n} M_i^2 \right) + \sum_{i=1}^{n} \mu_i^1 M_i^1 + \sum_{i=1}^{n} \mu_i^2 M_i^2 + \sum_{i=1}^{n} \delta_i^1 (M_i^{1\,max} - M_i^1)$$

$$+ \sum_{i=1}^{n} \delta_i^2 (M_i^{2\,max} - M_i^2);$$

(9.2)

with the Kuhn-Tucker conditions:

$$\frac{\partial \mathcal{L}}{\partial M_i^j} = 0 \rightarrow C_i'(M_i^j) + \lambda^j - \mu_i^j + \delta_i^j = 0, \forall i = 1, \ldots, n;$$
$$j = 1, 2.$$

(9.3)

and the slackness conditions:

$$\mu_i^j M_i^j = 0, \ M_i^j \geq 0, \ \mu_i^j \geq 0, \forall i = 1, \ldots, n;$$
$$\delta_i^j (M_i^{j\,max} - M_i^j) = 0, \ (M_i^{j\,max} - M_i^j) \geq 0, \ \delta_i^j \geq 0, \forall i = 1, \ldots, n;$$
$$j = 1, 2.$$

(9.4)

Solutions are:

$$
\begin{aligned}
&(a)\ C'_i(\cdot) = -\lambda^j - \delta^j_i \text{ for those } i \text{ for which } \mu_i = 0,\ \delta^j_i > 0;\\
&(b)\ C'_i(\cdot) = -\lambda^j \text{ for those } i \text{ for which } \mu_i = 0,\ \delta^j_i = 0;\\
&(c)\ C'_i(\cdot) = -\lambda^j + \mu^j_i \text{ for those } i \text{ for which } \mu_i > 0,\ \delta^j_i = 0,\\
&j = 1,\ 2.
\end{aligned}
\tag{9.5}
$$

It is clear that the solutions (9.5) are, in each hour, $j = 1,2$, equivalent to those in Equations (8.13). In other words, the problem of a time-varying load in two hours can be analyzed by considering each hour as independent and treating it in the same way as the cost minimization or the welfare maximization problem, one per each hour.[1] Consequently, there are two SMC, one per each hour, $\lambda^1$ and $\lambda^2$. Therefore, as in Chapter 8, the solution of the dispatching problem, at each hour, depends on the level of the load at that hour. We can represent this visually. For instance, if there were three power plants, and the load was such that in hour 1 the three plants are all needed, while in hour 2 only two plants are needed, this would appear as in Figure 8.3, with capacity (MW) on the x-axis instead of energy (MWh), and the left panel denoting the equilibrium during hour 1, the right one during hour 2.[2]

## 9.3　The Case of T Hours

It is straightforward to extend the analysis to the general case of several T periods. We leave it to the reader to work out the equations, and point out that the solutions are exactly equivalent to those in Equation (9.5), for $j = 1, .., T$.

It is interesting to represent the equilibrium in a graph. We must first consider the load, since the solution depends on the level of the load $M^j$. Recall that the variation over time of the load is described by its LDC. Let us use the following example:

---

**Example 9.1** Load: Assume there is a load that has the following features: all days of the year are equal, but throughout the day it oscillates from a minimum $M^{min}$, in a given hour, say hour 1AM, to a maximum $M^{max}$ at 12AM, and then back to the minimum. The LDC would have the shape described in Figure 9.1.

---

From this point onward we shall assume that the maximum installed capacity is constant over time. This is equivalent to considering short-run cases in which installed capacities do not change over time: $M_i^{j,max} = M_i^{f,max} = M_i^{max} \forall j, f = 1, \ldots, T$. By reporting the marginal costs of the power plants on a Cartesian space with money (dollars per energy) on the y-axis and power on the x-axis, it is possible to identify the different equilibrium solutions, namely, the various SMCs. Assume, for example, that there were three power plants as in the following examples, that continues Example 9.1.

---

[1] This is true under the assumptions of costs and utility additivity over time.
[2] Recall from Chapter 7 that it is possible to represent a time-varying load by means of the LDC. In this case, the LDC would be very simple, comprising only two levels of capacity, $M^1$ and $M^2$, with $M^1$ having a probability of 0.5, i.e. its capacity factor (or better its load factor, being $M$ a load) would be 0.5.

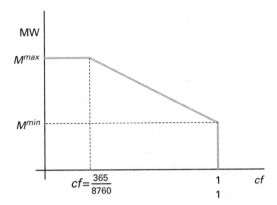

**Figure 9.1** The LDC of Example 9.1

---

**Example 9.1 (cont.).** Capacity: there are three power plants ranked such that $VC_1 < VC_2 < VC_3; FC_1 > FC_2 > FC_3$.

---

The welfare maximization problem of Example 9.1 is represented as in Figure 9.2. The hourly loads in a given day, are represented by the shaded area comprised between $M^{min}$ to $M^{max}$. The marginal costs of plants are constant throughout the day. The SMCs would be given by the intercept of the load with the marginal cost of the plants (i.e. are represented by the segment of the marginal costs of plants 1, 2 and 3 in the shaded area).

Note that Figure 9.2 is represented in the money–capacity space. Recall that solving the welfare maximization problem we obtain the $cf$ of each plant, at the equilibrium, which depends on the load and plants' costs. Thus, there are three variables linked in the analysis:

1. the cost of the power production from the power plants;
2. the load;
3. the capacity factors that arise from the welfare maximization (or cost minimization) problem.

Figure 9.2 links the costs (measured in money per energy, e.g. $/MWh) to the load (measured in power, e.g. MW). The LDC in Figure 9.1 relates the load to the capacity factor. It is also possible to link the cost and the capacity factor, by using the ACC (see Chapter 7). The ACC of plant $i$ plots the cost of the plant, measured in money per energy ($/MWh) to its capacity factor. Figure 9.3 shows the ACC curves of the power plants described in Example 9.1.

ACC curves are straight lines. Note the fixed costs of the plants reported on the $y$-axis. Variable costs, which coincide with marginal costs, are given by the slope of the ACC curves. In the figure, for instance, $\alpha = C_3'(\cdot)$. The ACC curves end where the capacity factor equals 1, since a capacity factor greater than 1 would have no meaning. In the

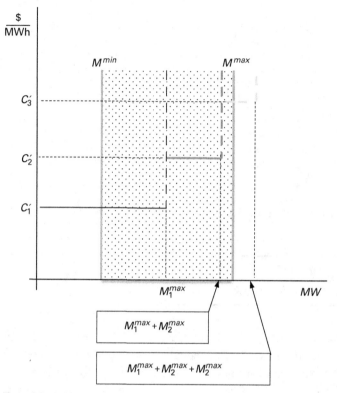

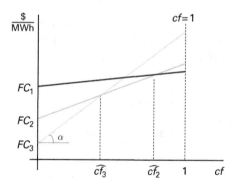

**Figure 9.2** Welfare maximization with time-varying load and three power plants

**Figure 9.3** ACC curves of Example 9.1

figure, there are two specific capacity factors, denoted as $\widehat{cf_2}$ and $\widehat{cf_3}$. They correspond to the point at which the ACC curve of plant 1 intercepts the ACC curve of plant 2, i.e. $ACC_1 = ACC_2$, and where $ACC_2 = ACC_3$.[3]

---

[3] Recall that from Equation (7.6) and (7.9) the yearly total cost equation is just the ACC function multiplied by the length of the time spell and the capacity of the plant. Thus, both functions measure total cost, expressed, for the yearly total cost function in terms of money per year ($/y), while for the ACC in terms of money per energy ($/MWh).

In Figure 9.3 we can observe the total cost as a function of the technology of a given plant and the number of hours that it can work over the time spell (i.e. its capacity factor). For instance, if plants are to be used with a capacity factor that is in the range $0 \le cf < \widehat{cf_3}$, the cost of power production associated with plant 3 is lower than the cost of producing with plant 2 and 1. That is because the impact of the fixed costs overtakes that of variable costs for such a limited time of usage, and plant 3 has the lowest fixed costs. At $cf_3$ the cost for the system is equivalent if energy is produced with power plant 2 or 3. For the range $\widehat{cf_3} < cf < \widehat{cf_2}$ the technology that minimizes total cost is that of plant 2. At $\widehat{cf_2}$ plants 2 and 1 provide the same total cost. In the range $\widehat{cf_3} < cf \le 1$ plant 1 minimizes the total costs, since, even if it has the highest fixed costs, it has also the lowest variable ones and it is producing for so many hours during the year that its total cost is the lowest.

## 9.4     Economic Dispatching

ACC curves thus can be used to assess which plant has to be dispatched in each hour, when load changes, in order to maximize welfare. When ACC curves are used to assess the merit order dispatching they are also called screening curves. Let us see how to use screening curves to assess the optimal dispatching. We put together Figures 9.1, 9.2 and 9.3 to represent graphically the welfare maximization problem of Example 9.1. In particular, we can see that the equilibrium capacity factors, $\widehat{cf_2}$ and $\widehat{cf_3}$ derive from the solution of the welfare maximization problem per each hour of the year, as load changes throughout the year. Consider Figure 9.4.

In the panel of the ACC curves, we see that when the load is at its minimum, plant 1 is dispatched, with a capacity factor of 1. In other words, for 8,760 hours, plant 1 produces, but with a capacity limited to $M^{min}$. Thus, for those hours it produces an amount of energy that equals $M^{min} \cdot 8760$. But it produces more. There are some other hours in which plant 1 is producing with a higher capacity, yet for a number of hours less than 8,760. For how many hours? For all those hours from 8,760 to $\widehat{cf_2} \cdot 8760$. Therefore, the whole area below the LDC from A to zero denotes the whole amount of energy that plant 1 generates.

Note that this amount of energy corresponds to a load that is almost always present throughout the year, or better, that is always present up to $M^{min}$ and that occurs with a high capacity factor, up to A. This is the baseload. The area from B to A below the LDC denotes the energy that is produced from plant 2 in the cost minimization problem. This is called mid-merit. The area from $M^{max}$ to B denotes the energy that is to be produced from plant 3 in order to minimize the cost. This is called peak load.

The solution of the welfare maximization problem that follows the merit order provided by the marginal costs is also called economic dispatching.

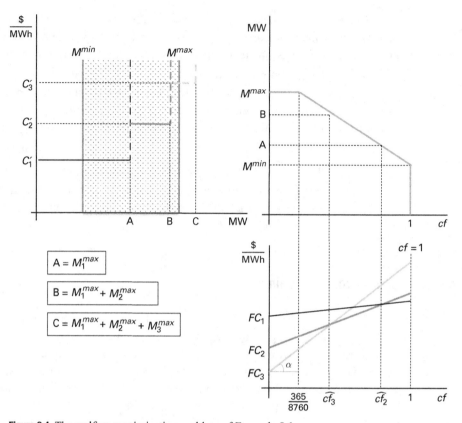

**Figure 9.4** The welfare maximization problem of Example 9.1

DEFINITION. *Economic dispatching: the dispatching of plants according to the merit order provided by the marginal costs.*

Economic dispatching, in the case of Example 9.1, provides the thresholds of baseload, peak load and mid-merit. This is a general feature that does not refer just to the case of three plants, but can be extended to the case of several plants. Let plants be ranked according to their ACC curves. If there is a plant whose ACC is not lower than any other plant for any $cf \in [0, 1]$, then that plant is not dispatched, since there will be no period of time in which its costs are the minimum costs for the system. If on the contrary, there will be a range of capacity factors such that the costs of plant $i$ are the lowest among all plants in that range, then that plant is to be dispatched for exactly that amount of time. For the energy that is needed with the capacity factor (load factor) between the mid-merit and the peak load threshold, the plant(s) whose technology has an intermediate marginal cost is (are) to be dispatched. This is (these are) the mid-merit plant(s).

The economic dispatching can be summarized as follows:

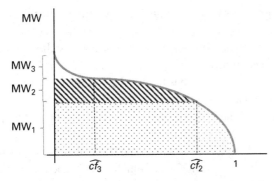

**Figure 9.5** Merit order dispatching with a generic LDC

---

**Result**

Economic dispatching corresponds to the following criteria:

a) Plants are to be ranked on the basis of their ACC.
b) The baseload is to be produced by the plant(s) whose technology has (have) the lowest marginal cost. Baseload plant(s) produces with a capacity factor that goes from 1 to the mid-merit threshold that corresponds to the capacity factor of the plants with mid-merit technology.
c) The peak load is to be produced by plant(s) with the highest marginal costs. This (these) plant(s) will not operate unless the load is high enough (i.e. it is higher than the level which is associated with the capacity factor threshold for the peak load).

---

Figure 9.5 shows the case of a generic LDC, still with three types of technology. The dotted area is the baseload and, with a slight abuse of notation, $MW_1$ denotes all the capacity levels associated with the baseload. The dashed area represents the mid-merit, whose capacity is $MW_2$; the white area is the peak load, with capacity $MW_3$.

## 9.5 Welfare Maximization with Capacity Constraint: Optimal Load Shedding

We have assumed so far that the installed capacity was high enough to cover demand for any possible levels of the load. This is too restrictive an assumption for real systems, since load changes over time and it can happen that at some point in time the installed capacity might not be able to serve the load. However, in electricity systems Kirchhoff's laws apply, which implies that at every point in time the energy produced has to coincide with the energy demanded.

So, what happens if the load demanded is higher than that which can be produced at that time? The solution to this problem has two dimensions. There is a programming, or *ex-ante* solution, and an *ex-post* solution. *Ex ante*, the problem corresponds to that of optimal planning of the electricity system, so that the load will not exceed the maximum installed capacity and for that load the production using that installed capacity minimizes the costs. This is the point of view of a central planner, or a monopolist, that can control both load and generation and that has to plan the production to maximize social welfare arising from the provision of energy. However, it can also happen that even if optimal planning has been implemented, in real time it occurs that some of the plants that were planned are not available, or that there is some extra load, or vice versa. Thus, there can be differences between the planned schedule and the realized one. As we saw in Chapter 5, this implies that there is an imbalance, which would generate an extra cost to the system. Again, it is the task of the dispatcher to manage this imbalance, in real time, and settle the payments *ex post*. We review the latter problem in Chapter 11. Here, we consider only the optimal planning problem with a time-varying load that needs to respect the constraint that it cannot exceed the maximum capacity available at each point in time.

The welfare maximization problem corresponds to maximizing utility of the load and minimizing costs to provide it. These two problems cannot be solved simultaneously. There are two variables that must be dealt with by the planner, the load and the cost to serve it. We assume that the maximum capacity is given. Thus, the planner must first optimize the load, setting it at the optimal level, for a given level of capacity installed in the system. Then, for given optimal level of load, the planner must minimize the cost. The welfare maximization problem is solved by first maximizing the utility of load provision, given the capacity constraint, and then minimizing the cost of provision of power, for the given (optimal) load.

As we saw in Chapter 7, load changes over time. When the installed capacity is fixed, in a given hour $j$ that level of capacity may or may not be enough to serve the load demanded at that hour. When, in a given hour, the capacity is enough to serve the load, we are back to the analyses performed in Paragraphs 9.2 and 9.3, considering just a single hour (i.e. the welfare maximization problem is the one presented in Equation (9.1), with just $j = 1$, for instance).

However, there will be some hours in which the maximum installed capacity $\sum_{i=1}^{n} M_i^{max}$ is not enough to fully serve the load that is demanded in that hour. Call $M^{j,max}$ the maximum possible level of the load at a given hour $j$. In those hours, $M^{j,max} > \sum_{i=1}^{n} M_i^{max}$.

Yet, the load has to be balanced, that is to say, the maximum amount of load that can be served, $M^j$, must be equal to the maximum amount of power injected in those hours:

$\sum_{i=1}^{n} M_i^j = M^j$ and more power cannot be injected than what is installed in the grid:

$\sum_{i=1}^{n} M_i^j \leq \sum_{i=1}^{n} M_i^{max}$. The remaining part of the load that cannot be served $(M^{j,max} - M^j)$ is to be shed. Thus, in a given time period, say a year, there will be some hours in which load is to be shed. The question that the planner must solve is thus, for a given installed capacity, what is the optimal amount of load that has to be shed and what is the value of the load shed?

In what follows we focus only on those hours in which the load is shed. Say that load is shed in a number of hours over the year that equals $T$-$g$. For instance, if $T = 8,760$ and $g = 8,755$, load is shed in five hours over the year.[4]

Formally, the planner must first solve the utility maximization problem, namely, finding the amount of load the maximizes utility, under several constraints: some of the load is to be shed; load has to be balanced and plants must respect the power generation constraints: $0 \leq M_i^j \leq M_i^{max}$, $i = 1, \ldots, n$.

$$\text{Step } 1 : \max_{M^j} U(M^j) - \sum_{i=1}^{n} C_i(M_i^j), \ j = g, \ldots, T; \text{s.t.}$$

$$a) \ \sum_{i=1}^{n} M_i^j = M^j;$$

$$b) \ (M^{j,max} - M^j) \geq 0;$$

$$c) \ 0 < M_i^j \leq M_i^{max};$$   (9.6)

$$d) \ M^{j,max} > \sum_{i=1}^{n} M_i^{max};$$

with $i = 1, \ldots, n; j = g, \ldots, T$;
where constraint ($a$) is the load balance constraint; ($b$) specifies that load cannot exceed the maximum, and together with ($d$) points out that at maximum load, it has to be shed; constraint ($c$) specifies that more power cannot be injected into the grid than is producible. The Lagrange Equation is:

$$\mathcal{L} = U(M^j) - \sum_{i=1}^{n} C_i(M_i^j) + \varphi^j \left( \sum_{i=1}^{n} M_i^j - M^j \right) + \psi^j (M^{j,max} - M^j), \ j = g, \ldots, T;$$

(9.7)

with the Kuhn-Tucker conditions:

$$\frac{\partial \mathcal{L}}{\partial M^j} = 0 \rightarrow U'(M^j) = \varphi^j + \psi^j, \ j = g, \ldots, T; \qquad (9.8)$$

and the slackness conditions:

$$\psi^j (M^{j,max} - M^j) = 0, \ (M^{j,max} - M^j) \geq 0, \ \psi^j \geq 0, \ j = g, \ldots, T. \qquad (9.9)$$

Notice that it cannot happen that $\psi^j > 0$: we would have $M^{j,max} = M^j$; this and constraint ($a$) of Equation (9.6) gives $\sum_{i=1}^{n} M_i^j = M^{j,max}$; from constraint $c$ we have

---

[4] This is an imprecise notation: so far index $j$ denoted the hour of the year; thus the notation we use would imply that for the hours $j = 1, \ldots, 8,755$ load is not shed, while load is shed only in the last five hours of the year. However, we do not mean this, since it is irrelevant in which hours of the year load is shed, provided that it is for exactly $j = T$-$g$ hours (for instance, just for five hours over the year).

$\sum_{i=1}^{n} M_i^j \leq \sum_{i=1}^{n} M_i^{max}$, and thus we would have $M^{j,max} \leq \sum_{i=1}^{n} M_i^{max}$ which violates constraint $d$. Thus, we have that $M^{j,max} > M^j$. In equilibrium, load has to be shed by an amount $M^{j,max} - M^j$. Condition (9.8) reduces to:

$$U'(M^j) = \varphi^j, j = g, \ldots, T; \tag{9.9}$$

See that in a given hour $j$, there are infinite $M^j$ for which $\sum_{i=1}^{n} M_i^j = M^j$ and thus $\varphi^j > 0$. However, having assumed that $U(\cdot)$ is an increasing function, the level of the load $M^j$ that maximizes the utility has to be the highest possible integer compatible with the constraint $M^j \leq \sum_{i=1}^{n} M_i^{max}$. Call this level $\widetilde{M^j}$. Note that since $M_i^{max}$ is time independent, also $\widetilde{M^j}$ is constant w.r.t. time. Thus we can neglect the superscript $j$ and call it $\widetilde{M}$. But this implies that also $U'(\widetilde{M})$ is constant and thus $\varphi$ is constant too. We can rewrite condition (9.9) as:

$$U'(\widetilde{M}) = \varphi. \tag{9.10}$$

Equation (9.10) shows that, when there is not enough capacity to serve the whole load and thus some load has to be shed, it has to be such that the level at which the marginal utility of the last watt serving the load is positive and equal to a parameter $\varphi$. But this parameter is the shadow value of constraint ($a$) in Equation (9.6), namely, the balanced-load constraint. In economic terms, $\varphi$ shows the value of relaxing by one unit of capacity the constraint that the installed capacity has to serve the load (i.e. the value of giving one unit more of power to the load). This value is the counterpart of the SMC, and is called the Cost of Unserved Energy, or Value of Lost Load (*VOLL*):

DEFINITION. ***Value of Lost Load (VOLL):** the value for the load, of having one marginal unit more of capacity installed in the electricity system.*

Equation (9.10) shows that the *VOLL* at the equilibrium corresponds to the consumers' willingness to pay to get one unit more of power when load is shed. The level $(M^{j,max} - \widetilde{M})$ provides the optimal load shed (i.e. the amount of lost load that solves the welfare maximization problem). Thus, we have the following result:

---

### Result

The optimal level of load shed is given by that amount of capacity, able to serve the load, such that the marginal utility of the load equals the *VOLL*.

---

Knowing the utility function of the load it is possible to calculate the marginal utility of the load and identify the optimal level of load shedding. From the latter, we derive the number of hours in which load is going to be shed ($g$, in problem 9.6), or the probability of having to shed the load, in a given time spell. This is called Loss of Load Expectation.

DEFINITION. *Loss of Load Expectation (LOLE): the number of units of time in a given period (e.g. hours of the year) in which it is expected that the load will be shed.*

The *LOLE* in the time spell $T$ is given by $I(M^j > \widetilde{M})\forall j = 1, \dots, T$, where $I(\cdot)$ is the indicator function. The fraction of those units of time in which the load is shed over the total period (e.g. the number of hours over the year), provides the probability that in that period the load is to be shed: $LOLE/T$. This is called Loss of Load Probability (LOLP).

DEFINITION. *Loss of Load Probability (LOLP): the probability that in a given time spell the load will be shed.*

Whenever needed, we shall denote the *LOLP* as $v_L$. Recalling the definition of the LDC, we see that the *LOLP* is a specific point on the LDC, namely, that level of the LDC that coincides with the maximum installed capacity, since it measures the probability that the load exceeds that level and thus it has to be shed. It can be interpreted as a capacity factor, or better a load factor, the load factor of the shed load.

The load shed has an (opportunity) cost for customers. This cost, that is expressed in terms of money, is summarized in a function, that depends on the value of the load for customers and thus the value of the lost load (*VOLL*), the number of hours in which the load is going to be shed (*LOLE*) and the amount of load that is going to be shed (optimal load shed):

$$DF = LOLE \cdot \left( M^{j,max} - \sum_{i=1}^{n} M_i^{max} \right) \cdot VOLL. \tag{9.11}$$

Equation (9.11) is called Customers' Damage Function or just Damage Function (*DF*). The product of the Optimal load shed and the *LOLE* is also called the Expected Energy Not Served (*EENS*), also called Expected Unserved Energy. Thus the *EENS* times the *VOLL* provides the economic value of the *EENS* (i.e. the Damage Function). See that the *DF* can also be expressed as a function of the *LOLP*, since $LOLE = v_L \cdot T$.

Once the optimal load shed is identified, the welfare maximization problem proceeds with step two, namely, the cost minimization problem of providing energy at each hour in which the load is shed, i.e. when the load is set at $\widetilde{M}$:

$$\text{Step 2}: \min_{M_i^j,} \sum_{i=1}^{n} C_i(M_i^j), i = 1, \dots, n; j = g, \dots, T, \text{s.t.}$$

$$a)\ \sum_{i=1}^{n} M_i^j = \widetilde{M};$$

$$b)\ \widetilde{M} = \sum_{i=1}^{n} M_i^{max};$$

$$c)\ M_i^j \geq 0;$$

$$d)\ (M_i^{max} - M_i^j) \geq 0. \tag{9.12}$$

It can be seen that the problem coincides with problem 9.1. Note, however, that in problem 9.12, $M^j$ is constant over time, and equal to $\widetilde{M}$, while in problem 9.1 we allowed for a different $M^j$ over time $j$. Thus, we can neglect the superscript $j$ since the solutions are constant over time:

$$
\begin{aligned}
&(i)\ C'_i(\cdot) = -\lambda - \delta_i \text{ for those } i \text{ for which } \mu_i = 0,\ \delta_i > 0;\\
&(ii)\ C'_i(\cdot) = -\lambda \text{ for those } i \text{ for which } \mu_i = 0,\ \delta_i = 0;\\
&(iii)\ C'_i(\cdot) = -\lambda + \mu_i \text{ for those } i \text{ for which } \mu_i > 0,\ \delta_i = 0.
\end{aligned}
\tag{9.13}
$$

See that solution $(iii)$ is ruled out since, if $\mu_i > 0$, it would follow that $M^j_i = 0$ and

$$
\sum_{\substack{t=1\\i\neq t}}^{n} M^{max}_t < \sum_{i=1}^{n} M^{max}_i,
$$

which violates constraint $b$.

Moreover, solution $(ii)$ cannot apply as well since it would yield $M^j_i < M^{max}_i$ and thus

$$
\sum_{i=1}^{n} M^j_i < \sum_{i=1}^{n} M^{max}_i,
$$

which would violate constraint $a$ and $b$. Thus, the only solution is solution $(i)$. Note that in solution $(i)$ for all plants $i, M^j_i = M^{max}_i$. The right-hand side is constant over-time so also $\delta_i$ is constant over time. Thus, we can write the solution simply as:

$$
C'_i(\cdot) = -(\lambda + \delta_i).
\tag{9.14}
$$

In solution (9.14), plants are dispatched with a capacity factor that equals 1, and produce at their maximum. This is as expected, for otherwise there would be some unused capacity that could generate power at a cost lower than its marginal value, which would be inefficient.

We can represent the solution of the optimal load shed using the same graphical tool as presented earlier. Let us continue Example (9.1) assuming that for some hours $M^{j,max} > \sum_{i=1}^{n} M^{max}_i$. Consider Figure 9.6.

The solution of the welfare maximization problem with capacity constraint implies first calculating the optimal load shedding. This is represented in the figure by the horizontal difference between $M^{max}$ and point $C = \widetilde{M}$. The *VOLL* is the horizontal line capping the load, and the dashed area represents the optimal load shed. The dotted area is the overall load expenditures. The LDC is bounded by the generation capacity installed: there are some hours in which the load could have gone to $M^{max}$ but it reached just $\widetilde{M}$. This is represented by the dashed segment of the LDC. Then for the given load, cost minimization applies. See that for all those hours in which the load could have gone to the theoretical maximum $M^{max}$, the load is limited to $\widetilde{M}$. Whenever the load is less than the installed capacity, there is no load shedding and the analysis would coincide to that shown in Example 9.1. Finally, note $v_L$, i.e. the *LOLP*, in the right panel of Figure 9.6, and the *DF* function (Equation 9.11) in the screening curves panel, expressed as a function of the *VOLL* ($\varphi$).

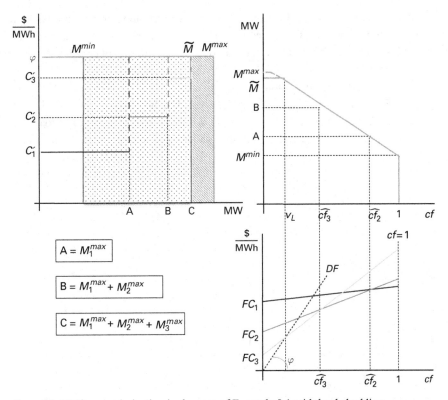

**Figure 9.6** Welfare maximization in the case of Example 9.1 with load shedding

## Learning Outcomes

- The welfare maximization problem with time-varying load is equivalent to the cost minimization, or the welfare maximization problem, of Chapter 8, whenever hours can be treated as independent from each other. The solution to the problem, in each hour, means it is possible to establish the optimal relationship between three variables: the costs of power production, the load and the optimal capacity factor of each plant.
- The ACC curves of the plants can be used to assess which is the plant that has to be dispatched when load changes, in each hour. They are called screening curves. Welfare maximization using cost functions and screening curves shows that plants have to be dispatched according to the merit order provided by the marginal costs. This is called economic dispatching.
- According to economic dispatching, the plants whose technology has the lowest marginal costs must produce the energy to serve the baseload. The peak load is to be produced by plants with the highest marginal costs. Between the baseload and the peak load there are the mid-merit plants.
- When there is not enough capacity installed to serve the load, a two-step solution applies: first the optimal level of load to be served has to be identified; then the cost to serve it must be minimized.

- The optimal level of load to be served can be found knowing the Value of Lost Load (*VOLL*), namely, the value of having one unit more of capacity installed in the system. The optimal level of load shed is given by that amount of capacity that serves the load, such that the marginal utility of the load equals the *VOLL*.
- The *VOLL* and the amount of installed capacity also allows calculation of the optimal level of the probability that the load will be shed, known as the Loss of Load Probability (*LOLP*). The *LOLP, VOLL* and the optimal level of load shed measures the customers' damages from load shedding, summarized in the Customers' Damage Function (*DF*).

# 10 The Market Solution to Optimal Dispatching

## 10.1 Introduction

In the previous chapters, we studied the problem of cost minimization (or welfare maximization) of load provision, from the standpoint of a central planner, or a perfectly regulated monopolist, who has to serve the load. This corresponds to the analysis of the vertically integrated industry in Chapter 4. Here we study what happens if we move away from it and introduce a market for power. We have already introduced in Chapter 5 the main characteristics of power markets, how they are organized and who participates. Here, we focus on what can be expected from market trades, namely, what is the equilibrium price and which plant is expected to produce. In Chapter 4 we introduced three models that relax the assumption of a monopolist, namely, the Single Buyer model, in which there are Independent Power Producers (Paragraph 4.2), the Wholesale market model (4.3) and the Wholesale and Retail markets model (4.4). From the standpoint of the analysis, the single buyer model coincides with the wholesale market under the assumption of a given rigid load. Recall that in the single buyer model the supplier (and dispatcher) acquires the electricity and transmits it to the end consumers, while several IPPs provide it. The Single Buyer is a monopsonist, while in the wholesale market, load is allowed to participate directly to the market. We do not evaluate the problem of the monopsonist's choice, when it is free to set the quantity or offer a price to producers. In this book, we focus on the specificities of power markets, not on the regulation of the monopoly. There is nothing specific of electricity markets for the case of regulating a monopsonist, thus we leave it to the analysis of the model that can be found in any book on industrial organization, such as Cabral (2000).

For the analysis of this chapter, the Single Buyer model of Chapter 4 corresponds to the case in which a given load is brought to the market, in the sense that producers compete among themselves to serve a load that, in a given time spell, is fixed. This level of load might be the optimal one for consumers, if the monopsonist is optimally regulated, or not; but nothing differentiates from the methodological perspective the single buyer model from the case of a wholesale market without demand-side participation. Therefore, in Paragraph 10.1 we consider the case of a given rigid load, regardless of whether this occurs because there is a monopsony (possibly regulated) or just a rigid load in a wholesale market. Then, in Paragraph 10.2 we remove this assumption and allow load to participate in the market together with generation. It is useful to specify the notation adopted in this chapter. Recall that, once the unit measure of time and the time-spell has been defined, framing the analysis in terms of power or energy is equivalent. For simplicity of notation, we will use the same terminology as in Chapter 8 (i.e. we refer to energy provision). Assume that plants want to maximize profits. Define as $p_i^j$ the price requested by plant $i$ at time $j$ to serve the load $Q^j$, $j = 1, \ldots, T$. Therefore $\pi_i^j = p_i^j Q_i^j - C_i(Q_i^j)$ is the profit function of plant $i$ at time $j$. This notation means that $p_i^j$ is not a function of $i$'s own production, which is equivalent to saying that $i$ has no market power. We shall assume that all plants are as such (i.e. the market is perfectly competitive). This assumption will be removed and we will study what happens when there is market power in Part IV. Finally, note that whenever the superscript denoting the time reference is not needed, we will omit it, meaning that all variables refer to a generic hour.

## 10.2    The Case of a Fixed Rigid Load

Assume there are $n$ power plants with a capacity installed such that at any point in time $\sum_{i=1}^{n} Q_i^{max} \geq \overline{Q}$. Note that it cannot be that the installed capacity is less than the given load $\overline{Q}$ for otherwise the load would be shed. For simplicity, we start with the case of three plants, $n = 1, 2, 3$ whose costs are as in Equation (7.1), and then extend this to a generic number of plants.

Assume producer $i$ has to choose the quantity $Q_i$ that maximizes profit:

$$\max_{Q_i} \pi_i = p_i Q_i - C_i(Q_i), \text{ s.t } 0 \leq Q_i \leq Q_i^{max}. \tag{10.1}$$

The Lagrange Equation is $\mathcal{L} = p_i Q_i - C_i(Q_i) + \mu_i Q_i + \delta_i(Q_i^{max} - Q_i)$, with the usual slackness conditions $\mu_i Q_i = 0$, $Q_i \geq 0$, $\mu_i \geq 0$; $\delta_i \geq 0$, $(Q_i^{max} - Q_i) \geq 0, \delta_i(Q_i^{max} - Q_i) = 0$. It is immediate to see from the F.O.C. that the solution of the problem 10.1. is $p_i = C_i'(\cdot) + \delta_i$, $i = 1, 2, 3$. In a market equilibrium there is a single price. Thus, we can write the equilibrium price relations as:

$$p = C_i'(\cdot) - \mu_i + \delta_i, i = 1, 2, 3. \tag{10.2}$$

First, see that it cannot happen at the same time that $\mu_i > 0$ and $\delta_i > 0$, for otherwise we would have $Q_i = 0$ and $Q_i = Q_i^{max}$ which is impossible. Thus, if $\mu_i > 0$, it must be that $\delta_i = 0$. Now, take any two plants $i$, $k$. $i = 1, \ldots, n$; $k = 1, \ldots, n$; $i \neq j$. Before considering the different possible cases, the following two important principles have to be established.

> **Result**
>
> If plants $i$ and $k$ are equal, in the sense that have the same marginal costs $C'_i(\cdot) = C'_k(\cdot)$ they must be treated in the same way, namely, they either are both off or are both running at some level.

*Proof.* Assume plant $i$ is off: $Q_i = 0$, $\mu_i > 0 \rightarrow p = C'_i(\cdot) - \mu_i$. Then, since $C'_i(\cdot) = C'_k(\cdot)$ also $\mu_i = \mu_k > 0$. If the plant is running, then $p = C'_i(\cdot) + \delta_i$. As before, since $C'_i(\cdot) = C'_k(\cdot)$ also $Q_k = Q_k^{\max}$. Q.E.D.

> **Result**
>
> If the two plants are different, in the sense that their marginal cost can be ranked such as $C'_i(\cdot) < C'_k(\cdot)$, then: 2.a) if plant $i$ is off, also plant $k$ must be off; 2.b) if plant $k$ is fully dispatched, i.e. $Q_k = Q_k^{\max}$, then also plant $i$ is fully dispatched.

*Proof of 2.a):* let $Q_i = 0, \mu_i > 0 \rightarrow p = C'_i(\cdot) - \mu_i$. Assume plant 2 is not off; we would have $p = C'_k(\cdot)$ and $C'_i(\cdot) - \mu_i = C'_k(\cdot)$. But $C'_i(\cdot) < C'_k(\cdot) \rightarrow C'_i(\cdot) - \mu_i < C'_k(\cdot)$, which contradicts the assumption.

*Proof of 2.b):* if plant $k$ is fully dispatched $Q_k = Q_k^{max} \rightarrow \delta_2 > 0$. Assume plant $i$ is not fully dispatched: $\delta_1 = 0$. Then, from Equation (10.1) we would have $C'_1(\cdot) = C'_2(\cdot) + \delta_2$ which is impossible since by assumption $C'_1(\cdot) < C'_2(\cdot) \rightarrow C'_1(\cdot) < C'_2(\cdot) + \delta_2$. Q.E.D.

The latter result establishes an important relationship among plants with different costs. It rules out situations in which a more costly plant is fully dispatched with a less costly plant that is not, and a case in which a more costly plant is kept active with a less costly one kept off. In other words, it establishes a ranking of plants according to their costs, so that the plant with lowest cost is dispatched first, then the second least costly one, and so on, up to the load. It is thus the analytical support of the merit order dispatching, that we saw in the cost minimization chapter, and that also follows in the market solution that we are developing here.

Now, let us consider different cases.

> Case a. $VC_1 = VC_2 = VC_3 \rightarrow C'_1(\cdot) = C'_2(\cdot) = C'_3(\cdot)$.

Notice that $\mu_i > 0$, $i = 1,2,3$ is impossible since it would violate the constraint $Q_1 + Q_2 + Q_3 = \overline{Q}$. Thus, according to Principle 1, we set $\mu_i = 0$, $i = 1,2,3$. According to principle 2, $\delta_1 = \delta_2 = \delta_3 = \delta$.

Two sub-cases arise:

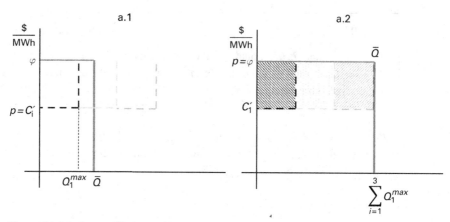

**Figure 10.1** Market equilibrium with equal marginal costs

a.1) $\delta = 0$; the equilibrium price is $p = C'_1(\cdot) = C'_2(\cdot)$. The price equals the (common) marginal cost. See that $\delta = 0$ implies $Q_1^{max} > Q_1$ and $Q_2^{max} > Q_2$. Both plants are producing with a $cf < 1$. Moreover, since $Q_1 + Q_2 = \overline{Q}$ we have that $Q_1^{max} + Q_2^{max} > \overline{Q}$: at the equilibrium, there is some spare capacity.

a.2) $\delta > 0$; the equilibrium price is $p = C'_1(\cdot) + \delta$. We have that $Q_1 = Q_1^{max}$ and $Q_2 = Q_2^{max}$, thus $Q_1^{max} + Q_2^{max} = \overline{Q}$. Producers generate at their maximum capacity, with $cf = 1$, and the equilibrium price is greater than the marginal cost: $p > C'_1(\cdot)$. What is the level of the equilibrium price? Having assumed that the marginal cost functions are constant, profit functions are univocally increasing in $p$. Thus, the equilibrium price would be the highest price at which the load is willing to be served. But we have already met this price, it is the *VOLL*. Thus, we have $p = \varphi$.

Figure 10.1 represents the two cases a.1. and a.2. The reader should not be confused by the picture of case a.1 in the figure; it looks as though plant 1 is fully dispatched, while plant 2 is partially dispatched and plant 3 is not dispatched. However, note that all plants are identical, so it is irrelevant in the figure where each plant's marginal cost curves are drawn (i.e. if plant 1, say, is the one to the left, the center of the right of the load in panel a.1). There is a random allocation of production to each plant, that respects the condition $Q_i^{max} > Q_i, i = 1, 2, 3$. The same is true for panel a.2, provided that $Q_i^{max} = Q_i, i = 1, 2, 3$.

---

Case b. $VC_1 < VC_2 < VC_3 \rightarrow C'_1(\cdot) < C'_2(\cdot) < C'_3(\cdot)$.

---

Assume for simplicity that load is such that two power plants are needed. According to Result 2, the power plant that must be off is plant 3. Thus, $\mu_1 = \mu_2 = 0$ and $\mu_3 > 0$, which implies that $\delta_3 = 0$. From Equation (10.1) and the slackness conditions we can see that the case $\delta_1 = 0$ and $\delta_2 = 0$ is ruled out, since we would have $p = C'_1(\cdot)$,

$p = C_2'(\cdot)$, thus $C_1'(\cdot) = C_2'(\cdot)$, which is excluded by assumption; similarly according to Result 2, the case $\delta_1 = 0, \delta_2 > 0$ is excluded.

There are only two cases.

Case b.1: $\delta_1 > 0$, $\delta_2 = 0$, $\delta_3 = 0$. In this case we have the following equations:

$$
\begin{aligned}
p &= C_1'(\cdot) + \delta_1; \\
p &= C_2'(\cdot); \\
p &= C_3'(\cdot) - \mu_3;
\end{aligned}
\tag{10.3}
$$

with $Q_1 = Q_1^{max}$, $Q_2 < Q_2^{max}$, $Q_3 = 0; cf_1 = 1, cf_2 < 1, cf_3 = 0$.

Notice that there is a price that equals $C_2'(\cdot)$, the marginal cost of the marginal plant. The rationale is clear. Plant 2 is the marginal plant, and is able to increase the production with its capacity. The marginal cost of this increase is equal to the marginal cost of the last watt-hour produced, so this must be the competitive price.

Case b.2: $\delta_1 > 0$, $\delta_2 > 0$. $\delta_3 = 0$. In this case we have the following price relations:

$$
\begin{aligned}
p &= C_1'(\cdot) + \delta_1; \\
p &= C_2'(\cdot) + \delta_2, \\
p &= C_3'(\cdot) - \mu_3;
\end{aligned}
\tag{10.4}
$$

with $Q_1 = Q_1^{max}$, $Q_2 = Q_2^{max}$, $Q_3 = 0; cf_1 = 1, cf_2 = 1, cf_3 = 0$.

See that in this case the equilibrium price is undetermined (since there are infinite $\delta_1$, $\delta_2$ and $\mu_3$ that satisfy Equations (10.4)). However, we can see that the price is bounded by an upper limit, determined by the marginal cost of plant 3, and a lower limit, the marginal cost of plant 2. The price is in between these two boundaries. This can be understood observing that, since the load is exactly equal to the generation capacity of plant 1 and 2, the latter plant has no spare capacity. Another way to put this is seeing that there is no proper system marginal price, since this should coincide with the marginal cost of generation, but the marginal cost of the last watt-hour produced (by plant 2) is lower than the marginal cost of the first watt-hour not generated (by plant 3).

Figure 10.2 represents the two cases b.1 and b.2, respectively. The case of $n$ plants extends naturally from the three-plants case. It is interesting to see what happens if there is no spare capacity from any plant: $\overline{Q} = \sum_{i=1}^{n} Q_i^{max}$. In this case, it can be seen that $Q_i = Q_i^{max} \forall i = 1, \ldots, n$. Thus, the price relations would reduce to

$$
p = C_i'(\cdot) + \delta_i, i = 1, \ldots, n.
\tag{10.5}
$$

Having assumed that costs functions are constant in $Q$, the profit function is increasing in $p$. Thus, the single price that can arise is the highest price compatible with Equations (10.5). This price is the *VOLL*.

The equilibrium price of a market is called system marginal price.

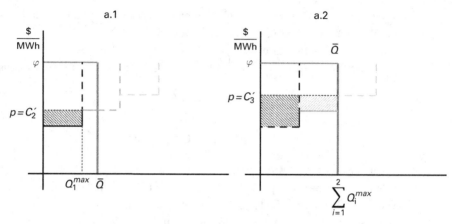

**Figure 10.2** Market equilibrium with plants with different marginal costs

DEFINITION. *System Marginal Price (SMP): the equilibrium price of the electricity market.*

It is termed as such to highlight that it is the price of the last unit of energy exchanged in the market, the marginal one. The solution of the plants' profit maximization can be summarized as follows:

---

Result

In a market equilibrium with rigid load, the System Marginal Price:

- coincides with the marginal cost of the producer that has the highest marginal costs, if there is some spare capacity and that producer is not fully dispatched;
- is higher than the marginal cost of the last unit fully dispatched, and lower than the marginal cost of the first unit not dispatched;
- is higher than the marginal costs of all producers and coincides with the VOLL if there is no spare capacity.

---

The graphical analysis is equivalent to that of Figures 10.1 and 10.2, with $n$ plants. The curve that is constructed by ranking all the marginal costs of the plants from the cheapest to the highest, thus respecting Results 1 and 2, is the supply curve.

It can be seen that a plant $i$ makes positive profit, in the short run, as long as $C_i'(\cdot) < p$. All plants except the marginal ones make profits. The latter make profits only if there is no spare capacity, since in this case the price goes to the *VOLL* and all plants make profits.

In Equation (10.5), $\delta_i$ measures the difference between the SMP and the plant's $i$ marginal cost. This difference measures so-called **supermarginal** profit. All plants apart from the marginal one have positive supermarginal profits. This is called *infra-marginal rent*, since it is positive for all plants except for the marginal one. For the latter, the supermarginal profit would be positive only if there is no spare capacity. The ratio between the price minus the marginal cost of a plant over the price, $\dfrac{p - C_i'(\cdot)}{p}$, is the

**price-cost margin.**[1] Using Equation (10.5), the price-cost margin can be expressed as $\dfrac{\delta_i}{p}$. Supermarginal profits, when present, are represented in Figures 10.1. and 10.2 by the dashed and dotted areas for the three plants.

## 10.3    The Wholesale Market Case: Variable Load

The analysis we have undertaken so far can represent a wholesale market equilibrium only for those markets in which load is not allowed to participate, or, if it is allowed, for the very short run in which it can be assumed as given. However, for more realistic cases we need to take into account that there are different buyers that can participate in the market. In this paragraph, we analyze the case in which there are M buyers of energy. To avoid confusion, we shall call them customers, even though in pure wholesale markets they are not final customers but suppliers or retailers (see the discussion in Chapter 4). Their demand is $Q^m$, $m = 1$, ..., M. The maximum level of energy that each of them can buy is $\overline{Q^m}$. Assume that the marginal utility of load is constant for $0 \leq Q^m \leq \overline{Q^m}$. As before, there are $n$ producers that compete to supply this load. Let us consider first the customers' problem. They want to maximize their utility, net of the cost of the energy they acquire. This cost is the price they have to pay multiplied by the quantity they buy. Call $p^m$ the unit price of energy bought. A customer $m$ faces the following maximization problem:

$$\operatorname*{Max}_{Q^m} U^m(Q^m) - p^m Q^m \ , \ \text{s.t.} \ 0 \leq Q^m \leq \overline{Q^m}. \tag{10.6}$$

As usual, writing the Lagrange Equation, denoting with $\rho_m$ and $\theta_m$ the co state variables of the constraints $Q^m \geq 0$ and $\overline{Q^m} - Q^m \geq 0$, respectively, with $\rho^m \geq 0$, $\theta^m \geq 0$, and solving the F.O.C. and the slackness conditions we have:

$$U^{m'}(\cdot) = p^m - \rho^m + \theta^m \ , m = 1, \ldots, M \tag{10.7}$$

Note that it cannot be that $\rho^m > 0$ and $\theta^m > 0$ for otherwise we would have $Q^m = 0$ and $Q^m = \overline{Q^m}$ which is impossible. Thus, we have three possible cases:

---

[1] We will discuss the concept of price-cost margins in Chapter 12.

a) $U^{m'}(\cdot) = p^m + \theta^m$ when $\rho^m = 0$ and $\theta^m > 0 \rightarrow Q^m = \overline{Q^m}$;          (10.8)

b) $U^{m'}(\cdot) = p^m$ when $\rho^m = 0$ and $\theta^m = 0 \rightarrow 0 < Q^m < \overline{Q^m}$;

c) $U^{m'}(\cdot) = p^m - \rho^m$ when $\rho^m > 0$ and $\theta^m = 0 \rightarrow Q^m = 0$.

Recall that $U^{m'}(\cdot)$ measures the marginal willingness to pay, namely, the willingness to pay for the last unit of watt-hour served. In case 10.8, (a) the customer expresses a marginal willingness to pay that is higher than the price of energy, and thus acquires all its desired load. In case (b) the marginal willingness to pay coincides with the price of energy, and the customer is indifferent between paying the load or saving the payment. In case 10.8, (c), the customer is willing to spend less than the price of energy, and thus does not consume.

Solution 10.8. applies to a generic customer $m$. However, in a perfectly competitive market the price customers have to pay will be equal across customers. Let us denote the price paid by customers as $p*$. It can be seen that the same rationale of the analysis developed for the plants in Paragraph 10.1 applies: customers' utility is the logical counterpart of plants' revenue and the counterpart of plants' costs is the cost that customers have to pay to acquire energy. The marginal revenue (i.e. the price received), is here the marginal utility; the marginal cost for plants corresponds to the unit price for customers.

The solutions are the same as in Paragraph 10.1: customers are ranked according to their marginal utility, that provides their willingness to pay. The last customer served is the marginal customer.

---

**Result**

In a market equilibrium with variable load, the System Marginal Price:

a) Coincides with the marginal utility of the customer that has the lowest marginal utility, if it is partially rationed, namely, some of its load is not served.
b) Is lower than the marginal utility of the last customer that is fully served and higher than the marginal utility of the customer that is fully rationed, i.e., whose load is entirely not served.

---

The curve that ranks customers' marginal utility in descending order is the market demand curve. Figure 10.3 shows the demand curve with three customers, ranked from A, the one with the highest willingness to pay, to C and the equilibrium price. See that customer C is not served while B is only partially served.

We can now put together the demand and supply in to the market. In equilibrium, there is just one market price. Thus, it is the marginal load and the marginal plant that determine the equilibrium price and consequently the equilibrium quantity. These are summarized in the following table:

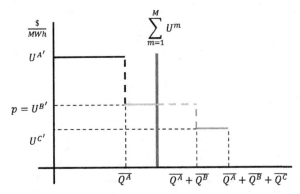

**Figure 10.3** An example of a market demand curve

---

### Results

In a market equilibrium with variable load, the System Marginal Price and the equilibrium quantity correspond to one of the following combinations:

1. The price is the highest marginal cost of those plants that are dispatched at a capacity lower than their maximum, if the marginal customer is fully served. The quantity is the maximum load demanded by the marginal customer.
2. The price is the lowest customers' willingness to pay if the marginal plant is fully dispatched and the marginal customer is not fully served. The quantity is the maximum quantity generated by the marginal plant.
3. The price is undetermined if the marginal plant and the marginal consumers are both fully dispatched and served. The quantity is the maximum quantity generated by the marginal plant, that coincides with the maximum quantity demanded by the marginal consumer.
4. The price is equal to the marginal cost if the marginal cost of the marginal producer coincides with the marginal utility of the marginal customer. The quantity is comprised between the minimum quantity demanded by the marginal customer and the maximum quantity generated by the marginal plant.

---

Figure 10.4 shows the four cases described in the table above. The solid line denotes the customers' demand curve, the dotted line the supply curve.

It is important to distinguish the concept of *load shedding* from the *load rationing* that occurs in the market equilibrium. The former occurs when there is a willingness to pay that is higher than the marginal cost to serve it, but it is not possible to serve the load since there is not enough capacity. The latter on the contrary, is the amount of energy that consumers would have required, but for which they would have been willing to pay a price lower than the marginal cost to generate it. And consequently, they have not been served.

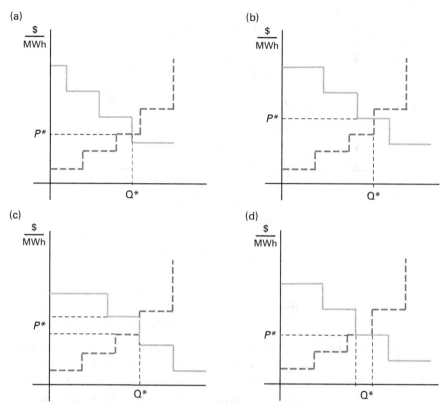

**Figure 10.4** The four possible market equilibria

## 10.4    Market Equilibria and Welfare Maximization

The careful reader has probably already noticed the similarities of the analysis developed in Chapter 9, for the welfare maximization problem and here. Indeed, under the assumptions made so far they coincide. Recall that in Chapter 9, we saw that $-\lambda$ is the system marginal cost (i.e. the marginal cost of the last unit of energy served). In Equation (9.13), we showed that at equilibrium the SMC was equal to:

$$(i)\ -\lambda = C_i'(\cdot) + \delta_i \rightarrow Q_i = Q_i^{max};$$
$$(ii)\ -\lambda = C_i'(\cdot) \rightarrow 0 < Q_i < Q_i^{max}; \tag{10.9}$$
$$(iii)\ -\lambda = C_i'(\cdot) - \mu_i \rightarrow Q_i = 0;$$

where here the subscript $i$ denotes the marginal plant and we have made use of the fact that in a given hour $Q_i = M_i$. In the market equilibrium, however, the price is such that:

$$(i) \ p = C_i'(\cdot) + \delta_i \rightarrow Q_i = Q_i^{max};$$ (10.10)

$$(ii) \ p = C_i'(\cdot) \rightarrow 0 < Q_i < Q_i^{max};$$

$$(iii) \ p = C_i'(\cdot) - \mu_i \rightarrow Q_i = 0.$$

It can be seen that Equation (10.9) and (10.10) coincide, and therefore the SMP in the market coincides with the SMC of the welfare maximization problem. Similarly, for the load, in the welfare maximization problem of Chapter 8, Equation (8.13), we had:

$$a) \ U^{m'}(\cdot) = \lambda + \theta^m \rightarrow Q^m = \overline{Q^m};$$ (10.11)

$$b) \ U^{m'}(\cdot) = \lambda \rightarrow 0 < Q^m < \overline{Q^m};$$

$$c) \ U^{m'}(\cdot) = \lambda - \rho^m \rightarrow Q^m = 0;$$

while in the market equilibrium, from Equation (10.8), when there is a single equilibrium price in the market ($p = p^m$) for the marginal customer $m$ the equilibrium conditions are:

$$a) \ U^{m'}(\cdot) = p + \theta^m \rightarrow Q^m = \overline{Q^m};$$ (10.12)

$$b) \ U^{m'}(\cdot) = p \rightarrow 0 < Q^m < \overline{Q^m};$$

$$c) \ U^{m'}(\cdot) = p - \rho^m \rightarrow Q^m = 0.$$

As before, $\lambda$ in the welfare maximization problem denoted the marginal value of one unit more of energy for the customer. Equations (10.11) and (10.12) are equivalent, thus the marginal value of one unit more of energy for the customer is equal to the equilibrium price in a perfectly competitive market. Putting together solution (i) and (ii) of Equation (10.10) with (a) and (b) of Equation (10.12) we have the four cases described in Figure 10.4.

Therefore, the welfare maximization problem developed in Chapter 9 provides the same solution as the market equilibrium of this chapter. In other words, as is well known from any intermediate microeconomics textbook (such as Varian, 2014), the market equilibrium coincides with a centrally planned one, or an optimally regulated one, under two assumptions: perfect competition, for the market, and no asymmetric information for the centrally planned or regulated monopoly.

Clearly, both perfect competition and the absence of information asymmetries assumptions are too restrictive, and not representative of the reality of both monopolistic power systems and market-based one. As noted, focusing on market analyses, we shall not discuss further the problem of regulation of the monopoly. We analyze market power in Part IV.

Also the graphical analysis considered here coincides with the one in Chapter 8, and the same conclusion arises. In the market, the optimal dispatching solution is the economic dispatching, and as a consequence the same screening curves and equilibrium capacity factors apply.[2] However, there is a caveat. One relevant difference between the market supply curve developed here and the cost minimization curve of Chapter 9 is that the latter is formed by marginal costs of plants and, if load is taken into account, the marginal utility of customers, while in the former plants, and load, bring to the market their willingness to produce, i.e. the cost at which they are willing to generate, and the willingness to buy energy. The market supply and demand curves are made of plants and customers' requests, not costs or utilities. These requests are often termed offers to sell or offers to buy, or simply bids, to highlight that a market setting is indeed an auction mechanism where the different offers are cleared at a market clearing price. It is the assumption of perfect competition that guarantees that these bids coincide with the marginal costs, for plants, and marginal utilities, for the load.

## 10.5    Market Equilibria in Different Hours

What we have seen so far refers to a given time unit $j$, that we have suppressed in our notation. However, we already saw that load changes over time. As before, this does not affect the rationale of the analysis: at each hour (or unit of time), the same analysis is reiterated, and an SMP (or a price between the boundaries of the marginal cost of the first watt-hour not served and the marginal cost of the last watt-hour served) is found for each hour. It is possible to plot in a graph the price that occurs in each hour, for a given time spell, for instance the year, as well as the cumulated relationship between prices and the hours (or the load factor, i.e. the capacity factor of the load). This curve shows the probability that for all hours over the time spell the price exceeds a given level. It is the price counterpart of the LDC that we have already presented in Chapter 6. It is called Price Duration Curve:

DEFINITION. *Price Duration Curve (PDC): The curve that shows the inverse of the cumulative distribution of the equilibrium prices over the time spell.*

The PDC can be used to assess the optimal level of investment in the electricity sector (i.e. the optimal level of capacity to be installed).

However, there is an important caveat about extending the results of the analysis to several hours. In the analysis we developed earlier, we have made a crucial implicit assumption, namely, that all hours were independent of each other. This is equivalent to assuming that the behavior of all the agents and the clearing of the market in a given hour, say $j$, does not depend on what happens in hour $j+k$ or $j-k$. This might not be the case. Consider power producers. Assume that there are two consecutive periods, $j$ and $j+1$. Suppose that, if a plant $i$ wants to produce in hour $j+1$, it must be on (i.e. dispatched, in hour $j$). For instance, it might be the case that the plant has a large heating time or a ramping constraint. Let the cost function of $i$ be a simple linear function such as $C_{ij} = a + bQ_j$. We focus on the short-run profits (i.e. we do not look at the fixed cost

---

[2] We shall see in Part VII, when we move from a short-run analysis (single hour) to a long-run one, that this will have important consequences for investment in capacity.

components $a$). Assume that plant $i$ does not expect positive short-run profit in hour $j$ since $p^j \leq b$. Let $p^j = b - \varepsilon$. For instance, when $\varepsilon = 0$, the plant expects to be the marginal one. However, let the short-run profit in hour $j+1$ be positive for $i$, since the price in hour $j$ is $p^{j+1} > b$ ($p^{j+1} > \dfrac{a}{Q_i} + b$ for the long-run profits). Set $p^{j+1} = b + \delta$. For instance, it might be that $i$ is a baseload plant, $j$ is a night hour in which the baseload technology is the marginal one and $j+1$ is the hour at which a large fraction of load turns on. If the plant was off in both hours, $i$'s profits would be $\pi_j + \pi_{j+1} = 0$. If it was on during both hours, its profits would be $\pi_j + \pi_{j+1} = (-\varepsilon + \delta)Q_j$, where for simplicity of notation we have assumed that the same quantity is to be dispatched in both hours $j$ and $j+1$ $((-\varepsilon + \delta)Q_j + 2a$ for the long-run profits). It can be seen that if $\delta > \varepsilon$ plant $i$ wants to be dispatched in both hours even if in hour $j$ it incurs a loss since the profits in hour $j+1$ more than compensate it. This implies that the plant is willing to bid below the marginal cost $b$, even if this implies a loss in that hour. We can summarize this result as follows:

---

### Result

When hours are linked, a producer can bid below the marginal cost in hour $j$ if it expects higher profits to be gained in subsequent hours and the possibility of being dispatched in those hours depends on being dispatched in hour $j$.

---

When bids of several hours are linked they are called **block bids**. Block bids imply, as we have seen, that plants can bid below marginal costs.

This is a general result that does not depend only on the fact that hours are linked because of costs. Whenever, in a given hour, there is an opportunity cost of not being dispatched in that hour, it is well possible that the plant wants to produce below its marginal cost in order not to incur it. Consider the following cost function:

$$C_{ij} = \begin{cases} -(a + \gamma_j) \\ a + bQ_{ij} \end{cases} if \begin{array}{l} Q_{ij} = 0 \\ Q_{ij} > 0 \end{array}. \tag{10.13}$$

Where $\gamma_j$ denotes the opportunity cost of not being dispatched in hour $j$. For instance, in the example above, it corresponds to the foregone profits of hour $j+1$. Plant $i$ profits are:

$$\pi_j = \begin{cases} -a - \gamma_j \\ (p^j - b)Q_{ij} - a \end{cases} if \begin{array}{l} Q_{ij} = 0 \\ Q_{ij} > 0 \end{array}. \tag{10.14}$$

it is immediate to see that plants' $i$ profit maximization solution corresponds to setting a positive quantity $Q_{ij} > 0$ iff $p^j > -\gamma_j/Q_j + b$. Note that there is no guarantee that the optimal solution $Q_{ij} > 0$ corresponds to the case of a positive price. If the module of the opportunity cost of being shut off, $|\gamma_j|$, is higher than the variable costs that the plant $i$ faces in order to remain active, $bQ_j$, the price $p^j$ would be negative, which means that the plant would be willing to pay up to $p^j$ in order to be dispatched and therefore remain active. This is summarized as follows:

> **Result**
>
> When there is an opportunity cost of being off, a power producer is willing to pay in order to be dispatched up to the difference between the opportunity cost of being turned off and the variable cost of producing and being on.

The rationale is simple. If, for the power producer, being shut off is more costly than being on and producing, the producer is willing to pay up to the difference between what it loses if it is off, namely, the opportunity cost of being off, and what it loses producing, given by the variable cost of production. Note that this opportunity cost can arise because of foregone profits, as in the example above, or for other reasons.

In a market setting, therefore, it is quite possible that plants make negative bids. Negative bids mean that plants are willing to pay in order to remain active. Following a similar rationale, the load can also express a negative willingness to pay (i.e. it wants to be remunerated to withdraw energy). This occurs whenever withdrawing more than what is needed creates a problem for the load, for instance because it implies some cost of wasting energy (such as extra Operation and Maintenance costs). In those cases, withdrawing energy for the plant is a drawback, not a benefit.

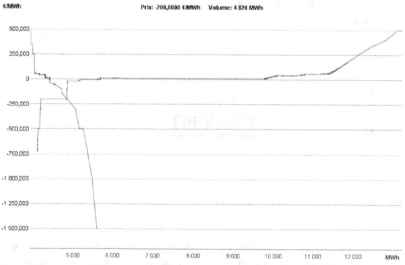

**Figure 10.5**  The market clearing of the French market on EPEX SPOT, hour 07–08, date June 16, 2013

*Source*: www.epexspot.com/fr/donnees_de_marche/dayaheadfixing/courbes-agregees/auction-aggregated-curve/2013–06-16/FR/07/3.

Therefore, in the wholesale (day-ahead) market, it is quite possible that the equilibrium of demand and supply meets at an equilibrium negative price. Figure 10.5, as an example, shows the equilibrium price and quantity of the French wholesale market (run by EPEX SPOT). We can see that the there is a negative (and very low) equilibrium price.

Negative prices have also occurred in the German market, in Texas (ERCOT) and in the California (CAISO) market. In the latter, for instance, during the first quarter of 2016, there were numerous examples of negative prices in the late morning and early afternoon hours due to low load and high levels of renewable variable generation (see Chapter 26).

## Learning Outcomes

- When load is fixed, plant bids are ranked according to their marginal cost of production, from the cheapest to the most expensive. The curve that ranks marginal costs is the supply curve.
- The equilibrium price arising in a market is the System Marginal Price. The marginal producer is the last producer to be dispatched. The equilibrium price is the marginal cost of the marginal producer if it is not fully dispatched. If it is fully dispatched, the system marginal price is higher than the marginal cost of the marginal producer and lower than the marginal cost of the first producer not dispatched. The system marginal cost is the VOLL if there is no unused capacity by any producers.
- When load has a different willingness to pay, the same principle of ranking costs for plants applies to the load. It is ranked according to marginal willingness to pay, from the highest to the lowest. This forms the demand curve. The marginal load is the load with the marginal willingness to pay. The equilibrium price coincides with the marginal willingness to pay if the latter is partially rationed. Otherwise, the equilibrium price is comprised between the willingness to pay of the last load served and the lower willingness to pay of the first unserved load.
- Putting demand and supply curves together, the market equilibrium provides the equilibrium prices and quantities. Market equilibria maximize welfare, provided the markets are competitive.
- When prices in several hours are linked, producers may bid below their marginal cost. They might be willing to pay in order to produce energy, whenever the variable cost of production is lower than the opportunity cost of not being active in the market. Also load might be willing to be paid to withdraw energy, since this might reduce its utility. As a result, negative equilibrium prices may occur.

# 11  Balancing Markets

## 11.1  Introduction

What we have seen in the previous chapters refers to the selling and buying of electricity *ex ante* (i.e. before it is delivered from the power plant to the end consumer). Therefore, the contractual arrangements that arise in the day-ahead market or the schedule of power plants defined by the single buyer or the monopolist according to the optimal dispatch rules, are indeed just lists of rights of injections and withdrawals of electricity into and from the grid. If all parties, in real time, were to fulfil those rights, there would be no difference between the scheduled *ex-ante* programs, arising at the wholesale level, and those effectively run in real time. However, as we have previously discussed, this is hardly the case in the electricity system. Power flows continuously in the system according to Kirchhoff's laws and not on the basis of contractual arrangements. If there is a difference between the two, there will be an imbalance that must be managed by the SO. When we consider the random nature of load and also of production and transmission, because of the impact of external factors on management and operational conditions, losses, efficiency rates, and so on, we understand that imbalances are normal occurrences of power systems. Their management by the SO requires the use of reserves. As we have discussed in Chapter 5, reserves are a part of ancillary services. These services can be exchanged in a market in real time, according to several possible rules and settings, from bilateral and long-term contracts to centralized market exchanges. Thus, in principle, the market analysis of ancillary services is similar to the market analysis of electricity; it seems that there would be no need to treat it specifically. However, there are two distinct features of ancillary services markets that require attention:

1. the counterpart of buying and selling those services is the SO;
2. not all plants (and load) can provide those services.

This explains the need to consider explicitly how the exchange of ancillary services takes place in real time. In this chapter we focus on balancing services since these are services which, as we shall see in Paragraph 11.6, can be exchanged in centralized marketplaces, and that are needed to manage imbalances. The other ancillary services are directly used by the SO and are either acquired on the basis of bilateral contracts between the SO and the service providers or are implicitly acquired, in the sense that plants that can provide those services are obliged to do so when they are allowed to be connected to the grid.[1]

We first describe in Paragraph 11.2 what imbalances are. Then, in Paragraph 11.3 we consider the welfare consequences of imbalances. In Paragraph 11.4 we describe the coexistence of day-ahead and real-time markets. In Paragraph 11.5 we present the double settlement process, also called the two-settlement system. Finally, in Paragraph 11.6 we describe how imbalances should be priced, and how it is possible to let imbalance prices emerge in a market setting.

## 11.2   Positive and Negative Imbalances

Balancing means all actions and processes through which the SO ensures, on a continual basis, the maintenance of system frequency within a predefined stability range. Balancing services comprise:

1) ensuring that the electricity sold to the buyer by the seller in the day-ahead can actually be injected into the grid;
2) ensuring that the electricity bought from the seller by the buyer in the day-ahead can actually be withdrawn from the grid.

Therefore, the SO provides the seller with the right to inject a certain amount of electricity into the grid and provides the buyer with the right to withdraw the same amount from the grid. However, in order to do so, the buyer who has the right of withdrawing the SO must also impose on the seller the obligation to inject that given amount of electricity, and vice versa. Thus, the SO can make sure that the buyer obtains exactly the amount sold by the seller only if both market participants fulfill their obligations. In this case, we say that they are balanced. If this does not occur, imbalances arise and the SO needs to intervene to clear the imbalances. As a consequence, in the execution phase, the exchanges between the seller and the buyer are split into two distinct trades: the exchange between the seller and the SO and the exchange between the SO and the buyer. All those who interact with the SO exchanging power become **Balancing Responsible Parties** (BRP).[2] BRPs acquire the right to be remunerated and the obligation to deliver energy that has emerged from the market clearing of the day-ahead market.

---

[1] In the bilateral contract case, the possibility of additionally selling ancillary services to the SO when investing in a power plant can be interpreted as a real option sold by the investor to the SO, that increases the value of the investment. If the investor is obliged to provide those ancillary services, this real option would not be valued, thus increasing the cost and reducing the amount of investment.

[2] In the terminology used in European network codes, sellers of balancing energy are called Balancing Services Providers (BSPs), while BRPs refer to the contractual counterpart of exchanges with the SO, which may or not be BSPs. Moreover, imbalances can be treated at unit level, or the BRPs can average out the imbalances in their portfolio of units (including possibly also load), eventually showing a net imbalance. For the sake of simplicity, we do not consider these differences here, and assume that BRPs and BSPs are the same and are equivalent to single units.

If a BRP does not fulfill its obligation, two distinct situations may occur:

a) there are negative imbalances: the amount of electricity injected into the grid (or withdrawn from the grid) is smaller (or larger) than the scheduled amount.
b) There are positive imbalances: the amount of electricity injected into the grid (or withdrawn from the grid) is larger (or smaller) than the scheduled amount.

In the event of a negative imbalance, the SO must replace the unfulfilled injection of a plant or the excessive withdrawal of some load with some other energy to be injected or load to be curtailed. It must look for this energy and acquire it, paying for it or compensating for the missed withdrawal.

In the case of a positive imbalance, the SO receives more energy into the grid than it has scheduled, or the load withdraws less energy than it has committed to. Therefore, the SO must either look for some extra load to be served or reduce the injection of some other plants.

It is important to understand that positive and negative imbalances are termed as such with reference to the sign of energy that either has to be injected (negative imbalance) or withdrawn (positive imbalance) in order to maintain the system balanced. A negative and a positive imbalance of the same amount cancel each other out.[3]

Imbalances are externalities to the electricity system. They have two impacts:

a. They imply a change in the realized schedule compared to the planned one. We can call this a wrong scheduling effect.
b. The cost of provision of extra energy or the loss of utility due to cutting load with a short notice is typically higher than the cost if the SO could plan it well ahead of delivery. We can call this a real-time effect.

Figure 11.1 represents imbalances due to generation and load, negative (panel a.1, a.2) and positive (b1 and b2), respectively. We focus on the impacts of imbalances on quantities of energy. However, imbalances can also have an effect on the price. We have ignored the price effect in the figure, by assuming that the load's greatest willingness to pay in real time is unaffected by the imbalances. We shall analyze the effect of imbalances on price further in Paragraph 11.5.

Throughout this chapter we adopt the following notation. A superscript * denotes the scheduled quantity. Note that when there are wholesale markets, the scheduled quantity derives from a market equilibrium. The effective quantity delivered in real time is denoted by superscript $ef$. The imbalance, which is the difference between the scheduled and the effective generation (or load) by superscript $imb$. Load $m$ is denoted as before as $Q^m$, and generation from plant $i$ as $Q_i$. The overall amount of load and generation that cleared the wholesale market, i.e. that was scheduled is $\overline{Q^*}$. The effective one that is injected and withdrawn in real time is $\overline{Q^{ef}}$. The aggregate imbalance is $\overline{Q^{imb}}$. The continuous line represents a quantity that has been effectively produced and/or withdrawn, the dashed line that which was scheduled.

---

[3] This is true if there is no congestion in the transmission lines, as it is assumed throughout this whole Part.

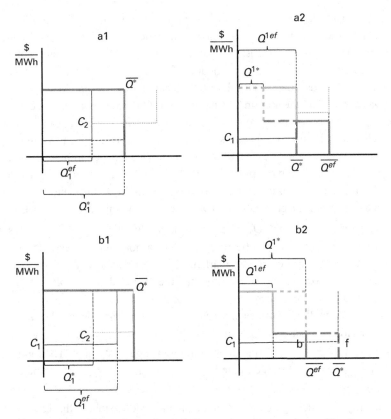

**Figure 11.1** Positive and negative imbalances due to generation and load

Consider panel (a1). The negative imbalance is due to plant 1, that was scheduled for $Q_1^*$ but has effectively produced $Q_1^{ef} < Q_1^*$. As a consequence, plant 2, described by a thin grey dashed line to the right of the load $\overline{Q^*}$ representing its marginal costs, is called by the SO to produce even if it was not scheduled in the wholesale market because of its higher cost. See that in the figure we have not represented the real-time effect, in order to avoid making the picture too complex. Indeed, this could have been described by drawing the marginal cost of plant 2, once called by the SO to clear the imbalance (the continuous thin light-grey line in the picture), at a higher level than the cost of the same plant at the day-ahead level.

Panel (a2) presents the case of a negative imbalance due to the load. In particular, load 1 (described by the thick light-grey continuous line) has withdrawn more energy than was scheduled (the thick light-grey dotted line). Therefore, load 2 is shifted to the right, and plant 2 (the dotted thin light-grey line), that was not scheduled because of its higher cost compared to plant 1, is called by the SO. Note that in the figure we have described the case of the cost of plant 2 being higher than the willingness to pay of load 2. This can happen since, as noted, the marginal cost of balancing energy can be quite high. The figure allows also us to show the difference between optimal scheduling and the effect of imbalances on scheduling. If, in the day-ahead market, load 1 had submitted the withdrawal plan that was then effectively implemented, namely, $Q^{1ef}$, the market would have cleared by calling just plant 1 and load 1, which have a willingness to pay higher than the marginal cost of energy provision. Plant 2 would not have been scheduled. However, load 2 was scheduled in the wholesale market (the dashed thick darker line), because load 1 had submitted a smaller program, and load 2's willingness to pay was higher than the marginal cost of plant 1. Once the imbalance occurred, then the SO can either call a plant that was not scheduled (as in the picture), or cut the load that was scheduled, if no new capacity serving the load existed (not shown in the picture).

Panel (b1) represents the case of a positive imbalance, due to plant 1 injecting more energy into the grid (the continuous thin black line) than it was scheduled to (the thin dotted black line). The graph shows the case of a fixed load. Since energy withdrawn and injected must be balanced, plant 2 that was scheduled to inject $Q_2^*$, is allowed in real time to inject just the amount $Q_2^{ef} < Q_2^*$ (the solid thin light-grey line). This is called a **curtailment**. Plant 2 has to be compensated for not having been able to execute the right that it had acquired in the market. If some extra load that was not scheduled (because of a lower willingness to pay than the marginal cost of plant 2) existed, then plant 2 needs not be curtailed.

Panel (b2) finally illustrates the case of a positive imbalance due to the load, in particular, load 1, that was scheduled for $Q^{1*}$ (the thick light-grey dotted line) but has withdrawn just $Q^{1ef} < Q^{1*}$ (the thick continuous light-grey line). The figure shows the case of a single plant that is curtailed: it was scheduled for $Q_1^*$ (the segment $C_1$ f, in the picture), but because of the positive imbalance, it is called by the SO to supply just the quantity $Q_1^{ef}$ (the segment $C_1$ b, in the picture). Notice that in this case load 2, which is shifted to the left (the continuous thick darker line), has a willingness to pay higher than the marginal cost of plant 1, but could have been depicted as well with a willingness to pay lower than the marginal cost of serving it.

## 11.3   The Welfare Effects of Imbalances

Let us focus now on the welfare effect of the imbalances. Recall that total welfare is the sum of consumer surplus and producer surplus. In a market, it is measured by the area below the demand curve and above the supply curve, up to the equilibrium quantity. For the electricity market, we have seen that the supply curve is given by the marginal costs of the plants, while the demand curve is provided by the utility of the load. At the day-ahead level, the equilibrium aggregate quantity is the scheduled one. However, in the case of imbalances the overall quantity that is injected and withdrawn in real time might differ from the quantity scheduled, being higher or smaller than the scheduled one in case of positive or negative imbalances, respectively. An increase in the costs (i.e. a reduction of supply), *ceteris paribus*, reduces total welfare. A reduction in the load (i.e. of the demand curve), *ceteris paribus*, lowers total welfare. Finally, either the overall quantity changes due to the variation in demand and/or supply derived from a market equilibrium, or if it does not correspond to the equilibrium one, the welfare is

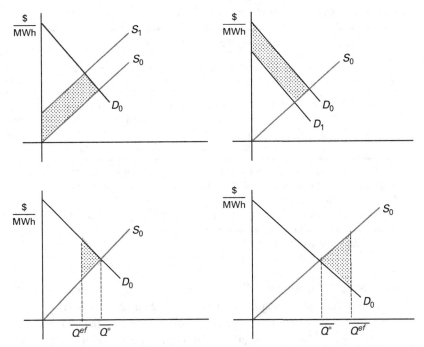

**Figure 11.2** Welfare loss due to reduction of supply, demand and aggregate imbalances in real time

reduced. Figure 11.2 summarizes these changes, using stylized linear demand curves for simplicity of drawing. The welfare loss is given by the dotted area.

Let us consider the change in welfare due to imbalances. Imbalances can be positive or negative, and due to generation or load. They impact the demand curve, if imbalances are due to load, or the supply curve, if imbalances are due to plants. Moreover, if the SO is not able to counterbalance the imbalance with a variation in generation or load of the opposite sign, there is an aggregate imbalance quantity effect. Consider, for instance, the case of a negative imbalance due to generation. The load curve (i.e. the demand curve), is not affected. The supply curve is reduced, since some plants that were not scheduled because they were more costly are called to replace the imbalance and so the cost of energy rises. The same is true when some other plants can fully replace the missing one; otherwise the delivered quantity in real time would be reduced compared to the scheduled one by cutting the overall load. This is the aggregate imbalance effect. The overall net effect on welfare is negative.

Table 11.1 summarizes all possible cases.

A negative net effect means that *ex ante* we can expect the total welfare to be reduced because of an imbalance of that sign and nature. Undetermined means that *ex ante* both a positive or a negative effect can arise, depending on the relative changes of the parameters. See that the negative imbalances due to generation, which are indeed the most frequent cases, cannot have a null aggregate effect. This is because in general the supply curved is always reduced by the imbalance. The only exception is the case in which the imbalance is due to the marginal plant and there are other plants with exactly

**Table 11.1** Impact on welfare of imbalances. All cases

| imbalances | due to | Impact on welfare due to changes in | | | |
| | | costs (supply curve) | load (demand curve) | aggregate imbalance | net effect |
|---|---|---|---|---|---|
| negative | generation | negative (a) | null | negative/null | negative (b) |
| | load | null | positive/null | negative /null | undetermined |
| positive | generation | positive/null | null | negative/null | undetermined |
| | load | null | negative (c) | negative/null | negative (d) |

(a) = it is null only if the imbalance was due to a marginal generator and there were other generators not dispatched with the same costs.
(b) = is null only in case (a).
(c) = it is null only if the imbalance was due to a marginal load and there were other loads not dispatched with the same level of utility.
(d) = is null only in case (c).

the same cost that were not dispatched because of insufficient load, a rather unlikely case. A similar argument applies for positive imbalances due to the load.

What we have seen in this paragraph is just the wrong scheduling effect. However, in addition, there is the real-time effect, that further increases costs or reduces utility. Thus, in reality, it is more likely that imbalances reduce welfare rather than increase it, since the negative impact on welfare is worsened by the real-time effect and the positive one is lowered.

## 11.4    The Coexistence of Day-Ahead and Real-Time Markets

Imbalances arise, by definition, because of differences between scheduled and realized programs of injection and withdrawal. If there were no scheduled programs and all exchanges were to take place in real time, there would be no imbalances. Thus, why not just have market exchanges in real time only? More generally, is it advisable having exchanges that take place both at the day-ahead level and in real time? In order to answer these questions, we need to look at the rationale of the coexistence of the exchanges of energy at the day-ahead level and in real time, as compared to day-ahead markets or real-time markets only. Consider the nature of imbalances. They can be due to deliberately reporting to the market a production (withdrawal) that is below the real level. However, there can be also involuntary imbalances, depending on elements that are not under the full control of power plants, such as climate, fuel availability, unforeseen circumstances and unexpected maintenance needs, and so on. Some of these could be reduced by applying proper forecasting techniques, reducing supply risks and in general applying the highest effort to minimize them.

Thus, different market designs can provide different incentives to reduce imbalances. There are two crucial parameters to be considered, namely, whether plants (loads) are paid (charged) according to the scheduled or realized programs, and at what prices imbalances are settled.

Let us consider the first aspect. Suppose that plants (loads) are remunerated (charged) just on the basis of the scheduled programs (i.e. those that result from the clearing of the wholesale market). Consider for the sake of simplicity the case of a negative imbalance. Assume that plant $i$ is scheduled for a production of $Q_i^*$. This means that in the wholesale market it has reported a bid for a quantity up to $Q_i^*$, and due to its cost it has been accepted. Suppose that the plant knew in advance that (in a given hour) it could produce just up to $Q_i^{ef} < Q_i^*$. If it was remunerated on the basis of the scheduled capacity, and not the one effectively released, it would have no incentive to report its true limit. If it did so, it would obtain the profit:

$$\pi_i = \left(p - C_i'(\cdot)\right)Q_i^{ef}; \tag{11.1}$$

where $p$ denotes the SMP of the market;[4] with the scheduled quantity the profit would be:

$$\pi_i = \left(p - C_i'(\cdot)\right)Q_i^*. \tag{11.2}$$

It can be seen that the profits in Equation (11.2) are higher than those in Equation (11.1).[5] Thus plant $i$ has no incentive to report its true production capability (i.e. to avoid generating imbalance). A similar argument can be made for positive imbalance, with a caveat. If plants (or load) were paid (charged) for the scheduled quantity, not the effective quantity, they would have no incentive to report to the market a lower (higher) level that the effective one. Thus, there would be no incentive to make a positive imbalance. Nevertheless, there would still be room for involuntary imbalances.

As noted above, at first glance a simple way to avoid imbalances would simply be to remunerate (or charge) plants (loads) on the basis of their realized rather than scheduled injections or withdrawals. For instance, in the case of Figure 11.1, panel (a2), load 1 would be charged for its effective withdrawal $Q^{1ef}$, load 2 would not be allowed to withdraw and plant 2 would not be called. *Ex post*, there would be just the settlement of quantity $Q_1^{ef}$ produced by plant 1 and withdrawn by load 1, as explained in Chapter 10.

However, such a solution implies that there would be no role for the day-ahead market, and thus there would be nothing allowing the emergence of the willingness to supply and the willingness to pay for electricity in each hour (or unit of time). But this is precisely the reason why a market is needed. We are referring to the well-known problem of the inefficiency of monopoly, or of vertical integrated industries, that is common to all industries that have these features (see any industrial organization textbook for an

---

[4] We have assumed for simplicity that the reduction in the schedule does not affect the SMP, which means that the plant has no market power. The argument would not change if it had market power, provided that $Q_i^*$ is defined as the profit-maximizing quantity, since then, either $\varphi = \bar{p}$ coincides with it, or by definition it yields a lower profit.

[5] This is immediate with linear cost functions, as we have assumed here. With more complex cost functions this might not be the case. However, if the quantity scheduled is the quantity that maximizes the plant's $i$ profits, then by definition profits cannot be higher for any other quantity $Q_i^{ef} \neq Q_i^*$.

analysis of these aspects, for instance Viscusi et al., 2005). In electricity systems, however, there is also a specific need for day-ahead markets. They ease the task of forecasting power flows in the grid for the SO, allowing it to see how much energy it can expect to be injected and withdrawn at each node by each operator. This allows congestion management of the grid. For this reason, the wholesale market is placed before real-time delivery, but sufficiently close to it allowing market operators to have sufficiently reliable forecasts of their real-time delivery possibility, and the SO checking the feasibility of these real-time deliveries. If operators in markets were not charged or paid on the basis of their supply and demand, there would be no incentive to report their true demand and supply to the market. Then, either these schedules would not be compulsory, which means that the market would be useless, or if used, the dispatching would be done on the basis of these market schedules; but then all power plants would have the incentive to report their costs as low as possible and their quantities as high as possible in order to be dispatched and all the consumers to report their willingness to pay as high as possible and their quantities as high as possible in order to be dispatched as well. The SO would then have schedules of energy to be injected and withdrawn that would be very different from the realized ones, and this would imply a lot of redispatching and balancing needs.

Therefore, the operators must be charged or remunerated on the basis of their scheduled plans submitted to the wholesale market, not the effective levels, but at the same time they have to be made responsible for their imbalances. This implies that operators must be settled both at the day-ahead level and for real-time deliveries and withdrawals. This is called **double settlement** (or two settlement). In order to do so, the price of the imbalance must be determined. We describe below the double-settlement mechanism, and show how prices of imbalances are determined.

## 11.5    The Double Settlement

In order to evaluate how energy is settled at both the day-ahead level and in real time, it is necessary to evaluate the effect of imbalances on the price of energy. Let us consider the following example, which refers to negative imbalances due to generation.

---

**Example 11.1  Double Settlement of Negative Imbalances Due to Generation** Suppose that there is a cheap plant, call it plant 1, which is scheduled in a given hour for 160 MW. Its cost of production is $10/MWh. The SMP of the day-ahead market is $30/MWh, thus plant 1 is not the marginal plant (assuming that the market is competitive). There is another plant 2, whose cost is $30/MWh, that is scheduled for 40 MWh in that hour even though its capacity is 50 MW. It is the marginal plant. The load is 200 MWh. The subsequent plant in terms of costs is plant 3, whose cost is $40/MWh with a capacity of 50 MW. It is not scheduled. The day-ahead schedule and profits, in a given hour, are reported in Table 11.2.

Notice that the superscript DA refers to the wholesale, day-ahead market. See that the total cost of optimal dispatching, at the day-ahead level corresponds to $2,800. Now,

**Table 11.2** Example of double settlement – 1

| Plant | Scheduled$^{DA}$ [MWh] | Unit costs [\$/MWh] | Total cost$^{DA}$ [\$] | Profits$^{DA}$ [\$] |
|---|---|---|---|---|
| 1 | 160 | 10 | 1,600 | 3,200 |
| 2 | 40 | 30 | 1,200 | 0 |
| 3 | 0 | 40 | 0 | 0 |
| Sum | 200 | | 2,800 | |

**Table 11.3** Example of double settlement – 2

| Plant | Scheduled$^{DA}$ [MWh] | Generated$^{RT}$ [MW] | Revenues$^{DA}$ [\$] | Costs$^{DA}$ [\$] | Exc.with.SO$^{RT}$ [\$] | $\pi_i^{RT}$ [\$] |
|---|---|---|---|---|---|---|
| 1 | 160 | 100 | 30×160 = 4,800 | 10×100=1,000 | −40×60 = −2,400 | 1.400 |
| 2 | 40 | 50 | 30×40 = 1,200 | 30×50=1,500 | 40×10 = 400 | 100 |
| 3 | 0 | 50 | 0 | 40×50=2,000 | 40×50 = 2,000 | 0 |
| Sum | 200 | 200 | | | 0 | |

suppose that plant 1 in that hour creates a 60 MWh negative imbalance. As discussed in the previous paragraph, because of the imbalance, 60 MWh cannot be produced at \$10/MWh, but plant 2 must be called for 10 MWh, and plant 3 for the remaining 50 MWh. The SO has to pay \$40/MWh to induce plant 3 to produce. Thus, now, total cost of generation is \$1,000 by plant 1 + \$1,500 by plant 2 + \$2,000 by plant 3 = \$4,500. There is an extra cost of \$1,700 due to the fact that more expensive plants had to be dispatched in real time. This is the wrong dispatching effect. This amount measures the inefficiency of the imbalance (net of the real-time effect that we are not considering here). Suppose now that each BRP is made responsible for its imbalances. Plant 1, which is creating an imbalance, is buying energy from the SO, while plants 2 and 3 are selling this energy to the SO. The price of this exchange is \$40/MWh. The double settlement corresponds to paying or receiving what is scheduled at the day-ahead level and what is being exchanged in real time. Consider Table 11.3.

See that the column *Exc.with.SO* denotes how much the plant has to spend or gain to buy or sell energy with the SO in real time; $\pi_i^{RT}$ denotes the profits after the settlement of real-time imbalances. Profits of plant 1 in day ahead are increased since it had revenues for 160 MWh at the SMP of \$30/MWh, while it had costs for just \$1,000 since it produces just up to 100 MWh. However, in real time, plant 1 has to pay the SO for the imbalance, and plant 3 receives the payment. Thus, profits in real time correspond to the SO charging plant 1 of 60 MWh of energy at \$40/MWh and using these revenues to remunerate plants 2 and 3. This is the double-settlement system. It internalizes the inefficiency of the negative imbalance. We can see this, comparing profits of plants without the imbalance (denoted as $\pi_i^*$) and after the settlement of real-time imbalances (denoted as $\pi_i^{RT}$). These profits are reported in Table 11.4.

**Table 11.4** Example of double settlement – 3

| plant | $\pi_i^*$ [$] | $\pi_i^{RT}$ [$] | $\pi_i^{\Delta} = \pi_i^{RT} - \pi_i^*$ [$] |
|---|---|---|---|
| 1 | 3,200 | 1,400 | −1,800 |
| 2 | 0 | 100 | 100 |
| 3 | 0 | 0 | 0 |
| Sum | | | −1,700 |

Because of the double-settlement system, plant 1 sees a reduction of profits of $1,800, while plant 2 has an increase of $100. The algebraic sum of the changes accrues to $1,700, which coincides with the loss in efficiency due to the extra costs. The fact that the figures coincide is not down to chance. Plant 1 has created a negative externality to the system since it has replaced 60 MWh of cheap energy at $10/MWh with a more expensive generation. The SO had to pay $40/MWh in order to induce all the plants it needed in order to cover the imbalance. Thus the value of the negative externality induced by plant 1 is (40 − 30)$/MWh × 60 MW, i.e. $1.800. This is internalized to plant 1 as a loss of profits. Plant 2, on the other hand, has produced a positive externality since its positive imbalance of 10 MWh costs $10/MWh less than the positive imbalance of plant 3. The positive externality worth $100 is internalized in its profits. Plant 3 generates no positive externalities since it is the marginal plant in real time. The sum of all profit losses and increase corresponds to the net effect of the negative externality of the imbalance.

Let us look now at the case of a positive imbalance. Again, an example helps to explain the double-settlement system. Let us see the case of a positive imbalance due to generation.

**Example 11.2 Double Settlement of Positive Imbalances due to Generation** Assume that costs are as in Example 11.1 and that the case is inverted: plant 1, 2 and 3 are scheduled for 100 MWh, 50 MWh and 50 MWh, respectively. Now the SMP of the day-ahead market is $40/MWh since plant 3 is the marginal one. Plants' profits are: $\pi_1^* = \$3,000$; $\pi_1^* = \$500$; $\pi_1^* = 0$. Plant 1 creates a positive imbalance of 60 MWh, thus 10 MWh from 2 and 50 MWh from 3 have to be curtailed. The reduction in overall costs generates a positive welfare change (i.e. a cost reduction of $1,700). Plant 1 sells this extra 60 MWh to the SO, which needs to compensate plant 2 and 3 for the missed schedule. The price of energy in real time is reduced. An easy way to see this latter effect is interpreting positive imbalances as sales of energy to the SO: whenever there is a positive imbalance, it is as if the BRP is implicitly selling to the SO the extra electricity that it is injecting or the reduction in the energy that it is not withdrawing. Similarly, negative imbalances can be interpreted as purchase of energy from the SO: if

**Table 11.5** Example of double settlement – 4

| Plant | Scheduled$^{DA}$ [MWh] | Generated$^{RT}$ [MWh] | Revenues$^{DA}$ [$] | Costs$^{DA}$ [$] | Exc.with. $SO^{RT}$ [$] | $\pi_i^{RT}$ [$] |
|---|---|---|---|---|---|---|
| 1 | 100 | 160 | 40×100 = 4,000 | 10×160=1,600 | 30×60 = 1,800 | 4,200 |
| 2 | 50 | 40 | 40×50 = 2,000 | 30×40=1,200 | −30×10 = −300 | 500 |
| 3 | 50 | 0 | 40×50 = 2,000 | 0 | −30×50 = −1,500 | 500 |
| Sum | 200 | 200 | | | 0 | |

**Table 11.6** Example of double settlement – 5

| Plant | $\pi_i^*$ [$] | $\pi_i^{RT}$ [$] | $\pi_i^\Delta = \pi_i^{RT} - \pi_i^*$ [$] |
|---|---|---|---|
| 1 | 3,000 | 4,200 | 1,200 |
| 2 | 500 | 500 | 0 |
| 3 | 0 | 500 | 500 |
| Sum | | | 1,700 |

there is a negative imbalance, it is as if the BRP is implicitly acquiring from the SO the electricity that it had scheduled but not injected or the load that it had not scheduled and has withdrawn. As a consequence of the positive imbalance created by plant 1, the latter sells energy to the SO. Plant 2 and 3 buys energy from the SO. For each unit of energy that is curtailed, they save the marginal cost of production of 40 and $30/MWh, respectively. Thus, these are the values of the curtailments for plant 2 and 3. The cheapest is the marginal value. In our case, it is $30/MWh. In the double-settlement system, plant 1 receives the scheduled amount of the day-ahead market (i.e. 100 MWh at $40/MWh). It is producing 160 MWh and thus incurs a cost of $1,600. Moreover, it sells 60 MWh of positive imbalances to the SO, remunerated at the value of the curtailments, $30/MWh: 30×60= $1,800. Table 11.5 summarizes the profits accruing from the double settlement for all plants:

Comparing profits of plants without the imbalance and after the settlement of real-time imbalances we see the changes reported in Table 11.6.

Plant 1 increases its profits, and the same is true for plant 3. The profits of plant 2 are unchanged. As before, the algebraic sum of the changes corresponds to the positive externality of the cost reduction (i.e. the positive externality is internalized by those who have created it).

Looking at Examples (11.1) and (11.2), we see that now plant 2 has no profit internalized, while a large share of positive externalities is captured by the profits of plant 3. This can be explained in light of the fact that the different imbalances have a different impact on the price of energy for the imbalances. In the case of Example 11.1 the increase of profits of plant 2 was due to the positive externality that was provided to the system by generating 10 MWh that are $10/MWh cheaper than those of plant 3. In the present case, the positive imbalance allows the SO to curtail 50 MWh of generation by plant 3 that are more expensive by $10/MWh than the marginal balancing energy provided by plant 2. Thanks to the curtailment of plant 3, the system saves $500, and this positive externality is internalized by the plant that has made it, plant 3. Plant 2 generates no positive externality since it becomes the marginal plant in real time. The internalization of the positive externality of plant 1 is worth $1,200. At first glance, this result seems wrong, since the extra energy produced by plant 1 costs $10/MWh, while the SMP of the day ahead was $40/MWh; thus there seems to have been a saving of $30/MWh. However, the calculation makes clear that even if the positive imbalance implies a net positive impact on welfare, it still comes at the cost of a mistake in scheduling *ex ante*. Had the SO known that plant 1 was going to produce 160 MWh, it would have changed the schedule, and as a result the SMP would have been set at $30/MWh, since the marginal plant would have been plant 2 and not plant 3. Thus, the effective saving induced by the extra production of plant 1 net of the price effect would have been just $(30 − 10)/MWh × 60MWh (i.e. $1,200), as shown in Table 11.6.

What we have seen in the examples can be made as a general point. As discussed in Paragraph (11.1), imbalances can be negative or positive. Let us denote the effect on the price of energy exchanged in real time due to the imbalances as $\omega = p^{imb} - p^*$, the difference between the price of energy exchanged in real time and the scheduled SMP. See that imbalances have the following effect:

A) Negative imbalances. Some extra energy that was not scheduled is called and this extra energy might be more costly. This is because of the optimal dispatch principle, that prescribes that plants are to be ranked according to their marginal costs. Thus, if the energy was not scheduled, this means that their marginal costs were not lower than those scheduled. Thus, for negative imbalances $\omega \geq 0$.

B) Positive imbalances. Some plants that were already scheduled, produce more. Being already scheduled means that their marginal cost was not higher than the marginal costs of the plants that were not scheduled. Thus, either the marginal cost of the marginal plant is not affected or the marginal cost is reduced: $\omega \leq 0$.

The profit of a plant $i$ that is charged or obtains a price $p^{imb}$ for the imbalance in the double-settlement system is:

$$\pi_i^{RT} = p^* Q_i^* - C_i(Q_i^{ef}) + p^{imb} Q_i^{imb}. \qquad (11.3)$$

Equation (11.3) applies for both positive and negative imbalances, since for the latter, $Q_i^{imb} = (Q_i^{ef} - Q_i^*) < 0$. If the imbalance is positive, plant $i$ pays the cost of producing the extra energy, and is remunerated from the SO. If it is negative, plant $i$ pays the SO. A similar equation can be written for imbalances due to the load, replacing the power plant's profits with the load utility function, recalling that the negative imbalance for the load is such that $Q^{l\,imb} = (Q^{l\,ef} - Q^{l*}) < 0$ and that the utility function of the load is as in Equation (10.5), i.e. $U^m(\cdot) - p^*Q^m$. Equation (11.3) can be simplified as:

$$\begin{aligned}\pi_i^{RT} &= p^*Q_i^* - C_i(Q_i^{ef}) + (p^* + \omega)Q_i^{imb}; \\ &= p^*Q_i^* - C_i(Q_i^{ef}) + (p^* + \omega)(Q_i^{ef} - Q_i^*);\end{aligned} \tag{11.4}$$

which gives:

$$\pi_i^{RT} = p^*Q_i^{ef} - C_i(Q_i^{ef}) + \omega Q_i^{imb}. \tag{11.5}$$

Equation (11.5) allows immediate calculation of the profits accruing in real time because of the double settlement, knowing the price of the day-ahead market, the cost function of the plant, the quantity scheduled and imbalanced and the impact of imbalances on the cost of energy exchanged in real time.

As we have see in Examples 11.1 and 11.2, the sum of all profit differentials between profit in real time and day-ahead profits internalizes the balancing externalities, i.e. provides an optimal dispatching on both day-ahead and real-time energy: $\sum_{i=1}^{n}(\pi_i^{RT} - \pi_i^*) = |\Delta W|$, where the r.h.s. denotes the absolute value of the change in welfare due to imbalances. As is well known from any microeconomics textbook (see for instance Varian, 2014), the welfare arising in markets in which all externalities were internalized is maximized (i.e. the market outcome is efficient). The following result summarizes how imbalances have to be treated in order to maximize efficiency:

---

**Result**

In the double-settlement system, BRPs are settled as follows:

- The BRP that has generated the imbalance is made responsible for it.
- The BRP is paid (or pays) the energy that it has effectively generated (or withdrawn) at the SMP of the day-ahead.
- The BRP pays or receives a payment for the imbalance that is equal to the quantity of energy that it has imbalanced, priced at the marginal cost of the marginal plant that in real time is called or curtailed because of the imbalance.

---

In a theoretical setting, if all costs could be observed *ex ante* and there was no real-time effect, $\omega$ can be calculated for every imbalance, since it corresponds to the difference between the marginal cost of the marginal plant that in real time is called or curtailed because of the imbalance, and the SMP of the Day-Ahead market. Recall that this analysis applies to every hourly price (or price in any other unit of time), and that we have not considered the real-time effect, which would further increase the cost and thus price of energy in real time.

In a real-world setting it can be complex to measure in every period of time the amount of net imbalances and their costs, in order to calculate the marginal price and the settlement of the imbalances. The SO can have difficulties in estimating or observing the real-time costs of energy provision (or the real-time value of withdrawals). This problem is exacerbated by the fact that imbalances can occur in time intervals that are shorter than those of the day-ahead market. Therefore, typically, what is calculated is the average imbalances' costs over a given period of time. This, however, implies that there is a welfare transfer across plants that provide energy in real time, and similarly for the BRPs that generate imbalances. Thus, the double settlement, applied *ex post* by calculating the average cost of imbalances in given periods and then using these prices in order to settle the imbalances, can generate welfare transfers across agents that can reduce the efficiency of the double-settlement scheme. A possible solution that reveals the costs and value of imbalances is creating a market, which shows the cost of balancing energy and willingness to pay for it.

## 11.6     A Centralized Imbalance Market

As we have seen, BRPs implicitly buy energy from or sell it to the SO. A market setting makes these exchanges explicit. A BRP that creates a negative imbalance buys energy from the SO in real time. The imbalance is created by supplying less energy in real time or withdrawing too much energy. Doing so, the BRP saves the cost of the energy that it is not generating, or gains the utility of the extra withdrawal in case of the load. Positive imbalances are generated by plants that supply more energy than the scheduled level, or load that withdraws less. By supplying more energy, plants incur extra costs of generation. By withdrawing less, load does not receive utility from the energy that it does not withdraw.

A centralized market for imbalances can be created, organizing the marketplace for demand and supply of imbalances. The market counterpart of imbalances is the SO. Thus, it is organized as a double auction in which the SO buys the imbalances from the sellers and sells imbalances to the buyers. Participants in the market have to be able to control imbalances. This requires the following characteristics.

A. Market participants are those that have participated in the day-ahead, since, by definition, the imbalance is the difference between what is scheduled at the day-ahead level and effectively withdrawn.
B. Plants and load must be able to increase or reduce their production or withdrawals compared to what is scheduled.
C. Imbalances must be standardized, i.e. a minimum unit measure of imbalances has to be set and plants and load must be able to exchange any multiple of this standard unit measure (for instance, 1 MWh).

For simplicity of notation, assume throughout this paragraph that $Q_i^{imb} = |Q_i^{imb}|$. In other words, we treat imbalances as positive quantities of energy, that can be sold (positive imbalances) or bought (negative imbalances) in a market by plants and loads.

Plant $i$, that acquires imbalance (i.e. makes negative imbalances), maximizes in the imbalance market the following profit function:

$$\pi_i^{IMB} = C_i(Q_i^{imb}) - p^d Q_i^{imb} \tag{11.6}$$

See that $i$ must pay the SO for the imbalances demanded, but it saves the cost of the energy that it is not supplying in real time; $p^d$ denotes the price of imbalances, which is a buying price. For the load, it maximizes the following utility function:

$$U^{mRT} = U^m(Q_i^{imb}) - p^d Q_i^{imb}. \tag{11.7}$$

The solution to the maximization problems in Equations 11.6 and 11.7 corresponds to $p^d = C_i'(\cdot)$ for the plant, $p^d = U^{m'}(\cdot)$ for the load. For all buying prices that are lower than the marginal cost of providing energy or of the marginal utility of withdrawing it, both plants and load are willing to demand imbalance energy from the SO. Thus the marginal utility of the load and the marginal cost of the plants, up to price $p^d$, provides the demand curve of imbalances. This confirms what we have seen in Example 11.2. The value of the curtailment, which is a negative imbalance, equals the marginal cost of the energy saved.

If $i$ creates positive imbalances it sells imbalances. It maximizes the following profit function:

$$\pi_i^{IMB} = p^s Q_i^{imb} - C_i(Q_i^{imb}). \tag{11.8}$$

Plant $i$ sells at $p^s$ the extra energy that it produces in real time, incurring the cost of generating it. $p^s$ is the supply price. For the load, it maximizes the following utility function:

$$U^{mRT} = p^s Q_i^{imb} - U^m(Q_i^{imb}). \tag{11.9}$$

As before, the solution to the maximization problems in Equations (11.8) and (11.9) corresponds to $p^s = C_i'(\cdot)$ for the plant, $p^s = U^{m'}(\cdot)$ for the load. For all selling prices that are higher than the marginal cost of providing energy or of the marginal utility of withdrawing it, both plants and load are willing to supply imbalance energy to the SO. Thus, the marginal utility of the load and the marginal cost of the plants, up to price $p^s$, provide the supply curve of imbalances.

In a market equilibrium, $p^d = p^s$. Recall that plants and load that participate in the balancing market are those that have participated in the DA. If all plants and load that participated in the day-ahead could do so in the balancing market (i.e. if they all respected conditions A–C above), and if the balancing market was competitive, as we have assumed throughout the whole of this analysis, an equilibrium price would arise given by the cheapest plant that was not dispatched in the day-ahead market and is called in the case of a negative imbalance or that was dispatched and then curtailed in the case of positive imbalances. This is described in the following result:

> **Result**
>
> In a competitive balancing market, the equilibrium price is given by either:
> i)  the marginal cost of the cheapest plant that was not dispatched in the DA and is called because of the negative imbalance, or the lowest marginal utility of the load that was scheduled and is being curtailed;
> ii) the marginal cost of the cheapest plant that was scheduled in the DA but is being curtailed because of the positive imbalance of the lowest marginal utility of the load that was not scheduled and is served.

Note, however, that a market for imbalances poses several questions. In real-market settings, not all plants that participate in the day-ahead can participate in it, since they might not all respect the criteria A–C above. Therefore, there might be a limited number of participants in the market. This might give rise to market power problems. For this reason, it is often common to set up markets for imbalances as pay-as-bid auctions (see Chapter 12).

## Learning Outcomes

- The flow of energy in real time can differ from what arises from market exchanges at the wholesale level. The differences are called imbalances.
- There can be negative imbalances, that oblige the SO to look for some extra energy to be injected or load to be curtailed to compensate for the lack of supply or excess withdrawal, and positive imbalances that require the SO to curtail some energy that was planned to be injected or look for extra load to be served.
- Energy balance belongs to the category of ancillary services. It is common to exchange ancillary services through long-term contracts, or impose supply obligations on those that can provide them. Imbalances however can be exchanged in real-time markets.
- Imbalances generate negative or positive externalities to the system. It is necessary to internalize them in order to maximize welfare accruing from energy exchanges. Joint settlement of energy exchanged at the wholesale level and also of the imbalances internalizes externalities, maximizing welfare. This is called double settlement.
- Double settlement requires defining the impact of imbalances on the energy cost exchanged in real time. This implies calculating both the wrong scheduling effect and the real-time effect accruing from imbalances.
- A market for imbalances can be created in order to reveal the marginal cost and the marginal utility of imbalances and define the equilibrium price of imbalances.

## Appendix to Part III: A Market Game of the Wholesale Electricity Market

To complete our analysis, we propose a web-based exercise that allows a deeper understanding of wholesale electricity market in practice. We refer to the wholesale market model (Chapter 4) organized with a power exchange. The reader will be guided through a tutorial explaining the basic functioning of an electricity producer that has to serve a demand (i.e. load) coming from retailers. This simple simulation of the electricity market is framed as a game with two producers, the player and the robot. The player must choose capacity first, make offers on the wholesale market and then choose production to meet demand. Demand comes from retailers that serve final consumers and it is exogenous.

The objective of the player is to maximize his profit, not to beat the robot The market is perfectly competitive, so each player cannot decide the selling price. This latter results from the market equilibrium (SMP). In particular, the market price is given by the last unit that is needed to cover the load. However, shortage, or load shedding, could occur. In this case, the price goes up to the maximum administrative price (price cap,) which can be interpreted as the *VOLL*. The game is repeated to cover a four-year period.

The game is designed to familiarize the reader with several concepts that we have explained in Part III:

- The technologies to produce electricity: they are characterized by a given maximum production capacity (called maximum production); investment costs (fixed costs); unit production costs (variable costs) that are assumed to be constant. Notice that average costs are calculated with respect to different operational conditions (i.e. with a plant that works at a 100 percent capacity factor, or 50 percent or 10 percent). Additionally, $CO_2$ emissions are calculated. Different technologies are introduced gradually, from gas plants, to coal, wind and hydro. This enables the player to think about their different technological characteristics and advantages (or disadvantages!) in the market game.
- Demand: load (i.e. demand) is exogenously given and is decreasing by blocks, representing preferences of different consumers/retailers, yet quite insensitive to price. It can be a peak or off-peak demand. In some cases, there is a slight uncertainty as to demand; that is, the realized load is different from that which the player was anticipating.

A pdf document detailing instructions for the game and the website where to play can be found at https://lud.io/resources/site/manual/nrj.pdf. This game is an introduction to more complete simulations that can be run on the website https://lud.io/energy-economics. Let's play and learn more about electricity markets!

# Part IV

---

# Competition in Wholesale Electricity Markets

The opening of the electricity market to competition and the different market design choices made around the world have been analyzed through different economic models. The latter have the objective of understanding the strategic interactions between plants and the impact on electricity pricing. The bottom line of the different modeling approaches is to understand whether and how market power can be exerted, in particular by incumbents. In most economics textbooks, market power is defined as the ability of a firm or group of firms to set market prices. Oligopolies (i.e. markets where firms possess some level of price-setting ability) are often compared with perfectly competitive markets in terms of their impact of on consumers' welfare and firms' profits. In practice, antitrust and regulatory agencies also require sound methodologies to understand if the ideal situation of "a level playing field," or fair competition among market participants, exists in reality.

Characterizing oligopolistic behavior in electricity markets is all the more complicated as models have to encompass different production technologies, capacity constraints, non-storability, inelastic demand, coordination between the market and the network in real time. Market design rules add further complexities to modeling competition in electricity markets.

Part IV tackles the issues of competition and market power in electricity markets, both on the theoretical and the empirical sides. We first analyze the main models of market power (Chapter 12) and then we turn to its practical measurement (Chapter 13).

Market power can lead to both allocative inefficiency (as electricity is not provided at marginal cost) and productive inefficiency (as higher-cost plants substitute for lower-cost plants and as higher-cost plants are induced to enter the market). The resulting transfers from consumers to producers can be substantial. Market power in electricity markets can be controlled, through a variety of policy interventions like policies that promote entry, promote real-time pricing, long-term contracting, further horizontal and vertical separation and well-targeted price controls. As Borenstein (2002, p. 198) writes: "The difficulties with the outcomes so far ... should not be interpreted as a failure of restructuring, but as part of the lurching process toward an electric power industry that is still likely to serve customers better than the approaches of the past."

One final word about what we do not consider in this book. We shall not deal with financial modeling of electricity pricing, which assumes perfect competition and focuses on time series econometrics. Moreover, we do not analyze electricity price forecasting. As noted in Chapter 7, electricity prices have complex periodic patterns, due to the seasonality of load and the randomness of primary energy sources that influence generation costs. We do not consider here the several econometrics techniques that have been used to perform such an analysis. A detailed survey of the financial approach to electricity prices and their forecasting can be found in Weron (2007). Finally, we do not deal with the ownership structure of the industry and its dynamics, such as mergers, acquisitions, partnerships, and similar aspects.

# 12 Wholesale Market Competition

## 12. 1 Introduction

This chapter analyzes competition at the wholesale market level (i.e. the day-ahead interaction). We focus on industrial organization models, after having summarized other types of models. Each of these models shows that electricity markets are vulnerable to market power, as electricity is not storable (or at least can only be partially stored and at very high costs,) demand is inelastic and generally, due to the capitalistic structure of the industry, few competitors serve consumers.

We detail the Cournot model, supply function equilibria and competition with uniform auctions. We focus here on short-term issues, in particular price formation in wholesale markets, introducing some notions about the relationship between the grid and market behavior. This latter topic will be also analyzed in Part IV. The long-run analysis and the role of competition in investments will be considered in Part VII.

## 12.2 Classification of Models

In order to analyze market power in electricity markets, we need to start by a taxonomy of different possible approaches to the analysis of market power. There are several studies in the literature that provide an overview of the modeling approaches used for electricity markets (see Nanduri and Das, 2007; Ventosa et al., 2005; Day et al., 2002; Kahn, 1998; Smeers, 1997). They have classified them according to some arbitrary criteria based on mathematical characteristics or on application orientation. In this book, following Ventosa et al. (2005), Day et al. (2002) and Smeers (1997), we group electricity market models according to their structure into three categories: optimization models, equilibrium models, and simulation models. These three categories can be further ordered according to the market environment assumed: perfect or imperfect competition. Figure 12.1 shows a schematic representation of this classification.

We review here below the three categories proposed.

### 12.2.1 Optimization Models

The main advantage of optimization models is the availability of optimization algorithms that allow large-scale modeling with a multitude of technical or economic

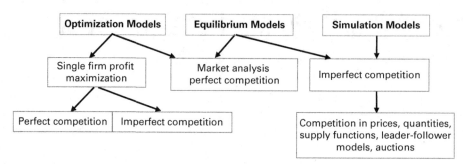

**Figure 12.1** A taxonomy of market power models
*Source*: our adaptation from Ventosa et al., 2005.

restrictions. However, the inclusion of rather complex scenarios in this framework comes at the cost of simplifying the market behavior of producers and consumers.

The simplest form of an optimization model is profit maximization under fixed deterministic market prices, as in perfect competition analysis. This problem can generally be expressed as a linear program or mixed integer linear program. The model type can be improved by introducing price uncertainty, under given distribution functions. Optimization models share the characteristics of risk management methods and thus allow analysis of hedging strategies. Another family of optimization models includes the possibility that a single firm fixes the market price, assuming the supply of its competitors as given. It is also possible to relax the single firm assumption, allowing for multiple firms, assuming however that each firm considers the other firms' output as given. Again, this approach can be differentiated in deterministic and stochastic models depending on the representation of the demand function (Ventosa et al., 2005).

The second branch of optimization models addresses whole markets by maximizing total welfare given supply and demand functions, or by cost minimization given a fixed demand level. The resulting price and quantity are numerically equivalent to a competitive equilibrium setting. However, the formulation via a welfare maximizing, or cost-minimizing, social planner considers aggregate supplies. The advantage of an optimization formulation lies in the simplicity of adding additional constraints (power-flow calculations, network constraints, etc.).

## 12.2.2    Equilibrium Models

Equilibrium models simultaneously satisfy each of the considered market participants' first order conditions of their profit maximization (Kuhn-Tucker conditions) and the market clearing condition equaling supply and demand. The Kuhn-Tucker conditions and market clearing define a mixed complementarity problem,[1] or can be formulated as

---

[1] A Mixed Complementarity Problem associates each variable, $x_i$ to a lower bound, $l_i$, upper bound, $u_i$, and an Equation, $F_i(x)$. The solution is such that if $x_i$ is between its bounds then $F_i(x)=0$. If $x_i$ is equal to its lower (upper) bound, then $F_i(x)$ is positive (negative).

variational inequalities.[2] The solution to an equilibrium problem (if it exists) satisfies the Nash equilibrium condition that no market participant wishes to alter its decision unilaterally (see Day et al., 2002). In this book, we develop the analysis building upon these equilibrium models, whose advantage, compared to optimization models, is that they address several market participants' profit-maximization problems simultaneously. Thus, some insights can be gained about the impact of strategic behaviors on market outcomes. The main drawback is that they require specific properties of the profit functions to guarantee that the Kuhn-Tucker conditions define an optimal solution and the existence of a market equilibrium. The convexity assumption does not hold for many specific problems in electricity markets, for instance, when there are quasi-fixed costs and unit-commitment problems (see Chapter 7). Moreover, it cannot be assumed when we consider the AC power flow dispatch problem.[3] Therefore, equilibrium models generally neglect these aspects. Similar to optimization models, solver algorithms for applied equilibrium models can handle large datasets and thus allow the application of strategic market models to large-scale approximations of real markets.

Following the game-theoretic approach to Industrial Organization analyses, the strategic interactions of competitors within the market can take several forms. Day; Hobbs and Pang (2002) identify the following types:

- Bertrand Strategy (competing in prices): the decision variable is the price offered by the firm;
- Cournot Strategy (competing in quantities): the decision variable is the supply by the firm given a demand function;
- Collusion: the principal idea is a maximization of joint profits among different firms; the concrete collusion design with possible side payments and penalties can vary;
- Stackelberg: a "leader" is defined that correctly accounts for the reaction of "followers" that do not consider how their reactions affect the leader's decisions;
- Conjectural Variations: the reaction of competing firms to a firm's decisions is anticipated via functional relations;
- Supply Function Equilibrium (SFE): firms compete by bidding complete supply functions instead of a single supply;
- Auctions: firms compete by submitting prices, and are dispatched according to the merit order ranking (uniform auctions) or are paid according to their offers (pay-as-you-bid auctions).

In addition to imperfect markets, equilibrium problems can also be applied to analyze a perfect competitive market by assuming that prices are fixed and the firms minimize costs. In Paragraph 12.3 we focus more deeply on these approaches, in particular on Cournot and Supply Function Equilibria. Moreover, we shall also review the Uniform

---

[2] A variational inequality is an inequality involving a function, which has to be solved for all possible values of a given variable, in a convex set.

[3] Note that we focus on direct current (DC) flow, except in Part V where we develop the network approach. However, a simplified DC equilibrium model that mimics the AC one can be constructed. For instance, optimal dispatch with AC network constraints can be simplified into a DC optimal dispatch model, called DC-Optimal Power Flow (DC-OPF).

Auction model, which reflects realistically the organization of the majority of wholesale electricity markets.

### 12.2.3     Simulation Models

The complexity of electricity markets often requires simplifications to obtain a solution within an equilibrium framework. Simulation models provide a flexible setting for market analysis when formal equilibrium approaches are no longer feasible. Agent-based models have emerged as a preferred tool for dynamic market analyses. Static equilibrium approaches typically neglect the fact that market participants base their decisions on historic information which accumulates over the market processes.

Agent-based approaches can overcome these drawbacks. The main feature of agent-based modeling is that market participants are modeled as computational agents that are goal-oriented and adaptive. In general, the procedure is as follows: (i) define a research question to resolve, (ii) construct an economy with an initial agent population, (iii) define the agents' attributes and the structural and institutional framework, (iv) let the economy evolve over time and (v) analyze and evaluate the simulation results. The majority of electricity-related papers focus on the market design analysis. According to Ventosa et al. (2005), agents learn from past experience, improve their decision making and adapt to changes in the environment (e.g. competitors' moves, demand variations or uncertain availability of primary energy sources, such as hydro inflows, for instance). This suggests that adaptive agent-based simulation techniques can shed light on features of electricity markets that static models ignore. The contribution of simulation models has been significant as they incorporate more complex assumptions than those allowed by formal equilibrium models.

## 12.3     Three Models of Market Power in Electricity Markets

We focus on the three main modeling approaches that analyze the strategies of power producers in wholesale markets. Cournot competition is the simplest approach that explains how firms compete by fixing quantities. The supply function model is one of the first that has been suggested to fit plants' strategies and encompass, under some assumptions, both competition in quantities and in prices. Finally, the model of uniform auctions reflects the rules used in many day-ahead markets.

### 12.3.1     Cournot Competition

We illustrate the basic model of Cournot competition with $n$ firms, specifying the hypotheses and the model solution.

**Hypotheses**

1) Electricity plants are characterized by cost functions of Equation (12.1):

$$C_i(Q_i) \quad i = 1 \ldots n; \text{ with } C_i'(Q_i) \geq 0; \tag{12.1}$$

where $Q_i$ is the quantity produced.

2) There are no production capacity constraints.
3) Consumers are represented by the demand function described in Equation (12.2), which depends on the total electricity produced $\sum_{i=1}^{n} Q_i = Q$:

$$p(Q) \text{ with } p'(Q) < 0 \tag{12.2}$$

**Model Solution**

Firms simultaneously choose their production. Each player assumes production by competitors as constant. The profit maximization is as follows:

$$\max_{Q_i} \pi(Q_i) = Q_i p(Q) - C_i(Q_i). \tag{12.3}$$

The first order condition (FOC) for profit maximization with respect to $Q_i$, is:

$$p(Q) + Q_i \frac{\partial p}{\partial Q} \frac{\partial Q}{\partial Q_i} - C_i'(Q_i) = 0. \tag{12.4}$$

Simplifying it, we can rewrite the FOC as follows:

$$\frac{p - C_i'(Q_i)}{p} = -\frac{Q_i}{p} \frac{\partial p}{\partial Q} \frac{\partial Q}{\partial Q_i}. \tag{12.5}$$

Notice that $\frac{\partial Q}{\partial Q_i} = 1$. Moreover, recalling the formula of demand elasticity $\eta$ (that is the degree to which demand responds to an infinitesimal change in price), i.e.:

$$\eta = -\frac{\partial Q}{\partial p(Q)} \frac{p(Q)}{Q}; \tag{12.6}$$

and multiplying the right-hand side by $\frac{Q}{Q}$ we can write Equation (12.6) as follows:

$$\frac{p - C_i'(Q_i)}{p} = \frac{1}{\eta} \frac{Q_i}{Q}. \tag{12.7}$$

The ratio $Q_i/Q$ is the *market share* of firm $i$, denoted by $s_i$.[4] The so-called individual *Lerner* index ($L_i$) is the firm individual mark-up:

$$L_i = \frac{p - C_i'(Q)}{p} = \frac{1}{\eta} s_i; \tag{12.8}$$

---

[4] Note that if all firms have the same marginal cost (firms are symmetric), that is $C_i'(Q_i) = C'(Q_i)$, all firms will sell the same quantity and therefore the market share will be $s_i = 1/n$.

which indicates a useful relationship between the price-cost margin $\left(p - C'_i(Q_i)\right)/p$, the firm market share $s_i$ and the demand elasticity $\eta$.[5]

The Cournot approach yields a simple outcome in terms of price and quantities, which depends on the demand function parameters. Under linear demand and cost functions, the Cournot model has a unique Nash equilibrium.[6]

Descriptions of the electricity market by assuming Cournot competition has frequently been used to analyze market power (Stanfield et al., 2008; Borenstein et al., 1995; Borenstein and Bushnell, 1999, for example). However, given the low demand elasticities in the electricity sector, the prices predicted are too high, and output too low. As Willems et al. (2009) argue, in Cournot models for electricity markets it is often assumed that a fixed percentage of sales is covered by forward contracts. This coverage factor is then used to adjust the model outcome. By varying the coverage factor, an infinite set of equilibria, ranging from perfect competition to standard Cournot outcomes, can be obtained.

## 12.3.2    Supply Function Equilibria

The Supply Function Equilibrium (SFE) shares with the Cournot model the assumption of profit-maximizing producers but differs in the assumption regarding the free choice variables and the behavior of the remaining market participants. In the SFE, each firm choose an entire supply function assuming that the supply function of the others remains fixed. Klemperer and Meyer (1989) showed that, absent uncertainty and given the competitors' strategic variables (quantities or prices), each firm has no preference between expressing its decisions in terms of a quantity or a price, as long as it faces a unique residual demand. On the contrary, when a firm faces a range of possible residual demand curves, it expects a higher profit expressing its decisions in terms of a supply function that indicates the price at which it offers different quantities to the market. To ease the calculations, we illustrate this model in a duopoly case.

### Hypotheses

1) Electricity plants $i$ and $j$ are characterized by the following cost function:

$$C_i(Q_i) \text{ with } C'_i(Q) \geq 0; \tag{12.9}$$

where $Q_i$ is the quantity produced.

2) There are no production capacity constraints.
3) Consumers are represented by a demand function which decreases in the price $p$. It varies over time $t$:

---

[5] This formula is used in Chapter 13 to obtain a measure of market power.

[6] The Nash equilibrium is a concept used in game theory. The Nash Equilibrium is the solution to a game in which two or more players have a strategy, and where each participant, considering an opponent's choice, has no incentive to change his/her strategy. Therefore, in the Cournot model, each producer finds the optimal quantity to be produced when considering the quantity choices of the other players.

$$D(p,t), \text{ with } D_p(p,t) < 0. \tag{12.10}$$

4) Firms, i.e. power producers, simultaneously submit Supply Functions $S_i$ (p) continuously differentiable and non-decreasing in $p$ :

$$S_i(p), \text{ with } S_i'(p) > 0. \tag{12.11}$$

The auctioneer determines the lowest equilibrium price $p^*$ such that each firm produces over its supply function and the market clears:

$$S_i(p^*) + S_j(p^*) = D(p^*, t). \tag{12.12}$$

5) $i$'s set of *ex-post* profit maximizing points can be described as a supply function, which intersects each realization of $i$'s residual demand curve once and only once (e.g. the residual demand curves shift in parallel).

We have the following:

DEFINITION. **Supply Function Equilibrium:** *A Nash equilibrium in supply functions is a supply function pair* $\{S_i(p^*),\ S_j(p^*)\}$ *such that* $S_i(p^*)$ *maximizes firm i expected profits, given* $S_j(p^*)$.

Market clearing implies that firms produce on their residual demand:

$$Q_i(t) = S_i(p^*) = D(p^*, t) - S_j(p^*). \tag{12.13}$$

## Model Solution

The profit maximization problem for firms is:

$$\max_p \; p[D(p,t) - S_j(p)] - C_i\Big(D(p,t) - S_j(p)\Big). \tag{12.14}$$

Differentiating profits with respect to $p$ yields the following First Order Condition (FOC):

$$\frac{dQ_j}{dp} = \frac{Q_i}{p - C_i'(Q_i)} + D_p(p,t). \tag{12.15}$$

In the symmetric case, $C_i'(Q_i) = C_j'(Q_j) = C'(Q)$. Therefore, we have:

$$\frac{dQ}{dp} = \frac{Q}{p - C'(Q)} + D_p(p,t). \tag{12.16}$$

Supply functions must be non-decreasing $\left( \dfrac{dQ}{dp} \in (0, \infty) \right)$ which implies that there is a continuum of equilibrium prices, whose boundaries are as follows:

$$C'(Q) \leq p \leq C'(Q) - \frac{Q}{D_p(p,t)} \tag{12.17}$$

Klemperer and Meyer (1989) have shown that price and quantity in any SFE are bounded by the Cournot and Bertrand outcomes. Bertrand equilibrium (i.e. marginal cost pricing), corresponds to a horizontal supply curve. Cournot equilibrium resembles a vertical supply function. This latter can be obtained assuming that the output of firm $j$ is not price responsive, as we show below. In fact, we would have the following problem:

$$\max_{p} \; p[D(p,t) - k_j] - C_i\Big(D(p,t) - k_j\Big); \tag{12.18}$$

whose solution gives, as F.O.C.:

$$Q_i + [\, p - C'(Q)]D'(p,t) = 0; \tag{12.19}$$

or

$$p = C'(Q) - \frac{Q_i}{D'(\cdot)}; \tag{12.20}$$

which formally coincides with the solution of the Cournot problem (Equation 12.5).

As Borenstein et al. (1999, p. 70) affirm: "The supply function model ... has some weaknesses that may limit its usefulness when applied to certain electricity markets. In some markets, trades do not occur exclusively, or even primarily, through a supply-function bid process. Bilateral trading of specified quantities is common in many restructured markets around the world, as are futures markets and different forms of spot markets ... The supply function approach also does not lend itself well to markets where there is a competitive fringe whose capacity may be limited due to either generation or transmission constraints. Overall the supply function approach approximates one important aspect of many restructured electricity markets more accurately than the Cournot approach, but it is not as flexible as the Cournot approach in incorporating other institutional aspects of these markets. Furthermore, the supply function approach produces multiple equilibria and the diversity of these equilibria grows as the uncertainty of demand is reduced. The Cournot equilibrium represents an upper bound on supply function equilibria and is generally easier to calculate, thus it may be a more appropriate screening measure of the potential for market power."

The SFE approach has been extensively used to describe and analyze the England and Wales market (Green 1996). For instance, Green and Newbery (1992) develop an asymmetric SFE model and show that the large firm finds price increases more profitable and therefore has a greater incentive to submit a steep supply function. The small firm then faces a less elastic residual demand curve and therefore deviates from its marginal costs. The SFE model, however, has some drawbacks, which mainly depend on its computational difficulties. Except in some specific cases, as for instance linear supply functions and constant costs or capacity constraints, the existence and uniqueness of a solution is hard to prove. This indeterminacy makes also difficult to understand firms' strategic incentives. The hypothesis of continuous non-decreasing differentiable functions is not realistic. In fact, as the Cournot model, the SFE approach does not consider some characteristics of real wholesale markets where market clearing is obtained through auctions.

## 12.4    Auctions

An auction is one of many ways that a seller can use to sell a product to potential buyers when the valuations of that product are unknown. Thus, the product is sold at a price determined by competition among buyers according to rules set in the auction format. When there are pools or power exchanges (see Chapter 5), important questions arise as to determine the market design in terms of number of auctions, lead time between auctions and frequency. Different methods have been proposed: single auctions, sequence of multiple auctions at different lead times, and continuous trading.[7]

In an electricity auction,[8] all agents simultaneously send their bids to the organizing entity, usually a market operator or the system operator. In their offers, agents declare the amount of energy in MWh, willing to sell/buy and at what price. Subsequently, the entity who organizes the market aggregates these offers according to economic merit-order criterion. That is, sale offers are ranked in ascending order of price, while purchase offers are ranked in descending order of price. Market clearing is then calculated at the point of intersection of both curves. A clearing volume of energy and a final equilibrium price are obtained. The equilibrium price is termed System Marginal Price, as we have seen in Chapter 10. The difference between the amount of money that buyers were willing to pay whose offers have been retained less the amount they pay is called consumer surplus, and similarly for producer surplus.[9]

In the energy markets, we found basically two different types of auction formats.[10]

- The pay-as-cleared or **uniform auction** (also called uniform price auctions). The auctioneer ranks the bids in increasing order, assuming that bids are the true marginal (linear) costs. The highest accepted bid, such that demand equals supply, determines the system marginal price (SMP). All the producers that have bid below the SMP will be remunerated with that price.
- The **pay-as-bid** auction, in which each cleared bid is remunerated at the bid (i.e. the price offered in the auction).

We compare these two formats in detail, first under perfect competition and then considering the possibility of market power. Table 12.1 focuses on the power plants' bids under perfect competition (PC). If power producers have market power, the comparison is modified as shown in Table 12.2.

---

[7] Continuous trading could be approximated to a sequence of infinite auctions. It should also be noted that by virtue of the first-come, first-served principle, clearing is of the type pay-as-bid.

[8] In power markets, in addition to auctions in which the product is electricity (in MWh), there are also auctions for related products such as long-term markets and also ancillary services or capacity mechanisms. For simplicity, at this point we will refer only to auctions for electricity, which occur, for instance, at the day-ahead level. Auctions can be considered as an efficient market design choice to implement the first-best competitive outcome, although, as we explain here, producers' strategic behavior may not be circumvented.

[9] There are other auction formats that are not covered here, including second-price auctions (also called Vickrey's auctions).

[10] It is also a frequent occurrence, especially in US markets, that additional side-payments take place for different reasons. In such cases we would speak of a discriminatory pricing rule.

**Table 12.1** Comparison of auction formats under perfect competition

| Uniform auction (PC) | Pay-as-bid (PC) |
| --- | --- |

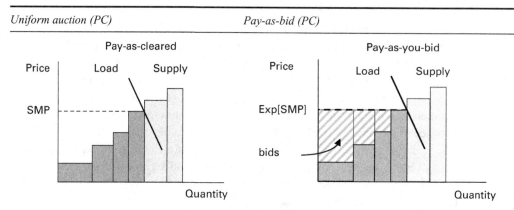

1) The optimal strategy for a power plant consists in bidding at its marginal cost in order to have every possible chance of being cleared in the auction.

→ By bidding, plants reveal their marginal costs.

1) The optimal strategy for a power plant consists in bidding at the market price that it anticipates. Under perfect and complete information, all agents manage to perfectly anticipate this equilibrium price.

→ By bidding, plants reveal information about their expectations on the equilibrium price (Exp[SMP] in the figure).

We can see that both auction formats may be prone to market power, but uniform auctions seem to be more vulnerable to withholding, as we explain in the following section.

### 12.4.1    Uniform Auctions and Market Power

Analyzing the link between market power and uniform auctions is not straightforward. However, a strand of research has addressed this issue, considering strategic equilibrium pricing in the wholesale market in uniform auctions (von der Fehr and Harbord, 1993; Wolfram, 1997; Cramton, 2004; Crampes and Creti, 2005; Fabra et al., 2006; among others). Regardless of some modeling differences, all the models point out the existence of two sets of strategic equilibria: if demand is sufficiently low, firms (i.e. plants) cannot sustain any price above a competitive bid equal to their marginal production costs; if demand is high, the maximum price attainable in the market is reached. We illustrate this fundamental result in a duopoly model with symmetric firms.

### Hypotheses

1) Power plants $i = a, b$ are characterized by the following linear cost function:

$$C_i(Q) = cQ_i \text{ with } C'_i(Q) = c \tag{12.21}$$

where $Q_i$ is the quantity produced.

**Table 12.2** Comparison of auction formats under imperfect competition

| *Uniform auction (imperfect competition)* | *Pay-as-bid (imperfect competition)* |
|---|---|
| 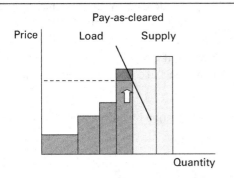 | 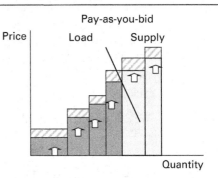 |

1) **Market power in prices**: A producer who anticipates being marginal has an incentive to bid above its marginal costs, as high as possible while cleared.

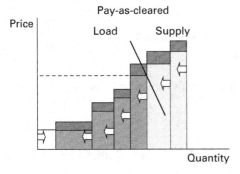

1) **Market power in prices:** A producer who anticipates being marginal has an incentive to bid above its marginal costs, as high as possible while cleared. However, it is more difficult for an agent to anticipate the price than in the case of uniform auction.

2) **Market power in volumes**: Producers with a diversified generation mix have an interest in withholding volumes offered in order to artificially shift the supply curve to the left and thus increase the equilibrium price.

→ Producers in their bids do not reveal their exact marginal costs and available volumes.

2) **Market power in volumes**: Not easy to exert because all agents have an interest to offer their production capacity.

→ Producers do not reveal exactly either their information, their marginal costs and available volumes, but exerting market power is more difficult than under uniform auctions.

2) There are (exogenous) symmetric production capacity constraints $M_a^{max} = M_b^{max} = M$.

3) Consumers are represented by a totally inelastic demand $D < 2M$.

4) Firms simultaneously submit price bids $B_i$.

5) The maximum price is the price cap $\hat{p}$ (this price cap can coincide with the *VOLL* or not).

6) Firms' bids are ranked in increasing order. This will form the supply function, increasing and discontinuous in blocks.

The market price equilibrium in a uniform price auction corresponds to the following rule:

1) all participants are awarded the market price, defined by the marginal unit that equates demand and supply at the highest accepted price (i.e. the SMP).
2) The lowest bidder is awarded all the demand, up to its capacity.
3) The highest bidder serves the residual demand, if any.
4) If firms bid the same price, they will split the demand equally (proportional rationing rule).

We can summarize the above rule for price formation by the equations below:

$$Q_i(D,\ B_i) = \begin{cases} \min\{D,M\} & B_i < B_j \\ \frac{1}{2}\min\{D,M\} + \frac{1}{2}\max\{0,D-M\} & \text{if} \quad B_i = B_j \\ \max\{0,D-M\} & B_i > B_j \end{cases} \qquad (12.22)$$

This is the equation that specifies the quantity attributed to each bidder at the equilibrium.

$$p^* = \begin{cases} B_j & \text{if} \quad B_i < B_j \text{ and } D > M \\ B_i & \text{otherwise} \end{cases}. \qquad (12.23)$$

This is the equation the summarizes the price formation rule, and that gives rise to the System Marginal Price.

### Model Solution

To solve the model, we look for Nash equilibria in the price bids. Consider two cases:

### Low Demand, i.e. D < M.

In this case, either firm can serve the demand (or stated differently, there is excess supply). Therefore, if one competitor bids above marginal cost, the other can undercut to get the whole demand. The bids adjustment stops at $p^* = c$, which corresponds to the outcome of the so-called "Bertrand equilibrium."[11]

We have the following:

---

Result 1

In a uniform price auction with low demand, i.e., $D < M$, the SMP is $p^* = c$.

---

### High Demand, i.e. $D > M$.

In this case, no firm can serve the demand alone. Each firm calculates its own profits taking the action of the others as constant. According to the rules of equilibrium

---

[11] The Bertrand model examines the interdependence between rivals' decisions in terms of pricing decisions, when goods are homogeneous. See Cabral, 2017.

formation, firms optimally find their profit-maximizing strategy by comparing the following profits ($i = a, b, i \neq j$):

$$\pi_i(B_i, B_j, M) = (B_j - c)(D - M) \text{ if } B_i > B_j, \tag{12.24a}$$

$$\pi_i(B_i, B_j, M) = (B_i - c)(D/2) \text{ if } B_i = B_j, \tag{12.24b}$$

$$\pi_i(B_i, B_j, M) = (B_i - c)D \text{ If } B_i < B_j. \tag{12.24c}$$

The profit in (12.24b) is Pareto-dominated by (i.e. lower) than the one in (12.24c), as in this region $D < 2 M$. Thus, each firm would prefer having the other one setting the SMP. Therefore, firm $i$ (respectively firm $j$) has to choose the bid that makes firm $j$ (respectively firm $i$) indifferent between (12.24a) and (12.24c). Notice that (12.24a) and (12.24c) are both increasing with bids, hence each firm has the incentive to bid the price cap as long the competitor bids below it. There are therefore two sets of Nash equilibria[12]:

- firm $a$ bids $B_a \in \left( c, c + (\hat{p} - c)\dfrac{D - M}{M} \right)$, firm $b$ bids the price cap $\hat{p}$;
- firm $b$ bids $B_b \in \left( c, c + (\hat{p} - c)\dfrac{D - M}{M} \right)$, firm $a$ bids the price cap $\hat{p}$.

In either of these equilibria, we have the following:

---

**Result 2**

In a uniform auction with high demand, i.e., $M < D$, the SMP is $p^* = \hat{p}$.

---

For the simple model we have solved here, Results 1 and 2 coincide with the economic dispatching solution of perfectly competitive markets, that we described in Chapter 10. Thus, a perfectly competitive uniform auction provides the same solution as a perfectly competitive market's allocation. This is straightforward: auctions are tools to make explicit and transparent the process of market clearing, thus, they provide the same solution and suffer from the same drawbacks as a centralized market. The simple auction we have defined here can be extended to different cases, such as asymmetric costs and capacities, elastic demand, multi-unit auctions, several bidders, endogenous available capacity (see Fabra et al., 2006 or Crampes and Creti, 2005). The equilibrium pricing outcomes remain similar: either marginal cost, if there is excess capacity, or the price cap, if demand is high and all suppliers are needed to cover it.

Uniform auction models have also been extensively used to compare different auction formats (in particular with respect to pay-as-you-bid, as in Bower and Bunn, 2000, Rassenti et al., 2003), incentives to invest (Fabra et al., 2011), collusion (Dechenaux and Kovenock, 2007). They still constitute a solid economic tool to describe wholesale markets with some degree of realism.

---

[12] More precisely, these are the pure-strategy equilibria.

## Learning Outcomes

- Three types of models are used to describe producers' strategies in the wholesale electricity market, with a specific focus on market power: Cournot, Supply Function Equilibria and Uniform Auction models. They are the most commonly used approaches when assessing competition in empirical approaches.
- The Cournot equilibrium is a vector of price and quantity, which depends on the demand function parameters. In Supply Function equilibria, firms choose an entire supply function, assuming that the supply function of the others remains fixed. Auctions are tools to reach an equilibrium, by submitting bids to the auctioneer. Auctions in electricity markets can be uniform auctions or pay-as-you-bid.
- There are similarities and differences between the three models considered, in terms of hypotheses, equilibrium concepts and firms' strategic behavior.

# 13 Market Power in Electricity Markets

## 13.1 Introduction

As argued in the previous chapter, electricity markets have special characteristics that make them vulnerable to market power. Borenstein and Bushnell (1999, pp. 285–286) summarize these aspects as follows:

"In most markets, there are other constraints that keep a single firm with a fairly small percentage of production from driving up the price by a large amount. If the good is storable, the buyers, or marketers in the middle, can store product to defend against such vulnerability. If end-user consumers receive the price information before buying, their own hesitancy to pay extreme prices discourages the seller from asking such a price. If there is supply elasticity, one firm demanding a high price for its output will just shift market share to another supplier. Each of these attributes is much less prevalent in electricity markets than in most other industries. The result is that the ability of firms with even modest market shares to exercise market power is greater than in most markets."

In assessing the competitiveness of electricity markets, regulators and antitrust authorities, as for instance the Federal Energy Regulatory Commission (FERC), define market power as *the ability to profitably raise prices for sustained periods of time*, for instance several hours if we refer to the wholesale market. As we have seen in Part III, price spikes are quite frequent in electricity markets, but this does not necessarily mean that the marginal firm setting this price is exerting market power: a sudden weather change, unplanned maintenance, network congestion or change in load profile may also explain price jumps. Therefore, understanding whether and how electricity firms affect prices is not an easy task.

Over the period 1996 to 2014, the European Commission has taken twenty-three antitrust enforcement actions in electricity markets to tackle abusive conduct by dominant incumbents; exploitative abuses by dominant incumbents and incentives to set similar prices (collusive behavior). For example, the Commission investigated E.ON's suspected abuse of its dominant position on the German wholesale market in 2008. There were concerns that E.ON may have withdrawn available generation capacity from German wholesale electricity markets (to raise prices), and may have deterred new investors from entering the generation market. The case resulted in a substantial commitment by E.ON to divest 5,000 MW of generation plants along with its extra-high voltage distribution network that structurally changed the German electricity market for the benefit of consumers.

Antitrust enforcement in the electricity sector has also included interventions to prevent restrictions on trade in electricity between EU countries (e.g. the Swedish interconnectors case, 2010). In 2014, the Commission imposed fines totaling €5,979 million on EPEX SPOT and Nord Pool Spot – the two leading European spot power exchanges – for agreeing not to compete with one another.

Many studies of market power and concentration have been carried out in wholesale electricity markets, especially in the United Kingdom and California. A substantial body of evidence has emerged that some plants have exercised market power in the past. In California, although costs increased substantially between the summer of 1998 and the summer of 2000, market power increased even faster, increasing total payments to plants from $1.7 billion in 1998 to over $9 billion in 2000 (Borenstein, 2002; Borenstein et al., 1999).

In general, the concept of market power in electricity markets can be interpreted in two ways:

1. Structural market power, which refers to the ability of a firm to profitably raise the price in an electricity market because of the market's settings, such as the number of firms, the level of demand, the type of product on sale, and similarly, regardless of whether or not firms have effectively taken specific actions to raise the price.
2. Behavioral market power, which refers to the explicit actions taken by firms in order to raise the price.

We discuss here how plants may exert behavioral market power and how to measure it in electricity markets, by using the implication of the competition models summarized in Chapter 12.

## 13.2    Physical Withholding to Exert Market Power

Physical withholding refers to the act of keeping power generation capacity out of the market, particularly during times of high demand. It is possible that by subtracting capacity from the market, firms can create price increases and through this obtain higher profits. Therefore, in a market with capacity constraints, demonstrating the presence of market power requires showing both that the market price is higher than the marginal cost of all the firms in the market and that at least one firm is operating below its capacity. Example 13.1 illustrates this case.

---

**Example 13.1 Physical Capacity Withholding in a Market with Four Power Plants**
Assume there is a market in which there are the four power plants, whose capacity and costs are as follows:

- Plant A, has a capacity constraint at 10 MWh and a constant marginal cost of $10/MWh.
- Plant B, has a capacity constraint at 20 MW and a constant marginal cost of $20/MWh.

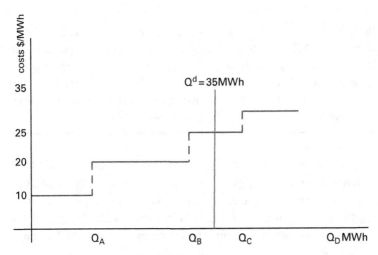

**Figure 13.1**  Wholesale market with four plants

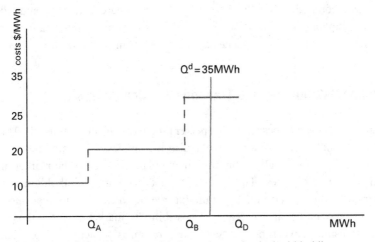

**Figure 13.2**  Wholesale market with three plants: physical withholding

- Plant C has a capacity constraint at 25 MW and a constant marginal cost of $25/MWh.
- Plant D has a capacity constraint at 10 MW and a constant marginal cost of $35/MWh.

There are no fixed costs. The load in the market is 35 MWh, as shown in Figure 13.1.

If the four power plants belong to separate companies that behave competitively and each of them makes supply offers to the market at its own marginal costs, the System Marginal Price (SMP) will be $25/MWh. Now, suppose there is a firm owning plants A and C. Under the scenario shown in the figure, this firm would earn profits of ($25/MWh – $10/MWh) · 10 MWh = $250 on Plant A and no profit on Plant C, which is the marginal supplier in this market. But suppose that the firm decides to remove plant C from the market, and thus does not submit a supply offer for it at all. The physical withholding of plant C would result in the System Marginal Price increasing to $35/MWh, as shown in Figure 13.2.

Following the withholding of plant C, profits accruing from plant A would be ($35/MWh – $10/MWh) · 10 MWh = $350. Plant C does not produce, but removing that plant from the market results in additional profits for the company that owns both plants A and C. By withholding plant C, its owner has both the incentive and the ability to exert market power. Notice that we have assumed that firms bid at their true marginal cost, so we could say that they still behave competitively.

Crampes and Cretì (2005) model the situation described in Example 13.1 in a strategic game, and find that profitable capacity withholding, leading to the possibility of exerting market power, is most likely to arise in off-peak hours, when the potential gains from effecting the market prices are highest. In this case, withholding will avoid SMP at marginal cost of the marginal plant and create the opportunity for the price cap to become the SMP.

This example shows that, in order to measure market power, several factors must be taken into account: the number of firms, their market share, their costs and bids, and the SMP. We explain in the next section how information on these parameters is used effectively to measure the presence and the extent of market power.

## 13.3    Economic Withholding and Transmission Constraints

Example 13.1 showed a case in which power producers do not submit bids. This is called physical withholding, in order to distinguish it from cases in which power plants can affect prices by strategically submitting manipulative offers to the market, in order to artificially increase prices. The latter is termed economic withholding, since plants might remain dispatched but, by saturating the network capacity, can insulate some segment of the market and increase the possibility to market power in those segments. The relationship between power generation, transmission network, electricity pricing and market power will be further developed in Part V. However, we introduce in the example below a simple case showing how the transmission constraint might be used strategically to enforce market power.[1]

**Example 13.2 Economic Withholding in a Two-Nodes System** Consider the two-nodes network in the figure below. The marginal cost of plant 1 is $10/MWh and the marginal cost of plant 2 is $20/MWh. We ignore fixed costs. The demand is located for simplicity just at Node 2, and is given by $P = 200 - (Q_1 + Q_2)$. There is a 50 MW limit on the transmission line.

Under perfect competition, the price at Node 1 is $10/MWh, while the price at Node 2 is $20/MWh. Plant 1 will produce 50 MWh (saturating the transmission line, as demand

---

[1] In Part V we will further develop the concept of nodal prices that we apply schematically in this example.

is located at Node 2), while plant 2 produces 130 MWh, since at $P = 20$, with $Q_1=50$, $Q_2=130$. The total demand served is 180 MWh. However, there is no reason for plant 2 to submit a competitive offer. Plant 2 can immediately see that, since only 50 MW can be transferred across the transmission line, it has a monopoly on serving any level of demand higher than 50 MWh, which is its residual demand. This monopoly power results specifically from the low capacity of the transmission line. If the capacity of the transmission line were to be increased, this would erode some of the market power possessed by plant 2. The residual demand curve is: $PQ_2 = 150Q_2 - (Q_2)^2$. Plant 2, being a monopolist on it, sets the quantity at which marginal revenue equal marginal costs. Revenues are $PQ_2 = 150Q_2 - (Q_2)^2$. The monopolistic quantity at node 2 is $Q_2 = 65$ MWh, with a corresponding price of \$85/MWh. At node one, we have assumed for simplicity that plant 1 behaves competitively, so total consumption is 135 MWh. This is the typical monopolist distortion, in that prices are higher and quantities are lower relative to the competitive market outcome.

## 13.4 Detecting and Measuring Market Power

Different metrics can be used empirically to appraise market power. A first set of measures, called concentration measures, refers to the preconditions that make market power more likely to be exercised. Thus, concentration measures look at the structure of the sector. Other indexes of market power are either linked to the price-cost margins and market shares, or the relationship between residual demand and individual market share. Let us start with concentration measures.

### 13.4.1 Measures of Concentration

In order to measure concentration, it is possible to measure either the number of firms, or the concentration ratio. The latter is given by the coefficient $CR_m$, which measures the sum of the market shares of the $m$ biggest firms. The number of firms is a very rough indicator of market power, since it does not say anything about the relative market share of each of them. Therefore, it is preferable to use a concentration ratio. There are several concentration ratios, depending on $m$. For each of them, a threshold has to be identified beyond which an industry can be said to be concentrated. It is common to use $CR_4$, and assume a threshold of 50 percent. Thus, a $CR_4$ greater than 50 percent would be regarded as evidence of a concentrated industry. This is, for example, the case for the wholesale markets of most European countries (DG Energy, 2016). Measures of concentration are insensitive to the symmetry between firms, which are an important feature of oligopoly models. According to the properties of the Cournot model, if firms have the same marginal cost, they will have an equal market share. If a firm is more efficient, it will have a bigger market share than the others.

The indicators of market share cannot take into account these characteristics of market outcomes. This can lead to similar measures, which have very different underlying distribution of market shares, and possibly competition. For instance, in a market there can be eight equal firms, each having a market share of 12.5 percent, or a situation in which there is one large firm having 41 percent of the market, and nineteen other equal firms with an equal market share of 3.1 percent each. In both cases,[2] $CR_4$ is 50, but with a very different market structure.

### 13.4.2     Measures of Market Power

The main indicators of market power that can be used for power markets are the Lerner Index, the Herfindahl-Hirschmann Index, the Pivotal index and the Residual Supply Index.

**Lerner Index.**

The model of Cournot competition allows some simple metrics of market power. Recall that the individual Lerner index is:

$$L_i = \frac{p - C_i'(Q_i)}{p} = \frac{1}{\eta} \, s_i, \qquad (13.1)$$

Where $s_i$ is firm $i$'s market share, i.e.: $s_i = Q_i/Q$ . See that the following properties hold true:

- $L_i > 0$ means that the plant can charge a price above its marginal cost;
- The lower the number of firms, the higher the individual market share $s_i$, the higher $L_i$ and so the higher distortion with respect to perfect competition.

In the Example 13.2, the Lerner Index for plant 1, that prices competitively, is ($10 − $10)/$10 = 0. The Lerner Index for plant 2 is ($85 − $20)/$85 = 0.76, which denotes the existence of market power.

From the individual Lerner index, it is possible to construct the aggregate or sectorial Lerner index, by taking the average of $L_i$ calculated with respect of the weight that each firm has in the market (i.e. its market share):

$$L = \sum_{1}^{n} s_i L_i. \qquad (13.2)$$

In Example 13.2, the industry Lerner index would be $L = 0 − 57 \times 0.76 = 0.43$.

**The Herfindahl-Hirschmann Index (HHI).**

The Herfindahl-Hirschmann Index is defined as the sum of the square of the market shares of $n$ firms in a given sector:

$$HHI = \sum_{1}^{n} (s_i)^2. \qquad (13.3)$$

---

[2] In the second case $CR_4$ has been rounded.

It is common to use market shares expressed as percentage terms in order to calculate HHI, or, alternatively, to multiply it by 10,000. The Antitrust Division of the Department of Justice (DOJ) in the United States uses the following levels:

- HHI < 1,000: non-concentrated industry;
- between 1,000 and 1,800: low-concentrated industry;
- 1,800: concentrated industry.

Assuming that firms compete in quantities, as in the Cournot model, it is possible to relate the HHI to the industry Lerner Index. Recall the definition of the industry (or sectorial) Lerner index presented in Equation (13.2). Substituting in it the definition of the individual Lerner index calculated in Equation (12.8), we have the following relationship:

$$L = \frac{(s_i)^2}{\eta} = \frac{HHI}{\eta}. \tag{13.4}$$

In the words of Borenstein et al. (1995, p. 232):

Cournot competition does not fully describe the options available to firms in an electricity market. Plants are not forced to bid quantities in a spot market, but are, in fact, free to bid any supply curve, with a quantity bid corresponding to the special case of a vertical supply curve. However, an estimate of a static Cournot equilibrium of the electricity market would still provide a rough estimate of competitive behavior if firms face little demand uncertainty. When there is no uncertainty, it turns out that of the many Nash equilibria that are possible, the one produced by quantity bids (the Cournot strategy) is the most profitable. Thus, if there were no uncertainty and cost data were available, an estimate of the price-cost margin from the Cournot model could take the place of a structural index such as an HHI calculation.

For example, Cardell et al. (1997), using 1994 data, calculate HHI values for 112 regions based on State boundaries and North American Electric Reliability Council (NERC) sub-regions. At that time, approximately 90 percent of these regions had HHI values above 2,500.

However, using the HHI to assess market concentration, in power markets can produce misleading results. In these markets, as we have seen, plants typically have capacity constraints. This implies that different market structures can yield different HHIs, but this might not affect the equilibrium pricing. Consider the following example of a power system with a mix of two technologies:

---

**Example 13.3  A Power Market with Different HHIs and the Same SMPs** Suppose that in the electricity markets there are two technologies, a baseload one (e.g. a nuclear power plant), and a peaker (e.g. a fossil-fuel one). Let us consider first the case in which there is a single baseload producer: The nuclear producer has a capacity constraint of 40 GW, and a marginal cost $c_1$; the fossil-fuel producer has a capacity constraint of 60 GW, with a marginal cost $c_2 > c_1$; we leave out fixed costs for the sake of simplicity. There is a fixed load of 50 GW. The system marginal price (SMP) will be $p = c_2$. Plant 1 has a market share of 40GW/50GW = 0.8, and plant 2 of 10GW/50GW = 0.2. So the HHI is 6,800. Suppose now that there are two nuclear producers, of 20 GW each. Each nuclear power plant has a 40 percent market share, with the fossil fuel one having the remaining 20 percent. The HHI is $(40)^2 + (40)^2 + (20)^2 = 3600$. Still the equilibrium price has not changed.

---

Example 13.3 shows that the relationship between market structure (HHI) and market power, as measured for instance by the Lerner index, is not linear, due to the impact of capacity constraints on market outcomes. In order to overcome this problem, in the electricity sector an HHI adjusted by the capacity constraints can be used (OECD, 2003). Suppose that there are $m$ capacity constrained firms whose market share is denoted by $\bar{s}$.

By definition $\sum_1^n s_i + \bar{s} = 1$. By multiplying the RHS of Equation (12.8) by $(s_i + \bar{s}/n)$, and summing up over $i$ ($i=1 \ldots n$) we get

$$\sum_1^n \left(s_i + \frac{\bar{s}}{n}\right) \frac{p - C_i'(Q_i)}{p} = \frac{HHI^{adj}}{\eta}; \tag{13.5}$$

where

$$HHI^{\,adj} = \sum_1^n s_i \left(s_i + \frac{\bar{s}}{n}\right). \tag{13.6}$$

Notice that if there is only one firm unconstrained, the adjusted HHI of the market is then simply equal to the market share of that firm, since the market shares of the other firms are irrelevant.

## The Pivotal Supplier Index

The Pivotal Supplier Index (PSI), proposed by Borenstein et al. (1999), is an attempt to incorporate the concept of marginal supplier into the empirical analysis and the measurement of market power in electricity markets, including demand conditions. This indicator examines whether a given producer or power plant is "pivotal" or necessary in serving demand at a given point in time, in the sense that absent this plant, load would have to be shed. The PSI can be defined as the ratio of all the hours (or different units of times) in which the plant is pivotal over a given period. For instance, if the period is a year and the unit of time is hours, the PSI of plant $i$ is:

$$PSI_i = \sum_{j=1}^{8760} I \left( Q^{dj} - \sum_{\substack{f=1, \\ f \neq i}}^{n} Q_f^{max} \right) / 8760 \tag{13.7}$$

Where $Q^{dj}$ denotes the load of hour $j$ and $I(\cdot)$ is the indicator function. While the *HHI* is a measure of overall market concentration, the pivotal supplier index is a measure of the concentration of the system capacity surplus, that is, the possibility of matching total system supply and demand at any particular time period. Example 13.4 shows how to apply the PSI index of Equation (13.7).

**Example 13.4 The Pivotal Supplier Index** Suppose there are two plants, with the following capacity installed (and available): $Q_1 = 450MW$; $Q_2 = 550MW$. Assume that in hour 1 the load is $Q^{d1} = 400$ MW. No plant is pivotal in that hour. Now suppose that in hour 2 the load is $Q^{d2} = 500$. Also in hour 2, plant 1 is not pivotal. However, in hour 2, plant 2 becomes pivotal: $PSI_2 = 1$, since, if plant 2 withheld its entire quantity, plant 1 would not have enough capacity to serve the entire load (thus 50 MW would have to be shed). Then $PSI_2$ in the overall period would be $\frac{1}{2} = 0.5$ (i.e. plant 2 has been pivotal for 50 percent of the time, while $PSI_1 = 0$, i.e. plant 1 has never been pivotal).

The ability of this index to represent situations of market power may also be limited. There can be situations in which no plant is pivotal, and plants can still control the price. Consider the following example:

**Example 13.5 Market Power with Zero PSI** Suppose a system has the following capacities and load:

- 25 GW of power provided by equal CCGT plants, whose marginal costs is $40/MWh,
- A very large number of small, equal suppliers, whose total capacity amounts to 30 GW, that are less efficient than the CCGT. Their marginal cost is $100/MWh,
- demand of 20 GW.

There would be no pivotal plants. This is true regardless of the number of CCGT plants, since the other less efficient plants can always cover the load. However, if there were fewer than five CCGT plants, each of them could exert market power by withholding capacity and controlling the price. Suppose there are four CCGT plants. They could form a cartel, by entering into the following agreement: they would rotate in entirely withholding the capacity of each of them every fourth hour: in hour 1, CCGT plant 1 would withhold its capacity, in hour 2 CCGT plant 2 would do so, etc., up to hour 5 in which plant 1 restarts withholding capacity, and so on. By doing so, they could always set the price at $100/MWh, and benefit from extra profits equal to $(100 - 40) \times 3 = \$180/MWH$ every four hours. Still, the PSI would be zero.

## Residual Supplier index

The pivotal index is a binary variable, taking the values zero or one. It measures just whether there are other plants that can serve the load, but not by how much a plant is pivotal, in the event that it is so. This can be done, by measuring the ratio of the load that has to be shed if a pivotal player withheld the capacity. This is called Residual Supplier Index *(RSI)*:

$$RSI_i = \sum_{\substack{f=1, \\ f \neq i}}^{n} Q_f^{max}/Q^{dj}. \tag{13.8}$$

The RSI measures if in a given hour, the plant is pivotal, and if so, by how much. See that if in hour $j$ plant $i$ is not pivotal, $RSI_i > 1$, meaning that the plant can be replaced because the supply capabilities of all other suppliers are sufficient to meet demand. If on the contrary, plant $i$ is pivotal, $RSI_i < 1$. The smaller the RSI, the greater the load that has to be shed, which implies that plant $i$ has a higher market power. From a practical perspective, for example, both the FERC and the EC Competition Commission consider that if a plant displays an RSI below 1.1 (or 110 percent), more than 5 percent of the time, there is too little competition.[3]

Still, these indexes should be used with caution. In Example 13.8, for instance, with four CCGT forming a cartel, the price would be 100, while the RSI of each CCGT would be = (30+18,75)/20 = 2,43, well above 1.

In both the PSI and the RSI, the examples show that these indexes cannot accurately represent situations of market power that arise because of the behavior of the agents rather than the structure of the market. The former can be seen, observing how producers operate in the market (i.e. their bids).

## 13.4.3    Inferring Market Power by Bids

In a market with uncertain demand, the situation is different. A producer will face many possible demand levels, even when it knows its competitors' production levels. Firms then engage in supply curve competition, discussed in Chapter 12 under the Supply Function Equilibrium framework. As we have seen, in the SFE model, firms undertake a supply curve competition. Suppliers are not bidding simple quantities as specified by the Cournot model but entire supply curves, leading to a continuum of equilibria in between Bertrand equilibrium (marginal cost pricing) and Cournot equilibrium. The introduction of demand uncertainty could therefore mitigate the effects of market power.

Twomey et al. (2006) point out that under the supply curve competition other, more sophisticated methods of measuring market power exist. They consist in simulating electricity markets, estimating with complex econometric techniques bid-cost margins and firms' strategies, as predicted by the Supply Function Equilibrium model. Green and Newbery (1992), Lucas and Taylor (1993), von der Fehr and Harbord (1995), Wolak and Patrick (1996), Borenstein and Bushnell (1999) and Borenstein et al. (1999) have followed this strand of research. The common factor of these studies is to analyze

---

[3] See that the threshold is set at a value higher than 1 since it includes a 10 percent security margin on the available capacity. This is done to take into account possible random increases of the load or reductions of available capacity.

firms' strategies enforcing market power, as well as measuring the impact on consumers of such non-competitive behaviors.[4]

## Learning Outcomes

- Despite the disparities in the methods and indexes, there is enough evidence that electricity markets are prone to market power, even if it is not always easy to distinguish price spikes that emerge naturally from Load Shedding from high prices due to exertion of market power.
- There are several measures of market power: Concentration ratios, Lerner indexes, HHI, Pivotal Supplier Index, Residual Supplier index.
- Concentration indexes refer to the market share of the first $m$ firms in the market. The individual Lerner index measures the price-cost margin of a given plant. The Industry Lerner index measures the weighted average of the individual Lerner indexes of all market participants. The HHI measures the dispersion of market shares across market participants. The Pivotal Supplier index measures whether a supplier is necessary, in order to avoid having to shed the load. The Residual Supplier Index adds to the Pivotal index the measure of by how much a given producer is necessary.
- A correct assessment of market power in the electricity market must be performed by using several indexes and measurement tools, as all these approaches are complementary.

---

[4] Excellent surveys on studies about market power in the United Kingdom and California can be found in OCDE (2003) and DOE (2000).

# Part V

# Introducing Transmission Networks: Network Congestion and Electricity Import-Export

In Part III, we analyzed the market setting of the electricity system under the simplifying assumptions that there is no network, and load and production are directly linked. Clearly, this is a simplifying assumption. As explained, the high voltage electricity network is the backbone of the electricity system, and its nature and development have determined the way electricity systems and markets are designed and operate. Network systems are thus extremely important, in terms of both their physical extensions and their economic values. For instance, in Europe, ENTSO-E regroups 312,693 km of high-voltage lines (ENTSO-E, 2015). As ENTSO-E states, "if laid, out, these lines would circle the earth circumference more than 7 times." The economic value of these lines is of considerable importance. At the beginning of 2016, the share of the network component in electricity pricing for households spanned from 65 percent in Sweden to 15 percent in Malta (Eurostat Energy Data, 2017) and generally a few percentage points less for industrial consumers.

Part V focuses on the economic analysis of power transmission and its coordination with electricity markets. We start by setting a simple model where production and consumption are connected by a single line (Chapter 14) and explain network pricing. In Chapter 15, we then introduce externalities due to Kirchhoff's laws in more complex networks. Transmission facilities are used by all firms competing in the electricity market. Therefore, granting non-discriminatory third-party access to transmission is the most important and necessary condition for any liberalized and competitive electricity market to be established and work properly. In such a setup, where the transmission segment remains organized as a regulated monopoly, it becomes crucial to fix the prices to use the existing network in the proper way. Chapter 16 details network pricing in practice and shows the different options that have been taken in several countries.

In Chapter 17 we move to transmission capacity expansion, investigating the optimal value of investment in the grid and the incentives to invest.

In Chapter 18 we introduce market instruments that can be used in order to manage transmission capacity, namely, transmission rights. We discuss these, and show how they can be used to hedge against price risks due to congestion.

# 14 Electricity Transmission: Basic Principles

## 14.1 Introduction

In this chapter, we extend the analysis of Part III by introducing the grid into the economic analysis of electricity markets. We start from a simplified two-nodes transportation network which links production and consumption. We also assume, for simplicity, that generators operate in a perfectly competitive environment. The network is represented as an independent operator, the System Operator (SO), under the crucial assumption that it has no role in electricity production. Under these hypotheses, producers will be remunerated by the SMP, as shown in Chapter 10.

What is the right price of the transmission network? The nodal pricing model has been developed, in order to answer this question (Caramanis et al., 1982; Bohn et al., 1984; Bohn et al., 1988; Schweppe et al., 2013; Joskow and Tirole, 2000). Nodal pricing works through the Direct Current Optimal Power Flow (DC-OPF) model. In this model, a given network is replicated, treating power lines as if they were Direct Current lines, and the cost minimization problem is solved assuming linear constraints due to Kirchhoff's laws. As before, the cost-minimization problem coincides with welfare maximization, providing the optimal dispatching solution that guarantees the efficient operation of the electricity system. This is the framework to which we refer. We assume that generation capacity is given, and is large enough not to induce any load shedding. Thus, the solution to the optimal dispatching provides short-term network pricing, for given transmission capacity, under the hypotheses that there are neither market distortions (such as imperfect information or market power), nor capacity constraints on the generation side.

## 14.2 Optimal Dispatching with Transmission Constraints and Nodal Prices

The economic analysis of natural monopoly explains how network services should be priced (see Chapter 6). Networks generally exhibit economies of scale, which means that when a single SO builds and operates the infrastructure the total cost of the infrastructure is lower than if there were several networks, which would increase the costs of the service.

Nodal prices are the prices that enable the attainment of the welfare-maximizing solution of the dispatching power problem in the network, in a decentralized way. The optimal dispatching of a system is the net quantity that should be injected and withdrawn at each node in order to maximize social welfare, for a given load and the technical, economic and locational features of power generation and transmission.

Thus, optimal dispatch represents the allocation that would be decided by a benevolent and perfectly informed SO exclusively concerned with the efficiency of the system, but untouched by any distributional concern. In other words, it is assumed that the SO does not own any power plant and does not care about the consequences in terms of prices that arise for load and power producers, as a solution to the OPF problem.

To calculate network pricing, it is necessary first to provide a synthetic description of the network configuration, given that for nodal prices it is crucial to specify where power is introduced or withdrawn from the system (i.e. at which node plants and consumers are located). Therefore, the underlying assumption is that all plants at the same node are paid the local uniform price, associated to that node; the same is true for the load. We start by the simplest case, namely, there is a single plant and a single load, in the simplest possible network configuration. We describe a simple radial configuration, where only one line connects consumers to producers. Then we introduce different power plants characterized by asymmetric costs. Finally, we consider line losses.

## 14.2.1   Case 1: A Single Power Plant

We shall use here the same framework as in Chapter 8, and in particular the one used in Paragraph 8.4, which makes explicit the link between utility maximization and cost minimization, written in terms of energy; recall, however, that for a given unit of time (the hour) energy and capacity coincide. We assume that there is just one consumer. We ignore the superscript $m$ denoting different consumers, but use the superscript $d$ to help to distinguish the load $Q^d$ from production. We start from the simplest case in which there is just one plant $i$. The plant and consumers are located at two different nodes. For the sake of simplicity, we ignore the case of production capacity constraint. The crucial point here is that there is a production node and a consumption node and one transmission line that links production to load. The transmission line sets the constraint that the load must take into account. What follows summarizes the hypotheses and the framework:

### Hypotheses

- The Electricity plant $i$ is characterized by the following simplified linear cost function: $C_i(Q_i) = c_i Q_i + FC_i$ . For simplicity, we shall focus on short-run analysis, and neglect fixed costs, setting $FC_i = 0$.
- There are no production capacity constraints.
- The Consumer is represented by the utility function $U(Q^d)$, with $U'(\cdot) > c > 0$.
- The usual load-balance constraint deriving from the Kirchhoff's laws applies: $Q^d = Q_i$.

- The transportation line has a capacity such that, at a given time, at most $K^{max}$ MWh can flow.[1] Kirchhoff's laws imply the following constraint: $Q_i \leq K^{max}$.
- There are no physical losses due to the electricity flow.

To obtain network pricing, we proceed by maximizing social welfare. The first-best solution gives the optimal quantities to be produced. Network pricing implements the first-best solution. The social planner maximizes:

$$\max_{Q^d, Q_i} U(Q^d) - C_1(Q_i), \text{ s.t. } a) \ Q^d = Q_i; \ b) \ Q_i \leq K^{max}; \ c) \ Q_i \geq 0. \tag{14.1}$$

The first and third constraints are the usual load-balance and positive supply constraint. The second constraint refers to the transmission line, which can operate at its full capacity or not. If it operates at full capacity, we shall say that the line is congested.

The Lagrange Equation is as follows:

$$\mathcal{L} = U(Q^d) - c_i Q_i + \lambda(Q_i - Q^d) + \chi(K^{max} - Q_i) + \mu Q_i. \tag{14.2}$$

The Kuhn-Tucker conditions at the equilibrium are:

$$\frac{\partial \mathcal{L}}{\partial Q^d} = 0 \rightarrow U'(\cdot) = \lambda;$$

$$\frac{\partial \mathcal{L}}{\partial Q_i} = 0 \rightarrow c_i + \chi - \mu = \lambda; \tag{14.3}$$

and the slackness conditions:

$$\mu Q_i = 0, \ Q_i \geq 0, \mu \geq 0; \tag{14.4}$$

$$\chi(K^{max} - Q_i) = 0, \ Q_i \leq K^{max}, \chi \geq 0. \tag{14.5}$$

Equation (14.3) provides the solution of the optimal power flow problem. For an internal solution, $Q_i > 0$, thus $\mu = 0$. However, it is possible that the transmission line is congested or not. Thus, there are two possible pricing solutions:

If there is no congestion, $K^{max} > Q_i$ and $\chi = 0$. Thus, the equilibrium price is reached at that level of production where $U'(Q^*) = c_i$. It follows that the equilibrium price coincides with the marginal cost (of the marginal plant), as is the case for any competitively supplied commodity.

If there is congestion, $K^{max} = Q_i$ and $\chi > 0$. Thus, the equilibrium price is reached at that level of production where $U'(Q^*) = c_i + \chi$. See that now the Lagrange multiplier $\chi$ is positive, signaling the value of the network whose capacity is saturated. In fact, from Equation (14.2) it is clear that $\chi = \dfrac{\partial \mathcal{L}}{\partial K^{max}}$. The multiplier $\chi$ represents the shadow value of the transmission constraint, from a social perspective: its value is the increase in utility due to a marginal rise in the transmission capacity, which clearly is positive only if

---

[1] Notice that transportation capacity is generally defined in MW. In a given time unit, typically an hour, it is measured in MWh.

the line is congested. Therefore, $\chi$ represents the value of the transmission line. Nodal pricing can be summarized as follows:

---

**Result**

When there is no congestion on the transmission line, the equilibrium price coincides with the marginal cost (of the marginal plant).

When there is congestion on the transmission line the equilibrium price is above the marginal cost, and also includes the value of the transmission line.

---

This result coincides with that for economic dispatching in competitive market presented in Chapter 10 without transmission lines. Indeed, when the line is not congested, it does not constrain the optimal allocation of power across plants. An important consequence of this can be summarized as follows:

---

**Result**

When a transmission line is not congested, it has no economic value.

---

Figure 14.1 illustrates the optimal solution without (panel a) and with congestion (panel b), under assumption of a decreasing linear utility function.

### 14.2.2    Case 2: Asymmetric Plants, Located at Different Nodes

With respect to the previous case, we now allow for the existence of two production plants. We assume that there is an efficient producer located at node 1. Its marginal production cost is below that of the inefficient plant located near consumers, denoted by subscript 2: $C'_1(Q_1) = c_1 < c_2 = C'_2(Q_2)$. See that now, the subscript denotes both the

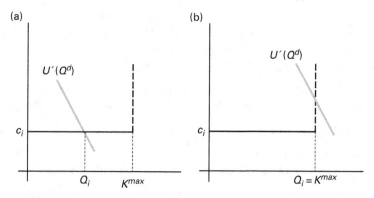

**Figure 14.1** An example of equilibrium with a non-congested (panel a) and a congested (panel b) transmission line

plant and the node at which the plant is operating. As in the previous case, the optimal dispatching is obtained by welfare maximization, under the load-balance, transmission and positivity constraints.

$$\max_{Q^d,Q_1,Q_2} U(Q^d) - c_1 Q_1 - c_2 Q_2, \text{s.t. } a)\ Q^d = Q_1 + Q_2;$$

$$b)\ Q_1 \leq K^{max};\ c)\ Q_i \geq 0, i = 1, 2. \tag{14.6}$$

The Lagrange Equation is as follows:

$$\mathcal{L} = U(Q^d) - c_1 Q_1 - c_2 Q_2 + \lambda(Q_1 + Q_2 - Q^d) + \chi(K^{max} - Q_1)$$
$$+ \mu_1 Q_1 + \mu_2 Q_2. \tag{14.7}$$

The Kuhn-Tucker and slackness conditions are as follows:

$$\frac{\partial \mathcal{L}}{\partial Q^d} = 0 \rightarrow U'(\cdot) = \lambda; \tag{14.8}$$

$$\frac{\partial \mathcal{L}}{\partial Q_1} = 0 \rightarrow c_1 + \chi - \mu_1 = \lambda; \tag{14.9}$$

$$\frac{\partial \mathcal{L}}{\partial Q_2} = 0 \rightarrow c_2 - \mu_2 = \lambda; \tag{14.10}$$

$$\mu_i Q_i = 0;\ Q_i \geq 0;\ \mu_i \geq 0; i = 1, 2; \tag{14.11}$$

$$\chi(K^{max} - Q_1) = 0;\ Q_1 \leq K^{max}; \chi \geq 0. \tag{14.12}$$

Equations (14.8) to (14.12) allow us to derive some useful properties of the optimal dispatch model with transmission constraints:

---

**Result**

Both power producers are active at the equilibrium if the line is constrained (necessary condition).

---

The result can be easily proved. If both $Q_1 > 0$, $Q_2 > 0$, then $\mu_1 = \mu_1 = 0$, by the slackness conditions (14.11). By equating the Kuhn-Tucker conditions, we get $\chi = c_2 - c_1 > 0$, therefore $Q_1 = K^{max}$.

---

**Result**

If there is excess transmission capacity, the inefficient plant is not dispatched (sufficient condition).

---

First-order conditions of the constrained maximization problem together with the slackness conditions prove the previous result. Excess transmission capacity implies

$Q_1 < K^{max}$, which in turn means $\chi = 0$. Therefore, by equalizing the two first-order conditions (14.9) and (14.10), we get: $c_2 - c_1 = \mu_2 - \mu_1$. See that : $c_2 - c_1 > 0$. Now, we have three cases: i) $\mu_1 > 0, \mu_2 > 0$: it is ruled out since we focus on interior solutions; ii) $\mu_1 > 0$, $\mu_2 = 0$, impossible given the non-negativity constraint of multipliers; iii) $\mu_1 = 0, \mu_2 > 0$, it implies $Q_1 > 0, Q_2 = 0$.

From the previous results, we have:

---

**Result**

When both plants are active and there are asymmetric production costs, the transmission lines between the two plants have a positive social marginal value.

---

The result immediately follows from the previous ones, considering that the positive social marginal value of the transmission line is measured by $\chi$, which is the value of the marginal increase in the transmission line.

Nodal prices are calculated as prices that maximize welfare. The most efficient plant should serve consumers as long as there is no congestion and the demand is sufficiently low. Line congestion implies a price above marginal cost of the efficient producer. When we consider the possible levels of load, we see that there are three possible situations depending on the relative balance between demand and supply: no congestion, relative congestion and absolute congestion.

- *No congestion*: electricity demand is below the transmission capacity of the line. In this case only the efficient plant will be dispatched at $U'(\cdot) = Q_1 < L^{max}$. The nodal price coincides with the marginal cost $p = c_1$.
- *Relative congestion*: similarly to the previous case, but the production of the efficient plant saturated the line $Q_1 = K^{max}$. The nodal price is $p = c_1 + \chi$. The shadow value of the transmission constraint here is positive: $\chi = U'(K^{max}) - c_1$.
- *Absolute congestion*: the inefficient plant is called into operation to serve the load above the production of the efficient one, which is constrained by the line capacity. One can also interpret this situation by saying that the consumption nodes require electricity from the inefficient plant that complements the import of more efficient production. The nodal price is aligned to the marginal cost of the inefficient plant: $p = c_2$. The shadow value of the transmission constraint is $\chi = c_2 - c_1$.

See that when there is absolute congestion, the value of the transmission line is equal to the differential between the marginal cost of the two interconnected nodes. Since the analysis assumes that the network configuration is given (i.e. it is a short-run one), nodal pricing is also called Short Run Marginal Cost (SRMC).

Figures 14.2 illustrates these three cases.

In panel (a) of Figure 14.2 we can see that the intercept between the demand function, namely, the load, and the marginal production cost of plant 1 corresponds to an equilibrium quantity $Q_1$ below the line capacity constraint. In panel (b), electricity consumed is exactly equal to the line capacity, whereas in panel (c) the inefficient

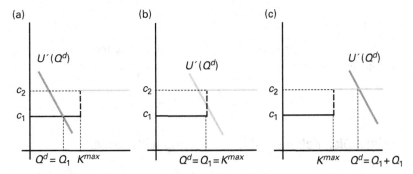

**Figure 14.2** Equilibrium with no congestion (panel a), partial congestion (panel b) and absolute congestion (panel c)

plant 2 provides the complement to what can be produced by the efficient plant 1, which cannot transfer more than the line capacity constraint $K^{max}$.

## 14.3    Transmission Constraints and Line Losses

Electricity transmission is constrained not only be line capacity, but also from the physical laws regarding power transmission and power losses. Recall that, as explained in Chapter 2, when electrons flow, there is an energy loss in the form of unused energy, namely, heating, which is (roughly) proportional to the line resistance.[2] Considering the main parts of a typical transmission and distribution network, the average values of power losses at the different steps can be calculated as follows:

1–2 percent – Step-up transformer from generator to Transmission line;
2–4 percent – Transmission line;
1–2 percent – Step-down transformer from Transmission line to Distribution network;
4–6 percent – Distribution network transformers and cables.

The overall losses between the power plant and consumers are then in a range between 8 and 15 percent. For instance, the U.S. Energy Information Administration estimates that electricity transmission and distribution losses average about 5 percent of the electricity that is transmitted and distributed annually in the United States.[3]

Transmission losses can be modeled as differences between production and consumption. Let us consider here how losses can be modeled and impact nodal pricing. Focusing on the impact of line losses, we assume that there is no transmission constraint. In a simplified scheme, that neglects external factors, voltages, and so on, losses can be represented by the following equation:

---

[2] For the sake of simplicity, in this book we use "resistance" as a general term, even though in AC circuits the proper concept is impedance.
[3] *Source*: EIA, www.eia.gov/tools/faqs/faq.php?id=105&t=3.

$$L(Q^d) = h(R)Q_i^2; \tag{14.13}$$

where R is the line resistance, with $h'(R) > 0$. Notice that marginal losses $L'(\cdot)$ and average losses $L_M$ are proportional:

$$L'(Q^d) = 2h(R)Q_i = 2L_M. \tag{14.14}$$

## 14.4     Optimal Dispatching and Nodal Pricing with Losses

Due to the losses, electricity consumption is below electricity generation:

$$Q^d = Q_i - L(Q^d). \tag{14.15}$$

We focus on losses for simplicity, thus neglect the quantity and transmission capacity constraint. The welfare maximization problem (14.1) becomes:

$$\max_{Q^d, Q_i} U(Q^d) - C(Q_i) \text{ , s.t. } Q^d = Q_i - h(R)Q_i^2. \tag{14.16}$$

See that now the load-balance constraint includes losses, given by Equation (14.13). The Lagrange Equation is:

$$\mathcal{L} = U(Q^d) - c_i Q_i + \lambda \left( Q_i - h(R)Q_i^2 - Q^d \right). \tag{14.17}$$

Solving it, we have the following F.O.Cs:

$$\frac{\partial \mathcal{L}}{\partial Q^d} = 0 \rightarrow U'(\cdot) = \lambda;$$

$$\frac{\partial \mathcal{L}}{\partial Q_i} = 0 \rightarrow c_i = \lambda \left( 1 - 2h(R)Q_i \right); \tag{14.18}$$

which can be simplified as:

$$U'(\cdot) = c_i \left( \frac{1}{\left( 1 - 2\frac{L(\cdot)}{Q_i} \right)} \right); \tag{14.19}$$

where we have made use of the following relation: $2h(R)Q_i = 2h(R)\frac{Q_i^2}{Q_i} = 2\frac{L(Q^d)}{Q_i}$. Notice that the average line losses are an increasing function of electricity generation. In terms of nodal pricing, we get:

$$p = \frac{c_i}{\left( 1 - 2\frac{L(\cdot)}{Q_i} \right)}; \tag{14.20}$$

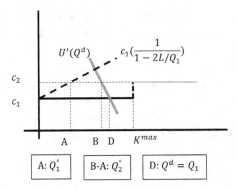

**Figure 14.3** Inefficient dispatching due to transmission losses

The presence of losses alters the optimal dispatching of Power plants. Let us consider, as an example, the case represented in panel (a) of Figure 14.2, assuming that now there are losses $L(Q^d)$ when importing energy in node 2. This is described in Figure 14.3. Equation (14.19) shows that the marginal cost of the energy imported in node 2 now becomes an increasing function of the quantity imported, due to the losses which are proportional to the quantity imported. Let us describe the equilibrium with losses with a superscript °. Figure 14.3 shows the new equilibrium and compares with the equilibrium without losses, point D in the figure. The existence of losses implies that beyond $Q_1^\circ$ it becomes optimal using plant 2 in node 2 in order to serve the load, instead of continuing to import energy from plant 1. Therefore, some of the load is now served by plant 2, for a quantity equal to $Q_2^\circ = Q^d - Q_1^\circ$. It is clear that losses imply an inefficient equilibrium, for two reasons: 1) the amount of energy $Q_2^\circ$ that was produced, with no losses, by plant 1 at a marginal cost $c_1$ is now produced by plant 2 at a higher marginal cost; 2) the amount of energy, that in Figure 14.3 equals D-B, which is not produced at all since in node 2 the price of energy is now increased to $c_2$. What is shown in Figure 14.3 can be generalized as follows.

---

**Result**

When there are asymmetric production costs, the existence of transmission losses makes the efficient plant less competitive, altering the optimal dispatching without losses and inducing inefficiency.

---

## Learning Outcomes

- Nodal prices are the simplest way to implement the first-best solutions, corresponding to welfare maximization, which gives optimal quantities.

- If there is no congestion, the price coincides with the marginal cost of the electricity producer, as is the case for any competitively supplied commodity. If there is congestion, the price is above the marginal cost, which signals the scarcity value of the line.
- When plants with different costs supply the load and the relatively more efficient ones must use the transmission facility, the inefficient plants are dispatched only if load is above the line capacity (absolute congestion). If the demand is exactly equal (or less than) the transmission capacity, only the efficient plants produce energy.
- Line losses have an impact on the marginal production costs of plants. Losses can make more efficient plants less competitive, if they have to transport electricity, altering the optimal dispatch and inducing inefficiency.

# 15 Meshed Networks and Congestion

## 15.1 Introduction

In this chapter, we detail how electricity moves when different lines connect producers and consumers. There are two possible configurations for power transmission lines. Recall that in a System, lines connect nodes. Whenever the grid is made of lines such that electricity can flow from one node to another on a single path only, we shall call this network **radial**. The simplest radial network comprises two nodes and a single line connecting them. If in the system there is more than one path that power can take to go from one node to another the network is defined as **meshed**. We analyze the simplest meshed configuration, a three-nodes network. Electricity may create a "loop," or a circle in a simple circuit with three-nodes with production and consumption. The question is the same as in the Chapter 14: given a congested line, how does electricity flow into the circuit and how can this be revealed by nodal prices?

We extend the nodal prices methodology to answer these questions and find optimal electricity prices in a three-node network, where one line can be congested. We also explain that congestion may create market power, eliciting strategies that include production capacity withholding, but also more complex behavior.

The real situations under which physical laws constrain network transmission, occur not only within a system, but also among all the interconnected systems. This latter case is crucial, for instance in building integrated electricity markets among different countries, where loops may cause surcharge and congestion. How electricity markets cope with the issues of cross-border transportation and congestion will be reviewed in light of the theory of nodal prices, taking European markets as an example.

## 15.2 From Two-Nodes to Three-Nodes Systems

In the previous chapter, we described the optimal allocation problem in a system comprising just two nodes. When we extend the network configuration to a three (or more node) system, taking stock of the transmission capacity constraint becomes more complex. Indeed, what matters for power transmission is the power line resistance, which is linked to voltage and current through Ohm's law (see Chapter 2). The magnitude of the current flowing in a given path, for a given voltage, depends on the resistance. If we assume that lines connecting nodes are made of the same material (same resistivity) and are of equal length, the length of the path determines the resistance and thus the power flow. The following example helps to clarify the role of resistance in the network.

---

**Example 15.1 Equilibrium in a Two- and Three-Nodes System** Suppose that there is a system made of two nodes, node 1 and node 2. In node 1 there is a net supply of power (i.e. a difference between supply and demand), of 100 MW. For instance, $Q_1 = 400$ MW and $Q_1^d = 300$. In node 1, there is a net demand of 100 MW. Suppose, moreover, that there are two interconnecting lines between the two nodes. Let us denote for simplicity by $fl_{i,k,j}$ the flow of energy on the path from node $i$ to node $j$, which might pass through node $k$, if present. Each line would transmit half the power flowing from node 1 to node 2: $2fl_{1,2} = 100$ MW, thus $fl_{1,2} = 50$ MW. This is represented in Figure 15.1.

   This result, however, depends crucially on the fact that the two lines are equal and follow the same path. Suppose, in fact, that instead of linking node 1 and 2, one line passes through node 3. In other words, there is a single line between node 1 and 2, but there is another interconnected node 3. Let us assume that node is a neutral node, in the sense that in node 3 production and load are balanced. Moreover, for simplicity, we standardize to one the length of a path and assume that all lines have the same length. The resistance of the three-nodes network is thus standardized to three, which is also the total length of the path that electricity follows. The direct path from the generation node 1 to the consumption node 2 is half as long as the indirect path from node 1 to node 3 and then from node 3 to node 2. As a consequence, it also has half of the resistance. Therefore, the power flowing on the indirect path from 1 to 2 through 3 is half that of the power going directly from 1 to 2; the ratio of the power on the direct path over the indirect path is 2/1. Even if node 3 does not add to, or subtract energy from, the system it still has an impact on the maximum energy transferrable, due to Kirchhoff's laws. The sum of the capacity installed is the sum of maximum

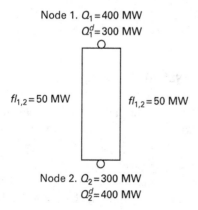

Node 1. $Q_1 = 400$ MW
$Q_1^d = 300$ MW

$fl_{1,2} = 50$ MW          $fl_{1,2} = 50$ MW

Node 2. $Q_2 = 300$ MW
$Q_2^d = 400$ MW

**Figure 15.1** Equilibrium in a two-nodes system

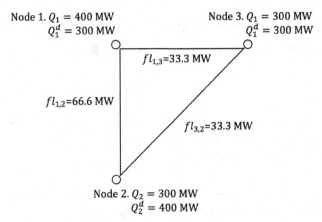

Node 1. $Q_1 = 400$ MW
    $Q_1^d = 300$ MW

Node 3. $Q_1 = 300$ MW
    $Q_1^d = 300$ MW

$fl_{1,3}=33.3$ MW

$fl_{1,2}=66.6$ MW

$fl_{3,2}=33.3$ MW

Node 2. $Q_2 = 300$ MW
    $Q_2^d = 400$ MW

**Figure 15.2** Equilibrium in a three-nodes system

transmission capacity of all paths, and the resistance of the path 1–3–2 is twice as much as that of the path 1–2. Thus, from Kirchhoff's laws, we have the following system of equations:

$$fl_{1,2} + fl_{1,3,2} = 100\text{MW};$$
$$fl_{1,2} = 2fl_{1,3,2}. \tag{15.1}$$

Solving it, we have $fl_{1,3,2} = 33.3\text{MW}, fl_{1,2} = 66.6\text{MW}$. This system is represented in Figure 15.2.

Whether the equilibrium flow in a three-nodes system is admissible or not depends on the capacity limit of each line and on their resistance. Let us show this. We replicate the problem (14.1), adding the constraint of the three-nodes network described in Example 15.1, with node 1 as the production node, node 2 the consumption node, and the load-neutral node 3. Moreover, as in the Example, we suppose that the capacity constraints on all lines are equal and that there is just one transmission capacity constraint that can be binding, the one on the line 1–2, since the ratio of the power on the direct path over the indirect path is 2/1, and all lines are supposed equal. The welfare maximization problem writes:

$$\max_{Q^d, Q_i} U(Q^d) - C_1(Q_1), \text{ s.t.}$$

a) $Q^d = Q_1$;
b) $Q_i \geq 0$;
c) $fl_{1,2} \leq K^{max}$;
d) $fl_{1,2} + fl_{1,3,2} = Q_1$;
e) $fl_{1,2} = 2fl_{1,3,2}.$

$$(15.2)$$

The first and second constraint are the usual load-balance and positive supply constraint. Constraints (c), (d) and (e) are given by Kirchhoff's laws. Simplifying them, we can rewrite the capacity constraint as $\frac{2}{3}Q_1 \leq K^{max}$ and replicating the usual analysis, when the line is congested, we reach the equilibrium condition:

$$U'(\cdot) = c_1 + \frac{2}{3}\chi \tag{15.3}$$

Comparing solution (15.3) with that in Chapter 14, we see that the nodal price in node 2 is reduced. It is clear that with the transmission constraint of Example 15.1 the flow described in Figure 15.2 is not feasible.

---

**Example 15. 1 (cont.)**  The line from node 1 to 2 in Figure 15.2 has a maximum capacity of 50 MW. The solution in the meshed line would not be feasible. In the optimization problem the constraint $fl_{1,2} = 50$ MW must be added, which implies that $fl_{1,2,3} = 25$MW. The entire 100 MW of net demand in node 2 cannot be served, but just 75 MW from node 1 to node 3 can be transmitted.

---

## 15.3        Nodal Prices in Three-Nodes Networks

In meshed lines, the existence of the externality implies that the first best equilibrium might not be attained. However, it is important to take into account that power flow is a contracted quantity. This means that the flow of power from node 1 to 2, counterbalances the flow of power from node to 2 to 1. As a consequence, when there is a meshed network and there are plants that are located at different nodes, several effects occur. When a less efficient plant produces, this increases the cost of energy provision, as we already know. However, in a multiple-nodes network, it is possible that the energy produced by a less efficient plant counterbalances the flow of energy in the opposite direction on a given path, and this might reduce the power flow constraint on that path. As a consequence, this might induce a higher level of production from a more efficient plant. In other words, energy production in a multiple-nodes system can produce positive externalities if they relieve congestion on the lines. It is quite possible that the extra cost due to the production of a less efficient plant is more than compensated by the positive externality arising from congestion relief, and therefore the overall cost of production is reduced. Let us show this, adapting an example from Crampes and Laffont (2001). Suppose that there is a three three-node network with the same configuration as the three-node network described in Example 15.1. In particular, suppose that the resistance of the direct path is 1/2 the resistance of the indirect path. Assume that there are two plants, located at node 1 and node 3. Plant at node 1 is more efficient than plant at node 3: $c_1 < c_3$. Node 2 is the consumption node. For power production of plant 1, constraints are as in problem (15.2): $fl_{1,2} = \frac{2}{3}Q_1; fl_{1,3,2} = \frac{1}{3}Q_1$. For the power

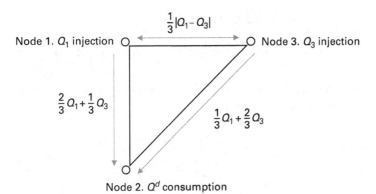

**Figure 15.3** A three-nodes system with positive externality

production of plant at node 3, the constraints work on the two paths from node 3 to node 2, namely, the direct one 3–2 and the indirect one 3–1–2: $fl_{3,2} = \frac{2}{3}Q_3$; $fl_{3,1,2} = \frac{1}{3}Q_3$. Figure 15.3 represents the power flows.

See that on path 1–3 the flow of energy from plant 1 counterbalances the flow from plant 3 on the reverse path. Thus, the net effect depends on the module of the difference between the two flows. Assume now that there is a transmission capacity constraint just on the line connecting node 1 and 3. Kirchhoff's laws imply $\frac{1}{3}|Q_1 - Q_3| \leq K^{max}$. Thus, the welfare maximization problem now becomes:

$$\max_{Q^d, Q_1, Q_3} U(Q^d) - c_1 Q_1 - c_3 Q_3, \text{s.t.}$$

$$a) \; Q^d = Q_1 + Q_3;$$
$$b) \; \frac{1}{3}(Q_1 - Q_3) \leq K^{max};$$
$$c) \; Q_i \geq 0, \; i = 1, 3.$$

(15.4)

The Lagrange Equation is as follows:

$$\mathcal{L} = U(Q^d) - c_1 Q_1 - c_3 Q_3 + \lambda(Q_1 + Q_3 - Q^d) + \chi\left(K^{max} - \frac{1}{3}(Q_1 - Q_3)\right)$$
$$+ \mu_1 Q_1 + \mu_3 Q_3.$$

(15.5)

The Kuhn-Tucker and slackness conditions are as follows:

$$\frac{\partial \mathcal{L}}{\partial Q^d} = 0 \rightarrow U'(\cdot) = \lambda;$$

(15.6)

$$\frac{\partial \mathcal{L}}{\partial Q_1} = 0 \rightarrow c_1 + \frac{1}{3}\chi - \mu_1 = \lambda;$$

(15.7)

$$\frac{\partial \mathcal{L}}{\partial Q_3} = 0 \rightarrow c_3 - \frac{1}{3}\chi - \mu_3 = \lambda;$$

(15.8)

$$\mu_i Q_i = 0; \quad Q_i \geq 0; \quad \mu_i \geq 0; \quad i = 1, 3; \tag{15.9}$$

$$\chi \left( K^{max} - \frac{1}{3}(Q_1 - Q_3) \right) = 0; \quad \left( K^{max} - \frac{1}{3}(Q_1 - Q_3) \right) \geq 0; \quad \chi \geq 0. \tag{15.10}$$

From the solution of the system of equations, assuming that both plants are active, i.e., $\mu_1 = \mu_3 = 0$, we derive the nodal price equations:

$$\begin{aligned} p_1 &: c_1 = p_2 - \frac{\chi}{3} \\ p_2 &: U'(Q^d) = \lambda \\ p_3 &: c_3 = p_2 + \frac{\chi}{3} \end{aligned} \tag{15.11}$$

As before, without congestion $(\chi = 0)$ all the prices are aligned to the marginal consumption utility. In case of absolute congestion, i.e. when $\frac{1}{3}(Q_1 - Q_3) = K^{max}$, nodal prices will be such that $p_3 > p_2 > p_1$. Prices encourage generation at node 3 which is costlier but allow using cheap generation originated at node 1. Plant injecting power into the grid at node 3 creates a counter-flow that alleviates congestion in the network. Because of this positive externality, the optimal dispatch solution can require a high-cost plant to generate power despite the availability of cheaper generating capacity elsewhere in the network. In the case of meshed networks, the flow of electricity is more complex than in the two-nodes configuration: as long as cheap generation is available, it will deliver energy to reach consumers, even if this implies that a higher cost plant is active at the equilibrium. For this same reason, in contrast to the one-node model, in a meshed network the shadow value of the transmission capacity constraint is no longer exactly equal to the difference in the marginal costs of generation at the two nodes. In the case of positive externalities, the latter is lower than the shadow value of the transmission constraint, or conversely, the marginal value of the transmission capacity is higher than the cost differential:

$$c_3 - c_1 = \frac{2}{3}\chi \rightarrow \chi = \frac{3}{2}(c_3 - c_1) \tag{15.12}$$

One of the objectives of network pricing is precisely to share the cost burden of the network between consumers and line owners, as we will explain in the following Chapter.

## 15.4    Transmission Congestion and Loop Flows: Some Examples

Network congestion occurs very frequently in electricity networks, due to the density of the lines and the multiple locations of generation and consumption. As an example, the European Commission (2001) distinguishes two phases of network usage that may create congestion, namely the determination of available capacity and the capacity allocation mechanism steps.

Transmission congestion costs arise from the fact that when transmission lines represent a bottleneck, as we have shown, it is not possible to generate electricity from the cheapest sources. One way to allow the value of the constraint posed by the network to emerge, as we have seen, is using nodal pricing. However, in reality, nodal pricing creates several practical issues. Indeed, it requires calculating a price at every single node. Electricity networks are quite complex, and often composed of thousands of nodes. Thus, from a practical point of view, in order to solve the DC-OPF problem some nodes are grouped together, on a proximity basis and/or depending on their nature (load or injection nodes). Thus, even where nodal pricing is in use, some criterion must still be adopted to group nodes and allow congestion to emerge and price it. The set of different nodes that are grouped together is called a **Zone**. In a given zone, a single price arises. Clearly, the more nodes are grouped in a zone, the larger the zone but the less the DC-OPF is representative of the true network topology, and thus the less the congestion pricing adheres to the true underlying value of each single line. Zonal pricing will be discussed in Chapter 16.

How does congestion pricing occur in practice? There are two interesting yet different examples of congestion pricing implementation in the United States. California is divided into congestion zones. Transmission constraints are small within each zone, but large between zones. A usage charge is imposed on all customers who send energy across zones. The charges are determined from bids voluntarily submitted by a scheduling coordinator to increase or decrease power generation in their zone at a specified cost. In New England, in contrast, congestion charges are calculated on the cost of out-of-merit dispatch. Costs are allocated to each load based on the percentage each load represents of the total load. Although this method is simple to implement, it does not produce price signals on how to alleviate the congestion. However, New England ISO does not have a significant transmission congestion problem.

Another interesting case study is the United Kingdom, in Europe, where the biggest source of bottlenecks is network capacity between Scotland and England. There is a surplus of cheap energy in Scotland, which cannot always be transmitted to England. This bottleneck is worsened by the rise of zero marginal cost wind generation in Scotland, which further widens the price disparity between Scotland and England and Wales, increasing the opportunities for profitable flow of electricity southwards and worsening the transmission congestion. Congestion costs increase the balancing costs and are averaged over all producers and consumers on a pro rata per MWh basis, included in Balancing Services Use of System charges. However, since there is no locational element to this cost, there is scope for competition and efficiency to be enhanced (Competition and Market Authority, 2015).

Congestion can be associated to internal or cross-border transmission. However, since interconnections between national transmission systems have not been built with the primary objective of facilitating energy exchange among countries, congestion arises more frequently on cross-border lines. As the energy moves freely through the grid from generation to consumption, imported/exported electricity flows do not necessarily correspond to commercial flows. The components of AC transmission systems are mostly passive elements that do not allow any control of the power flows across them.

Rather, the pattern of power flows is determined naturally by the parameters of lines and transformers, the network topology (i.e. the way lines and transformers are connected in substations), and the pattern of power injected into or withdrawn from the network by the producers and consumers. We have seen in Chapter 2 that there are some instruments for influencing power flows, such as voltage controllers, transformer tap changers and switches at substations, but the means to control power flows without affecting power quality or increasing power losses are very limited. This is often the case for power flows on interconnection lines across borders. Two kinds of flows can be considered:

- *Transit flows:* the physical flows due to the commercial relationships between one zone to another zone, on the basis of the contract path of electricity delivery.
- *Loop flows:* physical flows due to internal energy transfers in a given pricing zone.

It is not possible in a meshed AC network to identify those specific power injections or extractions that contribute to the power flow on a specific line, because practically all injections and withdrawals affect each line flow to some extent. Thus, some indirect measure has to be taken to identify these flows. For example, Elia, the Belgian SO, calculates the expected values of loop flows by cancelling all commercial exchanges on the interconnectors, and considering the remaining flows as loop flows on an hourly basis. This calculation is based on two days ahead forecast data. Loop flows at the Belgium borders (toward the Netherlands and France) may range from approximately 200 MW to 1,400 MW on an hourly basis.[1]

The relevance of the cross-border flows has been documented by various studies. For instance, Singh et al. (2016) report that about 50 percent of commercially scheduled transactions between Germany and Austria flow through interconnections with other countries, with Poland and the Czech Republic being the most affected. The study estimates that the unplanned power flows from Germany into the European region occur approximately 17 percent of the time in a year when the commercial schedules between Germany and Austria exceed 3,000 MW. The primary reasons identified for the unplanned flows in the continental Europe grids region are: insufficient coordination of cross-border markets, allocation of transmission capacity and increased renewable generation in Germany. Loop flows create external costs on the host area (i.e. that receives the flow) when the grid is not able to accommodate the flow and when the scope of scheduled flows within the host area must be reduced. These impacts include increased costs of security of supply and system services, as well as reduced capacity for market trade within the host country or between the host country and other areas.

An interesting question is how loop flows are managed in the different systems. In Europe, for instance, cross-border transmission access has traditionally been dominated in the past by the "contract path" principle: market parties had to determine a path of control areas from the transaction source to its destination, acquiring rights for each interface on its path. However, with increased interconnections between countries in the internal energy market, EU-wide rules have become increasingly necessary to manage electricity flows effectively. These rules, known as network codes, are Regulations

---

[1]  See www.elia.be/~/media/files/Elia/Grid-data/Interconnections/New-Loop-Flows-calculation.pdf.

containing legally binding rules to access networks for cross-border electricity exchanges (European Commission, 2009).[2]

If congestion can be anticipated by the System Operators because the transmission demand across a specific network interface exceeds the existing capacity more or less permanently, the only solution will be to allocate the existing capacity in advance to market participants. Typical examples are auctioning procedures or reservation procedures based on priority rules. This allocation imposes limitations on activities but saves excessive costs for later congestion management. A permanent market splitting occurs with the creation of a zone, which can eventually be modified on the basis of the evolution of the network topology.

As we shall see in Chapter 21, SOs also have to assess network security as part of their operational planning activities, as soon as actual information about the planned generation dispatch is submitted by the market parties. If network congestion is detected at this stage (i.e. if secure network operation based on the submitted schedules is not considered possible), it is up to the SOs to initiate countermeasures to relieve the congestion and thus to facilitate secure network operation. This stage of the process is referred to as **congestion management**. Typical countermeasures to be taken are adjustments of the network topology or devices like phase-shifting transformers that have an influence on power flows, or adjustments of generation dispatch by the SOs (i.e. redispatching) (see Chapter 5).

## Learning Outcomes

- In meshed networks, physical laws governing electricity transfer across the lines have to be integrated as constraints in the welfare maximization.
- Going from two- to three-nodes networks implies that Kirchhoff's laws become crucial in assessing the constraint to the optimal power flow, which depends on the lines' resistance.
- When at least one line is congested, in a three-node network, prices at the different nodes differ and the marginal valuation of the network is proportional to the nodal price difference. The example of the three-nodes network illustrates that the nodal pricing in a three-nodes network differs from that of two-nodes networks, because of the effect of the network externalities.
- Inefficient power plants can be called on to produce because this might reduce the congestion on a line and thus generate positive externalities, reducing congestion.
- The creation of large zones requires specific rules to measure and manage congestion, especially when it occurs across borders.

---

[2] To achieve non-discriminatory network access, the European directives seeking to ensure liberalization of electricity markets require the formerly vertically integrated electric utilities to unbundle at least their accounts with respect to transmission and distribution network operations. In particular, for the transmission level, an independent (at least in management terms) Transmission System Operator (TSO) must be designated in each country or area to ensure non-discrimination in system use between incumbents and new entrants.

# 16 Transmission Pricing in Practice

## 16. 1 Introduction

In competitive electricity markets, where any party selling or buying electricity connects to and make use of the transmission network, regardless of who owns and operates the power grid, network regulation encompasses two dimensions: access and pricing. In order to achieve non-discriminatory network access, it is generally required that the formerly vertically integrated electric utilities unbundle at least their accounts with respect to network operation and any other activities. For the transmission level, the SO must ensure non-discrimination access to the network between the incumbents and new entrants (Laffont and Tirole, 1996; see also Chapter 6 on regulation). Our focus here is on transmission network pricing attached to transmission usage. We detail some examples of network pricing implementation and we briefly conclude on congestion management rules that will be further discussed in Chapter 17.

## 16.2 Network Pricing Classification

All the theoretical findings reported in the previous chapters on network pricing rely on the key hypothesis that an efficient market exists which, at any time, delivers optimal nodal spot prices. Nothing seems less realistic when one explores the real-world electricity markets: with some exceptions, the models implemented in practice adopt simpler solutions which, of course, depart from the most efficient one. The most commonly used pricing rules are a mixture of two main classes (Crampes and Laffont, 1996):

- In the **Open Market model**, payment at one point gives access to the whole network. The point-of-connection tariff could be nodal, that is, linked to the costs of producing electricity, or based on the accounting costs of assets.
- In the **Transportation model**, tariffs are related to distance. For instance, in the contract path, entry and exit points are specified and the price refers to the cost of the assets on the agreed transmission path.

Within this classification, transmission pricing methods can be classified in two categories: cost-based methods, which are methods driven by transmission investment costs and value-based methods, which are driven by generation costs.

In the cost-based methods we can find the following methods:

- postage-stamp;
- contract-path;
- MW-mile;
- investment cost related network pricing (ICRP);
- area of influence and tracing methods.

In the value-based methods there are:

- zonal prices;
- short-run marginal cost (SRMC);
- long-run marginal cost (LRMC).

In this chapter, we discuss postage stamps for the cost-based methods and zonal prices for value-based methods. For the cost-based methods, postage stamps are the most widely used solution. For value-based methods, the theory of the SRMC has already been introduced in Chapter 14 and 15. Note that SRMC is also referred as Locational Marginal Pricing (LMP). Transmission LRMC is the investment and operation cost of transporting one additional MW across the network when transmission capacity can be altered. This will be analyzed in Chapter 17. However, before focusing on postage stamps and zonal prices, we provide a brief review of the other methods as well.

Contract path and MW-mile methods were developed at the end of the 1980s and used extensively mainly in the United States (Green, 1997). In the contract path method, the SO and the customer agree on a fictitious path (contract path) for the service. The contract path interconnects the points of injection and withdrawal, although it is defined virtually, regardless of the effective power flow. Once the contract path has been determined, all or a part of the transmission cost related to the specified path is assigned to the transaction, and transmission charges are calculated.

MW-mile can be calculated depending on the distance or the electricity flow. In the distance-based method, transmission charges are allocated according to the magnitude of transacted power and the geographical distance between the points of delivery and withdrawal (i.e. the product of power of the specific transaction and the distance that this power virtually travels in the network). This is the case with the **flow-based** pricing scheme, progressively introduced in Europe by the Regulation establishing a guideline on Capacity Allocation and Congestion Management (CACM), which entered into force in 2015. In this method, energy exchanges between bidding zones are limited by power transfer distribution factors and available margins on critical network elements.

ICRP method was developed by the National Grid Company (UK) and it is currently used for calculation of the Transmission Network Use of System Charges in England and Wales. The method is based on a transportation model to determine the optimal capacity of the network. It is based on the marginal investment cost of additional demand or generation, using a DC load flow transportation model.

The Area of Influence method was developed in Chile at the beginning of the 1990s and it is currently in use in Chile and Bolivia. It requires the calculation of a pro-rata quantity to allocate the cost of the transmission assets included in the area of influence among the users that share the same common area, this latter defined as the set of lines, substations and other facilities affected by the power production of one generation unit. The basic toll is a fixed charge that contributes to the maintenance and investment of the lines serving the influence area. Tracing methods to allocate transmission system costs over producers and demand have been studied from the academic point of view, but they are not in practical use. These methods decompose the network flows into components associated with individual customers. Distribution factors for such flows are defined through a sensitivity analysis and indicate the relation between a change in power injection in a certain bus and a change in the power flow in a particular line. An optional tracing method using generalized generation distribution factors has been used in Chile to calculate the pro-rata quantity among users that share the same common Area of Influence (Rudnick et al., 1999).

## 16.2.1    Postage Stamps

The postage stamp method is widely used worldwide. For instance, in the European Union, most SO implement a national postage stamp system, which has hardly any reference to nodal prices. A postage stamp rate is a fixed charge per unit of energy transmitted within a particular zone, regardless of the distance that the energy travels. Postage stamp rates are based on average system costs and may have a variety of rate designs, based on energy charges (cents per kWh), load charges (cents per kW), or both energy and load charges. Rates often include separate charges for peak and off-peak periods, may vary by season, and, in some cases, set different charges for weekday versus weekend and holiday usage. Transmission services are also generally offered on both a firm-basis and non-firm basis. Firm in energy transmission means that the SO guarantees service subject to emergency curtailments or system congestion. In contrast, non-firm transmission services are more economical than firm service, but are subject to curtailment or interruption, often with little or no advanced notice by the SO.

Like the postal service, postage stamp does not depend on the distance; the price is independent of the connection point and it is not directional. All nodes are viewed as belonging to a wide unique zone, which is often identified with the national territory. The main argument in favor of this kind of pricing is that it is very simple to implement and maintains some sort of equity between all system users. But such schemes are not efficient, since they have no relation with the power flow and the injection and withdrawal nodes. Furthermore, in cross-border exchanges, multiple transmission fees can apply for a single transaction. This accumulation of access charges, called **pankcaking**, is clearly inefficient and penalizes long-distance power deliveries.

Although postage stamp tariffs continue to be a commonly used solution, for instance for the case of the ENTSO in Europe, there is a trend in the opposite direction of economic signals. This is the case with the most recent guidelines contained in the European Regulation 1228, where it is stated that "a proper system of long-term locational signals would be necessary based on the principle that the level of network access charges should reflect the balance between generation and consumption of the region concerned,"[1] and that "it would not be appropriate to apply distance-related tariffs."[2] Moreover, the regulation makes clear that "congestion management methods implemented by Member States shall deal with short-run congestion in a market-based, economically efficient manner, whilst simultaneously providing signals or incentives for efficient network and generation investment in the right location,"[3] and "price signals that result from congestion management systems shall be directional."[4] These are the features of the flow-based model that is being adopted by various European counties.

## 16.2.2 Zonal Prices

As noted above, a zone is a set of nodes that are properly grouped. Zonal pricing aggregates several nodes into a predetermined number of zones. This solution was first proposed by Hogan (1998). Under zonal pricing, the power system is divided into several zones and the costs are evaluated within each zone. Within each zone, the price of access to the grid is uniform (as in the Open Market model), while the price of transferring energy from one zone to the other is related to distance (as in the Transportation model). The optimal size of the zones should be the result of a trade-off between more competition among power producers (and consumers) and the loss of efficiency in the dispatching of the grid.

In each zone, price is formed following the principle of economic dispatching that we have already introduced (Chapter 10). In order to identify zonal prices, nodes are first grouped in possible subsets (i.e. zones). Then, the market is considered as unique (i.e. all nodes are grouped together: if the day-ahead production/consumption plan respects all network constraints across all possible subsets zones, there is no congestion and a single price for the whole network emerges). The equilibrium price corresponds with the intersection of national (or system-wide) demand and supply curves, as in an unconstrained optimization. On the contrary, if a network constraint is saturated, then the geographical market is divided into two sub-markets, each one aggregating all the zones above and below the saturated constraint. Then market demand and supply curves are constructed for the sub-markets (taking into account the quantity that can flows between zones up to the transmission limit) and the process of market clearing is reiterated in each zone. If no further congestion occurs, two zonal prices result. In the case of permanence of network saturation, the process of splitting out the markets continues until all constraints are satisfied. When there is no congestion in the grid, we say that the market is coupled, or that there is **market coupling**. When more than a single zone arises, we say that the market is split, or that there is **market splitting**.

Figure 16.1 presents an example of unconstrained network. Zone A is dispatched by a total of 700 MWh coming from two plants, 1 and 2, which produce at a marginal cost of €20/MWh and €30/MWh, respectively. Zone A load is 650 MWh, therefore 50 MW can

---

[1] Regulation EC No. 1228/2003, (12), p. 2.   [2] Ibid., (14), p. 2.   [3] Ibid., Annex, Art. 1, p. 9.
[4] Ibid., Annex, Art. 4, p. 9.

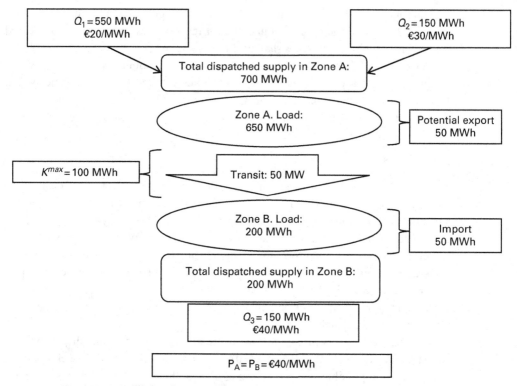

**Figure 16.1** Equilibrium in a zonal market: market coupling

be supplied to zone B. This is the potential export. Transmission limits are 100 MW, thus the potential export is within the limits. In zone B, load is 200 MWh. Plant 3, producing at a marginal cost of €40/MWh provides the additional 150 MWh, dispatched to zone B. In the merit order approach, the SMP is €40/MWh and, since the line is not saturated, there is no congestion and a single price arises. There is thus a unique market, namely, market coupling.

If now plant 1 increases its supply to 700 MWh the line becomes saturated. See Figure 16.2. Zone B demand will be served by the electricity that transits on the network and by an additional 100 MWh coming from plant 3. There is market splitting: the market is split in two zones, with different prices. Zone A price is €30/MWh and zone B price is €40/MWh.

In multiple zone networks, the process of market splitting can give rise to different market configurations, depending on which line is congested and thus which constraint is binding, as described in Figure 16.3.

Markets that are based on zonal pricing are formed by repeating the process described above, and observing how many zones emerge through market splitting. If it comes to pass that one zone, for instance, on average over a relevant period of time, is split, this means that there are relevant transmission limits between that zone and the other ones. Thus, that zone is fixed as a market zone. Over time, market zone configuration can

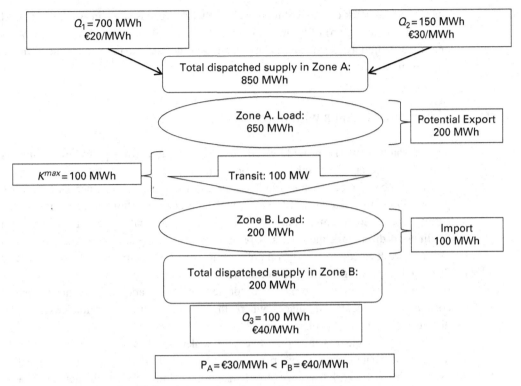

**Figure 16.2** Equilibrium in a zonal market: market splitting in two zones

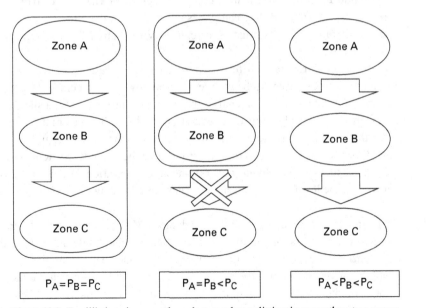

**Figure 16.3** Equilibrium in a zonal market: market splitting in more than two zones

change to take stock of the evolution of the network. For instance, in Australia's NEM the zone (called region) of Snowy was abolished and split between New South Wales and Victoria. In Italy, the Calabria market zone was merged into the South zone, forming a larger market zone.

## 16.3    Distributional Issues with Network Pricing

Transmission networks provide electricity transportation from plants to consumers located at different geographical locations on the network. Generation facilities are generally located close to the primary sources of energy, for instance hydroelectric power plants are located beside rivers with appreciable inflows and height differentials, coal-fired thermal plants are located close to coal mines or harbors with facilities to disembark the coal and sea water for cooling, and combined-cycle gas turbines are located close to gas pipelines city-gates. Consumers are geographically dispersed depending on the economic activity they perform, for instance, residential and commercial customers are located in cities and towns and industrial consumers are located in places where they optimize transportation costs of the different production factors.

Since assets of the transmission network are sunk costs, these costs must be charged to the users of the network (producers and consumers). Indeed, the grid provides positive externalities to network users, and from a theoretical point of view, the network charge should be tailored to internalize those network externalities. As for positive externalities, there is clearly a free riding problem: nobody in the energy market would wish to pay a higher transmission charge than its competitor, on the one hand, and no one would wish to reveal its true value, if they can play strategically, on the other hand. Therefore, the payment of those charges must be a regulatory obligation for all participants in the energy market.

Different countries take different approaches in allocating the total costs of transmission network services to be recovered from power producers and load customers. The split of total transmission charges between generation and load should take place according to the total benefits that generation and load obtain from the grid. However, given that estimating these benefits may turn out to be very difficult, in most cases, a 50/50 split of costs between the two groups may be adopted. System authorities can limit the costs to be paid by producers, since their operational decisions may be more sensitive to the level of transmission charges than those by loads (Olmos and Arriaga, 2009).

In practice, different solutions are adopted. Many countries apply transmission charges only to load (e.g. Germany and the Netherlands) while others (e.g. the United Kingdom) choose to split charges between plants and load. A similar issue arises in relation to investments to deliver security of supply, with one caveat: to the extent that security of supply is mostly required by the demand side, due to the higher economic impact of power outages on consumers rather than plants, service criteria can be allocated to consumers only.

## 16.4    Transmission Pricing: Some Experiences

This section illustrates a few instructive cases in the practical aspects of transmission pricing, namely, the United States, where different solutions are adopted, and Italy, as an example of zonal prices.

### 16.4.1    Transmission Pricing in the United States

The Energy Policy Act in 1992, introduced competition in the electricity sector and included provisions instructing the Federal Energy Regulatory Commission (FERC) to issue an order making transmission services available to any party. In 1996, FERC issued Order 888 and 889 which required utilities to unbundle transmission, distribution and wholesale generation services and established transmission service as a common carrier service. The orders also required jurisdictional utilities, which own, control or operate transmission lines, to file non-discriminatory open access tariffs to FERC for approval. Order 889, also known as the OASIS rule, requires utilities to share transmission capacity, pricing and other information necessary to grant an open non-discriminatory access transmission service. The order also notes that utilities may wish to go beyond functional separation and devote transmission to an Independent Systems Operator (ISO). The ISO would coordinate the use of the transmission system and ensure that the principle of non-discriminatory use of the transmission system is upheld.

The biggest operating ISOs[5] are: California ISO (CAISO); Electric Reliability Council of Texas (ERCOT); Pennsylvania, New Jersey, Maryland (PJM); ISO New England[6] (ISO-NE); New York ISO (NYISO); Southwest Power Pool[7] (SPP); Midcontinent ISO[8] (MISO).

The responsibilities of ISOs are very broad, going beyond the role of ensuring equal and fair access to the transmission system. ISO functions can be classified broadly under two categories: the facilitation of a wholesale power market, and pricing of the network and related facilities. The relative importance of the functions within these two categories and the details of how they are performed vary among ISOs.

Traditional transmission pricing in the United States is based on a routing scheme, the contract path or MW-mile. Much of the interest in transmission pricing reform involves moving away from utility-by-utility contract path pricing to regional transmission tariffs based on power flows and congestion pricing. The difference in nodal prices, namely, congestion costs, can either be assigned directly to those users that cause the congestion or shared among all users. The revenues that the ISO obtains from congestion, the so-called congestion rent, are distributed in different ways. In California, for instance, such revenues are used to reduce the access fees that all transmission customers pay.

[5] The ISO map can be accessed at www.ferc.gov/industries/electric/indus-act/rto.asp.
[6] ISO-NE serves Connecticut, Maine, Massachusetts, New Hampshire, Rhode Island and Vermont.
[7] SPP includes all or parts of Oklahoma, Kansas, Nebraska, South Dakota, North Dakota, Montana, Wyoming, Texas, New Mexico, Arkansas, Iowa, Missouri and Louisiana.
[8] MISO groups all or parts of Mid-West United States, Arkansas, Mississippi, Louisiana and Manitoba (Canada).

Another possibility is to create a system of transmission congestion contracts. These contracts would establish a comprehensive set of rights either to make power transfers, or to receive compensation for the inability to do so through redistribution of congestion rents to the holders of transmission congestion contracts (see Chapter 17 for a detailed description).

Most ISOs have proposed zonal pricing, considered as an interim method. The most noticeable exception is PJM, the biggest electricity pool in the United States, which implements nodal prices in the real-time market. These prices are calculated every five minutes, based on the actual system operations security-constrained economic dispatch. Separate accounting settlements are performed for the day-ahead market, where the settlement is based on scheduled hourly quantities and on day-ahead hourly prices, and the real-time market, where the settlement takes into account hourly integrated quantity deviations from day-ahead scheduled quantities and real-time prices integrated over the hour. The day-ahead price calculations and the real-time price calculations are based on the concept of nodal pricing.

Some regions use a megawatt-mile method for pricing transmission (e.g. SPP, MISO). This approach is a distance-based method that takes into account parallel power flows. This pricing approach gives no credit for counter flows and is administratively much more complicated than other methods, as each transaction must be calculated; rates must therefore be re-calculated for each change to a transaction or each additional transaction.

There are also firm transmission service contracts which are long-term contracts. Non-firm agreements can be either short or long term. Under the FERC Order 888, utilities are required to offer both location specific and network transmission service. Location-specific services have specified points of delivery and receipt, transmission direction, and quantities. Network service is typically negotiated through a longer-term contract and involves flexible delivery points and quantities.

Table 16.1 summarizes the main choices for transmission pricing in the United States.

### 16.4.2     Zonal Pricing in Practice

In Australia, NEM form a zonal market. In Europe, most countries use postage stamp tariffs. In Italy and in the Nord POOL, which groups several Nordic European countries, zonal pricing is adopted. The Italian market is an interesting case since it is a zonal market that spans the whole national market. It comprises six geographical zones (plus foreign virtual zones which represent transit flows with neighboring countries and poles of limited production in which there is limited load and bottlenecks to some relevant power plants). The twenty administrative regions which make up the Italian territory are aggregated into geographical zones (North, Centre-North, Centre-South, South, Sicily, Sardinia). Historically, the zone configuration was due to relevant bottlenecks, but prices across zones are converging, and zones are increasingly coupled. For example, over the year April 2016 to April 2017, almost all average zonal prices followed the same trend (increasing from €30/MWh to a maximum of €79/MWh at the beginning of 2017, then decreasing). A relevant exception is Sicily, which is an island with a limited transmission capacity with the continent, that suffered from relevant transmission

**Table 16.1** Transmission pricing in the United States

| ISO | Transmission rates | Congestion management |
|-----|--------------------|-----------------------|
|     | | Pricing |
| California ISO | Initially zonal (based on customers' service territory location), actually uniform pricing | Zonal; ISO may schedule voluntary trades; users pay for inter-zonal congestion, receive value for relief; adjustment bids for intra-zonal redispatch |
| ISO-New England | Postage-stamp access charge by region after transition period | ISO dispatches out-of-merit resources when capacity available, charges by hour and area |
| PJM ISO | Zonal (network service); ISO uses locational MP | Locational MP |
| New York ISO | Zonal (based on customers' service territory location) | Uses voluntary bids (increment or decrement); nodal pricing reflects congestion |
| Texas ISO | Access charge plus impact charge per MW-mile | Ensures redispatching; all users share costs (for planned transactions), individual users otherwise |
| Midwest ISO | Zonal rates (based on customers' service territory location) actually uniform pricing | ISO provides information for transmission customers; all users share costs incurred to avoid curtailment of firm supply |
| IndeGO (Northwest) | Access charge by region, capacity reservation for price certainty | Take bids on power purchase/sale to create reverse flow; paid by those causing congestion |
| DesertSTAR (Southwest) | Zonal | Take bids on power purchase/sale to create reverse flow; paid by those causing congestion |

*Source*: Adapted from NECA (2015).

congestion and due to the limited internal supply, experienced prices that remained on average around €52/MWh over that period.[9]

## Learning Outcomes

- Network pricing can be based on the open market model (if payment at one point gives access to the whole network), or the transportation model (if payment depends on the distance).
- Transmission pricing methods can be classified in two categories: cost-based methods (postage-stamp, contract-path; MW-mile, investment cost related network pricing, area of influence and tracing methods), and value-based methods (zonal prices, short-run marginal cost, theoretical long-run marginal cost).
- The international context in electricity transmission regulation shows a wide variety of pricing schemes. The most frequent types are methods based on Short Run Marginal

---

[9] Note that while producers receive zonal prices in the occurrence of congestion, buyers pay the National Single Price (PUN) for the electricity bought in the pool, which is an average of zonal prices weighted by the zonal purchases.

Costs at different locations on the network, such as transmission rights schemes in use in several systems in the United States; simple postage-stamp methods, used in many European countries; and zonal pricing, as in the Nord pool, in Italy and in Australia NEM.

- Cost reflectivity, which is one of the main objectives of transmission pricing, is not always achieved, even if there is a progressive movement toward increasing usage of nodal prices, as is the case for PJM in the United States.
- There are different approaches for allocating the total cost of transmission network services to be recovered from power producers and load customers, the 50/50 solution not being the most frequently used.

# 17 From Nodal Prices to Transmission Capacity Expansion

## 17.1 Introduction

The analysis we have performed so far in this Part was aimed at evaluating the impact of the transmission constraints on electricity prices, assuming the network capacity constraint as given. We have shown that the value of the marginal expansion of the grid equals the price differential among nodes due to the congestion, if any, weighted by the externalities that the grid generates. However, we did not consider the role of incentives to transmission capacity expansion. We shall do it here. In particular, in this chapter we investigate the optimal value of investment in the grid and the incentives to invest (Joskow and Tirole, 2005). We investigate these issues under the criterion of welfare maximization.

## 17.2 Interconnections and Net Export Curves

In order to evaluate the incentives to transmission capacity expansion, we start from the simple 2 node network described in Paragraph 14.2.2, namely, the case of two asymmetric plants (or set of plants), located at nodes, or zones, 1 and 2, whose cost functions are such that $C_1'(Q_1) < C_2'(Q_2)$, with $C_i'(Q_i) > 0$, $i=1,2$. Load is located at node 2, and is represented by a demand function $U(Q^d)$ large enough not to be satisfied by the power flowing just from node 1. Moreover, assume that there is permanent congestion on the transmission line. Denote as $p_i$ the market clearing prices for power generation at node $i$. We can define node 1 as an exporting node, and 2 the importing one. Notice that since at equilibrium the line is congested, $Q_1 = K^{max}$ and $Q_2 = (U'(p_2) - K^{max})$.

Under all these assumptions (and ignoring line losses), we follow the nodal price model, when the line is congested. The equilibrium nodal prices will be:

$$
\begin{aligned}
p_1 &= C_1'(K^{max}) \\
p_2 &= C_2'\left(U'(p_2) - K^{max}\right) > p_1
\end{aligned}
\tag{17.1}
$$

Let the SO receive as a remuneration for having made available and managing the grid the difference between the price at the exporting and the importing node, per each unit of energy that is being exported, which is limited by $K^{max}$. Therefore, its remuneration is: $(p_2 - p_1)K^{max}$. Such a remuneration is called congestion rent.

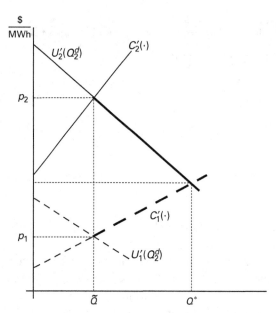

**Figure 17.1** Energy demand and supply in two zones

DEFINITION. ***Congestion Rent (CR):*** *the remuneration the SO receives from a congested line. It equals to the difference between the prices at the importing and the exporting node for the whole energy flowing on the congested line.*

Notice that the congestion rent is the value of each unit of energy flowing, multiplied by the flow on the line, this latter depending on the line capacity.

We can relax the assumption of no load in node 1 and provide a graphical representation of the generation and load at each node and the transportation capacity. This helps to visualize the congestion rent. Let there be two nodes, 1 and 2. From now onward, we shall use nodes and zones as synonymous. Each zone has its load and generation. Assume also that the cost of generation in zone 1 is cheaper than in zone 2. We start from a theoretical situation of no interconnection between zones 1 and 2. It would be the case of two purely separated markets. Let us plot the energy demand and supply curve of each of the two zones on a single picture, as in Figure 17.1.

We have represented a case in which the quantity cleared in zone 1 and 2 are equal, for ease of representation. In Figure 17.1 this quantity is $Q_1 = Q_2 = \tilde{Q}$. We can see that for zone 2 is exist a load above $\tilde{Q}$ that is not served because the willingness to pay for it is below the production cost. This quantity can be defined as the **net demand** of zone 2. Similarly, in zone 2 there are production possibilities that are not exploited because the willingness to pay in that zone is below the production cost. This is called the **net supply** of zone 1. Together, net demand curves and net supply curves are called **net export curves**. They are described in the figure as the thick part of the demand curve of zone 2 and supply of zone 1, respectively.

Assume now that some transportation capacity $K^{max}$ is added. Let us draw it on a graph with the net export curves. This is done in Figure 17.2. We can see that the energy

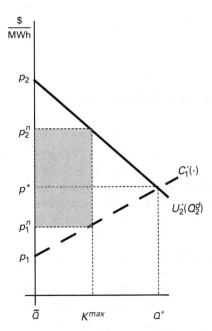

**Figure 17.2** Net export curves and congestion rent

price in zone 2 decreases, and the price at the export zone rises. The new price in zone 1 is $p_1^n$, the new price in 2 is $p_n^2$. However, as long as $K^{max}$ does not bridge the gap between the prices at the exporting and importing nodes, there would always be a positive difference between prices. This difference is what remunerates the owner and manager of the interconnecting line between 1 and 2, for all the energy that transportation capacity $K^{max}$ allows flowing on the line. Therefore, the remuneration of the SO is the Congestion Rent. In Figure 17.2, the congestion rent is the grey rectangle highlighted.

The welfare arising from power flow, including the SO, when there is a given level of transmission $K^{max}$ is $W = CR + Q_2^d - Q_1$. For marginal variations of $K^{max}$ we can neglect the impact of the change in the transmission capacity constraint on the equilibrium (nodal) prices; thus the welfare change would be given by

$$\frac{\partial W}{\partial K^{max}} = \frac{\partial CR}{\partial K^{max}} = (p_2 - p_1).$$

We already know this result from Chapter 14, namely, the welfare increases in a radial network with a congested line are given by the price differential on that line. Note, however, that this is a short-run result, since it assumes a given level of $K^{max}$ and consider just marginal variations of it. For this reason, as noted, it is referred to as the **Short Run Marginal Cost** principle, since under perfect competition the price equals the marginal cost of generation. We move now to the long-run, and investigate what the optimal level of $K^{max}$ is. Net export curves provide a simple answer to this question. We first investigate the optimal level of interconnection when there are no costs of investments in the line, and then what occurs if we take into account investment costs in interconnecting capacity. Let us start from the welfare analysis without transmission capacity investment costs.

## 17.3    Welfare Analysis in the Absence of Interconnection Costs

The area encompassed between the two net-export curves, absent transmission capacity, represents the amount of energy that can be usefully exchanged between the two zones, or nodes, if an interconnection line existed, and that cannot be transferred when there is no interconnection. Therefore, it is a loss from the social welfare point of view, summing the welfare losses of those who could export energy from zone 1 and those who could import it in zone 2 but cannot, through a lack of interconnection. For all this amount of energy, there are buyers willing to pay more than it would cost to produce and supply energy to them, but cannot acquire energy, without interconnection capacity. Therefore, from an economic point of view, the area between the two net export curves measures the deadweight loss that arises because of the inefficient dispatching due to the absence of interconnection capacity. What would be the optimal level of interconnection, if there was no cost of building or expanding the interconnection line?

We can answer this question by looking at the net export curves of Figure 17.2. Analytically, the area of welfare loss due to the absence of interconnection can be measured by the Harberger triangle, which approximates linearly the Deadweight Loss (DWL, also known as the congestion cost) in the two zones due to the lack of interconnection. When an interconnection capacity of amount $K^{max}$ is introduced, it allows the transfer of energy from zone 1 to zone 2; it also affects the prices, reducing the price of the exporting zone and increasing the importing zone. We cannot neglect such an effect, as we are considering relevant changes in transmission capacity. The area of the Harberger triangle is measured by the following equation:

$$DWL = \frac{1}{2} \left[ \left( p_2^n(K^{max}) - p_1^n(K^{max}) \right) \left( Q^* - Q_1(K^{max}) \right) \right], \qquad (17.2)$$

where $p_1^n(K^{max})$ denotes the price in zone 1 that is reached when an interconnection capacity of amount $K^{max}$ is introduced. It is therefore a function of $K^{max}$. Similarly for $p_2^n(K^{max})$; $Q^*$ is the amount of energy for which the price at zone 1 and 2 would coincide (i.e. the quantity that would eliminate congestion between zone 1 and 2); $Q_1(K^{max})$ is the quantity of energy that can be transferred from zone 1 to 2 thanks to the interconnection capacity of amount $K^{max}$. Equation (17.2) shows that the loss in efficiency due to the absence (or limited) interconnection depends on the price that can be reached at each node, when the line is introduced, times the amount of energy that can be transmitted, which is a function of the interconnection capacity.

The problem of maximizing welfare subject to a transmission capacity constraint is the solution to the corresponding dual problem of minimizing welfare losses due to insufficient interconnection (i.e. minimizing the DWL):

$$\min_{K^{max}} DWL = \frac{1}{2}\left[\left(p_2^n(K^{max}) - p_1^n(K^{max})\right)\left(Q^* - Q_1(K^{max})\right)\right]. \quad (17.3)$$

The F.O.C.s are:

$$\frac{\partial DWL}{\partial K^{max}} = 0 \rightarrow \frac{1}{2}\left[\left(p_2^n(\cdot) - p_1^n(\cdot)\right)\frac{\partial Q_1(\cdot)}{\partial K^{max}} - \left(\frac{\partial p_2^n(\cdot)}{\partial K^{max}} - \frac{\partial p_1^n(\cdot)}{\partial K^{max}}\right)\left(Q^* - Q_1(\cdot)\right)\right] = 0.$$

$$(17.4)$$

The term $\dfrac{\partial Q_1(\cdot)}{\partial K^{max}}$ measures by how much the power flow rises when one unit of transmission capacity is installed. In radial networks, when there are no losses and no security margin, we have $Q_1(K^{max}) = K^{max}$ (see Chapter 14) and therefore we can set $\dfrac{\partial Q_1(\cdot)}{\partial K^{max}} = 1$. Thus, Equation (17.4) simplifies to $\left(p_2^n(\cdot) - p_1^n(\cdot)\right) = \left(\dfrac{\partial p_2^n(\cdot)}{\partial K^{max}} - \dfrac{\partial p_1^n(\cdot)}{\partial K^{max}}\right)$ $(Q^* - K^{max})$.

Let us focus on the term between square brackets the above equation. It is clear to see that condition (17.4) is satisfied when $K^{max}$ is such that $p_1^n = p_2^n = p^*$ and $K^{max} = Q^*$. Denote as $K^{max*}$ this level of $K^{max}$. In other words, the optimal level of transmission capacity without any transmission cost would be at the level at which the interconnecting line is no longer congested (i.e. up to that level for which all the energy needed in node 2 can be transferred from node 1). This implies that both the DWL and the congestion rent are driven to zero.

---

### Result

In an hypothetical world with no transmission investment costs, the optimal level of investment in transmission capacity would be such that no congestion arises. As a consequence, both DWL and congestion rents would be eliminated.

---

The above result clearly depends on the assumption that there are no interconnection costs. It provides just a benchmark against which to compare the solution of the problem when there is a given transmission investment cost. We shall investigate what happens when transmission expansion costs are introduced in Paragraph 17.4. However, before doing so, we study the relationship between the investment remuneration scheme and the optimal level of investment. Clearly, if a planner could set up the optimal structure of the grid, it would choose $K^{max*}$. However, recall that the transmission service is a natural monopoly, managed by the SO. When the SO is remunerated for its activity on the basis of the congestion rent, can we expect the same benchmark solution of no DWL to arise? In order to answer this question, we investigate whether such a theoretical level would be reached, when the decision on grid building (or expansion) is left to the SO, in the benchmark case of no investment costs. We show below that this is not the case. If it was left free to choose the level of $K^{max}$ an SO would choose the level of investment in transmission capacity that would maximize its own rent. Such a level is below the optimal one. Assume that the SO wishes to maximize its own congestion rent, which is a function of the interconnection capacity $K^{max}$:

$$\max_{K^{max}} CR = \left[ \left( p_2^n(K^{max}) - p_1^n(K^{max}) \right) K^{max} \right]. \tag{17.5}$$

The F.O.C. of this problem is:

$$\frac{\partial CR}{\partial K^{max}} = 0 \rightarrow \left[ \left( p_2^n(\cdot) - p_1^n(\cdot) \right) + \left( \frac{\partial p_2^n(\cdot)}{\partial K^{max}} - \frac{\partial p_1^n(\cdot)}{\partial K^{max}} \right) K^{max} \right] = 0. \tag{17.6}$$

The optimal level of $K^{max}$ for the SO is that level of $K^{max}$ that solves:

$$\left( p_2^n(\cdot) - p_1^n(\cdot) \right) = - \left( \frac{\partial p_2^n(\cdot)}{\partial K^{max}} - \frac{\partial p_1^n(\cdot)}{\partial K^{max}} \right) K^{max}. \tag{17.7}$$

Notice that $\dfrac{\partial p_2^n(\cdot)}{\partial K^{max}} < 0$ and $\dfrac{\partial p_1^n(\cdot)}{\partial K^{max}} > 0$, thus $\left( \dfrac{\partial p_2^n(\cdot)}{\partial K^{max}} - \dfrac{\partial p_1^n(\cdot)}{\partial K^{max}} \right) < 0$. As $K^{max}$ rises, the price differential shrinks, which would induce a CR decrease. However, the RHS of Equation (17.7) also increases, which induces an increase of the CR. Call the level of $K^{max}$ that solves Equation (17.7) $K^{maxSO}$. The optimal level is such that $K^{maxSO} < K^{max*}$. The latter inequality can be simply deduced by observing that at $K^{max*}$, $\left( p_2^n(\cdot) - p_1^n(\cdot) \right) = 0$, which clearly cannot satisfy Equation (17.7), and $\left( p_2^n(\cdot) - p_1^n(\cdot) \right)$ is a positive decreasing function of $K^{max}$. Thus even in a hypothetical world of no investment costs, we cannot expect the SO to choose the optimal social level of transmission investments.

## 17.4    Optimal Transmission Investment with Investment Costs

We now introduce transmission investment costs. To keep the analysis simple, we assume that there are constant average costs of investments in transmission capacity: $(K^{max}) = \beta K^{max}$. As before, nodal energy prices fully reflect consumers' willingness to pay, all network externalities are internalized in nodal prices, transmission network constraints and associated point-to-point capacity are non-stochastic, and no plant has market power. Moreover, we consider congested lines in radial networks, thus $Q_1(K^{max}) = K^{max}$. The optimal expansion of the capacity with investment costs now becomes the problem of minimization of all costs, namely, of the welfare loss arising because of congestion (i.e. DWL and the cost of the expansion of transmission capacity). For the planner, the problem (17.3) becomes:

$$\min_{K^{max}} DWL + C(K^{max}) = \frac{1}{2} \left[ \left( p_2^n(K^{max}) - p_1^n(K^{max}) \right) (Q^* - K^{max}) \right] + \beta K^{max} \tag{17.8}$$

By replicating the analysis carried out earlier, we see that the equilibrium is reached at the level of $K^{max}$ that solves:

$$\frac{1}{2}\left[\left(p_2^n(\cdot) - p_1^n(\cdot)\right) - \left(\frac{\partial p_2^n(\cdot)}{\partial K^{max}} - \frac{\partial p_1^n(\cdot)}{\partial K^{max}}\right)(Q^* - K^{max})\right] = \beta. \quad (17.9)$$

Call $K^{max,\beta}$ the level of $K^{max}$ that solves Equation (17.9). Since $\left(p_2^n(\cdot) - p_1^n(\cdot)\right)$ is a decreasing function of $K^{max}$ and $\beta > 0$, it follows that $K^{max,\beta} < K^{max*}$. Therefore, the first best equilibrium is reached for that level of installed transmission capacity for which the congestion is not eliminated. In other words, when investment costs are taken into account, it is not optimal to expand transmission capacity up to the level that completely eliminates the congestion. On the contrary, the optimal investment is set at the level at which the marginal cost of the investment in the transmission capacity equals the marginal social gain in the reduction of the inefficiency due to the congestion. This is true for any two nodes linked through radial lines, and is termed **Long Run Marginal Cost**, since it refers to the long-run, when transmission capacity can be adjusted. The following result summarizes the findings:

---

### Result

When there are transmission investment costs, it is not optimal to expand the transmission line up to the level of capacity that eliminates congestion. The optimal level is set at that level at which the marginal cost of the investment in the transmission capacity equals the marginal social gain in the reduction of the inefficiency due to the congestion (Long Run Marginal Cost principle).

---

As before, if the SO is remunerated through the congestion rent, it chooses the optimal level that maximizes its congestion rent, net of the transmission investment cost. When the latter is positive, the SO further reduces the optimal amount of transmission capacity compared to the case of no investment costs. This can be seen by replicating the analysis of problem (17.5), under the assumption that the SO has to pay for the transmission capacity expansion:

$$\max_{K^{max}} CR - C(K^{max}) = \left[\left(p_2^n(K^{max}) - p_2^n(K^{max})\right)K^{max} - \beta K^{max}\right]. \quad (17.10)$$

Equilibrium is reached at that level of transmission capacity $K^{max}$ that solves:

$$\left(p_2^n(\cdot) - p_1^n(\cdot)\right) + \left(\frac{\partial p_2^n(\cdot)}{\partial K^{max}} - \frac{\partial p_1^n(\cdot)}{\partial K^{max}}\right)K^{max} = \beta. \quad (17.11)$$

Call the level of $K^{max}$ that solves Equation (17.11) $K^{maxSO,\beta}$. It follows that $K^{maxSO,\beta} < K^{maxSO} < K^{max*}$. Thus, the optimal level of investment chosen by the SO is such that the transmission line is constrained. Notice moreover that the larger the investment costs, the smaller the level of the capacity set by the SO.

With transmission capacity costs, we have that $K^{maxSO,\beta}$ can be higher, lower or equal to $K^{max,\beta}$. This can be seen observing that, at $K^{max,\beta}$, it must be that:

$$\left(p_2^n(\cdot) - p_1^n(\cdot)\right) = \left(\frac{\partial p_2^n(\cdot)}{\partial K^{max}} - \frac{\partial p_1^n(\cdot)}{\partial K^{max}}\right)(Q^* - K^{max}) + 2\beta, \tag{17.12}$$

while at $K^{maxSO,\beta}$, the following equation holds:

$$\left(p_2^n(\cdot) - p_1^n(\cdot)\right) = +\left(\frac{\partial p_2^n(\cdot)}{\partial K^{max}} - \frac{\partial p_1^n(\cdot)}{\partial K^{max}}\right)K^{max} + 2\beta. \tag{17.13}$$

Simplifying Equations (17.12) and (17.13), we see that $K^{max,\beta} = K^{maxSO,\beta}$ if and only if $\beta = -\left(\frac{\partial p_2^n(\cdot)}{\partial K^{max}} - \frac{\partial p_1^n(\cdot)}{\partial K^{max}}\right)$.

This implies that, when the investment decision on grid expansion is left to the SO, it is quite possible that it chooses a level that does not maximize social welfare, because it aims at maximizing its own profits. Only by chance can it be that the two levels coincide. Note that we have framed the analysis in a radial network framework, but this assumption is not necessary for the result. Oren et al. (1995), for instance, have shown that in a meshed network a capacity expansion, for instance a new line that transforms the network from radial to meshed, can indeed worsen the congestion. As a consequence, the SO (or whoever makes the investment on the basis of the maximization of the congestion rent), when selecting the investment level, need not choose the amount and type of capacity that maximizes welfare.

For this reason, in those systems in which the SO is remunerated on the basis of the congestion rent, and not on the basis of some cost-plus regulatory rule on the invested capital, investment decisions on transmission capacity expansion are not left to the SO but are regulated or agreed with or at least supervised by the responsible regulatory authority. This is, for example, the market design of the ISOs in the United States or the TSOs in Europe.

## 17.5    Transmission Capacity Expansion and Market Failures

The analysis of the previous paragraph assumed perfect competition at each node. What happens when there are imperfections in energy markets that create a distortion in price signals? There are a number of possible price distortions that can be obstacles to reaching the optimal equilibrium. Some of the possible reasons why market prices may turn out not to be optimal include market power, regulatory interventions like the imposition of price caps, the absence of a complete representation of consumer demand in the wholesale market, the discretionary behavior of SOs, or randomness in the load and or the costs.

Consider, for example, the role of market power. Assume that there is a plant with market power in zone 2, where import is constrained. When the producer exercises market power, it will do so by withdrawing capacity and increasing the price in zone 2. The market will therefore clear at a price in excess of marginal cost of plant in zone 2. In such a situation, the measured congestion rent will then overestimate the cost savings associated with the replacement of one unit of power generated in 2 by one unit of power

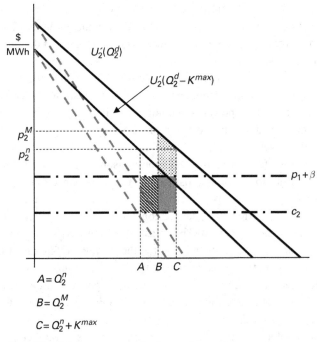

**Figure 17.3** Market power in the importing node

generated in 1, suggesting an over-incentive to reinforce the link and ignoring the potential impacts of the other market imperfections. As a result, market power in the importing area creates high incentives for transmission investment. This might even reduce total welfare.

Another fundamental problem is that a line expansion can improve competition and lower welfare at the same time. An example adapted from Brunekreeft and Newbery (2006) can help to illustrate this effect. Consider Figure 17.3.

Suppose that plant in node 2 is a monopolist, while plants in node 1 are under perfect competition. Assume that the marginal cost of generating power in node 1, $c_1$, plus the marginal cost of building the transmission line from 1 to 2, $\beta$, is higher than the marginal cost of power production in node 2, $c_2$. Because of the perfect competition assumption in node 1, $p_1 = c_1$. Moreover, assume for the sake of simplicity that $\frac{\partial p_1^n(\cdot)}{\partial K^{max}} = 0$. Let us compare the case of no transmission line with the case of a line of capacity $K^{max}$. Without transmission line, the price in node 2 is the monopolistic price $p_2^M$, to which corresponds an amount of energy $Q_2^M$. Let $p_2^M > p_1$. Suppose an SO can invest in the transmission line in order to obtain the congestion rent. From Equation 17.7, it would do so choosing the amount of capacity $K^{max}$ such that $p_2^M > p_1 + \beta$ (see that $p_1 = p_1^n$ by assumption). Indeed, $p_2^M$ would be the monopolistic price calculated by plant 2 on the residual demand, namely the demand net of the amount of energy imported from 1. The corresponding monopolistic quantity on the residual demand is $Q_2^n$. The overall amount of energy that load withdraws now in node 2 is $Q_2^n - K^{max}$. Now, compare the welfare effect of importing energy from 1 to the welfare without imports. The extra cost of energy imported from node 1, which includes the cost of building the line, compared to the cost of energy production node 2, is $[(p_1 + \beta) - c_2]K^{max}$. Indeed, due to transmission investments costs, it costs more to import energy from 1 than producing it in 2. This can be termed negative import effect. The extra import allows however reducing the DWL due to the monopolistic power, since now there is a higher energy to be used in node 2. This can be termed positive competition effect, since it represents the reduction in the monopolistic power of the plant in zone 2.

The net effect on welfare arises from the comparison of the two effects. When the latter is higher than the former, the expansion in the interconnection would be detrimental from a social welfare perspective. In Figure 17.3, the dashed area plus the grey area is the negative import effect; the positive competition effect is the grey area plus the dotted area. The grey area cancels out. The areas to be compared are the dashed and the dotted ones: if the former is larger than the latter, the overall welfare effect is negative. The positive competition effect would occur at the expense of higher cost of importing energy. It would have been better to regulate the monopolist in order to induce it to increase its production, rather than expanding the transmission line, even if this implies a reduced market power for the monopolist.

The overall effect of a capacity addition is determined by several factors:

- The higher the difference between generating costs in the two regions and the higher the costs of building the line $\beta$, the more likely it is that the overall effect is negative.
- The elasticity of demand is closely related to the competition effect: if demand is relatively inelastic, the competition effect of the line will be small.
- As the size of the line increases, the increase in welfare brought about by the competition effect decreases (due to downward sloping demand), whereas the decrease in welfare due to the negative import effect is constant (under the assumption of constant marginal costs). Thus, in this scenario, the overall effect of transmission is likely to be welfare decreasing beyond some critical size of the line capacity.

When there is market power, power plants can make strategic use of import constraints. A few models have addressed the link between transmission congestion and market power. Borenstein et al. (2000) show that, in the presence of transmission constraints, it can be profitable for plants to withhold output in order to constrain the transmission line that links those plants that would not have been constrained under perfect competition. Borenstein et al. (1995) cite empirical evidence from Northern California to this effect. Oren (1997) presents an alternative scenario with the transmission constraint located between two strategic plants in a three-node network. Stoft (2002) solves the corresponding Cournot game and Joskow and Tirole (2000) provide the following interpretation: the transmission configuration can turn the output of plants at two different nodes into "local complements." Therefore, in a duopoly, this situation increases the incentive for a plant to withhold output, as this limits the other producer's output and increases the price. Cardell et al. (1997) show that, if plants that behave strategically own generation assets at two production points in a three-node network, they might increase output at one node relative to a competitive scenario if this reduces the total energy delivered to the other node due to loop flows and therefore increases the price at this second location.

## Learning Outcomes

- In a congested network, the difference between nodal prices is called the congestion rent.
- When two zones are connected, the difference between demand and supply in each zone beyond the internal market clearing quantity generates net export curves. They can be used to display the congestion rent.
- The optimal level of transmission capacity without any transmission cost would be at the level at which the interconnection line is not congested. When transmission line expansion costs are introduced, it is no longer optimal to eliminate the congestion.
- The welfare maximizing network investment equates the value of a marginal reduction in inefficiency due to lack of transmission capacity to the marginal cost of investment.
- The SO would choose the investment level that maximizes its own rent (congestion rent). This level does not coincide with the socially optimal one.
- Market power exercised by firms in different interconnected zones distorts the optimal investment level. Firms can play strategically, creating congestion and insulating some zones where producers can set their prices. Network expansion that reduces monopolistic power in some zones can improve competition and simultaneously reduce total welfare.

# 18 Transmission Rights and Price Risk Hedging

## 18.1 Introduction

In the previous chapters, we have seen that it is not optimal to fully eliminate transmission congestions. Thus, in the grid it is possible to have transmission lines that are congested, that is, transmission capacity is a scarce resource. Like any scarce resource, transmission capacity has a value, and like any good that has a value, it can be traded in a market. By defining rights of using the scarce resource and commercializing them, the value of transmission capacity and the associated externalities can emerge. This is the role of markets for transmission rights. They are a way of showing the theoretical value of the transmission capacity that we have identified in the previous chapters.

Transmission rights can be seen as complementary tools to implement first-best allocation through nodal prices. Thus, not surprisingly, transmission rights markets have been implemented in markets based on nodal pricing, such as those in the northeast United States, such as PJM. In other countries, there have been intense discussions on the need for congestion hedging from transmission price risk. As reported by Kunz et al. (2016), in Europe, transmission rights between pricing zones used to be grandfathered in the form of Physical Transmission Rights (see below) between pricing zones (usually countries) to match commercial contractual arrangements for cross-border transactions, although this system is progressively being phased out. In the Nordic Pool and in Italy Financial Transmission Rights take the form of bilateral contractual arrangements with limited liquidity, since they are not issued by SOs.

In this chapter, we first explain what transmission rights are in Paragraph 18.2, distinguishing between financial and physical rights. Then in Paragraph 18.3 we show the equivalence between Physical Transmission Rights and Financial Transmission rights. In Paragraph 18.4 we show how financial transmission rights can be coupled with other financial products to hedge against price risk. Finally, in Paragraph 18.5, we point out the practical difficulties of providing the exact measure of transmission capacity limits.

## 18.2 Physical and Financial Transmission Rights

When there is congestion, a power exporter cannot be sure that its energy will be dispatched at the importing node. In other words, in order to deliver energy at the importing node, it needs to be able to use the transmission line. As we have seen, under congestion the transmission capacity is a scarce resource. How is this scarce resource to be allocated among different potential users? In other words, when there is more than one potential exporter, and not all of them can use the full transmission capacity since the amount that they require exceeds the transmission capacity constraint, how is this transmission capacity to be allocated among them? One simple way to answer these questions is to create a market for the scarce transmission capacity. An exporter that wants to use a transmission line to deliver electricity to an importing node, can do so by acquiring such a right in the market. These are called physical transmission rights:

DEFINITION. *Physical Transmission Right (PTR): a contract that gives to its owner the right to use a congested network along a predefined path.*

PTRs allow network users to inject or withdraw electricity at different locations in the grid. Thus, they are market mechanisms that can insure their owners against the delivery risk as a result of location-specific energy contracts (Bushnell, 1999). When there are PTRs, a power producer (consumer) must possess a given amount of PTR to have that amount of supply (load) scheduled or transported over the congested interface. Once it has such a right, there is no additional charge for using the transportation network, even if congested. The market for these rights, then, determines the market-clearing price of congestion.

However, creating a market for PTRs may be difficult. Apart from the market power in the market for rights that can distort congestion values, which is a common problem for all marketplaces, there are also electricity-specific issues. Electricity transmission is an unusual commodity. One issue with PTR is that transmission capacity must be measured *ex ante* and allocated. However, there is a time misalignment between the timing of the market exchanges of the PTRs and their usage. The allocation process of PTRs typically takes place in discrete periods, for instance every month. This occurs because there has to be enough time to group rights and perform the auction with a sufficient level of liquidity. On the contrary, the effective possibility of transmitting capacity in real time depends on the physical status of the grid at every point in time, which in turn depends on injections and withdrawals at every node, losses, and all the physical constraints of the grid. Thus, it is possible that a given PTR that has been commercialized cannot be used when needed since that capacity is not physically present at that moment. In this case, the PTRs would overestimate the effective capacity of the grid. However, the opposite problem can also occur. PTRs may underestimate the transmission capacity as this is very difficult, when assessing the amount of PTRs that can be issued, taking into account the fact that counter-flows actually increase the available transmission capacity. Finally, there is also a price signal risk issue. As noted, the buyers of PTRs must acquire them in advance of the delivery, on the basis of the expectations of the price differentials on the transmission lines. They must also communicate to the SO the fact that they intend to use their rights at some specific point in time, for instance in a given hour. This is called **nomination**. Nominations also take place before delivery, since the SO must timely check the feasibility of the dispatch schedule that arises in a given zone as a result of the nominations plus all the other internal supply and demand schedules. As a result, it is quite possible that, due to the result of the accepted schedule, the nominations go in the wrong direction, in the sense that the owner of the PTR, expecting that a line is congested from node $i$ to node $j$, nominates the capacity in order to export from $i$ to $j$, but the resulting equilibrium price is $p_1 > p_j$. Clearly, this would be inefficient since it would imply using the transmission capacity in the wrong direction (i.e. buying and using a PTR that is worthless).

PTRs are not the only transmission rights that can be used to price congestion. It is possible to tackle the problem of the allocation of scarce transmission capacity through a different approach. Buyers and sellers submit bids to the SO to buy and sell power at different nodes on the network. The network operator then chooses the lowest cost bids to balance electricity supply and demand, subject to the physical laws that govern electric power networks and the capacity of the network to carry power reliably. As explained in Chapter 12, the bid price of the last bidder selected at a given node becomes the market-clearing price at this node. Therefore, a power producer which is delivering electricity to customers and that is behind a congested line receives a lower net price than plants located downstream, next to consumers. As we have seen in Chapter 17, the price difference between the withdrawal and injection node gives rise to the congestion rent. Thus, one way to allocate scarce transmission capacity among capacity users is to transform the congestion rent into a financial product and commercialize it (Joskow and Tirole, 2000). This is what financial transmission rights are:

DEFINITION. *Financial Transmission Right (FTR): a contract that pays to its owner the real-time cost of transmission on a given path, entitling him/her to obtain the difference between the nodal prices of two interconnected nodes.*

On the basis of the rules, FTR can be grandfathered to users, if the SO wants or has to divest the CR to buyers (power plants and consumers), or sold through a competitive mechanism. In the latter case, the SO, by issuing an amount of FTR that is equivalent to the amount of energy transmissible on the congested lines, cashes in *ex ante* the expected value of the CR.

Those who have obtained or acquired FTR over the congested line receive a share of the congestion rent, equal to the share of the rights they hold over the total amount of shares issued to cover the congestion rent. An example can help to explain this aspect.

---

**Example 18.1 Financial Transmission Rights** Suppose that there is a transmission line whose capacity is 100 MW, that is always congested throughout a year. Assume that an FTR has a size of 1 MW. There are 100 FTR. Let the price differential on the two nodes be equal to $20/MWh per each hour of the year. The CR is $20[/MWh] × 100[MW] × 8760[h] = 17,520,000[$]. If a buyer acquires 50 FTR, it obtains a 50 percent share of the CR, i.e., 8,760,000[$].

---

If the price differential changes across hours, as normally happens, in the example above we would have to replace the price differential with the expected price differential over the entire time spell, but nothing else would differ.

## 18.3    Value Equivalence of PTRs and FTRs

At first glance, it seems that FTRs and PTRs are completely different objects. However, they provide the holders with the same service, namely, insuring them against the risk of energy not being dispatched due to congestion. Therefore, they have the same value. Let us show this result, first pointed out by Chao and Peck (1996).

Consider first the market equilibrium with PTRs.

Let us define the market clearing price of the PTR as $\eta_{PTR}$. When there is congestion and the transmission capacity is a binding constraint, the rights to use it has a market value $\eta_{PTR}$ that is greater than zero. Plants in the exporting node, node 1, receive for their power supply, in each hour, a price that corresponds to the difference between the price they receive from the customers in delivery node 2 (i.e. $p_2$), and the market value of each PTR they must acquire in order to deliver energy. Note that if the transmission right lasts for a time spell that equals $T$ (e.g. one year), in each time unit (e.g. one hour), the cost of the PTR would be $1/T$ of the overall costs of the PTR. For simplicity of notation, we normalize $T = 1$.

When both energy and rights markets are perfectly competitive, equilibrium prices at each node coincide with the marginal production cost at the exporting node and the marginal utility of consumption at the importing node, assuming for simplicity that there is no demand at node 1 and no supply at node 2. When there is congestion, the PTR has a positive value; thus there will be an amount of PTRs equal to the maximum amount of capacity tradable, i.e. $K^{max}$. The equilibrium value of the PTR arises as the solution to the following system of equations:

$$
\begin{aligned}
p_1 &= p_2 - \eta = C_1'(K^{max}) \\
p_2 &= U_2'(Q_2^d - K^{max}) \\
\eta_{PTR} &= (p_2 - p_1)
\end{aligned}
\tag{18.1}
$$

with $p_2 > p_1$ and $U_2'(Q_2^d - K^{max})$ denotes net demand at node 2, $C_1'(K^{max})$ net supply at node 1.

Let us compare the equilibrium in Equation (18.1) with that in the case of financial transmission rights.

Assume a system of FTRs is in place, and an amount equal to $K^{max}$ rights is issued. For simplicity, let the FTR be measured in the same unit measure of $K^{max}$, for instance 1 MW, thus $K^{max}$ denotes both the transmission capacity of a line and the number of financial rights issued on that line. As explained above, financial rights give holders a proportionate share of the congestion rent received by the SO when the transmission constraint $K^{max}$ is binding. In other words, holding one unit of financial rights entitles the owner to receive $(p_2 - p_1)T$, where $T$ denotes the duration of the FTR (e.g. one year). As before, for simplicity we set $T = 1$. Therefore, total payments to FTR holders will amount, in equilibrium, to $(p^{2*}-p^{1*})K^{max}$. Assuming again that there is no market power in the generation market and in the market for rights, the value of an FTR, call it $\eta_{FTR}$, is simply equal to the difference in the equilibrium (nodal) energy prices, i.e.:

$$
\begin{aligned}
p_1 &= C_1'(K^{max}) \\
p_2 &= U_2'(Q_2^d - K^{max}) \\
\eta_{FTR} &= (p_2 - p_1)
\end{aligned}
\tag{18.2}
$$

It is clear that $\eta_{PTR}$ in Equation (18.2) coincides with $\eta_{FTR}$ in Equation (18.1), thus the market value of the two types of rights coincides.

## 18.4    Transmission Rights and Risk Hedging

Financial rights are financial products. In particular, they are financial derivatives on congestion rent. They allow the risk of the nodal price difference to be shifted from the power producer to the issuer. As for any financial product, a properly built portfolio enables elimination of diversifiable risk, by founding an asset that is negatively covariate with it. In the case of financial transmission rights, the price risk can be fully hedged using FTRs and Contracts for Differences between power exporters and importers. Contracts for Differences are defined as follows:

DEFINITION. **Contract For Differences (CFD):** *a contract written between a plant, at the exporting node 1, and a consumer, at the importing node 2, such that the plant at 1 agrees to pay the consumer the difference between the negotiated strike price $p^S$ and the spot price, $p_2$, in exchange for a fixed payment.*

CFDs are financial products that shift price risk from power consumers to power producers. Suppose that a power producer, located at the exporting node 1, sells an amount $x$ of CFD to a consumer at the importing node 2. By agreeing to receive (or pay, if $p_2 < p^S$) $p_2 > p^S$ per each unit of time (e.g. each hour), the consumer would be exposed to a constant payment in the year (or any other period of validity of the CFD) equal to $p^S x T$. As before, let us normalize $T = 1$. If the spot prices at nodes 1 and 2 were always the same, there would be no price risk and no gain or losses between the producer and the consumer. The only CFD that the producer would be willing to sell is that with the strike price $p_1 = p_2 = p^S$ for otherwise it would incur a loss. However, for all those times in which prices at nodes 1 and 2 differ, the producer is exposed to a price risk. Whenever the spot price for power is higher at the consumer's node than at the producer's node, the customer pays the energy $p_2$ but is receiving back from the producer $(p_2 - p^S)x$. The overall expenditure for those hours would be $-p_2Q^d - (p_2 - p^S)x$. If the customer buy an amount of CFD, $x$, that equals the amount of energy it acquires, $Q^d$, it would thus gain $(p^S - p_2)x$, which corresponds to the transfer from the producer.

By building a portfolio with an amount of FTR, $K^{max}$ that equals the amount of energy exchanged through CDF (i.e. $x$), both producers and consumers can fully hedge against price risk (Bushnell and Stoft, 1996, 1997). This is shown in Table 18.1, where we have

**Table 18.1** Hedging portfolio of CFDs and FTRs

| | Payments | |
|---|---|---|
| | Producer (node 1) | Consumer (node 2) |
| | $Q_1 = Q$ | $Q^d = -Q$ |
| Electricity market | $p_1 Q$ | $p_2 Q$ |
| CFD $x$ at strike price $p^S$ | $(p^S - p_2)x$ | $-(p^S - p_2)x$ |
| Total | $p^S x - p_2 x + p_1 Q$ | $-p^S x + p_2 x - p_2 Q$ |
| FTR $K^{max}$ from 1 to 2 | $(p_2 - p_1)K^{max}$ | — |
| Total with $K^{max} = x$ (FTRs match CFDs) | $p^S K^{max} + p_1 Q - p_1 K^{max}$ | $-p^S K^{max} - p_2 Q + p_2 K^{max}$ |
| With optimal dispatch ($K^{max} = Q_1$) | $p^S Q$ | $-p^S Q$ |

assumed that the producer is located in node 1, markets clear, there is no load shedding, $Q^d = Q_1$, and signs before quantities denote production (positive) or withdrawals (negative). Note that, as we already know, when lines are constrained the optimal dispatch from congested lines coincides with the maximum capacity of the line, i.e. $Q_1 = K^{max}$.

Since CFDs and TCCs are both purely financial and thus unrelated to physical changes such as increased production or consumption, any deviations of the physical flows from the flows stipulated in the financial contracts only affect the settlement in the real-time market. Consequently, the hedging strategy has no impact on the decision to supply or consume an additional MW in real time. The nodal price affects this decision, and a competitive price leads to an efficient choice.

The correspondence between FTRs and power flows must be made explicit. This is done by issuing an amount of FTRs that is feasible, namely, that respects the constraints imposed by Kirchhoff's laws on power flow. A power flow on a network lists the power flowing on every line and its direction of flow. In a linear approximation of a network, two power flows can be measured by adding the flows on every line and taking account of cancellations due to counterflows. Some power flows are considered infeasible because the flow on at least one line violates that line's power-transmission limit. All other power flows fall into the category of the feasible ones. An FTR from node 1 to node 2 specifies that there will be a power flow from 1 to 2, but it does not specify the effective power that will flow on any line: this will be calculated given the characteristics and the shape of the grid, assuming that the unit measure of power of that specific FTR is injected at 1 and withdrawn at 2. Similarly, every set of FTRs corresponds to the sum of all the power flows corresponding to each FTR in the set. Any set of FTRs that corresponds to a feasible power flow is a feasible set; other sets are infeasible. The set of FTRs that are issued is restricted to be a feasible set. FTRs in a feasible set account for counterflows.

A final aspect refers to the issuing strategy. In particular, when FTR are grandfathered, the SO operator collects the congestion rent ($CR$) in the wholesale market and refunds much or all of it to the FTRs owners. If the SO sells the FTRs, it obtains a revenue. Call it $R_{FTR}$. We might ask under what conditions the $CR$ covers the overall amount of reimbursement of FTR holders, called Hedge Payments ($C_H$): $C_H < CR$. When this condition occurs, we say that there is revenue sufficiency. Indeed, $C_H$ are a cost to the SO. Without revenue sufficiency, the SO would go bankrupt or need to be subsidized to continue operating. There will be revenue sufficiency as long as:

$$C_H < CR + R_{FTR} \tag{18.3}$$

Hogan (1992) has shown that for a direct-current (DC) approximation to a meshed network, if the set of FTR distributed by the SO is feasible, condition (18.3) holds even when $R_{FTR} = 0$. In other words, the revenue sufficiency condition holds under grandfathering, provided the set of issued FTRs is feasible.

## 18.5     Measuring Transmission Capacity

In the analyses performed above, we always assumed that $K^{max}$ was a precise measure of the maximum transmission capacity. This is not the case. Measuring transmission capacity in the reality is a complex issue. Transmission capacity varies in real time, depending on the effective network configuration, including power injections and withdrawals and losses. Indeed, transmission capacity can be regarded as a stochastic variable, since it depends on stochastic factors, which implies taking into account expectations and risks. Thus, in real-life an issue arises about how to measure transmission capacity.

Different calculation methods can be applied to measure the transmission capacity. The most common one is the use of **Available Transmission Capacity** (ATC). This latter is defined as the Total Transfer Capability (TTC) less the Transmission Reliability Margin (TRM) and the sum of the existing transmission commitments (which includes retail customer service) and the Capacity Benefit Margin (CBM). The TTC is the amount of electric power that can be transferred over the interconnected transmission network in a reliable manner while meeting all specifically defined pre- and post-contingency system conditions. The TRM is the amount of transmission transfer capability that provides a reasonable level of assurance that the interconnected transmission network will be secure. TRM accounts for the inherent uncertainty in system conditions and its associated effects on ATC calculations, and the need for operating flexibility to ensure reliable system operation as system conditions change. The CBM is the amount of firm transmission transfer capability preserved for retailers where their load is located, to enable access to generation from interconnected systems to meet generation reliability requirements.

One alternative to the ATC is the usage of the **Operating Transfer Capability** Limit (OTC). The latter are the maximum value for the most critical system operating parameters(s), which meets: (a) pre-contingency criteria as determined by equipment loading capability and acceptable voltage conditions, (b) transient criteria as determined by equipment loading capability and acceptable voltage conditions, (c) transient performance criteria and (d) post-contingency loading and voltage criteria.

The two measures defined above are linked, since TTC cannot exceed the OTC. However, they provide distinct figures for $K^{max}$, a further difficulty that has to be taken into account when assessing investment and hedging strategies with transmission capacity.

## Learning Outcomes

- The creation and allocation of a system of tradable property rights over a network decentralizes congestion pricing in such a way that congested network lines are efficiently allocated. Transmission rights are complementary in the process of implementing the first-best allocation, together with nodal prices.
- Physical transmission rights are a contract that gives to its owner the right to use a congested network along a predefined path.
- Financial transmission rights are a contract that pays to its owner the real-time cost of transmission on a given path, entitling him/her to obtain the difference between the nodal prices of two interconnected nodes.
- Physical and financial rights have the same market value.
- Contracts for differences are contracts that insulate the holder from price fluctuation at its node. A portfolio of financial transmission rights and contracts for differences allows both power producers and consumers to fully hedge against price risk.
- Difficulties may arise in defining and measuring the amount of transmission capacity. There are different calculation methodologies that provide distinct information on real-time constraints.

# Part VI

# Economics of Electricity Retail Markets

In Chapter 4, we introduced the Wholesale and Retail model as the model in which all activities are fully liberalized, including electricity retail. The purpose of this Part is to review the characteristics and specific features of electricity retailing markets.

In general, in most industries, the role of retailers is to provide final customers with added-value services. The type and magnitude of costs and benefits from retailing activities vary widely across industries, final customers' characteristics, geographical locations and market structures. Electricity retailers perform two main activities: on one hand, they provide consumers with a complex service by aggregating inputs from all upstream actors (generation, transport and distribution); and on the other hand, they facilitate upstream firms' sales by finding, arranging and managing relationships with potential and actual buyers. However, in the electricity sector, retailing has some specific features that we will consider here. As we saw in Part III, wholesale electricity prices vary every hour. However, only a fraction of consumers are exposed to real-time pricing, with many customers, typically households, paying constant prices. Thus, a first element that retailers must take into account is that they are exposed to extremely volatile upstream prices, and rather rigid downstream ones. Secondly, electricity retailers' opportunities to provide value-added services seem more limited than in other sectors, unless innovation in electricity consumption occurs, since consumers buy a homogeneous, intangible and indistinguishable product, namely, the ordered flow of electrons called electricity. Thirdly, consumer behavior is quite passive in terms of looking for best deals when buying electricity, with many being reluctant to switch retailers. Finally, electricity is often considered a necessary good which must be provided in any circumstances and to all consumers that require it.

In Chapter 19 we focus on theoretical models of competitive electricity retailing activities, their impact on retail markets, and properties in terms of allocative efficiency. In Chapter 20 we underline some critical implementation issues and practical examples from different countries. We shall explain the extent to which retail competition delivers concrete advantages to consumers, from lower electricity pricing to faster innovation, and whether regulation is still needed to ensure customer protection.

# 19 Retail Competition: Supplying Electricity to Final Consumers

## 19.1 Introduction

There is no consensus in the literature on how to model markets and competition in electricity retail. A few models dealing with retail competition address specific features of retail pricing, in particular dynamic rates, under the implicit assumption that retail competition should lead to rates that are more sophisticated than flat prices. The existing models thus focus on the mix between fixed and fluctuating prices to end users. Additionally, the limited profit opportunities together with low switching rates question the benefits arising from introducing competition in electricity retailing (Pollit, 2008; Su, 2015). This chapter summarizes the very few models of retail competition that focus on the potential price distortions due to the coexistence of fixed and time-varying end users' prices. We also provide a brief overview of some experiences of retail competition and time-varying prices. Clearly, when one tries to evaluate the advantages of competing suppliers, it is difficult to disentangle the effects of incomplete deregulation from other barriers that avoid retail competition to deliver the desired outcomes.

## 19.2 Real-Time Pricing under Competitive Retail Markets

Some scholars (Borenstein 2005a and 2005b, Holland and Mansur 2006, Joskow and Tirole 2006) have analyzed real-time pricing together with fixed pricing and its consequences on reliability (Joskow and Tirole, 2007) and $CO_2$ emissions (Holland and Mansur, 2008). Competition in retail markets is generally seen as a slightly modified version of price setting (e.g. Bertrand) modeling, with the noticeable complexity of the time structure of retail pricing. This latter aspect is a crucial element of retail electricity markets. To understand why it is so, let us define the general characteristics of time-varying retail pricing.

According to Borenstein (2005a), time-varying retail electricity pricing has two main design issues:

a. *granularity of prices*: the frequency with which retail prices change within the day or week; and
b. *timeliness of prices*: the time lag between when the price is set and when it is actually effective.

Flat retail rates display no granularity, as there is a single price for days and nights, weekdays and weekends; and price setting is not timely as it is set months before some of the hours to which it is applied. The opposite hypothetical extreme would be a real-time pricing program in which prices change every minute and are announced only at the minute in which they are applied. This is the model that has been most extensively studied in the literature.

DEFINITION. *Electricity Real-Time Pricing (RTP): a system of retail pricing that has a very high degree of both price granularity and price timeliness.*

Under RTP, the frequency with which prices are defined changes within a day and the time lag is very short, for pricing to be effective.

RTP is not a specific feature of electricity retail markets only: there are other industries that see highly volatile wholesale prices and that adjust retail prices very quickly to reflect changes in the wholesale price of the good, such as the fresh food and gasoline industries, for instance.

In the electricity sector, as noted, in most cases retail electricity prices under RTP change hourly. Prices are typically set either a day ahead, or in real time. In the day-a-head formulation, the retail provider announces all twenty-four-hourly prices for a given day at one time on the prior day. In the real-time approach, the retail provider announces prices on a rolling basis, typically with the price of each hour determined between fifteen and ninety minutes prior to the beginning of that hour. Generally, RTP contracts are signed by large industrial consumers that optimize the costs of electricity as an input.

RTP, however, would expose consumers, particularly small and residential ones, to a price volatility that is difficult to manage for an essential commodity like electricity. Thus, in the real world, time-varying prices display limited granularity and timeliness. The types of possible time-varying prices that are applied in reality can be broadly classified as follows.

(1) *Time-of-use (TOU) pricing* is often used for large industrial and commercial customers. Under TOU, the retail price varies in a predetermined way within certain blocks of time. The rates for each time block, such as peak periods, intermediate periods and off-peak ones, for instance, are adjusted infrequently, only two or three times a year in most cases. Price is the same during a given period throughout the month or season for which the block is set.

(2) *Interruptible contracts* also present the features of time-varying prices. Customers served by this kind of contract accept curtailments when the system is short of capacity, against specific TOU prices or receive compensations.

(3) *Critical peak pricing (CPP)*, usually starts with a TOU rate structure, but then it adds one more rate that applies to specifically predetermined "critical" peak hours, that the retailer can call on short notice. While the TOU program has poor granularity and timeliness, as discussed above, CPP allows a very high price to be called at very short notice. Thus, CPP is similar to interruptible programs except that prices are not set so high as to cause most customers to reduce consumption to zero.

In practice, interruptible programs are usually proposed only to large customers, while CPP is envisioned to be used much more broadly.

## 19.3   Retail Competition and (In)efficiency of Real-Time Pricing

Let us analyze here RTP in retail competition, following the approach of Borenstein and Holland (2005) and Holland and Mansur (2006). In this paragraph, we show their main analytical result, namely, the inefficiency of having both RTP and flat-rate prices.

The authors consider an economy in which there are competitive retailers, and perfectly competitive wholesale markets. At the retail level, there are two types of consumer, those who are under RTP, and those who have a fixed time-invariant retail price. There is an exogenous fraction $\alpha$ of consumers who pay real-time prices that vary from hour to hour (i.e. $p_t$). The remaining fraction of consumers $1-\alpha$ pays a flat retail price that remain the same for every hour, that is, $p_t = \bar{p}$.

As we have seen in Parts I and II of this book, power demanded at the wholesale level must equal power supplied at every point in time. It is assumed that there are $T$ hours, and that the wholesale load in hour $j$ is represented by a demand curve which depends on prices at each hour:

$$Q^{dj} = Q^{dj}(p); \text{ with } \frac{\partial Q^{dj}}{\partial p} < 0. \tag{19.1}$$

The wholesale aggregate demand in a given hour is the sum of the demand of the customers in the two groups, which depends on the retail price that each of them faces, i.e. $p^j$ and $\bar{p}$:

$$\widetilde{Q^{dj}}(p^j, \bar{p}) = \alpha \widetilde{Q^{dj}}(p^j) + (1-\alpha)\,\widetilde{Q^{dj}}(\bar{p}). \tag{19.2}$$

Note that given the properties of the demand function, the aggregate demand decreases with respect to both real-time prices and flat prices. The demand curve elasticity depends on the fraction $\alpha$ of customer in real-time pricing. If $\alpha = 0$, the demand curve is vertical. The elasticity rises as $\alpha$ rises: having consumers with RTP confers price elasticity to aggregate demand.

Power plants are assumed to behave competitively and have the same cost structure as in Part III. The equilibrium of the wholesale market provides in hour $j$ the equilibrium wholesale price $p_j^*$. Note that as we have seen in Chapters 9 and 10, $p_j^*$ is either the marginal cost of the marginal plant or the VOLL.

Retailers are assumed to be in perfect competition in a retail market. They buy energy in the wholesale market and sell it to retail customers. In doing so, they face a time-invariant marginal cost of retailing $C_r'(\cdot) = c_r$ per each MWh supplied. Their profit function is:

$$\pi^{\mathrm{T}} = \sum_{j=1}^{\mathrm{T}}[\alpha(p^j - p_j^* - c_r)\widetilde{Q^{dj}}(\mathrm{p}^j) + (1 - \alpha)(\bar{p} - p_j^* - c_r)\widetilde{Q^{dj}}(\bar{p})]; \qquad (19.3)$$

where the first term represents the net profit from serving the flat-rate consumers and the second term is the retail profit from selling to RTP consumers; $p^j$ and $\bar{p}^j$ are the equilibrium retail prices, in each hour, for customers with RTP and under the flat-rate, respectively:

$$p^j = p_j^* + c_r; \qquad (19.4)$$

$$\bar{p} = c_r + \frac{\sum p_j^* \widetilde{Q^{dj}}(\cdot)}{\sum \widetilde{Q^{dj}}(\cdot)}. \qquad (19.5)$$

The price in Equation (19.4) is a time-changing price rate, which corresponds simply to the usual price equal to marginal cost rule, for the retailer. It is a mark-up on the wholesale price given by the marginal cost of the retailing activity. Price in Equation (19.5) on the contrary is a time-invariant plant rate. It corresponds to a mark-up on marginal cost of retailing, given by the weighted average of wholesale prices; weights are given by the relative weight of the load required by time-invariant customers in a given hour over their whole load for the entire period.

Borenstein and Holland show the following two results:

---

### Results

In a market with a positive fraction of customers who do not have retail RTP (i.e. with $\alpha \neq 1$), the wholesale competitive equilibrium is inefficient.

If the customers' distribution across types was such as that all retail customers face real-time prices (i.e. $\alpha = 1$), the competitive equilibrium is Pareto efficient.

---

The proof of result 1 rests on the consequences of the application of a well-known principle of competitive markets, namely, the *First Fundamental Theorem (FFT) of Welfare Economics:*

DEFINITION. *First Fundamental Theorem of Welfare Economics: when individuals are free to trade in a competitive marketplace and there are no externalities in production or consumption, the resulting distribution of resources in the economy is Pareto efficient: no person can be made better off without making some other person worse off.*

The FFT ensures the efficiency of the competitive equilibrium. In equilibrium, the price system is such as to indirectly coordinate the activities of all market participants, so that all resources move to their most highly valued uses.[1] In the case of the retail

---

[1] Work by Kenneth Arrow, Gerald Debreu and Francis Bator in the 1950s provided formal proof of the conditions under which the market equilibrium is Pareto-efficient (see Mas-Colell et al., 1989).

competition, the requirements of the welfare theorems are not met if $\alpha < 1$, since there is a missing market. Customers on flat retail prices cannot trade with customers on real-time prices or with producers, because all electricity transactions must occur at the same price for all flat-rate customers. In other words, there is a misalignment between trades at the wholesale level (which occur every hour) and trades with the flat-rate customers (which occur over a longer time scale, e.g. every year). This does not occur if $\alpha = 1$ since all trades would occur every hour, which explains result 2.

The main message of the Borenstein and Holland model is that, even if both the retail market and the wholesale market are competitive, this is not sufficient to provide an efficient allocation of resources: the fact that there are customers that do not respond to real-time wholesale prices at the retail level induces an inefficiency in the wholesale market. These authors also provide a number of other interesting results, that we describe in the next paragraph.

## 19.4    Retail Competition in the Borenstein and Holland (2005) Model: Specific Issues

Borenstein and Holland (2005) discuss other aspects of retail competition with RTP and flat rates that we summarize in this paragraph, focusing on their key messages. For simplicity, we neglect the (constant) marginal cost of the retail activity, i.e. we set $c_r = 0$ in Equations (19.4) and (19.5).

### 19.4.1    Second-Best Pricing

Borenstein and Holland show that when both RTP and flat-rate customers coexist, the second-best optimal flat rate would be equal to:

$$\bar{p}^{sb} = c_r + \frac{\sum p_j^* \left( \frac{\partial \widetilde{Q^{dj}}(\cdot)}{\partial \bar{p}} \right)}{\sum \frac{\partial \widetilde{Q^{dj}}(\cdot)}{\partial \bar{p}}}. \tag{19.6}$$

Equation 19.6, neglecting the marginal retail costs, differs from that in Equation 19.5 by the weights of the wholesale price. In particular, in the second-best equilibrium, the weights of the wholesale price are proportional to the relative slopes of the demand curves.

### 19.4.2    Fraction of Consumers on Real-Time Prices

In the short-run increasing the fraction of customers who are under RTP (i.e. $\alpha$), decreases wholesale prices during peak times and drives up wholesale prices during off-peak times, reducing volatility in wholesale prices. Specifically, whenever the wholesale price is above marginal cost pricing for the retailer, increasing the fraction of customers on real-time prices decreases quantity demanded and hence drives down wholesale prices, and vice versa.

### 19.4.3    Welfare Gains

Welfare gains from increasing the fraction of customers on real-time prices can be analyzed by dividing customers into five segments: existing RTP customers, customers that switch from flat rates to RTP, customers remaining on flat rates, power plants and retailers. They show that only existing RTP customers are made worse off by an exogenous increase in $\alpha$, because the reduced volatility in wholesale prices mitigates the gains that they previously made from shifting consumption to off-peak times. Power producers and retailers remain unaffected (competition keeps them at zero profit). Customers that switch to RTP must be weakly better off. Finally, customers that do not switch gain from the decrease in flat rate. The net effect on total welfare is ambiguous as long as some customers remain on flat rates. However, assuming linear demand the net effect on welfare of a rise in the share of RTP customers is unambiguously positive.

### 19.4.4    Endogenous Consumers' Switching

Borenstein and Holland also consider the incentives for consumers to switch from being under a flat-rate to a real time retail pricing scheme, assuming that it implies some costs, for instance of acquiring a real-time meter. Indeed, if switching was costless, all consumers would switch to RTP, and the only equilibrium would be with $\alpha = 1$. Even with a positive cost, if it was sufficiently low, all customers would still have an incentive to switch. However, as the cost of switching rises, an equilibrium area is reached in which some customers prefer not to adopt RTP. This result assumes homogeneous customers. With heterogeneous customers the analysis is more complex. There can be an elasticity effect, since the impact on the wholesale price of both RTP customers and customers on a flat rate depends on the elasticities of those who switch. Moreover, there can be an adverse selection problem: when RTP customers and flat rate customers coexist, those with high load in peak hours and relatively low load in off peak hours, that do not switch, are cross-subsidized by those with relatively low peak load and relatively high baseload. The latter customers have higher incentives to switch, but their switch might raise or reduce the wholesale price.

### 19.4.5    Long-Run Effects of Retail Competition

Borenstein and Holland also consider the relationship between retail competition and the long run analysis of wholesale markets (i.e. when power producers can choose the level of investments in capacity). In Part VII we show that perfectly competitive wholesale markets provide the correct long-run incentive for power plants' investments. However, when RTP is considered, the authors have shown that the wholesale equilibrium is not efficient. It is, therefore, no surprise that this inefficiency reflects the investment choice: because of the flat retail price, the first-best outcome is not achieved in both capacity investment and power production.

### 19.4.6    Empirical Evidence on RTP

Borenstein (2005b) uses data from the Californian market to calibrate and simulate the impact of RTP. The critical inputs for the simulation are load profiles, demand elasticities, and cost characteristics of the production technologies. The main findings of this study are as follows:

- The benefits of RTP outweigh the costs for the largest customers.
- The incremental benefits of putting more customers on RTP decline as the share of demand on RTP grows.
- Time-of-use rates are a poor substitute for RTP, as they capture only 20 percent of the efficiencies of RTP.
- Even with moderate demand elasticity, RTP will significantly change the composition of generation. The biggest effect will be a large decline in the amount of installed peak capacity. Mid-merit capacity would likely also decline and baseload capacity would increase, though these changes would be small compared to the potential for drastic reductions in peak capacity.

All in all, as long as flat rates persist, the benefits from retail competition and RTP seem difficult to reach.

## 19.5    RTP versus Two-Part Tariffs

Joskow and Tirole (2006) point out a few limitations of the Borenstein and Holland (2005) paper. First, it does not allow for two-part tariffs and instead assumes that all prices are single-rated. Secondly, it ignores the market distortions due to load profiling. Finally, the model assumes that customers are identical, whereas Joskow and Tirole extend their analysis to customers that vary according to a scale parameter.

Joskow and Tirole model equilibrium prices under retail competition with and without technical devices directly installed at the customers' place (smart meters) that allow the monitoring of real-time consumption and permitting real-time pricing. They extend Borenstein and Holland's paper by considering two-part tariffs, which outperform uniform rate tariffs, and load profiling (which is a specific form of TOU), rather than real-time pricing. Load profiling consists of measuring the load of a given customer at regular intervals, typically one hour, thirty or fifteen minutes, which leads to less efficient market outcomes than RTP.

The key message of the paper is that the first-best outcome is achieved with smart meters and real-time prices (i.e. prices that reflect market conditions in the wholesale market). Considering a monopolistic retail sector, instead of a perfectly competitive one, as in Borenstein and Holland (2005), Joskow and Tirole show that with customers using traditional meters, a two-part tariff achieves a second-best outcomes because electricity bills are calculated as weighted averages, thus not accounting for effective usage. Traditional meters and retail competition lead to a welfare level even below the second-best outcome, because retailers must rely on load profiling. When multiple firms share a customer base and effective time-varying usage is not known, retailers buy electricity in the wholesale market for their retail customers, based on average and not real customer usage, and they too face the wrong prices.

Joskow and Tirole also show that first-best outcomes are achieved with responsive customers, because the optimal retailer strategy is to pass wholesale prices on to consumers (i.e. charge real-time prices). When there are imperfectly reactive customers, who take into account transaction or information costs, retail competition provides a second-best outcome. The authors also consider a case where real-time meters are installed but real-time pricing by retailers is prohibited. Under the assumption that all customers are identical, retail competition leads to the second-best outcome achieved under traditional meters and load-profiling: the optimal uniform price allows customers to pay a price equal to the wholesale price weighted by the slopes of the individual demand curves.

## 19.6    Real-Time Pricing in Practice

Joskow and Wolfram (2012) note that despite its attractiveness, the adoption of RTP is difficult to generalize. They point out that, as shown by several studies, redistributive effects among consumers that adopt RTP and those who are served at flat rates might explain the persistent barriers to dynamic prices. Christen Associates in Energy Consulting (2016) report that fourteen US States and the District of Columbia presently have retail competition, and eight states have suspended or rescinded it. Because many states limit liberalization downstream, the dividing line among states is somewhat ambiguous. In US jurisdictions with retail choice, roughly half of commercial and industrial load has switched to competitive suppliers, while under 10 percent of residential load has done so. Retail competition is facilitating the diffusion of dynamic pricing programs.

Hu et al. (2015) point out that dynamic pricing adoption is quite different in the United States and Europe, due to seasonal characteristics of the electricity demand and the generation mix. The peak load in the EU usually occurs during the winter period. In contrast, the peak of the US electricity load occurs in summer and power consumption is usually the lowest in winter. The average peak-to-average ratio from 2009 to 2012 is 1.382 for the United States and 1.265 for the EU. High summer peaks due to air conditioning are very frequent. The United States insists on demand response in order to shave these peaks, whereas Europe has deployed smart meters to better monitor consumption.

Lack of consumer engagement and potential redistributive effects among different classes of consumers continue to explain resistance to RTP in Europe too. There are a few exceptions, however, as Eurelectric (2017) reports.

In Finland, consumers can choose dynamic pricing for electricity. In practice, this results in a price that is very transparently based on the Nord Pool spot price. The customer pays the hourly price, together with a retailer's premium and a monthly fixed fee. Approximately 10 percent of customers are on this tariff (as of over 3.4 million metering points, about 340,000 customers). The consumer can check the prices for each hour of the next day, for instance from a website. The prices are published according to the spot market timetable, so for the day-ahead at around 2pm the prices for the next twenty-four hours starting at midnight are "locked." The customer pays according to his/her hourly consumption times the price for that particular hour. This requires that the customer has hourly metering, which is the case for practically every consumer in Finland.

In Norway, about 65 percent (80TWh/year) of the electricity delivered is on dynamic pricing based on spot prices with hourly metering. This is mainly due to the fact that industrial customers using 100,000 kWh/year or more apply spot pricing with hourly metering.

## Learning Outcomes

- Competition in retail markets can be interpreted as a slightly modified version of price setting (e.g. Bertrand) modeling, under retail Real-Time Pricing (RTP).
- Retail Real-Time Pricing describes a system that has two main features: the frequency at which prices are set changes within the day, and the time lag for pricing is very short.
- The missing market arising because there are both flat retail price consumers and real-time consumers implies that the short-run competitive equilibrium is inefficient, unless there are only customers under RTP (possibly using smart meters).
- The long-run competitive equilibrium does not in general achieve the second-best optimal electricity allocation and capacity investment.
- Traditional meters and retail competition lead to a third-best outcome, because retailers must rely on load profiling.
- Competitive retailing with RTP is not yet widespread: a few examples exist in the United States and Europe.

# 20 Assessing the Benefits of Retail Competition

## 20.1 Introduction

Assessing the benefits of retail competition seems a difficult task. As highlighted in the previous chapter, there is no general model of retail competition that can be used as a reference. In the absence of a shared vision on the ideal competition benchmark, it is difficult to estimate and measure market performance at the retail level following the introduction of competition. Moreover, in the retail sector, economic efficiency must often be counterbalanced by the political need to ensure consumer protection and access to electricity, which is perceived or assumed to be an essential good. This latter goal can be achieved by specific regulatory interventions that also impact retail competition. For instance, the existence of specifically tailored tariffs for household consumers could be justified for redistributive purposes, even though these might lower or impede the contestability of the retail market.

In this chapter, we analyze in Paragraph 20.2 the potential gains from retail competition along three pillars: efficiency, product differentiation and innovation. Then in Paragraph 20.3 we consider the impact of consumer inertia on retail competition. Finally, in Paragraph 20.3 we discuss the regulatory provisions that ensure consumer protection and quality of the service. Some examples from different European countries illustrate the main arguments.

Overall, the literature review and its key messages summarized in this chapter suggest that the benefits deriving from retail competition to small consumers have been overstated with respect to what we observe in reality.

## 20.2 Benefits from Retail Competition

In addition to the standard argument that a competitive sector is efficient, we review here the other potential benefits from retail competition, which also encompass the quality dimension of the electricity service to end consumers.

### 20.2.1 Efficiency

Direct efficiency gains in electricity retailing services derive from a widespread adoption of cost-based pricing and a more efficient organization of retailing activities. Using 1996 data, Joskow (2000) gives an estimate of the potential saving for the average customer in United States of switching to a competitive retailer who is in charge of all retailing services. The competitive retailer is able to provide services at a maximum discount of 25 percent compared to existing tariffs of distributors. However, according to Littlechild (2009), efficiency gains may be more significant since they may originate not only from direct retail operations but also from upstream procurement, which is estimated to account for about 50 percent of the final retail price. In Littlechild's view, market forces acting over time are able to reintroduce the correct incentives to dynamic efficiency.

These papers suggest that when there is competition, only the best offers of the efficient suppliers can survive and expand at the expense of unwanted contracts or/and inefficient sellers.

Retail competition can help to solve the problem of double marginalization. Let us explain this point. When firms have market power, they will set price above marginal cost, which causes a welfare loss. This problem is accentuated when there is a firm with market power that buys an input from another firm that also has market power. The producer of the input will price above marginal cost when it sells the input to the other firm, who will then price above marginal cost again when they sell the final product that uses the input. This means the input is being marked up above marginal cost twice: once by the producer of the input, and once again by the firm that uses the input to make its final product, that is double marginalization. The elimination of this effect (Goulding et al., 1999) can generate efficiency gains. In the electricity sector, this effect is at stake when firms active along the ESC retain some degree of market power. From this perspective retail competition is seen per se as a positive element of liberalization reforms.

## 20.2.2 Pricing

In theory, efficiency gains may be passed through customers in the form of lower final prices. However, this effect is difficult to measure, as has been shown by several empirical studies.

In general, the energy component of electricity pricing encompasses both wholesale and retail pricing, therefore it is quite complex to disentangle the variation of wholesale prices from those on the retail margin.

Some authors have tried to estimate the impact of reforms such as privatization and liberalization on final prices and on efficiency (see for instance Newbery and Pollitt 1997, on British data, Steiner (2001) and Hattori and Tsutsui (2004) on OECD countries). Joskow's (2006) paper is the only one that properly accounts for retail competition. The author compares the changes in electricity prices between 1996 and 2004 in the US states that have introduced retail competition with those that have not. He finds evidence that households in the states where reforms have been adopted benefitted from larger reductions in prices (with the exception of Texas), while for industrial customers this trend does not show up. This result however cannot be completely attributed to retail competition, since in the same period several other reforms have been undertaken in the electricity sector (increased competition in generation, better regulation of distribution and transmission services, etc.). Borenstein and Bushnell (2015), stressing that retail restructuring have implied providing customers with the possibility of access to new providers who produced or acquired wholesale power for sale to end users, compare end-user prices of US states under full liberalization and those that have remained under some form of regulation and public interest power. Average rates in states that did not restructure have continued to increase since 2007, though at a slightly slower pace than between 1998 and 2007. Overall there is almost no difference in the change in average rates for the two groups over the full sample from 1998 to 2012. Gas prices seem to have driven retail electricity prices for both kinds of firms. Su (2015) finds that in those US states that have implemented retail competition, residential customers have bene-fitted from significantly lower prices. The price reduction, on average, ranges from 0:87 to 1:02 $/kWh. Commercial and industrial customers, on the other hand, have not benefitted from any significant price reductions associated with restructuring.

At the downside level (i.e. concerning competition among retailers to find, acquire and maintain their customers), several authors agree that retail competition can increase retailing costs, through rising advertising, and promotional, transactional and system duplication (e.g. billing or customer assistance) costs; there is no shared agreement, however, on the final balance between these costs and competition benefits. For instance, Littlechild (2000) affirms that in the long run efficiency gains may offset increased advertising and promotional costs, whereas Joskow (2000) and Defeuilley (2009) are more skeptical about this prediction.

### 20.2.3    Differentiation and Equipment Innovation

Retail competition is expected to bring to the market new offers and contractual arrangements, as well as widening the range of services, such as risk-hedging or energy management services. Furthermore, competitive pressure on retailers may indirectly force other players, such as distributors or equipment providers, to develop and install new measuring and reading devices and empowered equipment for quality services. However, according to several authors, this does not necessarily appear to be the case for the electricity retail sector. The potential for product differentiation and for developments in the range of value-added services for which small and residential customers are willing to pay an extra fee appears to be constrained in the electricity industry.

Empirical evidence in European countries partly disproves this negative view as to the limited room for product differentiation. If the demand for additional services such as energy management or multiple fuel contracts has been prompted largely by larger customers, competition in electricity retailing did stimulate demand for new types of products (mainly green options) and innovative contractual arrangements for pricing (wholesale price plus mark-up contracts, fixed-price contracts, standard variable con-tracts, flat-rate contracts) which were also available for small and residential customers. The diffusion of these products nonetheless remains heterogeneous. For a survey of newly introduced products see, for example, von der Fehr and Hansen (2010) on the Norwegian market and Littlechild (2002) on the UK market.

As an example of retail pricing and competition, we give some details of the European markets in the Box 20.1.

---

**Box 20.1** Retail Pricing and Retail Competition in Europe

**The Legislative Context**

In contrast to the price of fossil fuels, which are usually traded on global markets with relatively uniform prices, there is a wide range of electricity prices in Europe, twenty years after opening electricity generation and supply up to competition. Directive 96/92/EC and 2003/54/EC established that as of July 1, 2004 business customers were free to choose their supplier, extending this option as of July 1, 2007 to all consumers (including households). Some EU Member States anticipated the liberalization process, while others were much slower in adopting the necessary measures. In July 2009, the European Parliament and Council adopted a third package of legislative proposals (Directive 2009/72/EC) aimed at ensuring a real and effective choice of suppliers, as well as benefits for customers.

**Electricity Prices for Household Consumers**

For medium-sized household consumers, electricity prices during the second half of 2016 were highest among the EU Member States in Denmark (€0.308 per kWh), Germany (€0.298 per kWh) and Belgium (€0.275 per kWh), as shown by Figure 20.1. The lowest electricity prices were in Bulgaria (€0.094 per kWh), Hungary (€0.113 per kWh) and Lithuania (€0.117 per kWh). The price of electricity for households in Denmark and in Germany was more than three times as high as the price in Bulgaria. Note that the energy component of the retail price includes both average generation and retailing costs. The relative importance of the energy component together with the retail component, compared with network costs can be seen in Figure 20.1; the share of the latter was relatively low in Malta, Greece, Cyprus, Bulgaria, the United Kingdom, Spain, Italy and Ireland.

The EU-28 average price – a weighted average using the most recent (2015) data for the quantity of electricity consumption by households – was €0.205 per kWh.

Electricity prices for household consumers in the EU-28 increased in 2008, decreased in the first half of the year with the economic and financial crisis in 2009, but were stable in the second half of that year, and then increased continuously from the first half of 2010 to the second half of 2016, apart from a fall of 2.4 percent in the first half of 2016. One of the main reasons for these changes was the increasing support for Renewable Energy Sources, which is financed by levies on household prices. The relative amount of tax contribution in the second half of 2016 was smallest in Malta (4.8 percent) where a low VAT rate is applied to the basic price and no other taxes are charged to household consumers. The highest taxes were charged in Denmark where 67.8 percent of the final price was made up of taxes and levies.

**Box 20.1** (cont.)

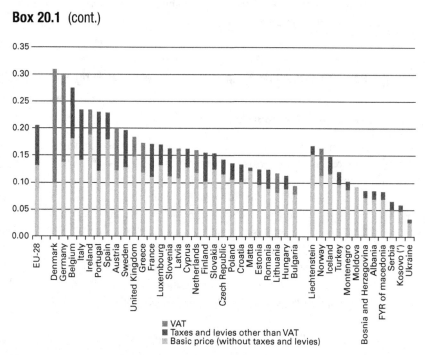

Note: annual consumption: 2,500 kWh < consumption < 5,000 kWh
(') This designation is without prejudice to positions on status, and is in line with UNSCR 1244/1999 and the ICJ Opinion on the Kosovo declaration of independence.

**Figure 20.1**  Electricity prices: households
*Source: Eurostat.* Available at: http://ec.europa.eu/eurostat/statistics-explained/index.php/
Electricity_price_statistics

### Electricity Prices for Industrial Consumers

During the second half of 2016, electricity prices for industrial consumers (with an annual consumption between 500 MWh and 2,000 MWh), were highest in Italy and Germany out of the EU countries. The EU-28 average price – a weighted average using the most recent (2015) national data for the quantity of consumption by industrial consumers – was €0.114 per kWh (see Figure 20.2).

Electricity prices for industrial consumers increased in 2008 and during the first half of 2009, decreased during the second half of 2009, and increased again each half year through to the first half of 2013. In the second half of 2013 the average price fell slightly, before increasing quite strongly (4.3 percent) in the first half of 2014 to reach a peak of €0.123 per kWh. From the second half of 2014 onwards, a decreasing trend was observed. The proportion of non-recoverable taxes and levies in the overall electricity price for industrial consumers is, in general, lower than for household consumers.

**Box 20.1** (cont.)

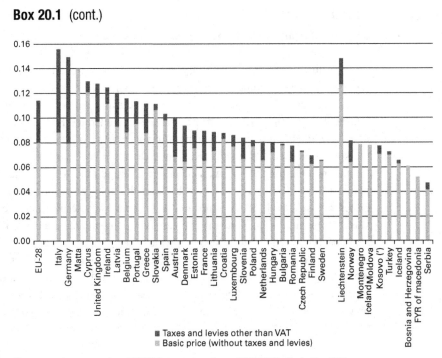

Note: annual consumption: 500 MWh < consumption < 2 000 MWh. Excluding VAT.
(') This designation is without prejudice to positions on status, and is in line with UNSCR 1244/1999 and the ICJ Opinion on the Kosovo declaration of independence.

**Figure 20.2** Electricity prices: industrial consumers
*Source: Eurostat.* Available at: http://ec.europa.eu/eurostat/statistics-explained/index.php/ Electricity_price_statistics.

## Relative Level of Competition

According to the Agency for the Cooperation of Energy Regulators (ACER/ CEER 2016), effective competition in retail energy markets requires, among other things, a sufficient number of suppliers, rivalry between suppliers, rewards – in the form of monetary gains and/or better services – for consumers active in the market, and simple, low-cost and timely switching processes. Based on a competition analysis (using a specific indicator computed by the Agency), the most competitive markets for household customers in 2015 were the retail electricity markets in Finland, Sweden, the United Kingdom, Norway and the Netherlands. Weak retail market competition was observed in household electricity markets in Greece, Bulgaria and Cyprus.

In comparison to 2014, changes in the competitive indicator for retail electricity markets were driven for most countries by dynamics in four sub-indicators: i) number of suppliers with market share above 5 percent; ii) average annual net entry; iii) numbers of offers per supplier; and iv) average annual mark-ups (i.e. the

> **Box 20.1** (cont.)
>
> degree of alignment over time between wholesale prices and the energy component of retail prices).
>
> According to the ACER, mark-ups could be used as an additional indicator for the effectiveness of competition in retail energy markets.
>
> The highest positive mark-ups in 2015, expressed in euros, were observed in the household segment of the electricity markets in the United Kingdom, Ireland and Greece, while the lowest positive mark-ups were observed in the retail electricity markets of the Czech Republic, Romania, Denmark and Hungary.
>
> In some countries with regulated prices, average mark-ups for the monitored period (2008–2015) were negative because the energy component of the retail prices was set at a level that appeared to be below wholesale energy costs. This was the case in Latvia, Romania and Lithuania. Negative average mark-ups were also observed in the Czech Republic, which does not apply regulated prices.
>
> Finally, ACER market monitoring results showed that many retail markets remain highly concentrated, with the average market share of the three largest suppliers in the EU exceeding 78 percent. The concentration effect is also reinforced by vertical integration between producers, often incumbents, and retailers.

## 20.3    Competition with Market Imperfections

Some authors claim that the presence of market imperfections, such as switching costs, informational complexity and consumer preference for not choosing, challenge the likely outcome of competition in the electricity sector, in particular for small and residential customers (Joskow, 2000; Brennan, 2006; Defeuilley, 2009; Hortaçsu et al., 2017). In the following sections, we review the main concerns arising from these market imperfections (see Concettini and Creti, 2014 for more details).

### 20.3.1    Switching Costs

In markets characterized by repeated interactions between buyers and sellers, a consumer who has previously purchased a product from a supplier may incur some costs when switching to a competitor, although firms' products are identical (Klemperer, 1995).

Switching costs arise for the following reasons:

- search costs to identify offers and suppliers;
- learning costs to become familiar with the supplier;
- transactional costs to sign and resolve a contract.

Switching costs may be real or perceived and lead to a situation in which "products that are *ex ante* homogenous become, after the purchase of one of them, *ex post* heterogeneous" (Klemperer, 1995, p. 517). These costs prevent customers from changing supplier even when a better-priced deal is available and they, therefore, impact on market dynamics in the same way as a barrier to entry.

In the electricity industry where consumers have long-lasting supply relationships with the incumbent, switching costs may act as a deterrent to full consumer mobility, leading to under-switching.

Giulietti et al. (2010) analyze the impact of searching and switching costs in the UK retailing electricity market by studying the trend in price convergence between new entrants and incumbents. The authors find that, in line with general predictions of competition models with switching cost, even after the entry of new competitors, incumbents are able to enjoy a consistent price advantage. Moreover, as soon as they are established in the market, new entrants tend to exploit searching and switching costs faced by consumers; over time the incentives that new firms have to lower prices in order to gain additional customers is more than counterbalanced by the benefits of keeping prices high to increase margins on previously served customers.

## 20.3.2    Informational Complexities

In some sectors, consumers may also be unwilling to change suppliers because they face difficulties in evaluating and comparing suppliers' offers. This may be the case for the electricity industry, where consumers are generally offered two or multi-part tariffs which reduce their ability to estimate the per-unit price of the product. This situation may be further complicated whenever supply contracts embed other advantages that cannot easily be translated into savings on electricity price (e.g. getting discounts on other purchases). This limitation may imply that:

- consumers switch to a more expensive supplier (over-switching);
- consumers switch to a cheaper but not the cheapest available supplier (inaccurate switching).

Errors made by consumers when deciding to switch affect their welfare directly, as they cannot take full advantage of retail offers.

Empirical evidence in the electricity sector is provided in Wilson and Waddams Price (2005). The authors use a sample of over 3,000 face-to-face surveys of UK households, 13 percent of which have switched supplier. They find that almost 30 percent of households who have switched have moved to a more expensive supplier, while inaccurate switching has led customers to benefit from only a quarter of the gain available on the market. The paper suggests that information overload and complexity may cause switching decisions to be less efficient when there is a large number of retailers and options in the market. As a consequence, while increasing the number of competitors may have a positive effect on the total gains available on the market, informational complexity may limit the ability of consumers to exploit such gains, with a negative net impact on equilibrium final prices.

### 20.3.3    Consumer Inertia

In open opposition to the assumptions of the standard economic model, Brennan (2006) attributes the likely scarce success of competition in electricity retailing market to a consumer preference for a lack of choice, which can be considered as a sort of market failure.

The move from a monopoly to the wholesale and retail market model has forced customers to make informed choices, which in turn presupposes increasing effort to understand and compare contractual conditions and terms of trade. However, the experience in the electricity sector seems to suggest that consumers do not always consider having more options as an advantage.

Brennan's opinion stems from an accurate analysis of the marketing literature which indicates that consumers generally show a limited propensity to go back on their choices or to change goods and services in their consumption bundle. More recently, Hortaçsu et al. (2017) find strong evidence for consumer inertia, analyzing data at the household level for the program "Power to choose" implemented in Texas in 2002 to help consumers select their retail provider.

### 20.3.4    Customer Segmentation

Some scholars notice that a possible side-effect of introducing competition in the retail electricity market is the segmentation of active and passive customers (von der Fehr and Hansen, 2010). Consumers are active in a market when they exercise their freedom of choice by switching suppliers, or by renegotiating their contractual conditions without changing retailer. Differences in the willingness of customers to switch suppliers or renegotiate contractual arrangements may create room for a two-tier retail market. This means that consumers are split into two categories: active and inactive consumers. Active consumers may benefit from the introduction of competition in retailing since they can have access to offers in which prices are more cost-reflective. Inactive customers, on the other hand, may end up by paying prices that are above what they were paying before the liberalization, since firms may use consumers' reluctance or inability to switch to cross-subsidizing their entry in the competitive sub-markets. Empirical evidence in Norwegian and United Kingdom markets seems to confirm this prediction (OFGEM, 2007; OFGEM 2012; von der Fehr and Hansen, 2010).

### 20.3.5    Innovative Processes

Some structural characteristics of the electricity industry may limit the scope for entry of new innovative firms that are supposed to be the main spur toward the achievement the benefits of competition, both in terms of price reduction and quality improvements. Defeuilly (2009) suggests that a careful analysis of electricity provision reveals that technological opportunities for new entrants in this retail sector are limited. Indeed, innovation investments seem to be characterized by a high level of appropriability and cumulativeness at firm level. Innovative processes in this sector are likely to be driven by large established firms, rather than by new entrants.

Moreover, innovation possibilities in electricity retailing seems to be triggered more by equipment innovations (installation of smart-meters devices), or upstream choices (investments in renewable sources) that are largely independent of competition in retailing, rather than by radical innovations in business management (new information technologies, improved customer management, etc.). However, the emergence of new entities such as aggregators, and new usages like self-consumption or distributed generation might foster innovation.

## 20.4    Equity Concerns in Competitive Retail Markets

As pointed out by some scholars "Throughout most of the history of electric utilities, retail pricing policy has been driven more by equity than efficiency considerations" (Borenstein and Bushnell, 2015, p. 438). This need for regulation does not disappear, even after the full development of competition.

Three situations are at stake:

- When competition is introduced in a market, customers can decide to switch to a new supplier or they can be passive and do nothing. In this case, the continuity of supply is ensured by assigning passive customers to a so-called Default Supplier (DS).
- Customers served by a competitive retailer may face the risk of being curtailed if the supplier becomes unable to provide the service, for instance because it is insolvent or bankrupt. In this case, regulators must arrange for the transition of customers to a temporary supplier, the so-called Last Resort Supplier (LRS), which secures service continuity. The LRS can be a supplier, or another entity.
- There may be vulnerable consumers, who struggle to find a counterpart in the market, notably because they are not profitable.

Each situation calls for a specific intervention. In the first two cases, the need to provide an uninterrupted service may be counterbalanced by the objective of ensuring a certain level of customer protection, especially in terms of price. An entire array of implementation patterns is feasible, according to the relative weight placed on these objectives and considering several possible providers. In addition, three procedures are available to assign these services to a retailer:

1. a direct *ex-ante* entitlement typically granted to the incumbent firm;
2. a random entitlement upon the competitive suppliers;
3. a bidding process based on the competitive selection of the provider.

For instance, when ensuring that continuity of supply is the only regulatory goal, the network system operator may provide Default and Last Resort services as part of its balancing activity. At the other end of the scale, if the regulator wishes to guarantee customer protection, Default and Last Resort services may be offered at a tariff and provided by a retailer or the local distributor.

The problem of vulnerable customers is slightly different and may be better understood in the framework of Universal Service Obligations (USOs) to ensure full market coverage at reasonable prices, including more costly market segments such as rural areas. Accordingly, some obligations have been imposed on network service providers in the form of restrictions on price discrimination ("non-discrimination" constraint), or obligations to provide the service regardless of customers' geographical location ("ubiquity" constraint). Often the two constraints have been combined, requiring retailers to ensure full market coverage at a uniform price.

From a theoretical point of view, when competition is introduced in markets with profitable and non-profitable end users, new entrants compete with the incumbent only for profitable customers, generating the so-called **cream skimming**, that is, serving high-value or low-cost consumers only. This phenomenon might force the incumbent to provide USOs by mean of cross-subsidies (Laffont and Tirole, 2000).

There is cross-subsidization when one type of customer indirectly pays for the consumption of a good or service of the other type. When there is no cross-subsidization, a firm sets subsidy-free prices. We can illustrate this concept through the following example.

---

**Example 20.1 Cross-subsidization** Assume that the cost of providing electricity to two consumers consists of three parts. One part of the costs is common to both consumers and has a per unit cost of 10. For the provision of retail services to consumer 1, the retailer incurs an incremental cost of 6 and for consumer 2, an incremental cost of 4. The total cost of retailing 1 unit is equal to $20 = 10 + 6 + 4$. The subsidy-free prices are such that every consumer pays at least for its additional costs, and that each consumer has a price less than the standalone cost. Define the price paid by consumer $i$, as $p_i$, $i = 1,2$. Prices are such that: $6 < p_1 < 10 + 6 = 16$ and $4 < p_2 < 10 + 4 = 14$. Additionally, if the regulated firm makes no profit, then the sum of the two prices is equal to the total cost of 20. These three equations specify the range of subsidy-free prices. If one of these conditions is not met, then there is cross-subsidization. If the price of consumer 2 is higher than 14 this consumer cross-subsidizes consumer 2 and vice versa, if the price of consumer 2 is below 4, consumer 1 is subsiding consumer 2.

---

Several authors (e.g. Anton et al., 2002; Choné et al., 2002; Mirabel and Poudou, 2004) have tried to assess the welfare effects and the distortionary impact of different regulatory instruments that governments may implement to allocate and finance USOs. However, none of these papers questions the truly economic rationale behind keeping USOs in liberalized markets. In particular, while the "ubiquity" constraint may continue to be imposed on the regulated network operators, "non-discrimination" constraint is at odds with the concept of competitive markets with efficient cost-reflective prices.

Panzar (2000) stresses that there is an unavoidable trade-off between competition and universal service provision in liberalized markets. Indeed, if the need for a universal service policy exists, this means that the competitive market cannot deliver socially acceptable allocations without a direct public intervention.

The literature seems to suggest that there is a need for USOs whenever the transition toward competitive retail markets excludes vulnerable or unprofitable customers from the trade of an essential good, such as electricity. However, in order to secure the risk of exclusion, more targeted and less distortionary interventions are to be preferred, such as social tariffs or direct transfers to customers.

In principle, the justification for universal service provision seems to rely on the need to avoid final customer exploitation due to retailers' market power after the introduction of competition (Littlechild, 2000; OFGEM, 2002; ERGEG, 2007). For instance, Vàsquez et al. (2006) affirm that a permanent well-calculated tariff including a shopping credit (i.e. the price against which new suppliers must compete if they want to attract customers) achieves the objective of guaranteeing the supply to all customers without deterring consumers' switching. Other authors such as Joskow (2000) and Littlechild (2000) are more skeptical about the benefits of including a shopping credit in regulated tariffs. It is likely, however, that consumers may be deterred from switching and new entry may be hampered if tariffs do not reflect underlying costs (Joskow, 2006; Wolak, 2014).

## Learning Outcomes

- There are several implementation issues relating to retail competition: the extent to which competition delivers advantages to consumers, from lower electricity pricing to faster innovation, and whether regulation is still needed to ensure customer protection.
- From experience to date, it is not possible to make a clear assessment of the advantages stemming from retail competition.
- Changing supplier creates switching costs: search costs to identify offers and suppliers; learning costs to become familiar with the supplier; transactional costs to sign and resolve a contract.
- Consumer inertia and reluctance to switch due to the above-mentioned costs may show that some advantages may not be achieved.
- The advantages of retail competition may be associated with the elimination of double marginalization and the introduction of smart meters and technical innovations that serve as a bridge toward time-varying prices that ensure cost-reflective electricity pricing.
- Some form of regulation such as Universal Service Obligations, Suppliers of Last Resort or Social Tariffs might still be still needed. Their effect on total welfare is, however, unclear.

# Part VII

---

# Investing in Power Generation

In Part III we analyzed the optimal dispatching solution and the market outcomes for power systems characterized by a given pre-defined topology, and in particular, installed generation capacity. Therefore, the analysis there was a short-run evaluation of the optimal operation scheme and the market study of an electricity system in which no new plants become operational, or old plants are mothballed. In this part, we remove the assumption of fixed generation capacity, and allow it to change over time. In other words, we move from a short-run analysis of the power system to a long-run analysis. As we focus on the generation investment decision, we shall not consider grid constraints or extension problems. In Chapter 21 we first analyze the optimal investment problem in a planned setting, namely, in a framework in which a central planner must decide the optimal level of investments. This approach, for the case of the long-run analysis, corresponds to the study of model 1, the monopolist, which for the short-run case we developed in Chapter 8 and 9. Then, we move on to the study of the long-run investment problem in a liberalized market setting (i.e. a situation in which power plants compete among themselves). This corresponds, for the long-run investment decision case, to considering models 2, 3 and 4, whose short-run study has been developed in Chapter 9. In Chapter 22, we discuss the difference between the first-best theoretical solution and the real-world problem of investment in power generation, and compare the optimal solution in markets without explicit remuneration for capacity, with the optimal solution where the latter exists. In Chapter 23 we present and discuss several alternative market design rules, with explicit remuneration for capacity, broadly defined as Capacity Remuneration Mechanisms.

# 21 Optimal Investment in Power Generation

## 21.1 Introduction

We consider here the problem of investment in generation capacity in the long run. The analysis is similar to that of Chapter 9, yet with a different focus. There, it was assumed that some level of capacity existed, and we studied how to serve the load in an efficient way in each hour of the reference period. Thus, it was a short-run analysis. Here, we consider the long-run case in which there is no preinstalled level of capacity, and we investigate the optimal level of investment. Thus, we shall not refer to a specific hour $j$, but to the whole period, say a year, and omit the superscript $j$. In the reference period, the load demands energy $Q^d$. This energy is produced by power plants. The energy supplied by plant $i$ is denoted by $Q_i^s$. However, this energy supply needs a capacity in order to be produced. The maximum level of capacity installed constraints the supply:[1] $Q_i^s \leq M_i^{max}$. Obviously, the overall installed level $\sum_{i=1}^{n} M_i^{max}$ constrains the maximum producible energy $Q^s = \sum_{i=1}^{n} Q_i^s \leq \sum_{i=1}^{n} M_i^{max}$. The usual load-balance constraints, stemming from the Kirchhoff's laws, apply: $Q^d = Q^s$. Investing in power plant has a cost. We shall consider yearly total cost functions as those described in Equation (7.1), with $c_i$ denoting the marginal cost of energy for plant $i$, for simplicity of notation.

## 21.2 The Optimal Investment Problem with a Single Technology

Let us consider the welfare maximization problem when there is just one single technology (i.e. all power plants have the same cost). How much capacity should be invested? The maximization problem for an average (reference) year is as follows:

---

[1] For the sake of simplicity, we ignore here the existence of probabilistic failures that are different from lack of capacity. In other words, we assume that if a capacity is installed it will be available. Introducing probabilistic failures would not change the rationale of the analysis: we would need to introduce a further figure, namely, the expected (average) available capacity in the period, which would be less than the installed one, and refer to this stochastic parameter as the effective capacity constraint.

$$\max_{M_i^{max},\, Q^d,\, Q_i^s} U(Q^d) - \sum_{i=1}^{n} C_i(Q_i^s, M_i^{max}), \text{ s.t.}$$

$$(a)\, Q^d = \sum_{i=1}^{n} Q_i^s;$$

$$(b)\, Q_i^s \geq 0;$$

$$(c)\, Q_i^s \leq M_i^{max}; \tag{21.1}$$

$$\forall i = 1, \ldots, n.$$

The Lagrange Equation is:

$$\mathcal{L} = U(Q^d) - \sum_{i=1}^{n} C_i(Q_i^s, M_i^{max}) + a\left(Q^d - \sum_{i=1}^{n} Q_i^s\right) + \sum_{i=1}^{n} b_i Q_i^s$$
$$+ \sum_{i=1}^{n} d_i(M_i^{max} - Q_i^s) \tag{21.2}$$

with the Kuhn-Tucker conditions:

$$\frac{\partial \mathcal{L}}{\partial M_i^{max}} = 0 \rightarrow \frac{\partial C_i}{\partial M_i^{max}}(\cdot) = d_i, \forall i = 1, \ldots, n;$$

$$\frac{\partial \mathcal{L}}{\partial Q^d} = 0 \rightarrow U'(\cdot) = -a; \tag{21.3}$$

$$\frac{\partial \mathcal{L}}{\partial Q_i^s} = 0 \rightarrow \frac{\partial C_i}{\partial Q_i^s}(\cdot) = -a - d_i + b_i, \forall i = 1, \ldots, n;$$

and the slackness conditions:

$$b_i Q_i^s = 0, \quad Q_i^s \geq 0, \quad b_i \geq 0, \quad \forall i = 1, \ldots, n;$$
$$d_i(M_i^{max} - Q_i^s) = 0, \quad (M_i^{max} - Q_i^s) \geq 0, \quad d_i \geq 0, \quad \forall i = 1, \ldots, n. \tag{21.4}$$

Considering only internal solutions and simplifying the constraints, we have:

$$d_i = \frac{\partial C_i}{\partial M_i^{max}}, \forall i = 1, \ldots, n;$$

$$d_i = \left(\frac{\partial U}{\partial Q^d} - \frac{\partial C_i}{\partial Q_i^s}\right), \forall i = 1, \ldots, n; \tag{21.5}$$

$$d_i(M_i^{max} - Q_i^s) = 0, \forall i = 1, \ldots, n.$$

See that the slackness condition is such as $d_i > 0$ when $(M_i^{max} - Q_i^s) = 0, \forall i = 1, \ldots, n$. Thus we can re-write the constraints as:

$$d_i = \frac{\partial C_i}{\partial M_i^{max}}, \forall i = 1, \ldots, n;$$

$$d_i = \left(\frac{\partial U}{\partial Q^d} - \frac{\partial C_i}{\partial Q_i^s}\right) I(M_i^{max} = Q_i^s), \forall i = 1, \ldots, n; \tag{21.6}$$

where $I(M_i^{max} = Q_i^s)$ is the indicator function denoting the number of hours, during the year, that the capacity will be fully used to provide energy. We can divide both equations by $T$, the number of hours of the year and solve them together, obtaining:

$$\frac{\frac{\partial C_i}{\partial M_i^{max}}}{T} = \left(\frac{\partial U}{\partial Q^d} - \frac{\partial C_i}{\partial Q_i^s}\right)\frac{I(M_i^{max} = Q_i^s)}{T}, \quad \forall i = 1, \ldots, n. \tag{21.7}$$

Comparing Equation (21.7) with Equation (21.5) and (7.3), we see that the left-hand side of Equation (21.7) is just the hourly rental cost of plant $i$, namely, the hourly discounted fixed cost per unit of capacity. The right-hand side, on the other hand, is the difference between the marginal utility of the load in the considered period (e.g. a year), and the marginal cost of provision of energy in that year, multiplied by the ratio of the number of hours in which the capacity of each plant is used at its maximum per each year over the total number of hours of the year. The sum of the capacity installed by each plant serves the whole load. Recall that in the given period – the year – load changes over time. We have already defined the Load Duration Curve as the curve that shows, in that period, the probability that for any possible level of total capacity installed, the load exceeds that level. Therefore, for a given $M_i^{max}$ per each plant and a given LDC, the term $\frac{I(M_i^{max} = Q_i^s)}{T}$ is the same for all plants and identifies a specific point of the LDC, namely, the probability (measured in number of hours over the year) for which load $Q^d$ exceeds the overall level of installed capacity $\sum_{i=1}^{n} M_i^{max}$ and thus load has to be shed.

Therefore, we can rewrite Equation (21.7) as:

$$hRC = \left(\frac{\partial U}{\partial Q^d} - \frac{\partial C_i}{\partial Q_i^s}\right)\Pr\left(Q^d > \sum_{i=1}^{n} M_i^{max}\right); \tag{21.8}$$

where we have omitted the subscript $i$ in the $hRC$ given that it is constant across plants.

We have already defined $\Pr(Q^d > \sum_{i=1}^{n} M_i^{max})$ in Chapter 9. It was the probability that in a given period load is shed: the *LOLP*. Moreover, from constraints (21.3), we see that the marginal utility of the load in equilibrium corresponds to the shadow value of the load-balance constraint, namely, the marginal value of having one extra unit of capacity able to serve the load. This concept has already been introduced in Chapter 9, namely, the *VOLL*. Thus, Equation (21.8) can be re-written as:

$$LOLP^* = \frac{hRC}{(VOLL - c_i)}; \tag{21.9}$$

where the superscript star over the *LOLP* denotes that it is an equilibrium value, namely, the level of installed capacity that solves Equation (21.8). Equation (21.9) has an interesting interpretation. It shows that, unless capacity had no cost, it would not be optimal to have as much capacity installed as the whole demanded load. It is optimal instead to have some hours of the year in which load will be shed. This result is similar to that obtained in Chapter 9, however, with different and stronger implications. There we showed that, for a given level of installed capacity, the load has to be shed up to the point in which the marginal utility of the load is equal to the value of having one marginal unit more of capacity installed. Here we show that the value of the marginal capacity in equilibrium must correspond to the marginal cost of that extra capacity. Thus, unless the marginal cost of capacity is equal to zero, there will always be some load shed, which implies that the marginal utility of the energy that the capacity generates will always be higher than the marginal cost of providing energy: $\frac{\partial U}{\partial Q^d} > \frac{\partial C_i}{\partial Q_i^s}$. This effect is the optimal rationing of energy.

Moreover, Equation (21.9) displays another interesting property of the optimal solution. Since installing a capacity has a cost ($hRC > 0$), it is worthwhile to do it only if $LOLP > 0$, i.e., the capacity is going to be fully used ($Q_i^s = M_i^{max}$). In other words, it is never optimal to install extra capacity if it not fully used ($Q_i^s < M_i^{max}$), as we would have expected.

It is possible to calculate how much capacity has to be installed and consequently for how many hours of the year we can expect to shed load. This optimal level of capacity is set at that level for which the extra cost of the last unit of watt installed, $hRC$, corresponds to the extra benefit, namely, the net expected marginal value of the last unit of watt installed. This latter is the extra value for the load accruing from the energy that the extra watt installed allows to generate (i.e. the $VOLL$), net of the marginal cost to generate it ($c_i$), multiplied by the probability that the extra capacity is effectively needed for otherwise the load would be shed (the $LOLP$).

Equation (21.9) can also be used to get a rough estimate of the optimal $LOLP$, using it, for instance, to compare if, *ex post*, the number of hours in which load was shed in a year in a given place corresponded to what was optimal or not, without any complex calculation. In reality, $VOLL$ values are typically of thousands of dollars per MWh, depending on which electricity system they refer to (see the discussion on the $VOLL$ in Chapter 3). The marginal cost is at a much lower scale (e.g. tens of dollars per MWh). Thus, we can omit $c_i$ and simply relate the $hRC$ to the $VOLL$ to perform a back-of-the-envelope estimation of the optimal $LOLP$:

$$LOLP \cong \frac{YRC}{VOLL}; \qquad (21.10)$$

Where YRC denotes the yearly capital rental cost. Equation (21.10) is generally referred to as peak load pricing[2] or **VOLL-pricing**, highlighting that at the equilibrium it is the product of $VOLL$ and $LOLP$ that provides enough incentives for investments.

---

Result

In a given electricity system, the optimal level of capacity installed must be such that the resulting $LOLP$ equals the ratio of the Yearly Rental Cost of the capacity over the Value of Lost Load.

---

[2] Terminology originally proposed by Boiteux (1960). See also Crew et al., (1995).

Example 21.1. shows how to use this formula in a simple calculation of the *LOLP*.

---

**Example 21.1 The Optimal *LOLP* and Capacity** Assume there are the following figures in a power system: yearly rental cost of capacity is \$43,800/MWy (i.e. \$5/MWh). The *VOLL* is \$5,000/MWh; marginal cost is \$40/MWh. On the basis of Equation (20.11) we can approximate the *LOLP* as 5/5,000 = 0.001, i.e. 0.1 percent of hours throughout the year, that is, 8.76 hours. Taking into account the marginal cost would not provide any relevant change since the difference between the two figures provided by Equation (20.11) and (20.10) is at the sixth digit. In order to convert *LOLP* into the optimal level of capacity to be installed, we need to know the LDC. For instance, let the consumption demanded be 52,560 GWh, and the LDC be the following linear function: LDC = 11,000 MW − 10,000 MW·*lf*, where *lf* $\in (0, 1)$ is the load factor (i.e. the capacity factor of the load, as defined in Chapter 7). It can be seen that the peak load is 11,000 MW, the baseload is 1,000 MW. The area of the LDC in the load factor space provides

the yearly load: $\int_0^1 LDCdlf = \frac{1}{2}(11000 + 1000) = 6{,}000\text{MWy} = 52{,}560\text{GWh}$. However,

all the load is not served. The optimal level of installed capacity is 11,000 MW − 10,000 × 0.001 = 10,990 MW. The load shed is 10MW × 8.76 hours × ½ = 43.8MWh.

---

We have assumed here that all plants have the same cost. However, if we remove this assumption, the main message of this Paragraph still holds. We show it here.

Allow plants to have different cost figures. In other words, we still assume that plants have the simple linear cost function as in Equation (7.2), but we assume that their marginal and fixed costs differ. For simplicity of notation, we consider the case of three plants, whose marginal costs are as $c_1 < c_2 < c_3$, and fixed costs are ranked as $hRC_1 > hRC_2 > hRC_3$. The case of $n$ plants follows naturally. The welfare maximization problem is the same as that stated in Equation (21.1), so we arrive at the solution stated in Equation (21.7), which we show again here for the sake of simplicity:

$$hRC_1 = \left(\frac{\partial U}{\partial Q^d} - c_1\right)I(M_1^{max} = Q_1^s)/T;$$

$$hRC_2 = \left(\frac{\partial U}{\partial Q^d} - c_2\right)I(M_2^{max} = Q_2^s)/T; \qquad (21.11)$$

$$hRC_3 = \left(\frac{\partial U}{\partial Q^d} - c_3\right)I(M_3^{max} = Q_3^s)/T.$$

Let us focus on the term $I(M_i^{max} = Q_i^s)/T$ for each of the three plants. Recall that from the optimal dispatching properties (see Chapters 8 and 9) we know that it is never optimal dispatching plant $i + 1$ if plant $i$ is not fully dispatched. Thus plant 1 is the baseload plant. The indicator function denotes the number of hours it is fully dispatched, so the ratio over $T$ denotes a specific point of the LDC, namely, the probability that the load exceeds the capacity of the baseload plant: $I(M_1^{max} = Q_1^s)/T = \Pr(Q^d > M_1^{max})$.

For plant 2, the indicator function over T denotes the probability that the load exceeds the capacity of both plant 1 and 2: $I(M_1^{max} = Q_1^s)/T = \Pr\left(Q^d > \sum_{i=1}^{2} M_i^{max}\right)$. For plant 3, it denotes the probability that the loads exceeds capacity of all three plants, so that load is shed: $I(M_1^{max} = Q_1^s)/T = \Pr\left(Q^d > \sum_{i=1}^{3} M_i^{max}\right) = LOLP$. Therefore, $\Pr\left(Q^d > \sum_{j=1}^{i} M_j^{max}\right)$ denotes the probability that a marginal unit of capacity $M_i$ is going to be used to serve the load, in the reference period.

The interpretation of condition (21.11) is the same as before for the case of equal costs, and can be generalized to $n$ plants. We summarize this below.

---

### Result

When capacity is costly, in equilibrium, it is optimal to invest in different technologies, having different costs, up to the point at which the marginal cost of the investment in the capacity equals the net expected marginal utility of the energy that can be generated using that capacity.

---

A corollary of this is that, since the probability of needing a plant of type $i+1$ is lower than that of plant $i$, being a point of the LDC to the left of the load associated to the probability of $i$, the capacity needed of technology $i + 1$ is lower than the capacity of technology $i$. Thus, the baseload plant has higher capacity installed than plant 2 type, the mid merit, whose capacity is higher than the plant 3 type, the peak load plants. The same result arises for the sum of all capacity installed: in equilibrium there is an optimal load shedding given by the *LOLP*.

## 21.3    The Cost Minimization Problem

We can derive interesting conclusions by looking at the solution of the optimal investment problem, namely, the levels of $M_i^{max}$ that solve conditions 21.11 below, from the point of view of cost minimization. As before, for simplicity we assume that there are three plants, with different costs functions. With a slight abuse of notation, we denote the LDC as $Q^d$ and let $Q^d - Q^s$ identify the loss of load because of shedding. We write the cost minimization problem, assuming that the load-balance constraint is met, so that if the LDC exceeds the overall energy injected, load is shed:

$$\min_{M_1^{max}, M_2^{max}, M_3^{max}} YRC_1 M_1^{max} + c_1 Q_1^s + YRC_2 M_2^{max} + c_2 Q_2^s$$

$$+ YRC_3 M_3^{max} + c_3 Q_3^s + v_L (Q^d - M_1^{max} - M_2^{max} - M_3^{max})\varphi. \qquad (21.12)$$

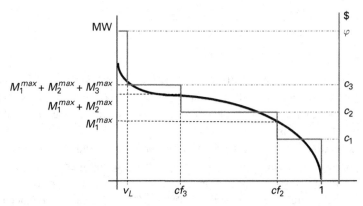

**Figure 21.1** The LDC and the PDC for the three plants case

Notice that the total system cost function includes the damage function arising from load shedding (see Equation 9.11), and $\varphi = VOLL$. The energy that each power plant injects into the grid depends on the LDC. Recall the definition of the LDC. A point of the LDC denotes the probability that the load exceeds a given level of capacity. Consider plant 1. Plants are ranked according to economic dispatching. This means that the optimal $M_1^{max}$ corresponds to that level of the capacity on the LDC for which the total cost of plant 1 and 2 coincides. This point is given by the capacity factor of plant 2: $cf_2$.

Another way to see this is simply noticing that, from the analysis run in paragraph 21.2, we know that the optimal $M_1^{max}$ is the level of capacity installed such that capacity is fully used to provide energy ($M_1^{max} = Q_1$). At that point the marginal plant becomes plant 2. Thus, for $Q^d < M_1^{max}$ the marginal plant is plant 1, producing energy at a marginal cost $c_1$. For $Q^d > M_1^{max}$, the marginal plant is plant 2, at marginal cost $c_2$.

The same reasoning applies to plant 2 for $cf_3$. For plant 3, the optimal capacity is given by the *LOLP*, $v_L$, on the basis of the marginal value of the loss load $\varphi$ (i.e. the *VOLL*). Therefore, from the LDC we can calculate and plot a Price Duration Curve (PDC). Figure 21.1 shows this, describing the LDC with regard to the left axis and the PDC on the right axis.

The energy that plant 1 is producing in the time period (e.g. the year) is $Q_1^s = M_1^{max} cf_2$. Consider now plant 2. It is the mid merit-one. It is called to produce only when load exceeds $M_1^{max}$. According to the LDC throughout the year it generates $Q_2^s = (M_1^{max} + M_2^{max})cf_3 - M_1^{max} cf_2$. Plant 3, the peaker, produces $Q_2^s = (M_1^{max} + M_2^{max} + M_3^{max})v_L - (M_1^{max} + M_2^{max})cf_3$. Substituting these relationships into problem (21.12) and solving it leads to the following FOCs:

$$YRC_1 + c_1 cf_2 + c_2 cf_3 - c_2 cf_2 + c_3 v_L - c_3 cf_3 - v_L \varphi = 0;$$
$$YRC_2 + c_2 cf_3 + c_3 v_L - c_3 cf_3 - v_L \varphi = 0; \qquad (21.13)$$
$$YRC_3 + c_3 v_L - v_L \varphi = 0;$$

which can be simplified as:

$$YRC_1 = cf_2(c_2 - c_1) + cf_3(c_3 - c_2) + v_L(\varphi - c_3);$$
$$YRC_2 = cf_3(c_3 - c_2) + v_L(\varphi - c_3);$$
$$YRC_3 = v_L(\varphi - c_3). \tag{21.14}$$

Let us consider the meaning of Equations (21.14). Consider plant 1. The extra unit of capacity $M_1^{max}$ has a unit cost of $YRC_1$. However, its marginal increase replaces the energy produced with a capacity factor $cf_2$ at a cost $c_2$ with one (marginal unit) of energy at cost $c_1$. Thus, cost is reduced by $cf_2(c_2 - c_1)$.

The extra capacity $M_1^{max}$ also rises $M_1^{max} + M_2^{max}$, and this allows replacement of energy produced by plant 3, with a capacity factor $cf_2$ and marginal cost $c_3$, with one marginal unit of energy produced at marginal cost $c_2$, thus saving $cf_3(c_3 - c_2)$.

Finally, there is also a rise in $M_1^{max} + M_2^{max} + M_3^{max}$, which allows replacement of one unit of energy that was shed at $LOLP$ (with a cost of $\varphi$) with one extra unit of energy at marginal cost $c_3$, thus saving $v_L(\varphi - c_3)$. The first Equation (21.14) shows that in equilibrium the net cost accruing from the investment in capacity 1 must be equal to the net gain in the cost of energy supply that the capacity allows to generate, including the reduction in the load shed. The same applies to technology 2 and 3.

Solving the system of three Equations (21.14) in the three unknowns $cf_1$, $cf_2$ and $cf_3$ yields the following solutions:

$$YRC_1 + c_1 cf_2 = YRC_2 + c_2 cf_2;$$
$$YRC_2 + c_2 cf_3 = YRC_3 + c_3 cf_3;$$
$$YRC_3 + c_3 v_L = \varphi v_L. \tag{21.15}$$

These are called **screening curves**. They coincide, for the entire time interval, to the ACC curves we have already introduced in Chapter 9.[3] They confirm the result found in Paragraph 21.2. Plant 1, the baseload, sees more capacity installed than the other plants. Solutions (21.15) show that it is optimal installing capacity $M_1^{max}$ up to the breakeven point $cf_2$, beyond which it is more convenient to install technology 2. The same holds for technology 2, *mutatis mutandis*, while for 3 the breakeven is given by the optimal load shedding.

Solution (21.15) comes from a welfare maximization-cost minimization problem. Thus it corresponds to the case of a regulated monopoly or a perfectly planned solution, as it was in Chapter 9. We see in the next paragraph that the same holds true in a competitive market.

## 21.4    The Competitive Solution to Optimal Investment

As before, we consider power plants with three different costs. However, we now assume that the price of the energy is set up in a competitive market. Each power

---

[3] See that in Chapter 9 the screening curves referred to a given hour $j$, therefore the fixed cost was the hourly rental cost; in this chapter, they are referring to the whole year, and therefore the fixed costs are the yearly rental costs.

producer wishes to maximize its own profit, and must decide whether to invest in capacity $M_i^{max}$ in order to do so. Clearly, profits depend on the price, which depend on the production of all power producers and the LDC. Let us consider the problem for each producer: plant 1, the baseload; plant 2, the mid-merit one; plant 3, the peaker.

Let us start from the last. For power plant 3, it produces only when $Q^d$ is above $M_1^{max} + M_2^{max}$. When the peaker is the marginal plant, in a competitive market, the SMP corresponds to $c_3$. This occurs for the following percentage of hours in the year: $(cf_3 - v_L)$. When load is shed, which occurs with a load factor given by the $LOLP$ (i.e. $v_L$) the price spikes to the $VOLL$ (i.e. $\varphi$). Therefore, revenues of the peaker are: $\varphi v_L M_3^{max} + c_3(cf_3 - v_L)M_3^{max}$. Costs are $YRC_3 M_3^{max} + c_3 cf_3 M_3^{max}$. Note that we can re-write the cost function as $YRC_3 M_3^{max} + c_3 v_L M_3^{max} + c_3(cf_3 - v_L)M_3^{max}$. The peaker's profit function is:

$$
\begin{aligned}
\pi &= \varphi v_L M_3^{max} + c_3(cf_3 - v_L)M_3^{max} - YRC_3 M_3^{max} - c_3 v_L M_3^{max} - c_3(cf_3 - v_L)M_3^{max}; \\
&= \varphi v_L M_3^{max} - YRC_3 M_3^{max} - c_3 v_L M_3^{max}.
\end{aligned}
\tag{21.16}
$$

Consider now the mid-merit plant. Replicating the same reasoning as above, we see that revenues are: $\varphi v_L M_2^{max} + c_3(cf_3 - v_L)M_2^{max} + c_2(cf_2 - cf_3)M_2^{max}$. Costs are $YRC_2 M_2^{max} + c_2 cf_2 M_2^{max}$, which, as before, can be written as: $YRC_2 M_2^{max} + c_2 cf_3 M_2^{max} + c_2(cf_2 - cf_3)M_2^{max}$. Thus, plant 2 profit function is:

$$
\begin{aligned}
\pi &= \varphi v_L M_2^{max} + c_3(cf_3 - v_L)M_2^{max} + c_2(cf_2 - cf_3)M_2^{max} - YRC_2 M_2^{max} - c_2 cf_3 M_2^{max} \\
&\quad - c_2(cf_2 - cf_3)M_2^{max}; \\
&= \varphi v_L M_2^{max} + c_3(cf_3 - v_L)M_2^{max} - YRC_2 M_2^{max} - c_2 cf_3 M_2^{max}.
\end{aligned}
\tag{21.17}
$$

Finally, for the baseload plant 1, revenues are: $\varphi v_L M_1^{max} + c_3(cf_3 - v_L)M_1^{max} + c_2(cf_2 - cf_3)M_1^{max} + c_1(cf_1 - cf_2)M_1^{max}$. Costs are $YRC_1 M_1^{max} + c_1 cf_1 M_1^{max}$, which can be written as: $YRC_1 M_1^{max} + c_1 cf_2 M_1^{max} + c_1(cf_1 - cf_2)M_1^{max}$. Plant 1 profits are:

$$
\begin{aligned}
\pi &= \varphi v_L M_1^{max} + c_3(cf_3 - v_L)M_1^{max} + c_2(cf_2 - cf_3)M_1^{max} + c_1(cf_1 - cf_2)M_1^{max} \\
&\quad - YRC_1 M_1^{max} - c_1 cf_2 M_1^{max} - c_1(cf_1 - cf_2)M_1^{max}; \\
&= \varphi v_L M_1^{max} + c_3(cf_3 - v_L)M_1^{max} + c_2(cf_2 - cf_3)M_1^{max} - YRC_1 M_1^{max} - c_1 cf_2 M_1^{max}.
\end{aligned}
\tag{21.18}
$$

The F.O.C.s of the profits' maximization problem of each producer with regard to $M_1^{max}$, $M_2^{max}$, $M_3^{max}$, respectively, in perfectly competitive market yield the following system of equations:

$$
\begin{aligned}
YRC_3 &= (\varphi - c_3)v_L; \\
YRC_2 &= (\varphi - c_3)v_L + cf_3(c_3 - c_2); \\
YRC_1 &= (\varphi - c_3)v_L + cf_3(c_3 - c_2) + cf_2(c_2 - c_1).
\end{aligned}
\tag{21.19}
$$

It is clear that conditions (21.19) are equal to conditions (21.14) of the optimal investment problem in a regulated (or planned) setting. Therefore, we have an important result:

---

**Result**

In a perfectly competitive market, profit maximization yields the same optimal level of installed capacity as in the investment planning problem.

---

See that the analysis of the screening curves in the optimal planned investment problem of paragraph 21.3 also holds for the competitive setting. We can interpret conditions (21.19) considering the PDC. Recall that $c_1$, $c_2$ and $c_3$ are the SMP whenever the marginal plant is, respectively, the baseload, mid-merit and peak load plant, while $\varphi$ is the equilibrium price when load is shed. Condition (21.19) shows that price volatility is necessary to finance the investment in capacity. When the investments are at their optimal level, all types of technologies see their fixed costs repaid. In particular, the peaker, which has a lower fixed cost, sees the (yearly) fixed costs repaid by all those hours of the year in which load is shed and price goes to the *VOLL*. For those hours, it cashes in the difference between revenues and variable costs, making supermarginal profits that are needed to cover investments costs. In other words, even if it has positive short-run profits, it has zero long-run profits. For the other technologies, the same holds true, with respect to their own costs. The mid-merit plant makes supermarginal profits whenever the peaker is called into operation (including when load is shed). This occurs for a number of hours more than the hours in which the peaker makes profits, but this is needed since the fixed costs of the mid-merit plant are higher. Finally, for the baseload, it is always producing but has only short-run profits when it is not the marginal technology. No plant makes positive long-run profits.

This analysis holds true for the planned equilibrium and for the perfectly competitive market. For the latter, it is the competition assumption that guarantees that the SMP, when the baseload is the marginal price, coincides with the marginal cost of the baseload, and similarly for the other levels of the SMP. For the planned solution, it is the planner who must set up prices (or cost of energy delivery to customers) in order to replicate the PDC of a perfectly competitive market.[4] Therefore, the following result holds:

---

**Result**

When installed capacity is at the optimal level and markets are perfectly competitive (or the monopoly is perfectly regulated), investors are able to repay exactly their investment costs. There are zero long-run profits.

---

This result is the usual zero-long-run-profit condition of any perfectly competitive (or perfectly regulated) market. As such, it does not imply that plants are not able to make

---

[4] This assumes that the central planner can observe the hourly costs and the hourly withdrawal from the grid (i.e. that there is real-time metering). This is a strong and rather unrealistic assumption. For a discussion of the consequences of lack of real-time metering see Chapter 19.

accountable profits. As is well known, profits are the fair remuneration for well diversified risks (see any finance textbook, such as Elton et al., 2014). Thus, in a theoretical setting, the long-run remuneration of the investment in power production, including risk-adjusted remuneration of the capital, equals the expected discounted sum of the profits accruing from electricity markets. However, the long-run analysis of electricity markets is based on the same assumptions on which any other perfectly competitive long-run evaluation is based. In the next chapter, we shall review them and discuss whether they are likely to be met or not in real electricity markets.

## Learning Outcomes

- In the long run, a planner aims for an optimum set-up of investments in capacity that maximizes total welfare. The solution to the problem shows that unless capacity had no cost, it is not optimal to install capacity in order to serve all possible levels of the load in a given time interval. Instead it is optimal to have some hours of the year in which load is shed.
- This result is independent of whether the costs of capacity are equal across all plant, or if costs are ranked. The optimal level of capacity is set at that level for which the marginal cost of the marginal plant equals the expected net marginal benefit of the energy that the capacity can generate.
- At equilibrium, in a given time period (for instance a year) the probability of not having load served (*LOLP*) equals the investment costs in that period (Yearly Rental Cost – YRC) over the net benefit of having load served. The latter is the *VOLL*, minus the marginal cost of producing energy. In practical analysis, *LOLP* can be approximated by the ratio of YRC over the *VOLL*.
- When costs differ across plants, the optimal level of capacity guarantees that the costs of energy provision and loss of load are minimized. The optimal dispatching is achieved by means of the screening curves. At equilibrium, baseload capacity has a higher share of capacity than the other types of technology and serves the load for a longer time interval; then the other types of capacity follow, ranked according to their marginal costs.
- When investors are profit-maximizing agents acting in competitive markets, they invest up to the capacity level that coincides with the level resulting from welfare maximization. At equilibrium, power plants make zero long-run profits and cover exactly the discounted investments cost.

# 22 Energy-Only Markets vs. Markets with Capacity Remuneration Mechanisms

## 22.1 Introduction

In the last chapter, we focused on generation capacity investments. It is important to point out that this is just one aspect of a broader concept, termed System Reliability or Security of Supply (European Commission, 2014):

DEFINITION. **Security of Supply (SoS)**: *the ability of the system to deliver electrical energy to all points of utilization within acceptable standards and in the amounts desired.*

SoS has two dimensions. The first, called **system security**, depends on the admissible flows in transmission lines and the availability of ancillary services and reactive power. We shall not deal with these aspects here. The second dimension is system adequacy:

DEFINITION. **System Adequacy:** *the power system's ability to meet demand in the long term*

When adequacy refers to the ability of generation capacity to meet demand, it is termed **Generation Adequacy**. In what follows, we shall refer to generation adequacy, although we should keep in mind that this is just a subset of the broader concept of system adequacy.

In the last chapter, we saw that the optimal level of investment to deliver generation adequacy in a theoretical setting can be reached regardless of whether energy is provided by a single regulated monopolist or if there are markets for power generation. In other words, the different models 1–4 of Chapter 5 have no impact on the investment level in the electricity system. However, this conclusion relies on a number of strong assumptions. In this chapter, we review them and consider how likely they are to be effectively met in real settings. This raises the concern that in the real world investments might not deliver an efficient outcome. In particular, it is often argued that there may not be enough generation adequacy. We review this problem in Paragraph 22.2. A natural question to ask when there are concerns about adequacy is whether it is possible to tackle them by adopting a specific market design for capacity. This question is answered in Paragraph 22.3, which explains the rationale for Capacity Remuneration Mechanisms that are analyzed in the next chapter.

## 22.2 Generation Adequacy in Practice

The optimal investment condition that we identified in Chapter 21 rests on the assumption of perfect competition. This means that there are no market failures. We discuss them here and assess to what extent they are likely to occur in electricity markets.

### 22.2.1 The Existence of Markets for Hedging Risks

In the previous chapter, we identified the investment optimality condition, without taking into account risk. In real electricity markets, there are uncertainties regarding plants' costs (due to fuel-price volatility, O&M costs, local investment risks, primary energy availability and so on) and on revenues. The optimal investment rule specifies that discounted fixed costs must equal the expected net benefit over the reference period, where expectations are taken with respect to the plant operating time. This rule can be extended by incorporating the expected figures of the stochastic (market and costs) variables. The equilibrium condition still holds: the yearly expected discounted costs of the plant must equal the yearly expected benefit. However, this implies that there must be markets in order to hedge these risks. In other words, investors must discount the fixed costs, which should also include the financial costs needed to invest in power plants. This is not a point that refers just to power markets: the efficiency of market remuneration for risk depends on the completeness and competitiveness of financial markets (see any finance textbook, such as Elton et al., 2014). In markets where it is hard to hedge against risk, the investment cost can be higher than the efficient level one.

This problem can be worsened by the time-nature of electricity markets. The equilibrium condition that we considered in the last chapter is framed with respect to a given time period, for instance a year. Power plants, however, last for more than a year. This is not a problem from a theoretical point of view: the yearly rental cost incorporates the discounting of the whole total costs throughout the whole expected life of the plant. Over a period of years, a plant sees its expected lifespan decrease. Because of amortization, its yearly rental costs decrease overtime. At the same time, recall that the marginal cost is $c_i = Fl_j \cdot a_{j,i}$, where $a_{j,i}$ is the efficiency rate of the plant. Over time, it is very likely that efficiency lowers (i.e. $a_{j,i}$ rises). The older a plant becomes, the greater its losses, as it needs time for maintenance, unexpected repairs and so on. Hence, the marginal cost of the plant rises over the year too. Moreover, there is also a technological obsolescence, as more modern and efficient technologies may replace older versions. For instance, this has been the case with combined-cycle gas turbines, that have higher efficiency rates than the old turbo-gas plants. Therefore, we can expect that over time at least some types of plants will move down the merit order ladder, as the more years pass by the more they become marginal plants. This reduces the expected number of hours in which they gain supermarginal profits. But again, this is what has to happen in an efficient market, since over time they experience a decrease in their residual fixed costs. At the end of economic life, when a plant is fully amortized, it has no residual extra costs and should not be dispatched, unless it is needed because of some new load. Thus, optimal investment also leads to dynamic efficiency.

However, such reasoning implies that all operators are able to forecast market outcomes and market evolution for the whole lifetime of the investment. In other words, when calculating optimal investments, the business plan must incorporate uncertainty over a long time period (e.g. 40 years), as regards all costs; and it must be able to foresee any possible evolution of technology, as well as any possible change in life expectancy of plants or variation in rules about market price formation and market design evolution. This is rather demanding assumption, which is not necessary. What is necessary, however, is that financial markets incorporate all the uncertainties, including technological and regulatory issues in the investment risk. This implies that the financial cost for the invested capital invested in power plants might be extremely high and it might induce a sub-optimal level of investments.

### 22.2.2    Market Power

We saw that the optimality of perfect competitive markets relies on the assumption of no-market power. Market power in electricity markets was discussed in Part IV. However, we point out here that another consequence of market power in electricity markets is the possible distortion of investment in capacity. In any markets, price spikes signal situations of scarcity. We saw in Chapter 21 that price spikes are a normal phenomenon of electricity markets. It is exactly the existence of the periods where price goes to the *VOLL* that provides enough remuneration for the capacity invested. However, we also know that scarcity increases market power. Price goes to *VOLL* only when capacity is scarce; but when it is scarce, producers have greater market power.

This problem is exacerbated by the rigidity of short-run electricity demand, which implies that withdrawing even a small share of capacity from the market during scarcity events can be extremely profitable for plants, as it might result in huge increases in the market clearing price. In practical terms, this means that it can be extremely hard in power markets to distinguish situations of effective price scarcity from situations of market abuse. It is true that in principle revenues accruing from market power and investment incentives are counterbalancing trade-offs. High prices accruing from periods of scarcity can induce new capacity to become operational, and this should reduce scarcity periods. However, it is not enough to see room for profit in a power system for an investor to build capacity and generate power. This decision must be taken in agreement with (or following the specificities set up by) the SO (which also decides on mothballing plants). The investment process takes time and this may create investment boom-and-bust cycles that could hinder efficiency. Moreover, it can be hard to disentangle effective scarcity from strategic scarcity. For this reason, several measures have been established in many European and US markets in order to mitigate market power such as price caps, supply obligation measures and market monitoring. These measures can interfere with investment decisions. Price caps limit the possibility to repay investment costs.

This problem is known in the literature as the **missing money** problem. We shall review it in Paragraph 22.3.1.

## 22.2.3    Lack of Coordination and Asymmetric Information

Asymmetric information is a typical cause of market failure, which can also arise in electricity markets. It is clear that the optimal planned equilibrium of Chapter 21 depends on the possibility of observing, or correctly estimating costs, prices and the operation of power plants. Thus, unless a central planner has perfect information about these figures, it is quite possible that the planned equilibrium is non-optimal. This problem is not specific to electricity markets. Indeed, the tendency to substitute regulation by markets derives from efforts to enhance efficiency in several regulated industries. When a market is set, it is the interaction among agents that makes apparent the willingness to pay and to produce among all of them. For electricity markets, however, it can be extremely hard to achieve efficient market equilibria. In terms of generation, we have already discussed in Chapter 13 the possibility that bids do not reflect marginal cost. For load, we have seen in the previous chapter that it is necessary to identify the marginal evaluation of the load in order to identify the optimal level of capacity to be installed. However, when demand is rigid there is no way to observe it from the market clearing value. It is necessary to set a highest level of load willingness to pay in order for the market to clear, whenever load exceeds available supply and it must be shed.

So far in this book we have solved this problem by assuming a given level of the *VOLL*. However, estimating the *VOLL* is a complex exercise for the following reasons: a) it can be difficult to identify individual consumers' *VOLL*, in particular at the transmission level, since it can be hard or impossible to discriminate across consumers when load is shed; b) estimating *VOLL* implies estimating utility of electricity; however, electricity is an intermediate good; consumers might measure its value through the value of the services they use thanks to electricity, but this latter depends on several factors; c) the relationship between load and utility might be more complex than we have assumed so far: the same level of load can have different levels of utility, perhaps depending on some external factors (in mathematical terms this means that the utility function might not be a function but a correspondence), or it might not be a monotone function (which gives rise to multiplicity of equilibria). For example, consumers strongly object to marginal episodes of load shedding, but become used to such episodes after a while. Eventually they react adversely if the load shedding is repeated too often over time, and finally choose to disconnect from the grid if load becomes entirely unreliable.

Note that if we allow the value of the load depending on the electricity system, we fall into a circularity of reasoning: the optimal dispatching and investment depends on the value of the utility, which in turns depends on the operation of the grid and the amount of capacity installed. In practical terms, this circularity is solved by assuming a rather high level for the marginal value of the utility, which caps the demand bids in the market and guarantees that the market clears at all prices, including when load is shed. But again, as for the case of market power, there is no guarantee that the chosen level of *VOLL* coincides with the theoretical one.

Asymmetries of information also have another important impact in power markets. So far, we have focused only on generation adequacy. However, as we have noted generation adequacy is just one aspect of system adequacy. As we saw in Part V, when a system is importing energy, lack of transmission capacity implies that demand cannot be fully served. Thus, both transmission and power production capacity affect system adequacy. Load control can also provide system adequacy. In the analyses we have performed so far, we have considered transmission and generation investment independently. In Part IV we discussed optimal grid structure, with generation capacity given, while in Chapter 21 we defined the optimal level of investments, for a given grid. However, decisions on generation and grid investment are interdependent. A lack of transmission capacity can hinder investment in generation, and different types and amount of generation capacities change the network constraints. In a centrally planned system, investment in the grid and in power plants are taken together in order to minimize system costs. However, in electricity markets, decisions on production and transmission are separate. Investments in generation need to assume a given system topology, and transmission expansion needs depend on actual and forecast evolution of power plants. There is therefore an issue about coordinating independent choices. This implies that a priority rule must be adopted. For instance, it might be decided that network investments should follow the expansion of generation investments in order to minimize inefficiency from network losses. However, this strategy might not be optimal whenever the transmission capacity and the generation capacity are substitutes. For instance, a new transmission line able to increase electricity import in a network constrained zone might be less expensive than installing a new power plant. Again, the problem is not a theoretical but a practical one. From a theoretical point of view, the coordination rule should imply that the investment with the highest cost-benefit ratio should be prioritized; however, in practical terms it might be hard to derive a single ranking for all possible system configurations that arise from the different choices. Any practical rules might induce a sub-optimal investment choice, and increase uncertainty about system evolution which would further affect investment optimality.

## 22.3     Electricity-Only Markets and Capacity Remuneration Mechanisms

Several authors (Cramton and Stoft, 2006; Joskow and Tirole, 2007; Joskow, 2007, 2008; Joskow and Wolfram, 2012; Cramton and Ockenfels, 2012; Cramton, Ockenfels and Stoft, 2013), on the basis of the arguments put forth in the previous paragraph, have conjectured that electricity markets might not provide enough incentives in practice to deliver optimal levels of capacity, and that a different market design has to be adopted. We have seen that the incentive to invest in capacity is provided implicitly by the price volatility of energy markets. Those markets that rely just on electricity markets to provide generation adequacy are termed **energy-only markets**, highlighting that it is the remuneration of energy that in equilibrium pays all costs, including the investment ones. There are, however, other possible market designs, in which generation capacity is explicitly remunerated. They are grouped under the broad name of markets with **Capacity Remuneration Mechanisms (CRMs)**.

Whether CRMs are effectively needed or not is debatable, depending on the effective relevance of the market failures highlighted in Paragraph 22.2. CRMs will be properly defined in the next chapter. Here, we show that, from a theoretical first-best setting, markets with and without CRMs provide the same level of investments. Suppose for simplicity of notation that there are just two technologies, 1 and 2. The first is the baseload, 2 is the peaker. From Equations (21.20), we know that at the equilibrium the optimal level of capacity, call it $M_i^*$, is such as that the following relationships hold true:

$$YRC_2 M_2^* = (\varphi - c_2) v_L M_2^*;$$
$$YRC_1 M_1^* = (\varphi - c_2) v_L M_1^* + (c_2 - c_1) c f_2 M_1^*. \tag{22.1}$$

When there is not enough capacity, there are too many hours in which load is shed. It is common to refer to situations in which load is shed because the amount of peak load capacity is lower than the optimal one as cases of **capacity-constrained systems**, while when there is not enough baseload capacity we refer to **energy-constrained systems**. We must stress that even if this is terminology is in common use, it is not quite accurate: in both cases there is not enough energy because there is not enough capacity, the only difference being the type of capacity that is lacking.[1]

As we saw in Paragraph 22.2, the capacity invested can be less than the optimal one because the figures for the cost do not incorporate all costs that the investor effectively faces, or because revenues are constrained since prices are not allowed to spike at the *VOLL* in situations of load shedding due to a price cap. We start with an analysis of the latter case.

### 22.3.1    Insufficient Capacity Due to Price Caps

Regardless of whether the system is energy constrained or capacity constrained, when there is a price cap and investments are explicitly remunerated, the same optimal allocation of the energy-only market setting without price cap can be reached, provided that the explicit remuneration for capacity is set at the optimal level. Consider a capacity-constrained system. This means that the effective level of peak load capacity installed is lower than the optimal one: $M_2^{ins} < M_2^*$. Denote the extra capacity that is lacking as $M_2^{mis} = M_2^* - M_2^{ins}$. For simplicity, assume that capacity of baseload is not affected: $M_2^* - M_2^{ins}$. Clearly this assumption is false since the loss in revenues would also affect the baseload, but we shall consider the baseload further below when we discuss energy constrained systems.

Let us show the *LOLP* corresponding to the optimal level of capacity as $v_L^*$, and the *LOLP* arising from the effective level of installed capacity as $v_L^{ins}$. Because of the lack of capacity, $v_L^{ins} > v_L^*$. The cause of the lack of capacity is the existence of a price cap on the electricity price $\bar{p} < \varphi$. Because of the price cap, plant 2 installs the amount of capacity $M_2^{ins}$ for which the *LOLP* solves the equation $(\bar{p} - c_2) v_L^{ins} = YRC_2$, while the optimal solution without the price cap was $(\varphi - c_2) v_L^* = YRC_2$. Since $(\bar{p} - c_2) < (\varphi - c_2)$ it follows that

---

[1] In capacity-constrained systems, a lack of peak load capacity is often coupled with a lack of flexible sources able to cope with imbalances, and of other ancillary services. We shall not consider these aspects here, except for the discussion of the operating reserve demand curve in Paragraph 23.5.

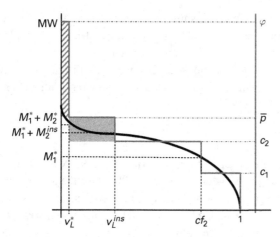

**Figure 22.1** Insufficient level of investment due to a price cap

$v_L^{ins} > v_L^* \rightarrow M_2^{ins} < M_2^*$. This is shown in Figure 22.1. Note that the price cap has a twofold impact on revenues: they are increased with regard to revenues of the optimal quantity $M_2^*$ since there is a higher number of hours in which load is shed. This is represented by the shadowed area in Figure 22.1 corresponding to $(\bar{p} - c_2)(v_L^{ins} - v_L^*)$. At the same time, plant 2 sees a reduction of revenues due to the limit in the price, which is the price (cap) effect. This is shown by the dashed area in Figure 22.1 that equals $(\varphi - \bar{p})v_L^*$. The net sum implies a reduction in revenues, which induces installing a lower amount of capacity, for otherwise $M_2^{ins}$ would have been the optimal quantity of capacity.

With installed capacity $M_2^{ins}$, plant 2 is having net earnings (i.e. revenues less operating costs) such as $(\bar{p} - c_2)v_L^{ins}M_2^{ins} = YRC_2M_2^{ins}$. Assume now there is a CRM that pays an amount $k$ per unit of capacity installed. With a CRM, plant 2 net earnings in equilibrium become:

$$kM_2^{ins} + (\bar{p} - c_2)v_L^{ins}M_2^{ins} = YRC_2M_2^{ins}. \tag{22.2}$$

What is the level of $k$ that maximizes social welfare (i.e. that provides the optimal level of capacity $M_2^*$)? We saw that the price cap implies lower revenues with regard to the revenues that the plant would earn without price cap or with a cap equal to the *VOLL*. Because of this loss, the amount of capacity invested is less than the optimal one. These missed earnings are $(\varphi - \bar{p})v_L^* - (\bar{p} - c_2)(v_L^{ins} - v_L^*)$. It is a transfer that is given directly to the firm through the CRM:

$$k = (\varphi - \bar{p})v_L^* - (\bar{p} - c_2)(v_L^{ins} - v_L^*). \tag{22.3}$$

Substituting Equation (22.3) for Equation (22.2) we have:

$$[(\varphi - \bar{p})v_L^* - (\bar{p} - c_2)(v_L^{ins} - v_L^*)]M_2^{ins} + (\bar{p} - c_2)v_L^{ins}M_2^{ins} = YRC_2M_2^{ins}. \tag{22.4}$$

Solving and simplifying it we obtain:

$$(\varphi - c_2)v_L^* M_2^{ins} = YRC_2 M_2^{ins} \rightarrow (\varphi - c_2)v_L^* = YRC_2. \qquad (22.5)$$

This is the same condition as Equation (21.19), leading to the same optimal solution.

Consider now an energy-constrained system. In our framework, it means that there is a price cap which provides lower revenues than the theoretical optimal one and this affects investment in the baseload technology only, not in the peak load one. The lower capacity installed by the baseload implies that the effective *VOLL* is higher because there is a lower amount of total capacity installed; moreover, the capacity factor of plant 2 rises, since it must be called for a larger number of hours. Replicating the reasoning above, we write the missing net earnings of the baseload as: $(\varphi - \bar{p})v_L^* - (\bar{p} - c_2)(v_L^{ins} - v_L^*) - (c_2 - c_1)(cf_2^{ins} - cf_2^*)$. Note that the last term refers to the extra hours in which price goes to $c_2$ because of the lack of baseload capacity.

The net earnings of the baseload with the CRM become:

$$kM_1^{ins} + (\bar{p} - c_2)v_L^{ins} M_1^{ins} + (c_2 - c_1)cf_2^{ins} M_1^{ins} = YRC_1 M_1^{ins}; \qquad (22.6)$$

and the optimal CRM:

$$k = (\varphi - \bar{p})v_L^* - (\bar{p} - c_2)(v_L^{ins} - v_L^*) - (c_2 - c_1)(cf_2^{ins} - cf_2^*). \qquad (22.7)$$

Substituting (22.7) into Equation (22.6) and simplifying we have:

$$\begin{aligned}
(\varphi - c_2)v_L^* M_1^{ins} + (c_2 - c_1)cf_2^* M_1^{ins} &= YRC_1 M_1^{ins} \\
(\varphi - c_2)v_L^* + (c_2 - c_1)cf_2^* &= YRC_1.
\end{aligned} \qquad (22.8)$$

Again, we get the same condition as Equation (21.19).

See that the optimal $k$ for the case of capacity-constrained systems set in Equation (22.3) can be re-written as:

$$k = (\varphi - c_2)v_L^* - (\bar{p} - c_2)v_L^{ins}; \qquad (22.9)$$

while the optimal $k$ for the energy-constrained case obtained in Equation (22.7) writes:

$$k = (\varphi - c_2)v_L^* - (\bar{p} - c_2)v_L^{ins} - (c_2 - c_1)(cf_2^{ins} - cf_2^*). \qquad (22.10)$$

Equations (22.9) and (22.10) have a nice interpretation. They show that the optimal CRM, per unit of capacity, must be equal to the extra remuneration that the plant would earn without the CRM in the energy-only market, net of any extra earning that they have already earned. These latter arise because of the price cap, and for the baseload plant also because of the effect that the smaller amount of baseload capacity installed has on the baseload price. This latter effect, $-(c_2 - c_1)(cf_2^{ins} - cf_2^*)$, corresponds to the effect of a baseload capacity withholding.

Note that in the energy-constrained case, we have assumed that the lack of baseload capacity was equal to the lack of capacity for the capacity constrained case, so that the impact on the *VOLL* was equal. Under these circumstances, since the lack of baseload capacity raises the baseload price and this partially counterbalances the lack of peak revenues, the optimal CRM for energy-constrained systems is smaller than the CRM of the capacity-constrained case. However, in more general settings, in order to compare the optimal CRM it is necessary to compare the impact on the *VOLL* of both cases and on the baseload price, if there is a lack of baseload capacity. As a consequence, the optimal $k$ in the two constrained systems can differ.

Equations (22.9) and (22.10) also show that the optimal level of CRM depends on the price cap level, but the price cap does not affect the optimal level of capacity installed. Let us see this. Consider the peaker. If the price cap was set at $\bar{p} = c_2$, the peaker would not have any incentive to install any level of capacity, without the CRM. In this case, the optimal CRM must be such as $k = (\varphi - c_2)v_L^*$, which is the same as Equation (21.20) for the peaker. The firm would earn no supermarginal profit in the energy market, but would see all its fixed costs components restored by the CRM. The same holds for the baseload, net of the capacity withholding effect. If on the contrary, the price cap was set at $\bar{p} = \varphi$, the supermarginal profits of the peaker in the energy market would be equal to $(\varphi - c_2)v_L^*$, and clearly the optimal CRM would be $k = 0$, since $v_L^{ins} = v_L^*$. The same is true for the baseload, since $cf_2^{ins} = cf_2^*$ too.

We can summarize what we have seen so far in the following:

---

### Results

- In a market where capacity is explicitly remunerated at the optimal level, the amount of investment in capacity coincides with the investment in a perfectly competitive energy-only market.
- When the energy price is capped, the optimal explicit remuneration for the capacity must equal the remuneration that the plant would have had if there had been no price cap, net of the supermarginal profits that plants have earned when there is a price cap.
- When the system is capacity constrained, the CRM must provide revenues for the peak load plants. When the system is energy constrained, the CRM must provide to the baseload plants the same revenues that they would obtain when load is shed, net of any increase in baseload price due to the lack of baseload capacity.

---

A corollary of this result is obviously that any price cap induces a distortion to the optimal theoretical level of investments in capacity, unless it is compensated by the optimal explicit remuneration for the capacity.

## 22.3.2    Insufficient Capacity Due to Extra Costs

Now suppose that there is an insufficient level of capacity because the investment costs are too high. By too high we mean that either the estimates are higher than the actual levels or there are financial costs higher than those that are competitive, for instance because financial companies have market power and thus risk-hedging tools are sold at

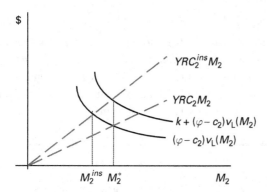

**Figure 22.2** Optimal and effective investment in the capacity-money space

a mark-up. In both cases, the situation is such that the assumed yearly rental costs $YRC_i^{ins}$ are higher than the optimal true ones $YRC_i^*$. As a consequence, there is less capacity installed. This can be shown in a graph, representing the fixed cost and the net revenues (gross revenues, minus operating costs) as functions of the capacity installed. Consider the capacity-constrained case. Recall that the $LOLP$, $v_L$, is a function of the capacity installed $M_i$. Thus, we can write the net revenue function as $R_i = (\varphi - c_2)v_L(M_i)M_i$ and the fixed cost function as $F_i = YRC_iM_i$. See Figure 22.2.

Note that the net revenue function depends on the marginal impact of the capacity on the $LOLP$. The slope of the net revenue curve changes depending on $\dfrac{\partial v_L}{\partial M_i}$. The picture shows that at equilibrium, because of the excessive yearly rental cost, the optimal amount of capacity installed is too low. Indeed, it is true that the lower level of capacity implies a higher $LOLP$. However, the extra revenues accruing from the higher number of hours in which load is shed do not compensate for the extra costs of investment and as a consequence the amount of load shed rises.

The equilibrium of the peaker without CRM is:

$$(\varphi - c_2)v_L^{ins}M_2^{ins} = YRC_2^{ins}M_2^{ins}. \tag{22.11}$$

With the CRM, it would obtain:

$$kM_2^{ins} + (\varphi - c_2)v_L^{ins}M_2^{ins} = YRC_2^{ins}M_2^{ins}. \tag{22.12}$$

The optimal level of $k$ is

$$k = (\varphi - c_2)(v_L^* - v_L^{ins}). \tag{22.13}$$

It is clear that condition (22.13) coincides with condition (22.3), when there is no price cap, i.e., $\varphi = \bar{p}$.[2] Substituting it into Equation (22.12) and simplifying it we have:

---

[2] Note, however, that there is a difference here. In condition (22.3), when there was no price cap, there was no distortion, and therefore $v_L^* = v_L^{ins}$. Here, the reason for the difference between the effective and optimal $LOLP$ rests on the excess fixed costs, and therefore $v_L^* \neq v_L^{ins}$ even if $\varphi = \bar{p}$.

$$(\varphi - c_2)v_L^* M_2^{ins} = YRC_2^{ins} M_2^{ins} \rightarrow M_2 = M_2^*. \qquad (22.14)$$

Optimality is restored. It is easy to see that the same holds true also for the energy constrained case. We leave the proof to the reader as an exercise. Therefore, the optimal CRM does not depend on the causes of the suboptimal investment, and the results of Paragraph 22.3.1 apply. In particular, result 2 holds true not just when there is a price cap, but also when there are wrong yearly rental cost figures.

---

### Result

When the fixed costs are wrongly set at too high a level, the optimal explicit remuneration for the capacity must be equal to the remuneration for the plants, had fixed costs been set at the correct level, net of any supermarginal profits that plants might have earned because of the wrong figures.

---

## Learning Outcomes

- The generation adequacy problem is a subset of the more general system adequacy problem, which must be solved to provide security of supply.
- In the real world, generation adequacy issues can arise due to the existence of several market failures. There may not be enough markets to hedge investment risks, or these markets might not be competitive. There can be market power in the wholesale markets, and this is favored by the nature of load, rigid in the short run and volatile.
- Price caps or any attempt to control prices at the wholesale level can give rise to a missing money problem (i.e. not enough supermarginal profits to cover investment fixed costs).
- There are also asymmetries of information on cost functions, on customers' willingness to pay and on the *VOLL* and the willingness to be shed. Finally, there are coordination issues between investments in generation and in transmission, which are both complements for the systems and substitutes in delivering Security of Supply.
- In several energy markets tools aimed at explicit remunerating capacity have been implemented. These are called Capacity Remuneration Mechanisms. Markets without CRMs are called energy-only. When there is not enough peak load capacity, the system is said to be capacity-constrained. When there is not enough baseload capacity, it is said to be energy-constrained. Insufficient levels of adequacy can arise because there is a price cap, or because there are mistaken costs estimates.
- Regardless of whether the system is energy or capacity constrained, and of the cause of the inadequate level of capacity, the optimal level of explicit remuneration for capacity can provide the same correct level of generation adequacy as perfectly competitive markets and optimally planned investments.

# 23 Analysis of Capacity Remuneration Mechanisms

## 23.1 Introduction

In the previous chapter, we saw that when there are distortions in energy markets, it is possible to retrieve the optimal level of capacity to solve a generation-adequacy problem by explicitly remunerating the capacity at the theoretical optimal level. In practice, there are several tools that have been designed to obtain such a result, which are grouped under the term Capacity Remuneration Mechanisms (CRMs).

Before analyzing them in this chapter, however, we need to explain what CRMs are. In principle, whatever affects the values of electricity provision either directly or indirectly could be classified as a CRM. A subsidy for renewables, for instance, increases their revenues, and thus foster investment in RES. The priority of dispatching also increases the profits of RES producers by reducing electricity market risks and thus inducing higher investments. Policies relating to primary energy fuels have an impact on their costs and therefore on the profitability of investments in power generation; the same is true for rules about the environmental impacts of power plants, or power supply rights or obligations. We review some of these issues in Part VIII. These tools should not be confused with CRMs, even if they have impacts on power investment. The latter can be defined as follows:

DEFINITION. *Capacity Remuneration Mechanisms (CRMs): all those policies whose aim is explicitly to remunerate capacity (or load) in order to provide the proper level of generation adequacy (including load reduction).*

The remuneration of capacity can also be made indirectly, for instance by fixing remuneration over a sufficiently long time period. The crucial feature that distinguishes CRMs from other support systems is their target: all those support systems whose aim is not directly to remunerate capacity (or load) to tackle an adequacy problem, but rather other environmental, social or distributional targets, are not classified as CRMs, even though they might have strong impacts on power investments.

In this chapter, we analyze the design of CRMs. In Paragraph 23.2, we propose different ways to classify CRMs. In Paragraph 23.3 we discuss capacity payments, capacity auctions, strategic reserves, capacity obligations and reliability options, highlighting the pros and cons of each of them. Finally, in Paragraph 23.4 we present a different tool that is not a CRM, but which can complement both energy-only markets and markets with CRMs, providing incentive-enhancing Security of Supply, the Operating Reserve Demand Curve.

## 23.2     Classifications of CRMs

It is possible to classify CRMs looking at different elements. In what follows, we present three distinct classifications of CRMs.

A first classification refers to the nature of the markets in which capacity is exchanged, and in particular, the characteristics of capacity demand. Let us explain this point. In Chapter 22 we showed that there is a problem of adequacy whenever the generation capacity invested is lower than the optimal one: $M_i^{ins} < M_i^*$ for some $i \in (1, \ldots, n)$. As a consequence, there is too high a load shedding: $v_L^{ins} > v_L^*$ (and also possibly load factors that are too high for non-baseload capacity if the system is energy-constrained). A theoretical optimal CRM can restore generation adequacy, remunerating, through a market, the capacity in terms of money per unit of capacity per time period, e.g. \$ per MWy (or any other unit measure of capacity in a given time period). Markets for capacity, as with any market, operate grouping demand and supply of capacity. As a result, a price and a quantity emerge at the equilibrium. Thus, the first classification of CRMs refers to the possibility of fixing *ex ante* the price of the capacity, its quantity (or volume requirement), or neither of the two. The case of a fixed price for capacity corresponds to a horizontal demand for capacity. The fixed quantity is a vertical demand for capacity. It is also possible to allow a demand for capacity that is neither perfectly elastic, nor inelastic, and let the market find the equilibrium price and quantity. Therefore, we have the following taxonomy: a) price-based CRMs; b) quantity-based CRMs; c) mixed CRMs. The latter are also termed option-based CRMs, since capacity is not bought or sold per se, but for its capability to deliver energy when needed; thus, capacity can be seen as an option to deliver energy. Note, however, that this terminology is highly imprecise, since all the capacity has the nature of an option, regardless of the characteristics of its demand.

A second taxonomy refers to whether or not CRMs are administratively set. There is a caveat here. All CRMs require some parameters to be identified. Capacity demand is expressed by those who have the responsibility to guarantee system adequacy. This is typically a task of the SO. Supply can be regulated too, for instance by predefining which type of capacity can participate in the market. In the last chapter we saw that $k$, the optimal remuneration level of the capacity, allows the system to reach $M_i^*$ and $v_L^*$. Thus, we shall say that a CRM is administratively set if $k$, or $M_i^*$, are fixed *ex ante* at some pre-determined level; otherwise the CRM is simply called market-based, and it is the market interaction that makes emerging the value of $k$ and $M_i^*$.

Another possible taxonomy refers to the allocation method through which capacity is remunerated, and in particular whether the capacity is exchanged in a centralized market, or through a system of bilateral contracts. The former is known as capacity market. The latter is referred to as a bilateral CRM or a CRM based on bilateral contracts.

A final classification refers to whether the CRM allows for the participation of external capacity, namely, capacity set outside the system to which the CRM refers to and to whether load can participate by providing load reduction. If external production and load is allowed, the CRM is said to be open to external production and load participation, respectively; otherwise the CRM is closed.

## 23.3    Typologies of CRMs

Several markets in the world have some type of CRM. In the United States there are CRMs in PJM, Midcontinent ISO (MISO), ISO New England (ISO-NE), New York ISO (NYISO) and California ISO (CAISO), while the Electric Reliability Council of Texas (ERCOT) and the Southwest Power Pool (SPP) do not have capacity markets. In Australia, the western states grouped under the NEM do not have CRMs.[1] The market of Western Australia has a CRM. New Zealand is an energy-only market.[2] In Europe, several national markets rely on some type of CRMs, the exceptions being markets in the Netherlands, Norway, Denmark, Estonia, Switzerland, Austria, Czech Republic, Slovakia, Bulgaria, Romania and the Balkan States (excluding Greece). In South America, there are CRMs in Brazil, Colombia, Chile and Peru.[3] Thus, CRMs are widely diffused. We present here the main typologies of CRMs and discuss their pros and cons. Clearly, every CRM has its own features, and can be attributed to different types of CRMs, on the basis of the different classifications presented above. However, what follows is a common way to group CRMs

### 23.3.1    Capacity Payments (CP)

Capacity payments (CP) are administratively set price-based CRMs. The price is awarded to all those producers who have some pre-determined features, through bilateral contracts set between the capacity buyer, generally the SO, and the power producers. It is also possible that producers are selected through competitive tender. In both cases, the price is fixed, and the market interaction between suppliers of capacity and the fixed demand determines the quantity of capacity that results. The payment in general is reserved to generation capacity. However, specific payments can also be dedicated to load reduction (i.e. to that load that sells to the SO the "right" to be the first to be shed in case of lack of capacity and is remunerated *ex ante* for this). In this case, the capacity

---

[1] Purely financial option contracts are also traded at the NEM.

[2] New Zealand is a largely hydro-based system. There are specific water usage regulations under extreme events and compensation schemes for planned load shedding that can be framed as targeted strategic reserves (see Paragraph 23.3.4).

[3] In South America, system adequacy in the region is usually pursued through long-term auctioning mechanisms. The product traded is often measured in terms of energy, and not capacity. However, the aim of those systems is to hedge investors' risk in large hydro-based power systems. According to our definition we could also classify them as CRMs, focusing on their purpose rather than their formal definition or characteristics.

payments are called payments for **interruptibility**.[4] Typically, capacity payments are closed to external participation, since, when there is a problem of SoS, the SO normally first cuts the cross-border transmission capacity. Therefore, the capacity that has been awarded the CP, but that is located outside a given system, might not be capable of delivering energy to the system that is constrained.[5]

CPs are or have been implemented in Greece,[6] Italy,[7] Ireland, Portugal, Spain, Poland, Chile, Peru and Argentina.

*Pro:* in general, CPs are quite simple tools to implement, since they require only the identification of the price to be paid and eventually the type of capacity that can be rewarded. The price can easily be set and adjusted, if needed. The regulation of a CP is somehow easier than for more complex tools, such as Reliability Options, for instance (see below).

*Cons:* the pros of CPs are also their cons. The price might not be set at the theoretical optimal level, but used instead to reach some other target, such as sustaining already amortized investments, or some specific technology, or investment in specific locations, and similarly. Moreover, it might not be effective, since the level of capacity that is incentivized by the CP depends on the supply, which might be wrongly estimated *ex ante* or changed over time *ex post*. Moreover, it is possible that the CP does not deliver the proper type of capacity if the CP is not differentiated by technology. The fixed payment has a marginal impact on the investment that is decreasing on the fixed costs of investments. This implies that the incentive provided by a given CP is higher for a plant that has the lower fixed costs and vice versa. But older plants, that are already amortized, also require more maintenance, have higher failures, and so on. Thus, it is possible that when needed, the capacity incentivized is not available. This phenomenon is informally known as **"paying for rust**." Also differentiating by types of technologies or plants can be problematic, since it can introduce rigidities in the regulation of the system, in the sense that *ex post* the amount of each specific capacity installed might not be the optimal (i.e. that which minimizes the total production costs). To avoid paying for rust, penalties for non-compliance can be introduced in CPs, as well as targeted CPs for specific technologies. However, they make the system more complex. For instance, if a penalty for non-compliance is introduced, the investor averages out the revenues accruing from the CP with the expected penalties that it can incur and might decide not to deliver energy if the latter is too low. Otherwise, the investments could be reduced if the penalty is set too high.

---

[4] These contracts have features in common with other CRMs, e.g. strategic reserves (see Paragraph 23.3.4).
[5] The practice of reducing cross-border transmission capacity might not be allowed in all interconnected systems, or may be specifically regulated, as it is in Europe.
[6] The CRM scheme in Greece is under revision and the adoption of Reliability Options (see below) is being considered.
[7] Italy is switching to a system of Reliability Options (see below).

## 23.3.2 Capacity Auctions (CA)

Capacity auctions (CA) are quantity-based CRMs, in which a subject, typically the SO, sets the quantity that is needed and the centralized market mechanism allows its value to emerge through an auction mechanism. CA can be closed or open. The auction can be set to deliver capacity with different possible time horizons, a short one, in which case auctions are repeated several times, or for a longer time spell. Several possible auction designs can be implemented. Moreover, even if they are quantity based, auction tools can be implemented, which makes them more similar to mixed systems than quantity-based ones. In particular, reservation prices and price caps can be set to the demand, as well as margins above and below the targeted quantity, with an associated maximum and minimum willingness to pay for the capacity. Example 23.1 shows the UK capacity auction.

---

**Example 23.1 The UK Capacity Auction** The UK capacity auction is a descending clock auction, in which bidders leave the auction whenever the price reaches the level beyond which they are no more willing to deliver the capacity. There are two distinct price caps, one for existing capacity, denominated "price takers," and another for new and refurbished capacity, which sets the auction price cap. The targeted quantity corresponds to the quantity that marginal wholesale producers are willing to install, having their fixed costs restored. This latter parameter is defined as **Cost of New Entrant (CONE)**. There is also a margin X above and below the targeted quantity. There is no price floor. The demand curve is represented in Figure 23.1.

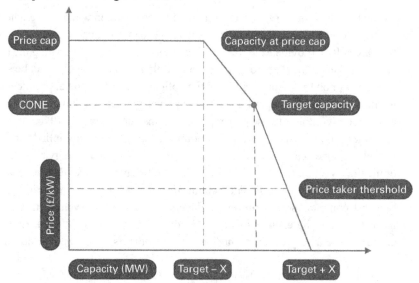

**Figure 23.1** Capacity demand curve, UK capacity auction
*Source*: OFGEM, 2017.

---

CA are in use in PJM,[8] NYISO, UK, Western Australia, Brazil, Peru and Chile.[9]

*Pro*: Capacity auctions, being targeted quantities, can help to deliver the required level of capacity. Moreover, they can be tailored to distinguish between types of capacity (e.g. between existing and new capacity), as well as open to demand-side participation. Moreover, they can help to stabilize investments, if they imply multi-year commitments. Finally, being centralized markets, they can benefit from higher liquidity than in decentralized settings.

*Cons*: The price is volatile, since it depends on the supply side. This can lead to investment instability, if it is perceived as too volatile, in particular if the auctions are repeated with a short time horizon. On the contrary, a long time horizon might deliver time commitments that are too long, unable to adjust to changing market settings, as for example, changes in the profile of the load duration curve. Moreover, they are very sensitive to the auction design and can be exposed to anticompetitive behavior by bidders. They are also subject to possible mistakes in the choice of several parameters that are administratively set and influence the result of the auctions, such as the price cap, the level of the targeted quantity and the related Cost of New Entrant (CONE) and the admissible margin, if any. Finally, on the basis of the market design, they can discourage some technologies or participants, if a single auction is set up, or require specific auctions or reservation prices for different types of participants (e.g. distinguishing between new entrants and existing capacity). Again, this might reduce liquidity, favor collusive behavior, increase rigidity and the risk of making the wrong choices in terms of parameters.

### 23.3.3    Capacity Obligations (CO)

Capacity obligation (CO) is a decentralized mechanism, in which those who participate in the energy market, either power producers or load suppliers, are required to show that they are able to provide *ex ante* a specific amount of energy, by owning the plants or the contracts that entitle them to make use of the plants. The obligation can be set on power producers or on load suppliers. When the obligation is set on power producers, they have to show that in order to participate in the power market they have to own the plants or a number of contracts to use power plants, for instance through VPP contracts or tolling agreements (see Chapter 4), for an amount of capacity that multiplied for a given time period (e.g. one year), gives rise to the predefined amount of energy required. When the obligation is set on load suppliers, they have to be able to cover their estimated demand in a given period by a sufficient amount of capacity for the entire period. The COs are bilateral contracts set by power producers and suppliers, even though a centralized market to ease the exchanges of those contracts can be established. Even if the CO appears to be a very different mechanism from others, it can be still be interpreted as

---

[8] This classification is somehow arbitrary. The CRMs of PJM, NYSO and ISO-NE share common aspects and have individual specificities as well. For a deeper analysis of US CRMs, see for instance Spees et al. 2012.

[9] In South America CAs have their specific features. In Brazil the products exchanged are long-term contracts fixing the price of energy. In Peru and Chile auctions set the energy price, while the remuneration for capacity is administratively set.

a quantity-based CRM, since the level of obligation is set in order to secure the required amount of capacity.

Capacity obligations exists in MISO[10] and CAISO.

*Pro:* The CO is a simple tool that requires little regulatory intervention, limited to predefining the admissible capacity types and how to fulfill the obligations, i.e. the characteristics of the capacity contracts, as well as the amount required. Moreover, when set on suppliers, this can incentivize load profiling by suppliers. For instance, suppliers can freely decide how to pass the cost of the obligation to their customers, for instance rewarding those customers that have a more reliable profile with a reduced price, or those that are properly grouped.

*Cons:* it is a rather short-run measure, since the time commitment of the CO is limited to each time period, for instance a year. This might not provide enough incentive for new capacity to be installed. It is true that the commitment is reiterated every year, but the level of the commitment can change and therefore the long-term incentive for new investment is lower than for other systems, such as CA or Reliability Options (see below) that can be set for longer delivery periods. On the contrary, the obligation period of the CO cannot be too long, as this reduces market dynamics, by freezing the possibility of entering into the market for potential entrants or exit for existing ones, either at the upstream level if the obligation is set on producers or among suppliers if they are under the obligation. When capacity is traded bilaterally, there can be market-power issues between buyers and sellers, in particular when there are few producers that can supply it. Moreover, CO favors vertical integration between power producers and suppliers, and this can affect the competitiveness of wholesale energy markets. It also limits entry into energy markets, in particular when the obligation it is set on suppliers. Rules must be established about tailoring the obligations for those who have not yet entered the market and thus do not have yet a record of load to be served. It is possible to impose obligations on newcomers similar to those of the existing suppliers, but this increases market risk for newcomers. If the obligation on newcomers is too strict they might not enter the market, while if the CO is too easily waived for newcomers it can alter competition among suppliers and endanger SoS. Finally, allowing the load to participate in CO can be inefficient. In principle, load could provide a CO by forecasting load reduction and selling it to those who have to buy the obligation. However, it is hard to disentangle the load reduction due to market events that are not under the control of the suppliers from a load reduction that is due to increased efficiency or better profiling of the load itself, therefore suppliers can be overrewarded or excessively penalized by the CO.

## 23.3.4    Strategic Reserves (SR)

Strategic reserves (SRs) refer to capacity that is directly attributed to or owned by the SO, which is allowed to use it whenever this is deemed necessary. They are quantity-based CRMs, in which capacity is generally selected through a tender mechanism.

---

[10] The MISO Resource Adequacy Requirement process is undergoing change. There is also a centralized CA.

Moreover, in order to avoid the SO influencing the wholesale market, the SR capacity is taken out of the market, in the sense that the SO cannot bid the energy produced through the SR into the day-ahead market (or the other intraday markets and balancing, if any). Generally, SRs refer to generation capacity; they can also include demand-response service. Moreover, the SO can also acquire load interruptibility contracts through tenders, and in this case interruptibility contracts can be seen as a technology-specific SR targeted to load reduction.

SRs are more tailored to cope with capacity-constrained systems than energy con-strained ones. The reason is that the capacity that is taken out of the market should be limited, so as not to impact on the functioning of the market, and be the marginal capacity of the market, since this is the capacity that works for fewer hours and whose cost is the lowest because it is already amortized. On the contrary, a baseload SR could interfere too much with the wholesale market, since it would largely reduce the market supply curve. If not taken out of the market, it would give rise to obvious risks of strategic playing by the SO, which can be tempted to dispatch its own capacity first. Finally, being the SR a capacity awarded to the SO, it has to be included in the SO control area, and for this reason generally no external participation is allowed.

SRs are in use in Belgium, Sweden, Finland, Germany, Poland and Lithuania. Tenders for interruptibility are in place in several European markets, as well as in New Zealand. In Brazil there is a targeted SR.

*Pro*: As the other quantity-based CRMs, it is easy to reach the targeted level of capacity. Moreover, it can be tailored to select the specific capacity that is needed (i.e. that which has the technical characteristics required, for instance in terms of flexibility). Moreover, SRs in general refer to a limited amount of capacity with low fixed costs, and thus also the expenditures accruing from SRs are low. If the capacity that is attributed to SR is the marginal or beyond marginal one, it also has a limited impact on the market, since it would only work by reducing the number of hours in which load is shed, but not its price. For the same reason, being used *ex post* by the SO, it is suitable to be used to reduce imbalances.

*Cons*: It is a CRM more targeted at existing plants that would otherwise be closed, rather than to new investments. Its incentive on the new capacity seems limited to just the possible impact that the expectation of relying on an SR at the end of the life cycle of the plant might have on the new investments, a rather limited one. As we have seen, it can hardly be used for energy-constrained systems. SRs subtract capacity from the wholesale market, thus there is a trade-off between large use of SRs and energy market liquidity. Moreover, there are wrong incentives for the SO or for policy makers to acquire too much capacity or playing strategically with it.

### 23.3.5    Reliability Options (RO)

We already pointed out that capacity has the nature of an option to provide energy. Reliability options (RO) are contracts that make this nature explicit, allowing the option provided by generation capacity (or load reduction) to be traded between sellers, namely, power plants (or the load) and the buyer, the SO. They are option contracts that have the form of call options, sold by plants (or load) and bought by the SO: the seller obtains *ex ante* the premium of the option, and in exchange gives to the SO the right to call such an option whenever required. This mechanism is similar to the SR case described earlier, yet with a crucial difference. With SR, the SO directly uses the capacity, while with the RO the SO implicitly asks the plant to produce, whenever the price of energy is higher than a predefined level.

This point requires careful explanation. In general, a call option is exerted by the holder only if the underlying fundamental of the option has a value higher than the predefined level, called the strike price. The non-negative difference between the value of the underlying fundamental and the strike price is known as the intrinsic value of the option. As is well known (see any finance textbook, such as Hull, 2015), the expected discounted value of the intrinsic value of a call, calculated with respect to properly risk-adjusted probabilities, provides the value of the call contract. In the case of energy markets and RO, the underlying fundamental of the capacity is the electricity production, which is sold in the market.

Consider the case of the marginal plant in the wholesale market. Suppose there are no RO. As we know from the analysis in Part III, if the price rises above the marginal cost, the power plant makes supermarginal profits, and, as shown in Chapter 22, in competitive markets this guarantees reaching the optimal level of investments. Now, suppose that an RO is sold by power producers, and that the strike price of electricity is set at the marginal cost of the marginal plant. In competitive RO markets, the value of the option is the expected risk-adjusted discounted value of the intrinsic value. But this intrinsic value is the price difference between the *VOLL* and the marginal cost times the *LOLE* (i.e. exactly the supermarginal profits of the peaker). Thus, RO works simply by shifting *ex ante* the supermarginal profits that producers would obtain *ex post* by participating in the electricity market. Whenever the price rises above the strike price, the sellers of RO have to give back to the SO the price differential, multiplied by the quantity of energy produced for those hours in which this occurs. This coincides with the supermarginal profits in case of no RO. Thus, sellers of RO have an incentive to make their capacity available to the market (or, if there is not enough of it, installing it), because whenever the SMP of the market spikes above the strike price of the RO they would have to give back the price differential. This is the implicit incentive embedded in the RO to produce energy. The example for non-marginal capacities works the same way: the baseload, for instance, would obtain just a fraction of the supermarginal profits (i.e. that capped by the strike price of the RO). Thus, the strike price of the RO works in the same way as the price cap analyzed in Chapter 22, and the analysis replicates that presented in Paragraph 22.3.

Reliability Options are in place in Colombia, ISO New England,[11] and Ireland, and are being introduced in Italy.

*Pro:* Their functioning does little to interfere with the wholesale market, limited to the price effect, due to the strike price. It enhances wholesale market liquidity and is

---

[11] The CRM of ISO_NE have specific features that induce Mastropietro et al. (2017) to question its classification as a proper RO.

technology neutral, in the sense that it does not discriminate across technologies. Thus, investments can follow over time the changes in load profile. A properly set lead time, (i.e. the lag period between option selling and the execution period), can favor new investments, in particular if the lead time is tailored to the expected delivery time of new power plants. Load can participate in auctions on a similar basis of production. Secondary markets can be established that enhance market liquidity and allow investors to hedge their investments positions. Moreover, the RO makes apparent the value of new capacity and the willingness to invest in it. If no new capacity is needed or the willingness to install is lower than the demand, which represents the social marginal value of the capacity, the price goes to zero. Therefore, the RO does not impose any rigidity in terms of price or quantity.

*Cons:* It is a complex system that requires several parameters to be established: a) Qualifying the capacity, defining which type of capacity can participate. For new investments, setting the guarantees that avoid strategic behavior, such as cashing in the RO and not providing the investments *ex post*;, setting explicit penalties for non-compliance and defining exclusion clauses, clearly specifying for instance the *force-majeure* causes that might delay or impede investments. For delivery of energy, deciding if and at what level explicit penalties for non-delivery of energy should be set. b) Establishing the demand curve and the possible participation of interconnectors (a problem in common with CA). c) Setting the strike price of the RO. The latter is the crucial parameter of the RO. The strike price must be properly set in order to provide the optimal incentive to investments. We have seen in Chapter 22 that the optimal CRM provides the same level of investment as the perfectly competitive energy-only market. For RO, this means that its value coincides with the sum of the supermarginal profits for all the hours of load shedding. Therefore, the optimal strike price should be set equal to the marginal cost of the marginal plants. However, this latter parameter changes over time, since load (and costs) changes over time. The strike price on the contrary is set in advance, since it is needed to identify the value of the call option when options are sold in the auction. This complicates setting and evaluating the RO. The theoretical correct strike price should be set equal to the average marginal cost of the marginal plants over the time period (e.g. a year). It can be difficult to calculate this parameter.

Strike prices that are too high lower the equilibrium value of the RO, since the value of a call option is inversely proportional to the value of its strike price. In turn, a value for RO that is too low may provide insufficient incentives for investment. On the contrary, strike prices that are too low may imply very limited supply of options in the tender, which can determine a very high value for the RO on the one hand, and interference with the wholesale market on the other hand, in the sense that the option would be called too many (unnecessary) times. To avoid fixing the strike price *ex ante* and for long periods, it is possible to adopt complex formulas, according to which the strike price can change over time being linked to some reference index. However, this makes the aspect of evaluating the option extremely complex, by introducing several sources of riskiness *ex ante*, since the strike price would also be perceived as a random variable. Moreover, the option evaluation is made worse by its complex nature. Capacity provides not just energy to be sold at the wholesale level, but also services that can have a value, for instance, by being marketed at balancing markets, or sold as ancillary services. This implies that the option cannot be treated as a simple call option, but as a bundle of derivatives written on several underlying prices, and again this adds complexity and risks that might not be fully hedged. Finally, as for other tender mechanisms, the market for RO can be subject to anticompetitive behavior among auction participants, which would distort the RO value.

## 23.4    Operating Reserve Demand Curve

The CRMs that we have discussed so far are aimed at providing enough incentives to deliver generation adequacy. Some types of technologies can provide not just power, but also other ancillary services, and in particular operating reserves. The latter is a generic term denoting both spinning and supplementary reserves (see Chapter 5). Operating reserves are generally set at a fixed level, tailored to the forecasted load and/or to the size and availability of existing power plants. In the literature (Hogan 2005, 2013, 2015), it has been argued that the missing money problem that we discussed in Paragraph 22.2 can impact not just power production, but also the provision of operating reserves. On the contrary, tackling this problem can also solve, or at least ease, the missing money problem and thereby incentivize the installation of capacity that can also provide enough generation adequacy. The tool that has been developed to reach this target is called the Operating Reserve Demand Curve (ORDC). Even though the ORDC is not a CRM, by providing incentives to install some technology-specific capacity (that which is able to provide spinning and supplementary reserve) the ORDC can complement energy-only markets to reach a long-run efficient equilibrium. Indeed, Hogan (2013) argues that it is a tool that can complement both energy-only markets and markets with CRMs.

The rationale of ORDC is overtaking the fixed requirement for reserves, that corresponds to a vertical demand curve, and constructing an elastic demand for operating reserves. This demand works in the short-run. Operating reserves are needed to replace exceptional load increase or failures of power supply in real time, with a very short time notice. Operating reserves are used by the SO. The elastic demand would thus be calculated by the SO, as follows.

Recall the analysis of Chapter 9. We saw that whenever capacity is higher than the existing load, the SMP is set at the marginal cost of the marginal plant. It goes to the *VOLL* when installed capacity becomes equal to or less than the load. In particular, it goes to the *VOLL* as soon as load equals capacity since this means that every single watt less of power injected implies an equivalent amount of load shedding. In a given period (e.g. a year), the VOLL-pricing of Equation (21.10) shows that in equilibrium there are enough incentives to install new capacity. However, Equation (21.10) and the analysis developed in Chapter 21 refer to the entire time period, for instance the year. In a single hour, as we have seen in Chapter 9, either the load is shed and the price goes to the *VOLL*, or the load is not shed and the price remains at the SMC. This ignores the role and importance of operating reserves. It is possible that the system is very close to load shedding, in the sense that the load almost equals the available capacity and there are very few operating reserves, or that there are large operating reserves, and thus enough capacity left to cope with sudden changes in demand or power plants' failures. In both cases, price remains at the SMC, since capacity to provide energy is not scarce. However, what differs in the two cases is the amount of the operating reserve, which implies that the two situations in terms of risk of load shedding are not equal. When there is little capacity left, there are also few remaining operating reserves and thus it is more likely that a given change in load or a power plant failure will determine a load shedding. On the contrary, when there are a lot of operating reserves, the system can cope with large and sudden changes in load or generation.

The ORDC overtakes this problem, extending the concept of $LOLP$ to measuring the risk of having load shed in a single hour (or a short-time period) based on scarcity of operating reserves. Recall that we defined the $LOLP$ as the probability that in the year the load is shed, measured by the ratio of number of hours in which load is shed over the year. The ORDC is based on the short-run $LOLP$ (i.e. $sLOLP$). The latter can be defined as the probability that in a given short-time period, for instance an hour, there will not be enough generation to serve the load: this depends on the expected outages rate of power plants, the standard deviation of the load and the amount of operating reserves available. For instance, if in a given hour $j$ the load has a standard deviation of 2 percent, that means that in that hour there is a 50 percent chance that the load rises by 2 percent and a 50 percent that it reduces by that much. This implies that the SO must hold an amount of reserves equivalent to at least 2 percent of the load to cope with these changes, for otherwise there would be a 50 percent chance of load shedding. If it had more reserves, the probability of load shedding would be lower, and vice versa. The $sLOLP$ is thus given by:

$$sLOLP = 1 - CDF(x); \tag{23.1}$$

where $CDF$ is the cumulative distribution function of errors in the estimates of the operating reserves $x$, defined as the differences between estimated and realized amount of the reserves. The ORDC in a given period is:

$$ORDC = sLOLP \cdot VOLL. \tag{23.2}$$

Administratively set elastic demand for Operating Reserves are in place in PJM, MISO, NYISO, ISO-NE. The ORDC describe here is in place at ERCOT. Figure 23.2 shows a representative ORDC at ERCOT.

The shape of the ORDC needs to be explained. It has a kink at 2,000 MW, and the value of $4,500/MWh. This is due to the introduction of a deterministic margin on the requirement of operating reserve. If the load and the power supply availability were such that the SO knew that every hour it needed at least $x$ MW of reserves, this amount would be the minimum security margin. It corresponds to the level of highest acceptable risk of load shedding, above which the SO behaves as if it has to shed load to preserve the minimum security level. For the ORDC of ERCOT, the security margin corresponds to 2,000 MW. For all levels of OR above it, every point of the ORDC depends on the given estimated level of the $sLOLP$. For instance, for a level of OR that equals 3,000 MW, the

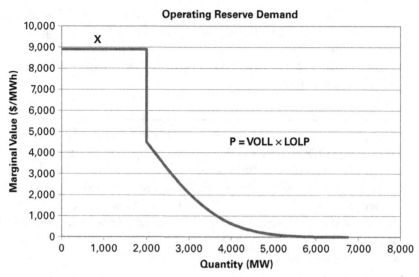

**Figure 23.2** The ORDC of ERCOT
*Source*: Hogan and Pope, 2017.

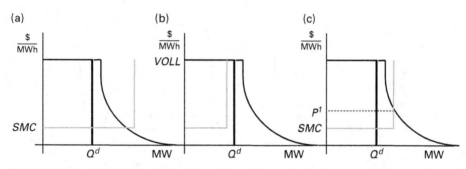

**Figure 23.3** The scarcity value of capacity and operating reserves using the ORDC

$sLOLP$ would be $3{,}000/9{,}000 = 0.33$. Note that there is not just one ORDC. At ERCOT, for instance, for each season, six ORDCs are calculated, each one for a four-hour block.

The ORDC can be added to the wholesale demand curve, to determine simultaneously the scarcity value of capacity and of operating reserves. This is called **scarcity pricing**. Consider the example represented in Figure 23.3.

We see that in panel (a) the demand of energy, including the ORDC, is not binding, in the sense that there is so much installed capacity that neither the capacity nor the operating reserves are scarce. Therefore, the equilibrium price is at the SMC. In panel (b), load is shed, and therefore there are no reserves, let alone capacity. The equilibrium price goes to the *VOLL*. In panel (c), there is enough installed capacity, thus the day-ahead price would clear at the SMC. However, there are few ORs, which implies that the risk of load shedding measured by $sLOLP$ is rather high. This gives rise to a price increase on top of the day-ahead price that represents the scarcity value of the ORs.

In particular, the price differential between the price with the ORDC (denoted as $P^l$ in Figure 23.3) and the equilibrium price without the ORDC (set at the SMC) signals the scarcity value of the ORs.

Example 23.2. shows the scarcity value of the OR, as expressed through the ORDCs, for ERCOT, in a tight week.

---

**Example 23.2 Scarcity Pricing in ERCOT** ERCOT calculates the price that would arise without the ORDC and the added price due to scarcity of operating reserves. This added price due to the scarcity of OR is called Price Adder. Figure 23.4 represents the load, the price of the day-ahead market (called DAM_LMP), the Price Adder (called RT Price Adder) and the price of the real-time market[12] (called RT_LMP) from August 4 to August 10, 2015. We can see, for example, that the first-day price rose because of scarcity of OR. On the contrary, the last-day price rose due to the equilibrium in the day-ahead market, but there was no scarcity of ORs.

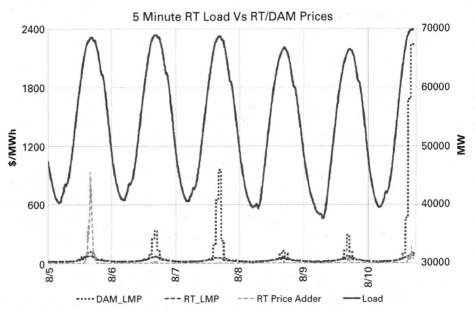

**Figure 23.4** Scarcity pricing in a tight week at ERCOT
*Source*: Surendran et al., 2016.

---

## Learning Outcomes

- Capacity Remuneration Mechanisms are tools that are set in order to explicitly remunerate capacity for the purpose of solving an adequacy issue. All other policy tools directly or indirectly supporting investments are not CRMs.

---

[12] See Chapter 5 for an introduction to real-time markets.

- CRMs can be classified according to whether they are price-based, quantity-based, or mixed; administratively set or market-based tools; centralized or not; open or closed to external participation and load participation. In the real word, there are several markets that have implemented some form of CRMs, as well as energy-only ones.
- The CRMs in use are: i) Capacity Payments; ii) Capacity Auctions; iii) Capacity Obligation: iv) Strategic Reserves; v) Reliability Options.
- The Operating Reserve Demand Curve is a tool that incentivizes the provision of operating reserves. It can complement both markets with and without CRMs. It is based on the short-run *LOLP*, that measures the probability of having to shed load in a given short-run period because of a lack of operating reserves. It facilitates attributing a price to the scarcity value of the operating reserve.

# Part VIII

# Environmental Challenges and the Future of Electricity Markets

The term "global climate change" refers to changes in the earth's climate brought about by a wide array of human activities. Because of predictions of a steady rise in average worldwide temperatures, global climate change is sometimes referred to as "global warming."

Much has been written on global climate change (see Tol, 2014). Put very simply, the greenhouse effect allows energy from the sun to pass through the earth's atmosphere and then traps some of that energy in the form of heat. This process has kept global temperatures on earth relatively stable, currently averaging 15.5°C and liveable for human populations. Nonetheless, jumps in emissions of carbon dioxide ($CO_2$) and other gases, such as methane, traced to fossil-fuel burning and other human activities, increase heat-trapping processes in the atmosphere, gradually raising average worldwide temperatures.

The Intergovernmental Panel on Climate Change (IPCC), the scientific advisory body created by the United Nations to analyze the science of global climate change, reports that unless the world takes drastic and immediate steps to reduce emissions of gases that are creating a magnified greenhouse effect, global temperatures could rise another 1.6 to 6.3°C by the year 2100. This would represent the fastest rate of warming since the end of the last ice age more than 10,000 years ago.

The relationship between global climate change and electricity markets is immediate: burning fossil fuels such as coal, oil and natural gas alters the climate by releasing carbon that has previously been locked up in coal, oil and natural gas for millions of years. The carbon in these fossil fuels is transformed into $CO_2$, the predominant gas contributing to the greenhouse effect, during the combustion process. Therefore, efforts to decrease $CO_2$ release in the electricity sector can play a major role in slowing global climate change. This is one of the major challenges that will shape the future of the electricity sector.

Part VIII presents different angles of such challenges, based on a large survey of the most relevant literature. In Chapter 24, we discuss how to decarbonize the electricity sector in the long-term scenarios that have been forecast in order to keep the temperature increase at 2°C by 2050. The impact on climate change on electricity demand, supply and price are also discussed. In Chapter 25, we turn to illustrate the share, costs and subsidies to renewables in electricity production. The latter are intermittent sources. This poses specific problems in terms of integrating the non-programmable energy sources in the electricity systems that are considered in Chapter 26. This effort will make the electricity sector "smarter," at different levels of the Electricity Supply Chain, mainly distribution and usage. This will be discussed in Chapter 27.

# 24 Global Warming and the Electricity Markets

## 24.1 Introduction

Quantifying efforts to decarbonize the electricity sector in order to control climate change and global warming is a difficult exercise. Scientists rely on building scenarios for the far future, which is the time scale of climate change occurrence. We discuss this issue in Paragraph 24.2 and present the Paris Agreement in Paragraph 24.3. Conversely, climate change may have some impacts on electricity demand and renewable energy sources (RES) production. We discuss such impacts in Paragraph 24.4. Looking more specifically at day-ahead electricity markets in countries where a carbon price exists, the relative competitiveness of fossil fuels may change, therefore putting upward pressure on electricity pricing. Paragraph 24.5 illustrates this effect.

## 24.2 Decarbonization of Electricity Production

Decarbonizing the electricity sector requires shifting from coal to gas, and more drastically to those technologies that produce no or few $CO_2$ emissions – solar, wind, geothermal and hydropower in particular. The first discussion about RES sources in economics was in the post-1973 oil shock era, when Nordaus, Houthakker and Solow (1973) and Dasgupta and Heal (1974) introduced the concept of **backstop technology**. Basically, the models with a backstop technology complete the Hotelling's (1931) result that the price of an exhaustible resource grows exponentially. The finite resource is used until its production costs exceed that of the inexhaustible backstop technology. When this latter is cheaper, it is introduced and it replaces the exhaustible one. However, if in theory renewable energies can be considered as a backstop technology to fossil fuels, assessing and forecasting their optimal deployment is not an easy task in practice.

Integrated Assessment Models are a tool to evaluate the long-term contribution to RES in mitigating the effects of climate change.

DEFINITION. *Integrated Assessment Model (IAM): a model which combines scientific and socio-economic aspects of climate change, assessing policy options to control climate change.*

The objective of IAMs is to provide a framework for understanding the climate change problem and for informed judgments about the relative value of different options dealing with climate change (Metcalf and Stock, 2015). IAMs draw knowledge and strengths from various disciplines studying climate change; contributions from each discipline rely on the mathematical representations of certain relationships connected to climate change. The models are based on a multitude of assumptions about the atmosphere and oceans, land cover and land use, economic growth, fossil fuel emissions, population growth, technological change, etc. However, making assumptions about what will happen in the future is a very difficult task. Therefore, there is a multitude of IAM, developed by universities, governments and institutions, that depend on the set of assumptions used, over a long timescale and geographical representation.[1]

IAM builds scenarios that prescribe a GHG stabilization level, to be achieved in the long-term future. Scenarios that have no constraint on GHG emissions are referred to as baseline scenarios. Comparing economic activity measures (e.g. macro-economic consumption) of baseline and mitigation scenarios allows the social costs of mitigation to be determined. Regarding in particular RES, their role can be assessed by comparing the social costs of mitigation under different assumptions of deployment (Edenhofer et al., 2013).

In order to provide robust insights into the role of RE sources in climate change mitigation, the IPCC Special Report on Renewable Energy Sources and Climate Change Mitigation (SRREN) reviewed 164 mitigation scenarios that were collected through an open call and were generated by sixteen different IAMs. There are multiple efficient pathways to achieve low-stabilization targets. This holds both in terms of emission trajectories over time and the magnitude of their economic potential. The economic potential of RES sources increases with the stringency of the mitigation target, particularly in the long term. RES should play an important role in climate change mitigation, but substantial uncertainty remains regarding estimates of the absolute economic potential of these sources. Despite the wide range of estimates, bioenergy accounts for a substantial share of the RES supply in 2050 in all scenarios. The role of geothermal energy is rather limited. This is also the case for hydropower. The median of the PV and wind share in the low concentration scenario (<440ppm) remains below 20 percent at the horizon of 2050 for most models. However, the ranges are wide. For instance, in the EMF 27 model comparison project (Luderer et al., 2014), half of the models report electricity shares from wind and solar greater than 40 percent after 2050 for medium to high constraints in the concentration of $CO_2$ (between 440 and 600 ppm).

The social costs of mitigation are quite difficult to calculate and compare, as they are highly dependent on the scenarios developed. For example, in a subset of models (the Report on Energy and Climate Policy in Europe, RECIPE),[2] aggregate consumption losses from 2005 to 2100 relative to the baseline scenario range from less than 1 percent to 5 percent. However, all these studies ignore the costs of intermittency of RES, an important issue which we will discuss in Chapter 26.

---

[1] For a methodological survey on IAM models and GHG scenario building, the reader should refer to Weyant (1996).

[2] See www.cmcc.it/projects/recipe-report-on-energy-and-climate-policies-in-europe.

## 24.3  RES and Energy Markets after the Paris Agreement

The Paris Agreement, signed in December 2016 and ratified at the United Nations on November 2017, is the most recent international framework to control climate change, both in developed and developing countries. In early 2018, the Agreement has been ratified by 174 countries out of the 195 that have signed it. "The Paris Agreement ... charts a new course in the global climate effort. The Paris Agreement's central aim is to strengthen the global response to the threat of climate change by keeping a global temperature rise this century well below 2°C above pre-industrial levels and to pursue efforts to limit the temperature increase even further to 1.5°C. Additionally, the agreement aims to strengthen the ability of countries to deal with the impacts of climate change. To reach these ambitious goals, appropriate financial flows, a new technology framework and an enhanced capacity building framework will be put in place, thus supporting action by developing countries and the most vulnerable countries, in line with their own national objectives" (UNFCC, 2017, p. 1). The Paris Agreement requires all parties to put forward their best efforts through nationally determined contributions. This includes regular reports on their emissions and implementation efforts. There will also be a global stocktake every five years to assess collective progress toward achieving the purpose of the agreement and to inform further individual actions by parties.[3]

The Paris Agreement has thus opened a new perspective for RES development. Many countries built on the momentum spurred by it, communicating their first Nationally Determined Contributions (NDCs). Of the 117 NDCs, fifty-five included targets for increasing renewable energy, while eighty-nine made reference to renewable energy more broadly. By late 2016 at the twenty-second Conference of the Parties (COP22) in Marrakesh, Morocco, more than 100 countries had officially joined the Paris Agreement, formalizing their commitments to sustainable development, often through decarbonization of the energy sector. At COP22, leaders of the forty-eight developing countries that constitute the Climate Vulnerable Forum, including COP22's host nation of Morocco, committed jointly to work toward achieving 100 percent renewable energy in their respective nations.

Based on the Paris Agreement objectives, IEA (2017b) and IRENA (2017) have developed core scenarios that would be compatible with limiting the rise in global mean temperature to 2°C by 2100 with a probability of 66 percent, as a way of contributing to the "well below 2°C" target of the Paris Agreement. Each of the IEA and IRENA analyses start with the same carbon budget (i.e. the cumulative amount of $CO_2$ emitted over a given time frame, for the energy sector). But the pathways to reaching the goal differ between the two analyses. The modeling analysis conducted by the IEA (2017b) aims to lay out a pathway toward energy sector decarbonization that is technology-neutral and includes all low-carbon technologies, taking into account each OECD country's specific circumstances. The analysis conducted by IRENA (2017), instead, maps out an energy transition that stresses the potential of energy efficiency and

---

[3] The text of the Paris agreement can be found at: http://unfccc.int/paris_agreement/items/9485.php.

renewable energy sources to achieving the climate goal, while also taking into consideration all other low-carbon technologies.

Limiting the global mean temperature rise to below 2°C by 2050 with a probability of 66 percent would require an energy transition of exceptional scope, depth and speed. Energy-related $CO_2$ emissions would need to peak before 2020 and fall by more than 70 percent from today's levels by 2050. The share of fossil fuels in primary energy supply would halve between 2014 and 2050, while the share of low-carbon sources, including renewables, nuclear and fossil fuel with carbon capture and storage (CCS), would more than triple worldwide to comprise 70 percent of energy consumption in 2050. The 66 percent 2°C scenario would require an unparalleled ramp-up of all low-carbon technologies in all countries and a set of ambitious policies, among which would be a $CO_2$ price reaching $190 per ton.

In the 66 percent 2°C scenario, aggressive efficiency measures would be needed to lower the energy intensity of the global economy by 2.5 percent per year on average between 2014 and 2050 (three-and-a-half times greater than the rate of improvement seen over the past fifteen years); wind and solar combined would become the largest sources of electricity by 2030. In particular, IRENA scenarios point out that the share of renewable energy needs to increase from around 15 percent of the Primary Energy Supply in 2015 to 65 percent in 2050. The reduction of energy intensity, defined as the share of Total Primary Energy Supply over GDP, must double, reaching around 2.5 percent per year by 2030, and continue at this level until 2050. Energy demand in 2050 would remain around today's level, due to extensive improvements in energy intensity. Around half of the improvements could be attributed to renewable energy from heating, cooling, transport and electrification based on cost-effective renewable power. This requires an increase of the share accounted for by renewables of about 1.2 percent per year, a seven fold acceleration compared to recent years. Total fossil fuel use in 2050 would stand at a third of today's level. The use of coal would see the greatest decline, while oil demand would be at 45 percent of today's level. Resources that have high production costs would no longer be exploited. While natural gas can be a "bridge" to greater use of renewable energy, its role should be limited unless it is coupled with high levels of carbon capture and storage. The amount of investment needed is of considerable importance: meeting the 2°C target requires an additional US$ 29 trillion of investment in the energy sector between 2015 and 2050 compared to the actual situation. These investments encompass the change in the energy mix, increased energy efficiency, but also improvements in the transmission and distribution electricity networks to make possible a very high RES penetration. So far, it is unclear if these perspectives are realistic.

## 24.4     The Impact of Climate Change on Electricity Demand and Supply

While the impact of electricity production on decarbonization and climate change has been extensively studied (for a survey see Fouquet, 2015), the reverse impact has received less attention in economics. However, some aspects are worth mentioning.

Global warming is characterized by a rise in average temperatures in most regions, changes in precipitation and seasonal patterns in many regions, the occurrence of extreme weather events and rises in sea level. These phenomena are expected to affect both energy supply and demand. There is a first, direct effect on power production:

---

### Result

Higher temperatures will imply lower demand for heating and higher demand for cooling.

---

Heating and cooling is measured by means of **heating degree days** and **cooling degree days**. Setting a base temperature as the temperature level at which there is no need for either heating or cooling, heating degree days are measured as the sum of negative deviations of the actual temperature from the base temperature over a given period of time; cooling degree days are the sum of positive deviations between the actual temperature and the base temperature.

This result is important since it can impact on the Load Duration Curve (see Chapter 7). The impact of climate change on heating and cooling has been documented for a number of different countries by Considine (2000) and Eskeland and Mideksa (2009). In the later study, in particular, a household demand model for electricity is estimated using panel data from thirty-one European countries for the period 1995–2005, and the projected changes in temperatures are considered. The results indicate that a 1°C change in temperature will change demand by 2 kWh per year per capita via the change in heating degree days, whereas for a unit increase in cooling degree days, the demand changes by 8 kWh per year per capita. This is a small effect when compared to current electricity use and to other estimates in the literature. Mansur et al. (2008) find, for the case of the United States, with warmer summers and cooler winters both households and firms consume more energy in the form of electricity, gas, and oil. They find that overall climate change will likely increase electricity consumption on cooling, but reduce the use of other fuels for heating. The net effect is that US energy expenditures will likely increase.

Changes in temperature also involve changes in thermal and non-thermal power production (Mideksa and Kallbekken, 2010). One important channel of transmission of the impact of temperature on power production concerns the technical efficiency with which the fuels are converted to electricity. As we have seen in Part II, how efficient a plant is in transforming fuels into electric power depends upon the temperature differential between the machine and the external environment. The higher the heat differential, the higher the efficiency of conversion and vice versa (see the Carnot machine of Chapter 1). Since climate change is likely to produce higher air and water temperatures, the heat differential between the machine and the environment will decrease, thus reducing the net power generated from a given amount of fuel. Durmayaz and Sogut (2006) investigate the impact of changes in cooling water temperature on the thermal efficiency of nuclear power plants using plant-level data and an engineering model. Their result suggests that a 1°C increase in the temperature of the environment reduces power output by approximately 0.45 percent points. Another effect of climate change on power production is the change on water inflow for power production. Golombek et al. (2012) find that Nordic European countries with a large market share for reservoir hydro may experience a rise of total annual production by 8 percent in 2030, reflecting an expected increase in inflow of water. Finally, several studies find increased production from wind power by 2050 (see Mideska and Kallbekken, 2010 for a more detailed survey).

If we consider the implications of such results on electricity demand in Europe, it is likely to fall in Northern Europe and rise in Southern Europe because of the changes in heating and cooling degree days in the next decades. Supply is likely to fall in countries where much of the electricity generation is based on thermal power, whereas it could increase where there is a large share and an increased potential for hydropower and wind power, as in northern Europe.

These, however, are just preliminary considerations. The impact of extreme weather events on the production and transmission of electricity, as well as on electricity demand in several parts of the world, is an active area of research that is under development and requires further investigation.

## 24.5     The Impact of $CO_2$ Prices on Electricity Markets

When there is environmental regulation to reduce carbon emission in the form of a carbon price,[4] it is possible that firms make some arbitrage in production and emissions in order to pass carbon costs through to final consumers. This issue has been extensively discussed in Europe, where a carbon market has existed since 2005, namely, the European Emission Trading Scheme or EU ETS (Ellerman and Joskow, 2008). Around 5,000 operators with approximately 12,000 production units participate in this attempt to reduce $CO_2$ emissions from four broad sectors:

- energy (electric power production, oil refineries, etc.);
- production and processing of ferrous metals (iron and steel);
- minerals (cement, glass, ceramics);
- pulp and paper.

The electricity sector is one of the broadest within the carbon market.

The issue of the interaction between carbon prices and electricity prices was discussed in particular at the outset of EU ETS trading, since in the period 2005–2007 electricity prices hit very high levels in several European markets. In particular, it has been argued that when the initial permit allocation is given for free, called **grandfathering**, instead of using an auction, windfall profits arise because

---

[4] For an extensive explanation of carbon prices and carbon markets, interested readers should refer to Kolstad, 2011.

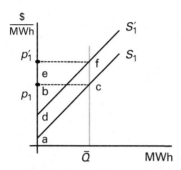

**Figure 24.1** Windfall profits accruing from grandfathering of emission permits
*Source*: adapted from Sijm et al., 2006.

producers pass on the market value of the emission rights to consumers via a markup on energy prices.[5] The main theoretical argument is that instead of using the free allowances, firms can sell them at the current market price. A company that receives free permits can always choose to cut production instead of using the allowances, and thus sell them in the market. There is an opportunity cost of electricity production accruing from the decision to generate power and thus consuming the allowances instead of selling them in the market. When producing electricity, the firm needs to recover this foregone opportunity cost in the electricity price. In other words, although a power plant does not have to pay for emission rights, it uses them to cover emissions when producing, and therefore it tries to pass on the extra opportunity cost arising from this forgone possibility of selling allowances to the final product price (Woerdman et al. 2009). On the contrary, when allowances are bought by power producers, costs rise due to the increase in the expenditures that producers face in order to generate. Thus, even if they pass these extra costs to the buyers of electricity, they do not experience any windfall profit. Figure 24.1 illustrates these effects.

The curve $S_1$ represents the reference case of either auctioning or free allocation, assuming perfect competition. Absent carbon costs, the equilibrium price is $P_1$ where the inelastic load $\bar{Q}$ meets the supply $S_1$. When emissions trading is introduced, the opportunity costs of carbon allowances are included into the other variable production costs, reducing the supply curve $S_1'$ and raising the equilibrium price $P_1'$.

The following effects are at stake:

- The power price increases from $P_1$ to $P_1'$. Hence, the pass-through rate is 100 percent since the change in power price is equal to the change in marginal production costs.
- The producer surplus before emissions trading is equal to the triangle **abc**. As we have seen in Part VII, in a competitive situation this surplus covers the fixed (investment) costs of power production, including some fair plants' profits.

---

[5] As of 2013, in the European emissions market, the power sector no longer receives free allowances; industrial sectors, such as cement and steel may receive free allowances of up to 100 percent of their requirements; and other sectors receive a free allocation of 80 percent of their share of the pollution cap, which will be reduced by 10 percentage points each year, phasing out free allocation by 2020.

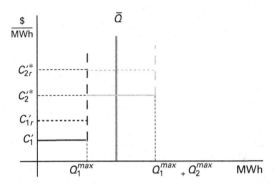

**Figure 24.2** Auctions and carbon costs without merit order switch

- After emissions trading, in the case of auctioning, when the power producers have to pay for the emission permits, the producer surplus is equal to **def**. The produce will gain after the increase of variable costs due to emissions if the area **def** is bigger than the area **abc**.
- The total emission costs are equal to the area **adfc**, which are fully passed on to consumers by means of higher prices, resulting in a similar consumer surplus loss.
- In the case of free allocation, producers get the allowances for free. Thus, even if their opportunity cost is increased, which justifies the shift from $S_1$ to $S_1'$, they are not charged for allowances, while still passing on the opportunity cost to the consumers. This results in an increase in their producer surplus by the quadrangle **adfc**. This increase in producer surplus due to emissions trading is the "windfall profit" resulting from grandfathering.

A crucial assumption is that power plants have market power in the wholesale market. However, as we have seen in Part III, the existence of different technologies implies that power plants are not treated equally when power is dispatched. Given the functioning of wholesale electricity markets, the effect on electricity prices of the emission trading costs, and more generally of the cost of $CO_2$ emissions relating to power production are complex, since one must consider the impact on the marginal technology that determines the system marginal price (SMP).

Consider the case illustrated by Figure 24.2, where we depict two technologies with different emission intensities. For the sake of simplicity, we draw the two technologies with two different grey scales (black and light grey) and identify the marginal cost curves before the emission trading with solid lines, after emission trading with dotted lines. Assuming perfect competition, the SMP before the carbon trading is the marginal cost $C_2'$.

After carbon trading, the technology $i$ ($i = 1,2$) must cover the $CO_2$ costs entailed by its usage, at the unit permit price $p$, proportionally to its emission factor $e_i$. Therefore every units of power costs $C_{ir}' = C_i' + e_i p$. In this case, it turns out that the merit order is unchanged; power plant 2 is still the marginal technology, and the equilibrium SMP after the introduction of pollution regulation is $C_{2r}'^*$ (the uppercase * denotes equilibrium). The electricity price difference is equal to the increase of marginal costs of the

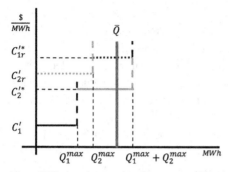

**Figure 24.3** Auctions and carbon costs with merit order switch

technology 2, that is $C'^*_{2r} - C'^*_2$. The opportunity costs are all passed-through to electricity consumers. If we compare the effect of buying the emission permits with grandfathering, as before, we see that in the case of grandfathering there will be windfall profits for both power plants due to the increase in the equilibrium SMP. However, it is quite possible that carbon pricing causes a merit order switch, as illustrated in Figure 24.3. In this case the carbon costs make technology 1 less competitive than technology 2. The SMP becomes $C'^*_{1r}$. See that the carbon costs of the "new" marginal technology are higher than the electricity price increase ($C'^*_{1r} - C'_1 > C'^*_{1r} - C'^*_2$). This implies that plant 1 is able to pass to consumers only a fraction of the increase in the cost, due to the emissions. There is an imperfect pass-through. Moreover, there is also an implicit cross-subsidization across plants, since plant 1 now becomes the marginal plant, while plant 2 sees an increase in its profits due to higher prices.

In general, with several plants, and different marginal impacts on plants' costs of the carbon pricing, the computation of windfall profits is challenging. Moreover, there can be other factors that affect cost pass-through rates, such as market power, elasticity of electricity demand and domestic supply. These factors have proven difficult to estimate in empirical work and have therefore been approximated by a range of measurable drivers that might be linked to them. The drivers include trade intensity, transport costs, tariff barriers and product substitutability, as well as indicators of market concentration and pricing power. Clearly, the exact extent at which costs are estimated to be passed through is highly dependent on the methods chosen and the data used. Most of the existing studies seem to indicate that even in the early days of the EU ETS, a major part of the scheme-induced carbon costs were passed through to power prices (Sijm et al., 2006). Nevertheless, higher fuel prices also played a role in electricity price increases, and some plants' profits reflected their ownership of low-cost nuclear or coal generation in areas where the market electricity price was set by higher-cost natural gas plants (Ellerman and Buchner, 2007; European Commission, 2015).

## Learning Outcomes

- Global warming mitigation necessarily constrains electricity production as the latter is one of the major sources of $CO_2$ emissions.

- Renewable Energy Sources can efficiently contribute to decarbonizing the electricity sector. Their long-term potential is difficult to assess. However, it increases with the stringency of emission caps. According to a majority of scenarios, photovoltaic and wind will not account for more than 40 percent of the OECD electricity mix in 2050.
- Global warming increases the demand for cooling and reduces demand for heating; it also reduces thermal plant efficiency and may endanger network safety due to extreme weather events.
- When carbon regulation exists, in the form of a market for permits, the $CO_2$ price raises electricity prices and may alter the relative competitiveness of electricity-producing technologies (the merit order). When the initial permits allocation is given for free (grandfathering), instead of using an auction, windfall profits may arise because producers pass on the market value of the emission rights to consumers via a markup on energy prices.

# 25  Renewable Energy Sources and Electricity Production

## 25.1  Introduction

According to the IEA (2017b), in 2016 renewables accounted for 22.8 percent of world electricity production, after coal (39.3 percent) and gas (22.9 percent), and ahead of nuclear (10.6 percent) and oil (4.1 percent). Geothermal, solar, wind and tide energy accounted for 4.8 percent, whereas the share for hydropower was 16 percent. In terms of annual growth rate, since 1990, renewable electricity generation grew 3.6 percent on average, that is, faster than the total electricity generation growth rate (2.9 percent). In 1990, the share of renewables for electricity generation was 19.6 percent and in 2015 it has reached 22.8 percent. Hydroelectric power saw its share of total world electricity production fall from 18.1 percent in 1990 to 16.0 percent in 2015. Taking out hydroelectricity from renewables, the share of the remaining renewable sources used to produce electricity grew from 1.3 percent in 1990 to 6.8 percent in 2015. Solar is the renewable electricity production source that has experienced the fastest growth rate as from 1990 (45.5 percent), surpassing the increase for wind (24.5 percent). Most new renewable energy capacity is installed in developing countries, and largely in China, the single largest developer of renewable power and heat over the past eight years. These figures show an interesting and rapidly changing landscape. What factors explain the deployment of renewables?

In this chapter we explain, in Paragraph 24.2, the reasons for choosing renewables as one of the pillars of the electricity system. Then we introduce the concept of Levelized Costs of Electricity (LCOE), which is used to assess RES competitiveness with respect to thermal technologies in Paragraph 25.3. RES are generally sustained by specific subsidies. We detail and illustrate them with recent figures in Paragraph 25.4.

## 25.2  The Reasons for Choosing Renewables

In the 1990s, the promotion of renewable energy sources was proposed as part of the solution to a number of environmental problems. The oil crises of the 1970s and the worry that these were manifestations of a fundamental depletion problem necessitated a switch to energy sources that had less impact on the earth's resources. The conventional solution to this problem – nuclear power – was perceived as presenting too many environmental, safety and security problems. For their proponents, renewables presented a clean and safe way of producing energy and reducing dependence on diminishing reserves of fossil fuels (Heal, 2009).

Different episodes of oil price slumps, as well as a more favorable perspective on oil, gas and coal reserve availability, have not been enough to reverse the trend. Renewables are still on the rise. The main reason is that they offer an alternative to the environmental damage caused by energy production and use. As fossil fuel contributions to $CO_2$ emissions have been identified as the principal challenge, renewables – together with conservation and in some countries nuclear power – have been seen as an important mechanism for medium- to long-term control of global warming.

As reported by McGowan (1991), at the end of the 1980s the only renewables that were used for electricity generation, both in the OCDE and in less developed countries, was large-scale hydro, followed by biofuels. R&D budgets were the only form of subsidy to renewables, and these were relatively low compared to those devoted to fossil fuels, and concentrated, from the beginning of the 1980s, in solar technologies. The United States and Germany have been the most active countries in subsidizing R&D in renewables. Even if the European Community had also started subsidizing R&D in renewables, with funding for security of supply, environmental and policy reasons, much higher funds were devoted at that time to nuclear energy.

Since that time, various exercises have been carried out to estimate the potential for electricity production from renewables, identifying a clear disadvantage in terms of costs of RES with respect to fossil fuels. The Brundtland Report (1987) for sustainable development noted this and recommended that renewables should become the basis for energy needs in the next century. However, it also warned against over-stating the role of renewables in energy balances.

The prospects for future electricity production that were estimated at the end of the millennium ranged from 6 percent to 20 percent. Admittedly, renewables were acknowledged as being extremely vulnerable to competing technologies. As long as it was possible to produce power at lower costs, without the incorporation of externalities, renewables were seen, and are still today, as less competitive generating technologies. This is further discussed in the next paragraph.

## 25.3     The Levelized Cost of Energy

Most RES, such as those based on wind or solar irradiation, have certain economic characteristics in common – large fixed costs and low or no variable costs, and intermittency. Consequently, average costs vary with output levels and availability of the primary energy source.

The common way to measure RES competitiveness is to calculate an indicator of the total cost of electricity produced for the whole time-life of the power plant that generates it, over the whole amount of energy that it can produce in that time span. This indicator is referred to as the Levelized Cost of Electricity.

DEFINITION. *Levelized Cost of Electricity (LCOE): the present value of the total cost of building and operating a generating plant over an assumed financial life time and duty cycle, converted to equal annual payments, in real terms.*

Levelized cost of electricity (LCOE) is often taken as a summary measure used to ease the comparison of the competitiveness across different generating technologies. It represents the per-MWh cost of building and operating a generating plant over an assumed financial life and duty cycle. Key inputs to calculating LCOE include capital costs, fuel costs, fixed and variable operations and maintenance (O&M) costs, financing costs, and an assumed utilization rate for each plant type. The importance of the factors varies among the technologies. For technologies such as solar and wind generation that have no fuel costs and relatively small variable O&M costs, LCOE changes in rough proportion to the estimated capital cost of generation capacity. For technologies with significant fuel cost, both fuel cost and overnight cost estimates significantly affect LCOE.

The basic LCOE formula for an investment in a given technology that has a time-life of $T$, with $t = 1, \ldots, T$ denoting a single time period (generally a year), can be obtained taking into account that, in competitive markets, the following relationship must hold:

$$\sum_t \frac{(Q_{i,t})(P_t)}{(1+r)^t} = \sum_t \left[ \frac{(Capital\ Expenditure)_t}{(1+r)^t} + \frac{(O\&M)_t}{(1+r)^t} + \frac{(Fuel\ Costs)_t}{(1+r)^t} \right], \quad (25.1)$$

where $Q_{i,t}$ denotes the electricity produced and sold in the market in $t$, $r$ is the discount rate applying over the time $t$ and $P_t$ is the price at which the electricity is sold (i.e. the annual average wholesale price). The left-hand side of Equation (24.1) is the total discounted revenues for the whole time-life. The right-hand-side is the total discounted cost of the plant. Then, Equation (25.1) shows that the total discounted (annual) revenues must cover the total discounted (annual) costs, taking into account the different types of expenditure.

By replacing the energy price at each time period $P_t$ with the average price over that period we can solve Equation (25.1). That is to say, we set $\sum_t \frac{P_t}{T} = \tilde{p}$, and thus we can write Equation (25.1) as:

$$\sum_t \frac{(Q_{i,t})\tilde{p}}{(1+r)^t} = \sum_t \left[ \frac{(Capital\ Expenditure)_t}{(1+r)^t} + \frac{(O\&M)_t}{(1+r)^t} + \frac{(Fuel\ Costs)_t}{(1+r)^t} \right]. \quad (25.2)$$

Equation (25.2) can be solved for the average energy price, providing the LCOE:

$$LCOE = \sum_t \left[ \frac{(Capital\ Expenditure)_t}{(1+r)^t} + \frac{(O\&M)_t}{(1+r)^t} + \frac{(Fuel\ Costs)_t}{(1+r)^t} \right] \Big/ \sum_t \frac{Q_{i,t}}{(1+r)^t}. \quad (25.3)$$

Thus, the LCOE, which is the ratio of the total discounted costs over the overall amount of electricity that can be sold, corresponds to a specific level of the average energy price: that level for which, in equilibrium, the total discounted costs corresponds to the total discounted revenue. This explains the use of the term "levelized," since costs are discounted, or "levelized," in order to equalize total revenues.

The basic LCOE formula can be completed by adding other terms in the right-hand side of Equation (25.3). For example, the availability of various incentives, including subsidies, can also impact the calculation of LCOE. The projected utilization rate, which depends on the load shape and the existing resource mix in an area where additional capacity is needed, is one such factor (EIA, 2017).

The existing resource mix in a region can directly impact the economic viability of a new investment through its effect on the displacement of existing resources. For example, a wind resource that would primarily displace existing natural gas generation will usually have a different economic value than one that would displace existing coal generation, since it would have a different capacity factor and thus a different amount of energy produced over its lifetime.[1] Therefore, depending on the cost factors considered, the time span, the region, LCOEs take different values (Borenstein, 2012).

As an example, the estimated LCOE for new generation resources, i.e. plant entering service in 2022 in the United States are as follows (in US\$, average levelized cost per technology, weighted by the new capacity coming online in each region, relative to capacity additions for each region projected in the period 2018–2022).

**Table 25.1** Estimated LCOE for new generation resources in the United States

| Gas-fired combined cycle | Advanced nuclear | Biomass | Onshore wind | Solar PV | Hydroelectric |
| --- | --- | --- | --- | --- | --- |
| 58.6 | 96.2 | 97.7 | 55.8 | 73.7 | 63.9 |

*Source*: EIA, 2017.

From the LCOE calculation derives the notion of technologies that are competitive. This competitiveness can be measured in different ways, but the most common indicator used is that called "grid parity."

DEFINITION. ***Grid parity for RES:*** *grid parity occurs when a RES can generate power at an LCOE that is less than or equal to the price of acquiring power from the grid.*

The price of energy purchased is given by the marginal cost of the marginal technology. Without RES, the marginal technology is a conventional plant. Thus, the definition above implies that RES reach the grid parity and become competitive and economically efficient once their LCOE drops below or at least equals those of conventional plants. Germany was one of the first countries to reach parity for solar PV in 2011. By January 2014, grid parity for solar PV systems was reached in at least nineteen countries (Deutsche Bank, 2016). Another important factor that can change the LCOE figures and thus grid parity is whether in the calculation of the LCOE the cost and benefits of reducing $CO_2$ emissions and other pollutants are factored in.

---

[1] Several LCOE calculators can be accessed on the web, for example Comello, S., Glenk, G. and S. Reichelstein (2017). Levelized Cost of Electricity Calculator. URL: http://stanford.edu/dept/gsb_circle/sustainable-energy/lcoe.

However, the grid parity criterion is criticized, as is the case for the metric of LCOE itself (Schmalensee, 2012; Borenstein, 2012). For instance, Joskow (2011) argues that, because electricity prices vary, revenues for power production from variable renewables depend on the specific time at which they are produced. The basic LCOE formula we introduced in Equation (25.3) does not consider in which periods electricity is produced, while the value or wholesale price of electricity varies widely throughout the day, week and year. Therefore, the LCOE approach tends to overvalue generation from wind – as its output is more heavily weighted to off-peak periods when electricity prices are relatively low – and to undervalue power production from solar, as it usually generates relatively more electricity during periods of the day when prices are relatively high. Moreover, the LCOE does not consider that, depending on the renewables location, grid-related costs will be different. In particular, other things equal, the economic value of electricity from offshore wind – which is often located at a distance from the load – is usually significantly lower than the electricity from solar PV produced next to the load center. The LCOE does not incorporate these values.

## 25.4    RES Support Policies

The economic reasons behind RES support policies encompass several objectives, which include:

- *Mitigation of climate change*, which has been the primary rationale justifying the substitution of fossil fuel in electricity generation, in order to limit $CO_2$ emissions. Subsidizing renewables corresponds to pricing unpriced fossil fuel pollution. This argument is reinforced by the *cost reduction* obtained by widespread RES adoption via learning by doing, i.e. the percentage of cost reduction when the capacity rises and economies of scale, i.e. the cost reduction when renewable electricity production increases (Edenhofer et al., 2013).
- *Local pollution.* In many countries, reducing local air pollution has also become a key driver. China, for example, announced in early 2017 that it would invest US$360 billion in renewables by 2020, due largely to the massive air pollution and health problems in major Chinese cities caused by coal generation.
- *Energy security*, which refers to uninterrupted energy supply and independence from export in energy provision. This is another driver, as it has been advocated both in Europe and in the United States. Energy security is also being considered more widely in the context of increasing energy system resilience to climate change impacts.
- *Sustainable growth* and *creation of domestic green jobs*. This is often claimed as a factor that strengthens interest in these technologies.

Multiple instruments can be used in order to achieve one more of these quite different objectives. The literature (Battle et al., 2012) clearly distinguishes between two broad categories of RES support mechanisms: **price-based** and **quantity-based** policies. We summarize their main characteristics here. Designing an optimal RES support policy requires knowledge of the welfare-optimal deployment level and the nature, dynamics and causality of all the effects that can induce market failures. This kind of global assessment has not been clearly performed to date. However, some pros and cons of RES support policies can be identified, highlighting the lesson learned by the practical implementation of different instruments.

### 25.4.1    Price-Based Policies

Price-based policies can be classified as follows:

*Feed-in tariffs (FITs)* reward any MWh produced from RES with a specific price, generally in the form of a contract lasting for a long time period (e.g. ten years), embedded in some specific laws or decrees or undersigned with the system operator. FITs can be "stepped," that is, tailored to each RES technology, or flat. They can also decrease as RES deployment develops, according to a pre-determined rate of decay or the growth of capacity installed.

*Pros:* FITs have the main advantage of securing a revenue stream over a medium-term horizon, regardless of electricity price level and fluctuations. FITs place a low administrative burden on regulators. Finally, FITs reduce barriers to entry since investors do not need to find any electricity buyers (e.g. a retailer or another plant).

*Cons:* FITs suffer from two major limitations. It is very difficult for the regulator to set the right FIT and the optimal time horizon, as there is imperfect information on RES costs and dynamics. Second, as FITs are not linked to price signals, they do not give incentives to non-intermittent (or dispatchable) renewables like biomass or hydro to improve their contribution to demand-supply imbalances.

*Feed-in Premiums (FIPs)* are payments guaranteed to RES as un uplift to the electricity market price on day-ahead markets. These extra payments last for a given time period.

*Pros:* They give RES plants an incentive to adjust their production in line with price signals, at least for dispatchable sources.

*Cons:* FIPs do not avoid the market risks associated with electricity price fluctuations; however, this can be mitigated by investing in a portfolio of technologies to attenuate the revenue variability. As for FITs, they can distort the market if set at levels that are too high/or low, and if their evolution is not tailored to the change of RES costs over time.

*Net metering/billing* supports the deployment of small-scale, distributed renewable energy systems by enabling plants to receive credits or payments for electricity generated, but not consumed on site.

*Pro:* They can be easily managed and measured, in particular if smart meters are employed.

*Cons:* They can be difficult to implement if smart meters are not deployed.

*Fiscal and investment incentives,* such as accelerated depreciation schedules, tax exemptions, tax credits or soft loans, or even import restrictions to favor local RES developers.

*Pros:* They can be effective from an equity perspective, as they can ease RES competing with fossil fuel technologies on the basis of their long-term profitability. They also tend to favor the entry of new players.

*Cons:* They do not necessarily guarantee a fixed electricity share produced by RES, and thus expose producers to market risk. They can distort competition across sources if they are set at the wrong level, or if their evolution does not follow the pace of evolution of RES costs.

## 25.4.2 Quantity-Based Policies

Quantity-based policies can be classified as follows:

*Renewable Portfolio Standards* (RPS) or *Tradable Green certificates* (TGC) or *Renewable Obligations* (RO) establish RES quotas for consumers and/or plants This means that a given share of the electricity consumption or production must be certified as sourced by RES. Tradable certificates are a guarantees of origin for electricity produced by RES and can be bought by those obliged to comply with the quota set by the RPS or the RO. RPS and RO can be accompanied by additional measures such as differentiated quotas according to RES type (banding provisions), non-compliance penalties, long-term contracting obligations, floor prices in TGC trade.

*Pros*: As for FIPs, quotas provide incentives to traditional plants to include RES in their portfolio. Allowing a predetermined share of RES production, RPS and other similar quota mechanisms set fair conditions for competition among RES and fossil fuel technologies.

*Cons*: They do not neutralize the risk of electricity price fluctuations; under the form of TGC, they can lead to oversupply, low certificate prices and overinvestment.

Government can set *competitive auctions* to award RES capacity to be built over a given period. The winner of the bid is then offered a long-term contract for production of renewable electricity. The characteristics of the auctions can depend on the RES plant size or technology.

*Pro*: Auctions share the same advantages as FITs, but with fewer burdens on regulators, in that auction participants reveal their cost in the process.

*Cons*: These mechanisms can be effective only if the technologies are mature and can easily achieve economies of scale.

Box 25.1 provides a recent overview of RES policies (according to the information in REN21 report, 2017).

---

**Box 25.1** RES Support Policies around the World

As at year-end 2016, renewable energy targets were in place in 176 countries. The majority of targets focus on renewable energy use in the power sector, with targets for a specific share of renewable power instituted in 150 countries, and economy-wide targets for primary energy and/or final energy shares in place in eighty-nine countries.

In 2016, the EU proposed a 2030 Framework under which it aims to achieve a share of at least 27 percent of total energy consumption from renewables and at

**Box 25.1** (cont.)

least a 27 percent improvement in energy efficiency (relative to a business-as-usual scenario) to help reduce greenhouse gas emissions by 40 percent in 2030 (compared to 1990 levels). At the national level, countries in Asia were particularly active in launching new targets, or revising existing targets. China's latest five-year plan sets an overall goal of increasing renewable energy capacity to 680 GW by 2020, accounting for 27 percent of total power generation.

FITs are in place in several countries for the deployment of small-scale installations. In an increasing number of countries, support for large-scale projects is shifting to auctions. Policy makers adjust FIT rates as the technologies become more cost-competitive.

Net metering policies are in widespread use in forty-one North American States, where they often overlap with RPS.

In addition to regulatory policies, several countries, such as India, have provided public funding through grants, loans or tax incentives.

Finally, countries that have issued carbon price policies (taxes or market for permits), implicitly give incentives to RES deployment in order to decarbonize the energy sector (as explained in Chapter 24), therefore using several overlapping instruments.

## Learning Outcomes

- There is no general consensus on how to calculate the optimal share of renewables and how renewables can be linked in practice to relieve climate change. However, several countries have set some form of target for RES deployment.
- The Levelized Cost of Electricity is a metric that is used to measure RES competitiveness with respect to fossil-fuel generation.
- Price-based and quantity-based instruments are used to subsidize RES. Both are used at the worldwide level, until RES can generate power at a Levelized Cost of Electricity that is less than or equal to the price of acquiring power from the grid.

# 26 The Integration of Renewable Energy Sources in the Electricity System

## 26.1 Introduction

Among renewable energy sources (RES), variable energy resources (VER) such as wind and PV are characterized by specific features that pose some serious challenges to their integration in the electric grid. Wind and solar generation is not programmable, which means that the grid operator cannot choose when to dispatch the electricity they produce. Only when the sun shines or the wind blows can electricity be generated. Thus, VER exhibit cyclical variations in output based on daily fluctuations in wind speed and solar irradiance. Although it varies by location, wind generation is often at its highest in the very early morning hours, and solar generation is often greatest around midday and early afternoon. Moreover, both wind and sun exhibit rapid changes in wind speeds and solar irradiance. Solar generation also tends to have a ramp-up in the morning and falls in the evening more steeply than wind. This implies that the actual amount of production at any given moment from a wind or solar facility may be difficult to forecast. Finally, provided that the wind is blowing and the sun is shining, the short-run cost of providing one additional kilowatt-hour of wind and solar generation, is nearly zero.

Hirth (2012, 2013) and Holttinen et al. (2011) claim that there is roughly a 15 to 20 percent limit to the level of penetration of VER generation in an electricity grid. With a VER penetration higher than 20 percent, managing the grid would become very difficult due to uncertainty about when the generation would occur and challenges in ramping programmable generation up and down to offset the fluctuations in VER generation. However, there are electric grids around the world today that manage extremely high levels of VER renewable penetration. They have shown that high levels of VER penetration are technically feasible with sufficient transmission capacity and connections with adjacent electricity grids. Still, VER utilization leads to specific costs that we consider below.

We define the main VER characteristics in Paragraph 26.2. From the perspective of the electricity system (market and networks), high shares of VER entail different issues. The connection of VER to the transmission and distribution networks may cause the so-called integration costs, a multifaceted concept that we discuss in Paragraph 26.3, whereas integration in the wholesale market is likely to shift the supply curve and to put downward pressure on pricing. This latter effect in known as merit-order effect and is explained in Paragraph 26.4. Since several studies have been conducted on a case-by-case basis to quantify integration costs and/or the merit-order effect, we refer to the most updated examples, both in the United States and in Europe.

## 26.2    Variable Energy Resources: Some Stylized Facts

The IEA has identified and discussed several specific characteristics of power generation from VER that appear to be relevant from the system integration perspective (IEA, 2014). We start by considering a possible definition of VER:

DEFINITION. *Variable Energy Resources (VER): energy resources whose output is variable, uncertain, location specific, modular and with low short-run costs.*

These characteristics can be described as follows:

- *Variable*: power output fluctuates depending on the availability of the renewable energy source, notably on the weather conditions (affecting wind speed and sun radiation). As a result, output from VER plants cannot be controlled or economically dispatched by system operators based on traditional economic criteria, in contrast to output from most conventional plants that can be turned on and off based on their economic attractiveness at every point in time to supply electricity and other system services according to real-time power demand and other system needs (Joskow, 2011). Note that technological development makes their usage in power production at least partially controllable downward, in the sense that their production can be reduced with regard to the maximum producible level; however, they remain variable in their nature since they depend on variable and uncontrollable (or partially controllable) primary energy supply.
- *Uncertain*: due to limitations in forecasting weather conditions, output from VER plants is less predictable and, hence, less certain than other, controllable plants.
- *Location-specific*: VER resources are not evenly distributed geographically and, in contrast to conventional fuels, cannot be transported to other locations. This may affect siting decisions and transmission needs, since generation sites with high VER output potentials may be located far from areas of high electricity demand.
- *Modular*: the scale of an individual VER production unit (wind turbine, solar panel) is much smaller than of a conventional (fossil-fuel, nuclear or large-hydro) plant. The increasing amount of smaller, distributed generation from VER has a major impact on the structure and operation of the transmission and distribution.
- *Low short-run costs*: once built, VER plants can produce electricity at very little cost as their short-run and marginal costs are close to zero.

Note that these characteristics do not refer just to RES. Some RES are not VAR, and some features of VAR, such as modularity, belong to conventional fossil-fuel plants too, or limited short-run cost, as with the case of nuclear power plants. However, the joint appearance of these features characterizes most RES.

One well-known example of the consequence of the combination of these factors is given by the evolution of the Californian net load, that is, overall consumption net of

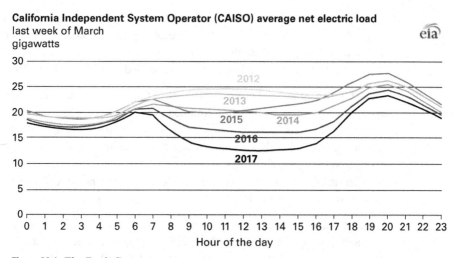

**Figure 26.1** The Duck Curve
*Source*: EIA. Available at: https://www.eia.gov/todayinenergy/detail.php?id=32172.

VER, in recent years. This is shown in Figure 26.1. As more solar resources have been added, net load has increasingly fallen during midday when solar output is highest, and peaks in the first hours of the morning and at the sunset. The recent addition of both utility-scale and small-scale solar plants has contributed to steeper morning ramp-down and evening ramp-up periods. Other types of generating units, like flexible thermal generation, decrease in the morning as solar generation increases with the sunrise and increase in the evening as the sun sets.

CAISO anticipated this evolution of the net load profile, often referred to as the "**Duck Curve**," back in 2013. Load profiles from March were used as the reference for a typical spring day, because seasonally low electricity demand makes the impact of solar and wind on net load more evident at that time of year. The Duck Curve is shown in Figure 26.1. The Californian Duck Curve clearly shows the impact on the load profile of VER. However, on top of the impact on the load profile, integration of renewables also challenges the grid. We discuss this in the next paragraph.

## 26.3    Integration Costs

Grid integration costs can be seen from two distinct points of view. On one hand, they can be interpreted as real economic costs accruing from integrating VERs, that may impact decisions by policy makers or electric grid operators regarding electricity sources. On the other hand, they trigger the use of emerging technologies, such as storage, which can smooth the variability of the grid. Moreover, integrating VER requires flexibility in the power system. This includes the flexibility of existing power plants (i.e. how fast they can adjust their output), the short-term responsiveness of demand, the availability of electricity storage and the quality and smartness of the transmission and distribution grid. The size and degree of interconnection are also relevant, since a larger and more interconnected system generally implies easier integration (Perez-Arriaga and Battle, 2012).

In the literature, there have been several possible definitions of integration costs:

1. the extra investment and operational costs of the non-wind part of the power system when wind power is integrated (Holttinen et al., 2011);
2. the additional costs of accommodating wind and solar (Milligan et al., 2011);
3. the marginal impact that additional wind or solar power has on the costs of the residual system (Hirth, 2012);
4. the additional system costs induced by VER that are not directly related to their generation costs (Ueckerdt et al., 2013).

These costs have been calculated in different ways, using a broad variety of methodology and assumptions. Despite these differences, integration costs have generally been decomposed in different categories (NEA, 2012; Hirth, 2013; Ueckerdt et al., 2013; Hirth et al., 2015). A possible common definition of VER integration cost is as follows:

DEFINITION. *VER integration costs: costs accruing from integration in the grid of VER, divided into balancing, grid related and adequacy costs.*

In greater detail, these costs are:

- *Balancing costs*, i.e. the impacts and costs due to the short-term variability and uncertainty of VER generation output, including costs arising from the need to hold and use more system operating reserves against higher uncertainty (errors) in forecasting output from VER plants, as well as from the (related) increase in ramping, cycling or other, less cost-effective operations of other power plants.
- *Grid-related costs*, i.e. the costs of VER deployment on transmission and distribution needs and the associated costs to extend and reinforce the network in order to meet these needs (including occasional benefits of lower grid needs and lower network losses at different VER penetration rates).
- *Adequacy costs*, i.e. cost deriving from the reduced deployment or utilization of conventional, non-VER plants, which might imply a lack of conventional capacity providing backup or safeguard services.

Based on a review of more than one hundred recent studies and surveys of the cost-related impacts of integrating VER into different power system around the word, Sijm (2017) reports the following findings:

1) The deployment of wind and solar power causes significant integration costs, in particular at higher penetration levels (i.e. > 10 percent). At 10–30 percent penetration, these costs range €10–30/MWh for wind and €25–50/MWh for solar. These amounts correspond to a range of 15–40 percent of LCOE for wind and of 15–35 percent for solar.

2) Balancing costs are generally the lowest component of total VER system integration costs, ranging from €1–6/MWh (i.e. 5–15 percent of total integration costs). The largest component consists of either grid-related costs or adequacy costs, depending on the specific case or study considered.

3) Apart from the cost definition and methodology used, estimates of the size and composition of VER integration costs are location-specific. They vary from country to country and from power system to power system, depending on a complex interaction of factors such as VER characteristics (power output profiles, load factors, penetration rates), electricity load characteristics (magnitude of peak load, load profiles, correlation with VER output), generation plant mix, geographical and balancing area size, transmission connections with neighboring regions, designs of the distribution networks, time perspective, etc.

4) Integration costs per MWh of VER output tend to increase with growing penetration rates. Integration costs may even be negative (benefits) at low penetration levels (1–3 percent), as they make transmission and distribution more efficient. Costs often become significant and tend to show a steep increase at 5–10 percent VER penetration. At higher shares of VER deployment, the increase in integration costs seems to decrease gradually.

Moreover, as regards the dynamics of these costs, they tend to decrease over time depending on the adaptation or transformation of the power system, including options to enhance the overall flexibility of the power system such as improving the flexibility of the power plant mix, enhancing demand responsiveness, extending and enforcing the grid infrastructure, introducing more flexible system and market operations, etc.

Who bears integration costs? Under perfect and complete electricity markets in long-term equilibrium, profile costs would show up as reduced revenues from the day-ahead spot market; balancing costs would arise from the net costs for intraday trading and imbalance charges; grid-related costs would appear as differentiated locational spot prices or differentiated grid fees. Thus, if markets are perfectly competitive and tariffs for network usage are optimally set, costs are borne by those who cause them (Hirth et al., 2015). However, in reality distortions, contract incompleteness, and practical implementation make the internalization of integration costs imperfect.

## 26.4   The Impact of VER on the System Marginal Price

In Chapter 11, we introduced the merit-order effect in balancing, namely, changes in merit order due to imbalances. VER can induce the merit-order effect in balancing markets, as well as changing the merit order at the day-ahead level. Indeed, the marginal cost of producing electricity from VERs such as wind and solar is nearly zero. Therefore, they will generally be prioritized by the grid operator over dispatchable generation that has a positive marginal cost of generation. This implies that the SMP of the day-ahead level is reduced because of the introduction of the VER.

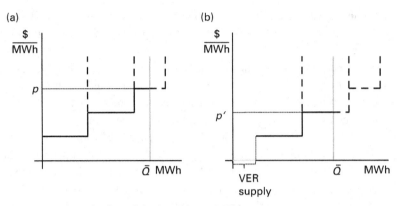

**Figure 26.2** The reduction of the SMP due to VER

The impact on the SMP is represented in Figure 26.2. The benchmark situation is shown in the left panel a. The introduction of VER supply (panel right b) displaces higher cost thermal generation and as a consequence, the SMP decreases to $p'$.The impact of the VER on the system marginal price depends on five important factors: (Hirth, 2012; IEA, 2014; Sjim 2017):

1. the VER penetration rate;
2. the slope of the merit-order curve;
3. the type of VER technology (wind or solar);
4. the geographical size of the market area;
5. the flexibility of the power system.

The first factor is a volume effect: a larger VER output has a larger impact on prices. The impact on the SMP rises as the slope of the merit-order curve increases, since a steeper curve leads to a stronger price drop when VERs are available. At higher VER generation rates, the wholesale price effect is usually higher for solar than for wind as solar generation generally fluctuates more significantly during the day. If a larger geographical area is integrated into one uniform price area, it helps to smooth the wind-generation profile, alleviating transmission constraints and reducing the wholesale price effect at higher penetration rates. Flexibility resulting from large-scale hydro reserves or generation plants that have quick cycling has a similar effect, absorbing the fluctuations of VER generation over time (IEA, 2014).

The wholesale price effect of VER deployment has been estimated by a large number of studies, including model simulations and empirical, historical price data analyses. There is a long tradition of quantifying market effects of VER, emerging in the 1980s. This empirical literature is quite heterogeneous with respect to methodology and focus.

An interesting survey of the empirical literature on the impact of VER on the SMP has been undertaken by Hirth (2013). The author has compared the calculations of more than thirty studies on several countries worldwide. These results are expressed in relative terms, i.e. as a percentage or ratio – called "*value factor*"– between an annual base price (the annual average of SMP price) and a relative average price earned by VER (the SMP price weighted by the volume of VER production). For instance, if the relative average price of VER was €49/MWh for wind power, and the average, reference price over a certain period was estimated at €70/MWh, the value factor of wind power would be 0.7 (or 70 percent). The complement of the value factor is the wholesale price effect. In this example, it would be 0.3 (30 percent) in relative terms and €21/MWh in absolute terms.

Hirth (2013) finds that, on average, at low penetration rates, VER value factors are generally close to unity. This means that all the impact on SMP, if any, is due to the volume of VER injected into the wholesale market. Wind value factors are estimated to drop to, on average, 0.7 at 30 percent wind penetration, while solar value factors are reported to drop faster, i.e. they reach 0.7 already at 10–15 percent solar penetration (although there is a large variation in both wind and solar value factors). Based on these findings and assuming a normalized, system-base price of €70/MWh in all studies surveyed, Hirth estimates that the wholesale price effect, in absolute terms, varies between €15–35/MWh at 30 percent wind penetration.

However, it is worth reiterating that these estimates are gross averages. Detailed figures depend on local specificities, such as grid structure and capacity, plant characteristics and costs, the existence and amount of interconnection, and load profile.

Increasing VER deployment also has important impacts on dispatchable plants. In principle, all conventional power plants will be affected by the VER-induced wholesale price effect (i.e. by lower electricity prices and, hence, lower revenues). This applies in particular for those baseload and mid-merit-order plants (gas plants) that are active during the hours in which VER plants produce substantial amounts of output. In addition, depending on the VER penetration rate, some conventional plants are also affected by reduced capacity factors, resulting in higher average production cost.

This is one of the additional effects of the energy transition toward low-carbon electricity generation that remains to be solved. How to ensure increasing penetration of VER in the system, minimizing its integration costs and the impact on thermal generation is an open question. In future, storage possibilities and the expansion of smart grids could perhaps balance these costs.

## Learning Outcomes

- Electricity output from wind and solar plants is variable, uncertain, location-specific, modular and has low short-run costs.
- Variable Energy Resources (VER) integration costs encompass balancing, grid related and adequacy costs. At 10–30 percent penetration, integration costs range from €10–30/MWh for wind and from €25–50/MWh for solar.
- It is possible to estimate, on average, the impact on system Marginal Price of increasing the electricity supply by integrating VER. At high penetration rates (i.e. over 30 percent), the SMP decreases on average by 30 percent. At 10–15 percent PV penetration rate, the SMP average decrease amounts to 15 percent. However, detailed figures depend on local specificities, such as grid structure and capacity, plant characteristics, costs, the existence and amount of interconnection, and load profile.

# 27 Smart Grids

## 27.1 Introduction

As we saw in Chapter 3, the "term" grid is used to characterize an electricity system that may support all or some of the following four operations: electricity generation, electricity transmission, electricity distribution, and electricity control. A Smart Grid (SG) is an enhancement of the traditional grid generally used to carry power from a few central plants to a large number of users or customers, and possibly also vice versa, when these end consumers become (generally small) producers (e.g. as in the case of small domestic photovoltaic production), that in certain circumstances can feed the grid. Thus, the SG uses two-way flows of electricity and information to create an automated and distributed advanced energy delivery network.

The SG refers to a modern electricity network that monitors, protects and optimizes the operation of the electricity system. It requires the deployment of various types of devices concerning the power infrastructure, electronic sensors, computer systems connected by fast communication devices, and standardized protocols. The need for SG follows different factors, such as increasing demand, ageing network infrastructure and the deployment of low-carbon technologies, such as electric vehicles and intermittent renewables (wind, solar PV, tidal and wave generation). The SG can encompass, adapt and manage events that take place anywhere in the grid, at the level of power generation, transmission, distribution, and consumption. It is therefore a technological improvement that can impact the energy system in a transversal way (Farhangi, 2010). For instance, if a medium voltage transformer failure event occurs in the distribution grid, the SG may automatically change the power flow and recover the power delivery service. Another example can be demand profile shaping (A. T. Kearney Energy Transition Institute, 2015).

In this chapter, we focus on the impact of SG on generation, transmission, distribution and supply. The economic aspects of Demand Response (DR) and the impact on retail competition were analyzed in Chapter 19.

Smart Grids integrate complementary components, subsystems, functions, and services under the control of automated systems. Therefore, the existing studies on SG involve technical aspects of grid functioning. We analyze the smart infrastructure system, namely, the energy, information, and communication infrastructure that underlies the SG that supports i) advanced electricity generation, supply and consumption; ii) and advanced information metering, monitoring, and management.[1] More precisely, the smart energy subsystem is responsible for advanced electricity generation, delivery, and consumption. It is responsible for advanced information metering, monitoring, and management, in the context of the SG.

Paragraph 27.2 details the definition and the applications of SG. Paragraph 27.3 discusses the economic benefits of Smart Grids. We conclude in Paragraph 27.4. by comparing SG deployment and R&D in Europe and United States.

## 27.2 Defining Smart Grids

The IEA (2011) defines SG as follows:

DEFINITION. **Smart Grid (SG)**: *a modern electricity network that monitors, protects, and optimizes the operation of its interconnected elements.*

Digital appliances such as microprocessors make possible two-way communication, from and to production centers and load. Renewables require the coordination with decentralized production. Smart Grid technologies offer a new solution to the problem of monitoring and controlling the grid's transmission system. New technologies called Phasor Measurement Units (PMU) sample voltage and current many times per second at a given location, providing a snapshot of electricity flows. PMU coupled with communications technologies allow measurements many times a second, offering dynamic visibility in the power system. Smart Grid technologies also offer new means of controlling the transmission network. New high-power electronics work essentially as large-scale versions of transistors, adding a new level of control. New technologies may also help reduce unwanted power oscillations and avoid unproductive flows of current through the grid that only serve to waste energy. The combination of new measurement and control technologies also enables a new automated approach to control the grid. Software could potentially monitor the grid in real time for potential disturbances that could lead to blackouts, and might be able to take action to check disturbances. Such monitoring software could act to dampen oscillations in the power grid, or it could even reroute power through the grid to avoid overloading a transmission line. In the event that a power line needs to be removed from service, control software could reroute the power in a way that causes minimal disruptions to the grid. This approach is often referred to as the **self-healing grid**. The ideal self-healing grid will involve a combination of transmission monitoring and control software and comparable measures for the local distribution systems that deliver power to consumers. In turn, this allows different usages of electricity to be accommodated, for example, including charging electric vehicles, using small-scale renewable energy to satisfy consumer needs, demand response.

Table 27.1 summarizes a brief comparison between the main features of existing grid and the SG.

[1] Other aspects of the SG system are surveyed by Fang et al. 2012 and the literature cited therein.

**Table 27.1** Comparison of the electrical system under the traditional grid and the SG

| Area | Traditional grid | Smart grid |
|------|-----------------|-----------|
| *Communication* | Electromechanical | Digital |
| | One-way | Two-way |
| *Power* | Centralized | Centralized and distributed |
| *Monitoring and control* | Few sensors | Self-monitoring |
| | Manual monitoring | Self-healing |
| | Manual restoration | Adaptive and automatic pervasive control |
| | Failures and blackouts | |
| | Limited control | |
| *Market* | Few customer choices | Many customer choices |

*Source*: Farhangi (2010).

As Table 27.1 shows, the innovations brought by SGs are pervasive, concerning all the areas of the electric system (communication, power, monitoring and control). SG are process innovations; they do not create new functions, but improve existing functions making them more efficient, thanks to the application of bi-directional communication devices. In SGs, there is a bi-directional communication and power flow Consumers also become producers of energy, for themselves (self-consumption) but also for others, having the possibility of injecting power into the grid. Therefore, the very distinction between consumers and producers becomes questionable. These new type of active consumers/producers are termed **prosumers.**

The SG can be used to accomplish different functions such as:

- *coordinating production units* and, whenever possible, storage option processes, via superconductors Dynamic Line Rating, Volt/VarControl;
- *enabling active consumer participation*, by giving access to information about electricity usage and sending signals to adjust consumption, via specific end-user devices (smart meters, net metering, demand-response);
- *optimizing costs*, with efficient operation of production units and advanced routing and operational algorithms;
- *self-healing and continuously detecting possible grid vulnerabilities*, via ICT systems, sensors and power electronics (Wide Area Monitoring and Control, Distribution Management System and Phasor measurement units).

All these functions are made possible thanks to the communication of operational measurements and control signals within each area. These signals are relayed either via wired infrastructure (e.g. power-line communication for the distribution grid or optic fiber for high voltage environment), or wireless networks (e.g. satellite, cellular or radio for wide areas).

We discuss a few specific applications along the ESC that use the SG properties, following the approach proposed by Fang et al. (2012).

## 27.2.1     Generation

In contrast to power generation in the traditional power grid, smarter power generation becomes possible, since two-way flows of electricity and information are integrated.

A key power generation paradigm enabled by SG will be **Distributed Generation (DG)**. Distributed generation consists of small-scale technologies often situated next to residential and industrial consumers, offering an alternative to large-scale centralized production, with the advantage of reducing power line losses. It also offers the possibility of self-sufficiency in production and consumption. DG takes advantage of distributed energy resource (DER) systems (e.g. solar panels and small wind turbines), which are often small-scale power plants (typically in the range of 3 kW to 10,000 kW) owned by prosumers, in order to improve power quality and reliability. For example, a **microgrid** (discussed in paragraph 27.2.3), which is a localized grouping of electricity plants and loads, can disconnect from the transmission grid, termed **macrogrid** to distinguish it from the former, the event of a disturbance, so that distributed plants continue to power the users in this microgrid without obtaining power from outside. Thus, the disturbance in the macrogrid can be isolated and the electricity supply quality improved.

IEA (2011) pointed out that a power system based on a large number of reliable small DGs can operate with the same reliability and a lower capacity margin than a system of equally reliable large plants. According to the IEA, power generation may evolve from the present system in three stages:

1. *accommodating DGs* in the current power system;
2. *introducing a decentralized system of DGs* cooperating with the centralized generation system;
3. *supplying most power by DGs* and a limited amount by central generation.

As DG enables users to deploy their own plants, the large-scale deployment of DG will also change the traditional power grid design methodology, in which plants are connected to the transmission grid.

In Chapters 4 and 13, we saw that VPPs are a tool to allow upstream competition in power generation. However, the coordination of *small* Virtual Power Plants (VPPs) can be considered as a form of DG, which enables the management of a large group of distributed plants with a total capacity comparable to that of a conventional power plant. DG, allowed by SG, enables clustering several VPPs as if they were collectively run by a central controller. The concerted operational mode can enhance efficiency by delivering coordinated peak load electricity or flexible power generation at short notice. Note that more flexibility allows the system to react better to fluctuations. However, a coordinated VPP is also a complex system requiring a complicated optimization, control, and secure communication methodology.

## 27.2.2     Transmission

On the power transmission side, factors such as infrastructure challenges (increasing load and quickly ageing components) and innovative technologies (new materials, advanced power electronics and communication technologies) drive the development of smart transmission grids. The smart transmission grid can be regarded as an integrated system that functionally consists of three interactive components: smart control centers, smart power transmission networks, and smart substations.

Based on the existing control centers, the smart control centers enable many new features, such as analytical capabilities performing evaluations, monitoring, and visualization of production and consumption profiles.

Smart power transmission networks are conceptually built on the existing electric transmission infrastructure. However, the emergence of new technologies (e.g. new materials, electronics, sensing, communication, computing and signal processing) can help to improve power utilization, power quality, system security and reliability, and thus drive the development of a new framework architecture for transmission networks.

Smart substations serve as the basis and backbone of the establishment of the SG. The automation level deployed at a substation allows the station's local functions (e.g. fault isolation) to be strengthened, improving the integrated performance with respect to security, reliability and quality.

With a common digitalized platform, in the smart transmission grid it is possible to enable more flexibility in control and operation, allow for embedded intelligence, and foster the resilience and sustainability of the grid.

## 27.2.3    Distribution

For the distribution grid, the most important problem is how to deliver power to better serve the end users. However, the evolution of distribution implies that many distributed plants will be integrated into the smart distributed grid. This, on the one hand, will increase system flexibility for power generation; on the other hand, it also makes the power flow control much more complicated, in turn necessitating the usage of smarter power distribution and delivery mechanisms.

The distribution network faces challenges provided by microgrids and the vehicle-to-power paradigm. Let us look at them more closely.

### Microgrids

A microgrid is a localized grouping of electricity generation, energy storage, and load. The term "microgrid" is a conventional term that does not refer to a predefined, fixed, scale, but to its functioning. Note, however, that when the microgrid becomes large, it is common to refer to it by different names, highlighting the different specifics and purposes. For instance, at the town level we talk of **smart cities**, composed of several microgrids interconnected with each other, which are generally designed to foster the use of renewables. There are also **super-grids**, which consist of several microgrids interconnected through the transmission network in different geographical areas.

Under normal operational conditions, the microgrid is connected to a traditional power grid, which is termed the macrogrid. The users in a microgrid can generate low-voltage electricity using distributed generation, such as solar panels, wind turbines, and fuel cells. The single connection point of the microgrid with the macrogrid can be disconnected isolating the former, for instance when there is a network disturbance. Under these circumstances, users within the microgrid continue to receive power from distributed generation, and not from the power plants located in the macrogrid. Thus, the multiple distributed plants and the ability to isolate the microgrid will provide highly reliable electricity supply. This intentional "islanding" of generation and load has the potential to provide greater local reliability than the level provided by the power system as a whole. Note that although users do not obtain the power from outside in the islanding mode, they may still exchange some information with the macrogrid. For instance, they may want to know the status of the macrogrid and decide whether they should reconnect to the macrogrid and obtain power from the electric utility.

The primary function of the islanding relates to technical and reliability problems. However, it is possible that future decisions on disconnecting from the microgrid will be taken on the basis of economic considerations. For instance, it is possible that further technical development of microgrids will also foster the development of **local energy communities**. Community energy projects are those in which a community comes together to develop, deliver and benefit from energy produced by green electricity. They can involve energy supply projects such as renewable energy installations and storage, and energy reduction projects such as energy efficiency and demand management. Community energy may include community-based approaches to selling or distributing energy.

### Grids and vehicles

As fossil fuels become more expensive, we can expect a rise in the popularity of fully Electric Vehicles (EV) or plug-in hybrid EV. These vehicles, however, can be seen from two points of view. On the one hand, they provide transportation services, in the same way as any other vehicle. However, being electric, they are also part of the grid. Therefore, there are two main approaches that can be followed when considering the relationships between EV and the grid in a scenario of a widespread diffusion of EV: the Grid-to-Vehicle (G2V) and the Vehicle-to-Grid (V2G) approach.

In G2V, EVs are seen as vehicles that need to be powered by electricity originally from an external power source, and thus need to be charged after the batteries deplete. From the perspective of the grid, one of the most important issues in G2V is that the charging operation leads to a significant new load on the distribution grids. One solution to mitigate the impact of EVs on the grid is to optimize their charging profile. In other words, peak power demand has to be as small as possible, taking into account the extra power consumption from the vehicle charging. This can be done by coordinating the charging operations of different EVs so that they are not charged at the same time.

In the V2G, EVs are seen as providers of new storage services and power supply. Under the V2G-scheme, EVs can communicate with the grid to deliver electricity into the grid, when they are parked and connected to the grid. There are three major delivery setups for EV providing V2G services:

- A hybrid or fuel cell vehicle, which generates power from storable fuel, uses its engine to produce power during some hours, for instance peak hours. These vehicles serve as a distributed generation system producing energy from conventional fossil fuels or hydrogen.

- A battery-powered or plug-in hybrid vehicle uses its excess rechargeable battery capacity to supply power at peak hours. These vehicles can then be recharged during off-peak hours at cheaper rates. These vehicles serve as a distributed battery storage system to store power.
- A solar vehicle uses its excess charging capacity to provide power to the power grid when the battery is fully charged. These vehicles serve as a distributed small renewable energy power system.

Note that G2V and V2G are not to be seen as substitute approaches, from the point of view of the SG. For example, V2G-enabled EVs can be used to provide power to help smooth the load profile, sending power to the grid when demand is high and charging when demand is low. This aspect is similar to the demand response case.

## 27.2.4 Supply

The Advanced Metering Infrastructure (AMI), which encompasses smart meters to read electricity consumption and automated meter readers to communicate data to the distributor via meter data management systems that allow bi-directional communication flows, enables control over electricity consumption. In particular, Demand Response (DR) allows the active participation of consumers. It is defined, according to the Federal Energy Regulatory Commission (FERC) as "Changes in electric use by demand-side resources from their normal consumption patterns in response to changes in the price of electricity, or to incentive payments designed to induce lower electricity use at times of high wholesale market prices or when system reliability is jeopardized" (FERC, 2017).[2]

DR programs enable DSOs to manage consumers' load profile in response to grid imbalances, primarily during times of peak demand or unexpected drop of supply. There are end-user Energy Management Systems that are programmed, on receiving a trigger signal from the DSO, to alter the demand of smart appliances at residential and building sites, or even the demand of electricity-intensive industrial plants that wish to cooperate. According to A. T. Kearney Energy Transition Institute (2015), the information flow from consumer to the DSO enables:

- real-time, non-aggregated DSO knowledge of consumer demand;
- improved DSO control over consumer bills (increased precision, cheaper reading by distance vs. manual reading);
- net metering billing;
- rewarding owners of DG systems (such as PV, EV) for the electricity they add to the grid.

The Information flow from the DSO to the consumers enables:

1. demand-response programs, thanks to the reception of dynamic pricing signals;
2. energy consumption visualization through in-house displays.

[2] See www.ferc.gov/industries/electric/indus-act/demand-response/dem-res-adv-metering.asp.

## 27.3    Economic and Environmental Benefits of Smart Grids

From the beginning of 2000s, it has been evident that there is a need for a methodological approach to estimating the costs and benefits of Smart Grids, based to the greatest possible extent on actual data from Smart Grid pilot projects. A study published by the Electrical Power Research Institute (EPRI) in 2010 and commissioned by the US Department of Energy (DoE), provided a framework for evaluating economic, environmental, reliability, safety and security benefits from the perspective of all the different stakeholder groups (utilities, customers and society). Its aim is the identification of easy-to-understand, directly measurable and quantifiable benefits. It is the first of its kind to develop a systematic way of defining and estimating the benefits of the Smart Grid.

In the same vein, in 2011 the European Joint Research Centre carried out the first comprehensive collection of Smart Grid projects in Europe to perform a qualitative and quantitative analysis of past and currently running projects and to extract results, trends and lessons learned. The study recognizes that the impact of Smart Grid projects goes beyond what can be captured in monetary terms, integrating economic analysis (monetary appraisal of costs and benefits on behalf of society) with a qualitative impact analysis (non-monetary appraisal of non-quantifiable impacts and externalities, e.g. social impacts, contribution to policy goals).

However, a formal analysis evaluating Smart Grid projects based on investment needs and resulting benefits can be difficult. The challenge is linked to three main reasons (Giordano and Sanchez, 2012):

- SG projects are typically characterized by high initial costs and benefit streams that are uncertain and often long term in nature. In fact, many SG benefits are systemic in nature (i.e. they only come into play once the entire smart electricity system is in place and new market players have successfully entered it).
- SG assets provide different types of functions to enable SG benefits. A variety of technologies, software programs and operational practices can all contribute to achieving a single Smart Grid benefit, while some elements can provide benefits for more than one SG objective in ways that often impact each other.
- The active role of customers is essential for capturing the benefits of many SG solutions, but is very often uncertain.

Moretti et al. (2017) report a summary of cost-benefit analyses of more than one hundred Smart Grids worldwide, looking at production, transmission and distribution. The main findings can be summarized as follows. The reported economic costs of SG systems ranged from 0.03 to 1143.14 M€/yr. The potential benefits of SGs varied from 0.04 to 804.41 M€/yr. On average, the costs exceeded the benefits by 59.1 M€/yr. The huge differences in estimates of costs and benefits are mainly due to the scope of the analysis, electricity prices, assumptions about the inclusion of tangible and intangible costs and benefits, the time horizon of interest, geographical area, discount rates, capacities, utility operating characteristics, and to a lesser extent, the data used for the different ICT devices. Regarding environmental benefits, the GHG emission reductions range from 10 to 180 $gCO_2$/kWh with a median value of 89 $gCO_2$/kWh, depending on the country grid mix, and assumptions on both the type and the level of penetration of renewable energy into the power grid, as well as on the boundary of the considered SG systems. GHG emissions benefits were larger in countries with a high share of fossil fuels in the grid mix and where a high level of penetration of renewable energy was assumed. GHG emission reductions due to energy losses on the electric network were three times smaller than emission reductions due to the penetration renewables. This finding clearly illustrates that the penetration of renewable energy sources is the key parameter for estimates of GHG savings of Smart Grid systems. Emission reductions were almost twice as high in studies focusing on only a segment of the electricity grid mix as those considering the full electricity grid mix.

## 27.4     The Deployment of Smart Grids

The various applications of Smart Grids make them very appealing. However, depending on several economic factors, including regulation and incentives, they are being deployed at different speeds worldwide.

In *Japan,* because its energy self-sufficiency is a mere 4 percent, the focus of SG plans is to build renewable-friendly power grids. Moreover, the Great East Japan Earthquake that struck in 2011, and the subsequent nuclear power plant accident, prompted the Japanese government to adopt reforms targeted at the power system; here, SGs provide stable power supplies and optimize overall grid operations from power generation to the end user. Moreover, Japan has developed SGs to achieve the $CO_2$ emission reductions stipulated in the Kyoto Protocol.

In *China*, high electricity consumption and distributed loads have appeared with the rapid development of the economy and a large and growing population, which result in a high demand for SGs. China prefers to renovate traditional power systems with modern information technology, while establishing a highly automated and widely distributed network for energy exchange to solve its energy balance problem.

As reported by Zhang et al., 2017, In the *United States*, SGs emphasize the reliability, safety and operational efficiency of power systems through the strong support of digital and other advanced technologies. In addition, the United States is also devoted to the reduction of power supply costs created by an ageing power infrastructure. In particular, the United States has launched massive investment as from 2009. In the American Recovery Investment Act, $4.5 billion has been devoted to Smart Grids (out of $21 billion in the energy sector overall). This program represents the most ambitious investment in research and development devoted to SG. One of the effects of this investment effort is the number of patents filed by the United States in the SG area. Over the 12,000 patents registered up to 2013, 43 percent have been filed by the United States and 15 per cent in Europe. The cumulative public and private R&D effort has amounted to $3 billion up to 2014 (A. T. Kearney Energy Transition Institute, 2015).

The US market has the biggest deployment of smart meters. In the United States, electric companies have installed 65 million smart meters, covering more than 50 percent of US households, as of the end of 2015. Deployment is projected to reach 90 million by 2020. More than thirty electric companies have fully deployed smart meters to improve grid operations, integrate renewables and provide innovative services to customers (Edison Foundation, 2016).

European innovative SG schemes attempt to reconcile two approaches of renewable energy development, namely, large-scale centralized approaches and small-scale, local decentralized approaches, so as to achieve a transition toward a fully low-carbon electricity system, while attempting to realize energy trading between European countries. To promote such objectives, the European Commission has also monitored SG projects, proposed guidelines for the cost-benefit analysis of SG projects and smart meter deployment, investigated the complexity features of smart energy grids, and evaluated the social dimensions of SG projects.

According to Colak et al. (2015), the value of Smart Grids in Europe can be estimated at $33 billion in 2012, and $16 billion in 2014 for digital technologies alone. Based on a survey of 950 Smart Grid projects originating in Europe, but also deployed in countries abroad, Gangale et al. 2017 report a cumulative investment of €4.97 billion, with €1.6 billion for R&D and €3.36 billion in technology demonstration activities. These Smart Grid projects involve 2,900 organizations, mainly DSOs, universities and technology manufacturers. The 800 implementation sites are spread across thirty-six countries, in particular Germany and Spain, with 140 and ninety-five sites respectively. These figures show the dynamism of these rapidly evolving activities.

## Learning Outcomes

- A Smart Grid (SG) system is the bi-directional integration of electricity and communication flows that impact all the segments of the electric sector.
- The economic benefits of SGs are difficult to measure in a standard form, as many of them do not have a clear market price. There are still reasons to justify government intervention in the form of R&D subsidies.
- GHG emissions benefits are larger in countries with a high share of fossil fuels in the grid mix and where a high level of penetration of renewable energy was assumed.
- Distributed generation, consisting of small-scale technologies often situated near residential and industrial consumers, allows savings on transmission and distribution costs.
- Electric vehicles represent not only a new use of electricity for charging needs, but can also be conceived as small storage devices that have the same impact on consumption as demand response.
- With increasing penetration of SG, renewables and other forms of decentralized energy production and demand response, the way to a more efficient and greener use of electricity has been paved, even if there are still some barriers to changing consumer behavior through economic signals.

# References

ACER/CEER (2013). Annual Report on the Results of Monitoring the Internal Electricity and Natural Gas Markets in 2012, November.

ACER/CEER (2016). Annual Report on the Results of Monitoring the Internal Electricity and Natural Gas Markets in 2015, November.

Aid, R. (2015). *Electricity Derivatives*. London: Springer Verlag.

Anton, J. J., Vander Weide, J. H. and Vettas, N. (2002). Entry Auctions and Strategic Behavior under Cross-Market Price Constraints. *International Journal of Industrial Organization*, 20(5), 611–629.

A. T. Kearney Energy Transition Institute (2015). Smart Grids (Introduction), Factbook.

Averch, H. and Johnson L. L. (1962). Behavior of the Firm under Regulatory Constraint. *American Economic Review*, 52, 1059–1069.

Batlle, C., Pérez-Arriaga, I. J. and Zambrano-Barragán, P. (2012). Regulatory Design for RES-E Support Mechanisms: Learning Curves, Market Structure, and Burden-Sharing. *Energy Policy*, 41, 212–220.

Baumol, W. J. and Bradford, D. F. (1970). Optimal Departures from Marginal Cost Pricing. *The American Economic Review*, 60(3), 265–283.

Benth, F. E., Benth, J. S., Koekebakker, S. (2008). *Stochastic Modeling of Electricity and Related Markets*. Singapore: World Scientific.

Biggar, D. R. and Hesamzadeh, M. R. (2014). *The Economics of Electricity Markets*. New York: Wiley-IEEE Press.

Blumseck, S. (2010). Introduction to Electricity Markets, available at www.e-education.psu.edu /ebf483/.

Bohn, E., Caramanis, M., Schweppe, F. and Tabors, R. (1988). *Spot Pricing of Electricity*. Dordrecht: Springer Science & Business Media.

Bohn, R. E., Caramanis, M. C., and Schweppe, F. C. (1984). Optimal Pricing in Electrical Networks Over Space and Time. *The RAND Journal of Economics*, 360–376.

Boiteux, M. (1960). Peak Load Pricing. *Journal of Business*, 33, 157–179 [translated from the original in French published in 1949].

Borenstein, S. (2002). The Trouble with Electricity Markets: Understanding California's Restructuring Disaster. *The Journal of Economic Perspectives*, 16(1), 191–211.

Borenstein, S. (2005a). Time-Varying Retail Electricity Prices: Theory and Practice. *Electricity Deregulation: Choices and Challenges*, 317–357.

Borenstein, S. (2005b). The Long-Run Efficiency of Real-Time Electricity Pricing. *The Energy Journal*, 93–116.

Borenstein, S. (2012). The Private and Public Economics of Renewable Electricity Generation. *The Journal of Economic Perspectives*, 26(1), 67–92.

Borenstein, S. and Bushnell, J. (1999). An Empirical Analysis of the Potential for Market Power in California's Electricity Industry. *The Journal of Industrial Economics*, 47(3), 285–323.

Borenstein, S., and Bushnell, J. (2015). The US Electricity Industry after Twenty Years of Restructuring. *Annual Review of Economics*, 7(1), 437–463.

Borenstein, S., Bushnell, J. and Knittel, C. R. (1999). Market Power in Electricity Markets: Beyond Concentration Measures. *The Energy Journal*, 20(4), 65–88.

Borenstein, S., Bushnell, J., Kahn, E. and Stoft, S. (1995). Market Power in California Electricity Markets. *Utilities Policy*, 5(3), 219–236.

Borenstein S., Bushnell, J. and Stoft, S. (2000). The Competitive Effects of Transmission Capacity in a Deregulated Electricity Industry. *The RAND Journal of Economics*, 31(2), 294–325.

Borenstein, S., and Holland, S. P. (2005). On the Efficiency of Competitive Electricity Markets with Time-Invariant Retail Prices. *The RAND Journal of Economics*, 36(3), 469–493.

Bower, J. and Bunn, D. W. (2000). Model-Based Comparisons of Pool and Bilateral Markets for Electricity. *The Energy Journal*, 1–29.

Brennan, T. (2006). Consumer Preference Not to Choose: Methodological and Policy Implications. *Energy Policy*, 35(3), 1616–1627.

Brundtland, G., Khalid, M., Agnelli, S., Al-Athel, S., Chidzero, B., Fadika, L. and Singh, M. (1987). Our Common Future, The Brundtland Report.

Brunekreeft, G., and Newbery, D. (2006). Should Merchant Transmission Investment Be Subject to a Must-Offer Provision? *Journal of Regulatory Economics*, 30(3), 233–260.

Bushnell, J. (1999) Transmission Rights and Market Power. *Electricity Journal*, 12(8), 77–85.

Bushnell, J. and Stoft S. (1996). Electric Grid Investment under a Contract Network Regime. *Journal of Regulatory Economics*, 10, 61–79.

Bushnell, J. and Stoft S. (1997). Improving Private Incentives for Electric Grid Investment. *Resource and Energy Economics*, 19, 85–108.

Cabral, L. M. B. (2000). *Introduction to Industrial Organization*. Cambridge, MA: The MIT Press.

Caramanis, M. C., Bohn, R. E. and Schweppe, F. C. (1982). Optimal Spot Pricing: Practice and Theory. *IEEE Transactions on Power Apparatus and Systems*, 9, 3234–3245.

Cardell, J. B., Hitt, C. C. and Hogan, W. W. (1997). Market Power and Strategic Interaction in Electricity Networks. *Resource and Energy Economics*, 19(1–2), 109–137.

Carlton, D. W. and Perloff, J. M. (2015). Modern Industrial Organization. Chapter 11, Natural Monopoly. London: Pearson Higher Education.

Chao, H. P. and Peck, S. (1996). A Market Mechanism for Electric Power Transmission. *Journal of Regulatory Economics*, 10(1), 25–59.

Choné, P., Flochel, L. and Perrot, A. (2002). Allocating and Funding Universal Service Obligations in a Competitive Market. *International Journal of Industrial Organization*, 20(9), 1247–1276.

Christen Associates in Energy Consulting (2016). Retail Choice in Electricity: What Have We Learned in 20 Years?, available at www.emrf.net/uploads/3/4/4/6/34469793/emrf_paper_re tail_choice_in_electricity_160202_february_2016.pdf.

Christensen, L. R., and Greene W. H. (1976). Economies of Scale in US Electric Power Generation. *Journal of Political Economy*, 84(4), 655–676.

Colak, I., Fulli, G., Sagiroglu, S., Yesilbudak, M. and Covrig, C. F. (2015). Smart Grid Projects in Europe: Current Status, Maturity and Future Scenarios. *Applied Energy*, 152, 58–70.

Competition and Market Authority (2015). Locational Prices in Great Britain, available at https://assets.publishing.service.gov.uk/media/54eb5da5ed915d0cf7000010/Locational_pricing.pdf.

Concettini, S., and Creti, A. (2014). Liberalization of Electricity Retailing in Europe: What to Do Next? *Energy Studies Review*, 21(1), 21–35.

Considine, T. J. (2000). The Impacts of Weather Variations on Energy Demand and Carbon Emissions. *Resource and Energy Economics*, 22(4), 295–314.

Crampes, C. and Creti, A. (2005). Capacity Competition in Electricity Markets. *Economia delle fonti di energia e dell'ambiente*, 2, 59–83.

Crampes, C. and Laffont, J.-J. (2001). Transport Pricing in the Electricity Industry. *Oxford Review of Economic Policy*, 17(3), 313–328.

Cramton, P. (2004). Competitive Bidding Behavior in Uniform-Price Auction Markets. In *System Sciences, 2004. Proceedings of the 37th Annual Hawaii International Conference on* IEEE, 11–15.

Cramton, P. and Stoft S. (2006). The Convergence of Market Designs for Adequate Generating Capacity. White Paper for the California Electricity Oversight Board, March 2006. Available at http://web.mit.edu/ceepr/www/publications/workingpapers/2006-007.pdf.

Cramton, P. and Ockenfels, A. (2012). Economics and Design of Capacity Markets for the Power Sector. *Zeitschrift für Energiewirtschaft*, 36(2), 113–134.

Cramton, P., Ockenfels, A. and Stoft, S. (2013). Capacity Market Fundamentals. *Economics of Energy & Environmental Policy*, 2(2), 27–46.

Crew, M., C. Fernando and Kleindorfer, P. (1995). The Theory of Peak-load Pricing: A Survey. *Journal of Regulatory Economics*, 8, 215–248.

Dasgupta, P. and Heal G. (1974). The Optimal Depletion of Exhaustible Resources. *The Review of Economic Studies* 41, 3–28.

Day, C. J., Hobbs, B. F. and Pang, J. S. (2002). Oligopolistic Competition in Power Networks: A Conjectured Supply Function Approach. *IEEE Transactions on power systems*, 17(3), 597–607.

Dechenaux, E. and Kovenock, D. (2007). Tacit Collusion and Capacity Withholding in Repeated Uniform Price Auctions. *The RAND Journal of Economics*, 38(4), 1044–1069.

Defeuilley, C. (2009). Retail Competition in Electricity Markets. *Energy Policy*, 37(2), 377–386.

Deutsche Bank (2016). Solar grid parity in a low oil price era, available at www.db.com/cr/en/concrete-deutsche-bank-report-solar-grid-parity-in-a-low-oil-price-era.htm.

DG Energy (2016). Statistical Pocketbook. Bruxelles, BG: European Commission.

DOE (2000). Horizontal Market Power in Restructured Electricity Markets, Report. Washington, DC: Department of Energy.

Durmayaz, A. and Salim Sogut O. (2006). Influence of Cooling Water Temperature on the Efficiency of a Pressurized-Water Reactor Nuclear-Power Plant. *International Journal of Energy Research*, 30(10), 799–810.

Edenhofer, O., Hirth, L., Knopf, B., Pahle, M., Schlömer, S., Schmid, E. and Ueckerdt, F. (2013). On the Economics of Renewable Energy Sources. *Energy Economics*, 40, S12–S23.

Edison Foundation (2016). IEI Report, Electric Company Smart Meter Deployment.

EIA (2017). Levelized Cost and Levelized Avoided Cost of New Generation Resources in the Annual Energy Outlook 2017, available at www.eia.gov/outlooks/aeo/pdf/electricity_generation.pdf.

Ellerman, A. D. and Buchner, B. (2007). The European Union Emissions Trading Scheme: Origins, Allocation, and Early Results. *Review of Environmental Economics and Policy*, 1(1) 66–87.

Ellerman, A. D. and Joskow, P. (2008). *The European Union's Emissions Trading System in Perspective*. Arlington, VA: Pew Center on Global Climate Change.

Ellerman, A. D., Convery, F. J. and De Perthuis, C. (2010). *Pricing Carbon: The European Union Emissions Trading Scheme*. Cambridge: Cambridge University Press.

Elton, E. J, Gruber, M. J., Brown, S. J. and Goetzmann, W. N. (2014). *Modern Portfolio Theory and Investment Analysis* (9th ed.). New York: John Wiley & Sons.

ENTSO-E (2015). Entso at a Glance, available at www.entsoe.eu/Documents/Publications/ENTSO-E%20general%20publications/entsoe_at_a_glance_2015_web.pdf.

Eskeland, G. S., Mideksa, T. K. (2009). Climate Change Adaptation and Residential Electricity Demand in Europe. *CICERO Working Paper*.

Eskeland, G. S., Rive, N. A., and Mideksa, T. K. (2012). Europe's Climate Goals and the Electricity Sector. *Energy Policy*, 41, 200–211.

Eurelectric (2017). Dynamic Pricing in Electricity Supply, Position paper, available at www.eemg-mediators.eu/downloads/dynamic_pricing_in_electricity_supply-2017–2520-0003–01-e.pdf.

European Commission (2001). Analysis of Electricity Network Capacities and Identification of Congestion – Final Report. Brussels.

European Commission (2009). Regulation (EC) No 714/2009 of the European Parliament and of the Council of 13 July 2009 on Conditions for Access to the Network for Cross-Border Exchanges in Electricity and Repealing Regulation (EC) No 1228/2003.

European Commission (2014). Identification of Appropriate Generation and System Adequacy Standards for the Internal Electricity Market. Final Report. Paper prepared by AF Mercados, E-Bridge, REF-E. EUR 2015.1392 EN. Luxembourg: Publications Office of the European Union. Doi:10.2832/089498.

European Commission (2015). Ex-post Investigation of Cost Pass-through in the EU ETS, CE Delft and Oeako Institute Report, EC Press.

Everett, B, Boyle, G, Peake, S. and Ramage, J. (2011). *Energy Systems and Sustainability. Power for a Sustainable Future* (2nd Edition). Oxford: Oxford University Press.

Fabra, N., von der Fehr, N. H. M. and Harbord, D. (2006). Designing Electricity Auctions. *The RAND Journal of Economics*, 37(1), 23–46.

Fabra, N., von der Fehr, N. H. M. and de Frutos, M. Á. (2011). Market Design and Investment Incentives. *The Economic Journal*, 121(557), 1340–1360.

Fang, X., Misra, S., Xue, G. and Yang, D. (2012). Smart Grid – The New and Improved Power Grid: A Survey. *IEEE Communications Surveys & Tutorials*, 14(4), 944–980.

Farhangi, H. (2010). The Path of the Smart Grid. *IEEE Power and Energy Magazine*, 8(1), 18–28.

Faulhaber, G. R. (1975). Cross-Subsidization: Pricing in Public Enterprises. *The Economic Review*, 65(5), 966–977.

FERC (2017). Staff Issues Assessment of Demand Response and Advanced Metering, Report available at www.ferc.gov/industries/electric/indus-act/demand-response/dem-res-adv-metering.asp.

Fouquet, R. Ed. (2015). *Handbook of Energy and Climate Change*, London: Edward Elgar Publishing.

Gangale, F., Vasiljevska J., Covrig F., Mengolini A. and Fulli G. (2017). Smart grid projects outlook 2017: Facts, figures and trends in Europe, EUR 28614 EN, doi:10.2760/15583.

Garfield, P. J., and Lovejoy, W. F. (1964). *Public Utility Economics*. Englewood Cliffs, NJ: Prentice-Hall.

Giordano, V. and Sanchèz, J. (2012). Guidelines for conducting a cost-benefit analysis of Smart Grid projects, JRC Reports, European Commission.

Giulietti, M., Grossi, L. and Waterson, M. (2010). Price Transmission in the UK Electricity Market: Was NETA Beneficial?, *Energy Economics*, 32(5), 1165–1174.

Goulding A. J., Rufin, C. and Swinand, G. (1999). The Role of Vibrant Retail Electricity Markets in Assuring that Wholesale Power Markets Operate Effectively. *The Electricity Journal*, 12(10), 61–73.

Green, R. J. (1996). Increasing Competition in the British Electricity Spot Market. *Journal of Industrial Economics*, (44), 205–216.

Green, R. J. (1997). Electricity Transmission Pricing: An International Comparison. *Utilities Policy*, 6(3), 177–184.

Green, R. J. and Newbery, D. M. (1992). Competition in the British Electricity Spot Market. *Journal of Political Economy*, 100(5), 929–953.

Golombek, R., Kittelsen, S. A. C. and Haddeland, I. (2012). Climate Change: Impacts on Electricity Markets in Western Europe. *Climatic Change* 113(2), 357–370.

Hattori, T. and Tsutsui, M. (2004). Economic Impact of Regulatory Reforms in the Electricity Supply Industry: A Panel Data Analysis for OECD Countries. *Energy Policy*, 32(6), 823–832.

Heal, G. (2009). *The Economics of Renewable Energy*. National Bureau of Economic Research, Working Paper No. w15081.

Hirst, E. and Kirby, B. (2001). Key Transmission Planning Issues. *The Electricity Journal*, 14(8), 59–70.

Hirth, L. (2012). Integration Costs and the Value of Wind Power: Thoughts on a valuation framework for variable renewable electricity sources, Potsdam Institute for Climate Impact Research and Vattenfall GmbH.

Hirth, L. (2013). The Market Value of Variable Renewables: The Effect of Solar and Wind Power Variability on Their Relative Price. *Energy Economics*, 38(2), 218–236.

Hirth, L., Ueckerdt, F. and Edenhofer, O. (2015). Integration Costs Revisited: An Economic Framework for Wind and Solar Variability. *Renewable Energy*, 74, 925–939.

Hogan, W. W. (1998). Nodes and Zones in Electricity Markets: Seeking Simplified Congestion Pricing. In: *Designing Competitive Electricity Markets*, Hung-po, C. and Huntington, H. G., Eds. New York: Springer.

Hogan, W. W. (1992). Contract Networks for Electric Power Transmission. *Journal of Regulatory Economics*, 4, 211–242.

Hogan, W. W. (2005). On An "Energy Only" Electricity Market Design for Resource Adequacy, Center for Business and Government, John F. Kennedy School of Government, Harvard University, Cambridge (MA). Available at www.whogan.com.

Hogan, W. W. (2013). Electricity Scarcity Pricing through Operating Reserves. *Economics of Energy & Environmental Policy*, 2(2), 65–87.

Hogan, W. W. (2015). Electricity Market Design Energy and Capacity Markets and Resource Adequacy, EUCI Conference, Capacity Markets: Gauging Their Real Impact on Resource Development and Reliability, Cambridge, MA. Available at www.whogan.com.

Hogan, W. W. and Pope, S. L. (2017). Priorities for the Evolution of an Energy-only Electricity Market Design in ERCOT. FTI Consulting. Report. Available at www.whogan.com.

Holland, S. P. and Mansur, E. T. (2006). The Short-Run Effects of Time-Varying Prices in Competitive Electricity Markets. *The Energy Journal*, 127–155.

Holland, S. P. and Mansur, E. T. (2008). Is Real-Time Pricing Green? The Environmental Impacts of Electricity Demand Variance. *The Review of Economics and Statistics*, 90(3), 550–561.

Holttinen, H., P. Meibom, P., Orths, A., Lange, B., O'Malley, M., Tande, J., Stanqueiro, A., Gomez, E., Söder, L., Strabac, G., Smith, J. and van Hulle, F. (2011). Impacts of Large

Amounts of Wind Power on Design and Operation of Power Systems, Results of IEA Collaboration. *Wind Energy*, 14, 179–192.

Hortaçsu, A., Madanizadeh, S. A. and Puller, S. L. (2017). *Power to Choose? An Analysis of Consumer Inertia in the Residential Electricity Market.* National Bureau of Economic Research, Working Paper no. w20988.

Hotelling, H. (1931). The Economics of Exhaustible Resources. *Journal of Political Economy*, 39(2), 137–175.

Hu, Z., Kim, J. H., Wang, J. and Byrne, J. (2015). Review of Dynamic Pricing Programs in the US and Europe: Status Quo and Policy Recommendations. *Renewable and Sustainable Energy Reviews*, 42, 743–751.

Hull, J. C. (2015). *Options, Futures and Other Derivatives* (9th ed.). Upper Saddle River, NJ: Pearson Prentice Hall.

Hunt, S. (2002). *Making Competition Work in Electricity.* Chichester: John Wiley & Sons.

Hunt S. and Shuttleworth, G. (1996). *Competition and Choice in Electricity*, Chichester, USA: John Wiley & Sons.

IEA (2011). *Technology Roadmap: Smart Grids*, International Energy Agency (IEA/OECD), Paris.

IEA (2014). *The Power of Transformation: Wind, Sun and the Economics of Flexible Power Systems*, International Energy Agency (IEA/OECD), Paris.

IEA (2017a). *Key World Energy Statistics.* Paris: International Energy Agency, OECD/IEA.

IEA (2017b). Renewable information. www.iea.org/publications/freepublications/publication/ RenewablesInformation2017Overview.pdf.

IEEE (1996). *IEEE Standard Dictionary of Electrical and Electronic Terms.* Piscataway, NJ: IEEE Std 100–1996, Institute of Electrical and Electronics Engineers.

IRENA (2017). Perspectives for the Energy Transition: Investment Needs for a Low-Carbon Energy System, Report, OECD Press.

Jamasb, T. and Pollitt, M. (2005). Electricity Market Reform in the European Union: Review of Progress towards Liberalization and Integration. *The Energy Journal*, 26(Special Issue), 11–41.

Joskow, P. L. (1996). *Introducing Competition into Regulated Network Industries: From Hierarchies to Markets in Electricity.* Cambridge. MA: The MIT Press.

Joskow, P. L. (2000). Why Do We Need Electricity Retailers? Or Can You Get It Cheaper Wholesale? MIT working paper.

Joskow, P. L. (2006). Markets for Power in the United States: An Interim Assessment. *The Energy Journal*, 27, 1–36.

Joskow, P. L. (2007). Competitive Electricity Markets and Investment in New Generating Capacity. In: *The New Energy Paradigm*, Helm, D., Ed. Oxford: Oxford University Press.

Joskow, P. L. (2008). Capacity Payments in Imperfect Electricity Markets: Need and Design. *Utilities Policy*, 16(3), 159–170.

Joskow, P. L. (2011). Comparing the Costs of Intermittent and Dispatchable Electricity Generating Technologies. *American Economic Review*, 100(3), 238–241.

Joskow, P. L. (2014). Incentive Regulation in Theory and Practice: Electricity Distribution and Transmission Networks. In *Economic Regulation and Its Reform: What Have We Learned?* Rose, N., Ed. Chicago: University of Chicago Press, pp. 291–344.

Joskow, P. L. and Tirole, J. (2000). Transmission Rights and Market Power on Electric Power Networks. *The RAND Journal of Economics*, 31(3), 450–487.

Joskow, P. L. and Tirole, J. (2005). Merchant Transmission Investment. *The Journal of Industrial Economics*, 53(2), 233–264.

Joskow, P. L. and Tirole, J. (2006). Retail Electricity Competition. *The RAND Journal of Economics*, 37(4), 799–815.

Joskow, P. L. and Tirole, J. (2007). Reliability and Competitive Electricity Markets. *The RAND Journal of Economics*, 38(1), 60–84.

Joskow, P. L. and Wolfram, C. D. (2012). Dynamic Pricing of Electricity. *The American Economic Review*, 102(3), 381–385.

Kahn, E. P. (1998). Numerical Techniques for Analyzing Market Power in Electricity. *The Electricity Journal*, 11(6), 34–43.

Kirschen D. S. and Strbac, G. (2004). *Fundamentals of Power System Economics*. New York: John Wiley & Sons.

Klemperer, P. (1995). Competition When Consumers Have Switching Costs: An Overview with Applications to Industrial Organization, Macroeconomics, and International Trade. *Review of Economic Studies*, 62(4), 515–539.

Klemperer, P. D. and Meyer, M. A. (1989). Supply Function Equilibria in Oligopoly under Uncertainty. *Econometrica*, 57(6), 1243–1277.

Kolstad, C. (2011). *Intermediate Environmental Economics: International Edition*. Oxford: OUP Catalogue (2011).

Kunz, F., Neuhoff, K. and Rosellón, J. (2016). FTR Allocations to Ease Transition to Nodal Pricing: An Application to the German Power System. *Energy Economics*, 60, 176–185.

Laffont, J.-J. and Tirole, J. (1993). *A Theory of Incentives in Regulation and Procurement*. Cambridge, MA: The MIT Press.

Laffont, J.-J. and Tirole, J. (1996). Creating Competition through Interconnection: Theory and Practice. *Journal of Regulatory Economics*, 10(3), 227–256.

Laffont, J.-J. and Tirole, J. (2000). *Competition in Telecommunications*, Cambridge, MA: The MIT Press.

Landon J. H. (1983). Theories of Vertical Integration and Their Application to the Electric Utility Industry. *The Antitrust Bulletin*, 28, 101–130.

Littlechild, S. (2000). Why We Need Electricity Retailers: A Reply to Joskow on Wholesale Spot Price Pass-Through, *Cambridge Working Paper in Economics*.

Littlechild, S. (2002). Competition in Retail Electricity Supply. *Journal des Economistes et des Etudes Humaines*, 12(2), 1–21.

Littlechild, S. (2009). Retail Competition in Electricity Markets: Expectations, Outcomes and Economics. *Energy Policy*, 37(2), 759–763.

Lyon, T. (1996). A Model of the Sliding Scale. *Journal of Regulatory Economics*, 9, 227–247.

Lucas, N. and Taylor, P. (1993). Characterizing Generator Behaviour: Bidding Strategies in the Pool: A Game Theory Analysis. *Utilities Policy*, 3(2), 129–135.

Luderer, G., Krey, V., Calvin, K., Merrick, J., Mima, S., Pietzcker, R. and Wada, K. (2014). The Role of Renewable Energy in Climate Stabilization: Results from the EMF27 Scenarios. *Climatic Change*, 123(3–4), 427–441.

Mansur, E. T., Mendelsohn, R. and Morrison, W. (2008). Climate Change Adaptation: A Study of Fuel Choice and Consumption in the US Energy Sector. *Journal of Environmental Economics and Management*, 55(2), 175–193.

Mastropietro, P, Rodilla, P. and Battle, C. (2017). Performance Incentives in Capacity Mechanism: Conceptual Considerations and Empirical Evidence. *Economics of Energy and Environmental Policy*, 6(1), 149–163.

McGowan, F. (1991). Controlling the Greenhouse Effect. The Role of Renewables. *Energy Policy*, 19(2), 110–118.

Metcalf, G. and Stock J. (2015). The Role of Integrated Assessment Models in Climate Policy: A User's Guide and Assessment. Discussion Paper 2015–68. Cambridge, MA: Harvard Project on Climate Agreements.

Mideksa, T. K. and Kallbekken, S. (2010). The Impact of Climate Change on the Electricity Market: A Review. *Energy Policy*, 38(7), 579–3585.

Milligan, M., Ela, E., Hodge, B.-M., Kirby, B., Lew, D., Clark, C., DeCesaro J. and Lynn, K. (2011). Integration of Variable Generation, Cost-Causation, and Integration Costs. *The Electricity Journal*, 24(9), 51–63.

Mirabel, F. and Poudou, J. C. (2004). Mechanisms of Funding for Universal Service Obligations: The Electricity Case. *Energy Economics*, 26(5), 801–823.

Moretti, M., Djomo, S. N., Azadi, H., May, K., De Vos, K., Van Passel, S. and Witters, N. (2017). A Systematic Review of Environmental and Economic Impacts of Smart Grids. *Renewable and Sustainable Energy Reviews*, 68, 888–898.

NEA (2012). Nuclear Energy and Renewables: System Effects in Low-Carbon Electricity Systems, Nuclear Energy Agency (NEA/OECD), Paris.

NECA (2015). Transmission Pricing: Summary of International Experiences. Internal Report.

NEMA (1995). American National Standard Preferred Voltage Ratings for Electric Power Systems and Equipment (60 Hz). National Electrical Manufacturers Association, approved by American National Standards Institute, ANSI C84.1–1995. Rosslyn, VA.

Nanduri, V. and Das, T. K. (2007). A Reinforcement Learning Model to Assess Market Power under Auction-Based Energy Pricing. *IEEE Transactions on Power Systems*, 22(1), 85–95.

Newbery, D. M. and Pollitt, M. G. (1997). The Restructuring and Privatisation of Britain's CEGB: Was It Worth It? *The Journal of Industrial Economics*, 45(3), 269–303.

Nordhaus, W. D., Houthakker, H. and Solow, R. (1973). The Allocation of Energy Resources. *Brookings Papers on Economic Activity*, 4(3), 529–576.

OECD (2003). Competition Issues in the Electricity Sector, DAFFE/COMP(2003)14.

OFGEM (2002). Review of Domestic Gas and Electricity Competition and Supply Price Regulation: Conclusion and Final Proposals, London.

OFGEM (2007). Domestic Retail Market Report, London.

OFGEM (2012). The Retail Market Review: Updated Domestic Proposals, London.

OFGEM (2017). Annual Report on the Operation of the Capacity Market in 2016/2017. Ofgem/ Ofgem E-Serve 9 Millbank, London SW1P 3GE, available at www.ofgem.gov.uk.

Olmos, L. and Pérez-Arriaga, I. J. (2009). A Comprehensive Approach for Computation and Implementation of Efficient Electricity Transmission Network Charges. *Energy Policy*, 37(12), 5285–5295.

Oren, S. S. (1997). Economic Inefficiency of Passive Transmission Rights in Congested Electricity Systems with Competitive Generation. *The Energy Journal* 18(1), 63–83.

Oren, S. S., Spiller, P., Varaiya, P. and Wu, F. (1995). Nodal Prices and Transmission Rights: A Critical Appraisal. *The Electricity Journal*, 8(3), 24–35.

Panzar, J. (2000). A Methodology for Measuring the Costs of Universal Service Obligations. *Information Economics and Policy*, 12(3), 211–220.

Pérez-Arriaga, I. J. Ed. (2013). *Regulation of the Power Sector*. Dodrecht and London: Springer Verlag.

Perez-Arriaga, I. J. and Batlle, C. (2012). Impacts of Intermittent Renewables on Electricity Generation System Operation. *Economics of Energy & Environmental Policy*, 1(2).

Pollitt, M. (2008). Liberalization and Regulation in Electricity Systems: How Can We Get the Balance Right? In: *Competitive Electricity Markets: Design, Implementation, Performance*, Sioshansi, F. P., Ed. Oxford: Elsevier Science.

Rassenti, S. J., Smith, V. L. and Wilson, B. J. (2003). Discriminatory Price Auctions in Electricity Markets: Low Volatility at the Expense of High Price Levels. *Journal of regulatory Economics*, 23(2), 109–123.

Rebours, Y. and Kirschen, D. (2005). *What Is Spinning Reserve?* Manchester: University of Manchester.

Rebours, Y., Kirschen, D. S., Trotignon, M. and Rossignol, S. (2007). A Survey of Frequency and Voltage Control Ancillary Services – Part I: Technical Features. *IEEE Transactions on Power Systems*, 22(1), 350–357.

REN 21 (2017). REN 21, Renewables: Global Status Report, available at www.ren21.net/gsr-2017.

Rudnick, H., Soto, M. and Palma, R. (1999). Use of System Approaches for Transmission Open Access Pricing. *International Journal of Electric Power and Energy Systems*, 21(2), February 1999.

Shepherd, W. and Shepherd, D. (2014). *Energy Studies* (3rd ed). London: Imperial College Press.

Schmalensee, R. (1989). Good Regulatory Regimes. *The RAND Journal of Economics*, 20, 417–436.

Schmalensee, R. (2012). Evaluating Policies to Increase Electricity Generation from Renewable Energy. *Review of Environmental Economics and Policy*, 6(1), 45–64.

Schweppe, F. C., Caramanis, M. C., Tabors, R. D. and Bohn, R. E. (2013). *Spot Pricing of Electricity*. Dordrecht: Springer Science & Business Media.

Siano, P. (2014). Demand Response and Smart Grids: A Survey. *Renewable and Sustainable Energy Reviews*, 30, 461–478.

Sijm, J., Neuhoff, K., and Chen, Y. (2006). CO2 Cost Pass-Through and Windfall Profits in the Power Sector. *Climate Policy*, 6(1), 49–72.

Sijm, J. P. M. (2017). Cost and Revenue Related Impacts of Integrating Electricity from Variable Renewable Energy into the Power System: A Review of Recent Literature. *Policy Studies*, Vol. 2016, p. 2015.

Sims, R. E. H., Schock, R. N., Adegbululgbe, A., Fenhann, J., Konstantinaviciute, I., Moomaw, W., Nimir, H. B., Schlamadinger, B., Torres-Martínez, J., Turner, C., Uchiyama, Y., Vuori, S. J.V., Wamukonya N. and Zhang, X. (2007). Energy Supply. In: *Climate Change 2007: Mitigation. Contribution of Working Group III to the Fourth Assessment Report of the Intergovernmental Panel on Climate Change*, Metz, B., Davidson, O. R., Bosch, P. R., Dave, R., Meyer, L. A., Eds. Cambridge, UK and New York: Cambridge University Press.

Singh A., Frei T., Chokani N. and Abhari R. S. (2016). Impact of Unplanned Power Flows in Interconnected Transmission Systems: Case Study of Central Eastern European Region. *Energy Policy*, 91, 287–303.

Smeers, Y. (1997). Computable Equilibrium Models and the Restructuring of the European Electricity and Gas Markets. *The Energy Journal*, 18(4), 1–31.

Spees K., Newell, S. A. and Pfeifenberger, J. P. (2013). Capacity Markets: Lessons Learned from the First Decade. *Economics of Energy & Environmental Policy*, 2(2), 1–26.

Steiner, F. (2001). Regulation, Industry Structure and Performance in the Electricity Supply Industry. *OECD Economic Studies*, No. 32, 2001/I.

Stoft, S. (2002). *Power System Economics*. New York: IEEE-Wiley.

Stanfield, B., Mansur, E. T. and Saravia, C. (2008). Vertical Arrangements, Market Structure, and Competition: An Analysis of Restructured US Electricity Markets. *The American Economic Review*, 98(1), 237–266.

Su, X. (2015). Have Customers Benefited from Electricity Retail Competition? *Journal of Regulatory Economics*, 47(2), 146–182.

Surendran, R. Hogan, W. W., Hui, H. and Yu, C. (2016). Scarcity Pricing in ERCOT, FERC Technical Conference, June 27–29, 2016. Available at: www.ferc.gov/CalendarFiles/20160629114652-3-FERC2016_Scarcity Pricing_ERCOT_Resmi Surendran.pdf.

Taylor, B. N. and Thompson, A. (2008). *The International System of Units (SI)*, NIST Special Publication 330, Gaithersburg, MD: National Institute of Standards and Technology.

Tol, R. S. J. (2014). *Climate Economics: Economic Analysis of Climate, Climate Change and Climate Policy*. London: Edward Elgar Publishing.

Twomey, P., Green, R. J., Neuhoff, K. and Newbery, D. (2006). A Review of the Monitoring of Market Power: The Possible Roles of TSOs in Monitoring for Market Power Issues in Congested Transmission Systems. *Journal of Energy Literature*, 11(2), 2005.

Ueckerdt, F. L. Hirth, G. Luderer, and Edenhofer, O. (2013). System LCOE XE "Levelized Cost of Electricity": What Are the Costs of Variable Renewables? *Energy*, 25, 178–190.

Varian, H. (2014). *Intermediate Microeconomics: A Modern Approach* (9th Edition). New York and London: W. Norton & Company.

Vàsquez, C., Batlle, C., Lumbreras, S. and Perez Arriaga, I. J. (2006). Electricity Retail Regulation in a Context of Vertical Integration: The Debate on Regulated Tariffs. IIT Working Paper, IIT-06-028A.

Ventosa, M., Baıllo, A., Ramos, A. and Rivier, M. (2005). Electricity Market Modeling Trends. *Energy Policy*, 33(7), 897–913.

Viscusi, W. K., Harrington, J. E., and Vernon, J. M. (2005). *Economics of Regulation and Antitrust*. Cambridge, MA: The MIT Press.

von der Fehr, N. H. M. and Hansen, P. V. (2010). Electricity Retailing in Norway. *The Energy Journal*, 31(1), 26–45.

von der Fehr, N. H. M., and Harbord, D. (1993). Spot Market Competition in the UK Electricity Industry. *The Economic Journal*, 103(418), 531–546.

von der Fehr, N. H. M. and Harbord, D. (1995). Capacity Investment and Long-Run Efficiency in Market-Based Electricity Industries. Competition in the Electricity Supply Industry: Experience from Europe and the United States. University of Oslo, Norway, Working Paper.

Weron, R. (2007). *Modelling and Forecasting Electricity Loads and Prices: A Statistical Approach*. Chichester: John Wiley & Sons.

Weyant, J. (1996). Integrated Assessment of Climate Change: An Overview and Comparison of Approaches and Results. In *Climate Change 1995: Economic and Social Dimensions of Climate Change*. Edited by J. Bruce, H. Yi, and E. Haites, 367–439. Cambridge: Cambridge University Press.

Willems, B., Rumiantseva, I. and Weigt, H. (2009). Cournot Versus Supply Functions: What Does the Data Tell Us? *Energy Economics*, 31(1), 38–47.

Wilson, C. and Waddams Price, C. (2010). Do Consumers Switch to the Best Supplier? *Oxford Economic Papers*, 62(4), 647–668.

Wolak, F. A., and Patrick, R. H. (1996). Industry Structure and Regulation in the England and Wales Electricity Market. In *Pricing and Regulatory Innovations Under Increasing Competition*, New York: Springer, pp. 65–90.

Woerdman, E., Couwenberg O., and Nentjes. A. (2009). Energy Prices and Emissions Trading: Windfall Profits from Grandfathering? *European Journal of Law and Economics*, 28(2), 185–202.

Wolak, F. A. (2014). Regulating Competition in Wholesale Electricity Supply. In *Economic Regulation and Its Reform: What Have We Learned?* Chicago: University of Chicago Press, pp. 195–289.

Wolfram, C. D. (1997). Strategic Bidding in a Multi-Unit Auction: An Empirical Analysis of Bids to Supply Electricity. National Bureau of Economic Research Working Paper no. w6269.

Zhang, Y., Chen, W. and Gao, W. (2017). A Survey on the Development Status and Challenges of Smart Grids in Main Driver Countries. *Renewable and Sustainable Energy Reviews*, 79, 137–147.

# Index

Printed in the United States
by Baker & Taylor Publisher Services